DATE DUE		
Nov 4 '75		
Nov 25 '75		
Dec 15 '75		
Apr 13 7 3		
May 6 '7 3		
GAYLORD M-2		PRINTED IN U.S.A.

University of Washington Publications in Anthropology, Volume XIII

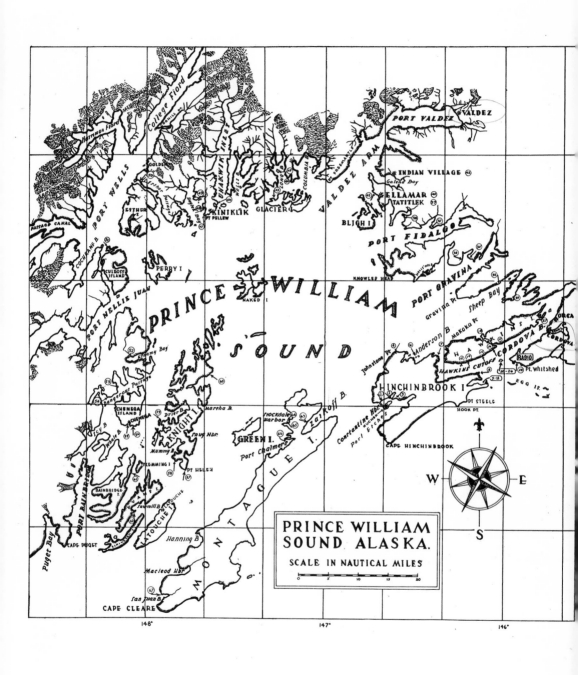

PRINCE WILLIAM SOUND ALASKA.

SCALE IN NAUTICAL MILES

0   5   10   15   20

Chugach Prehistory

THE ARCHAEOLOGY OF PRINCE WILLIAM SOUND, ALASKA

By Frederica de Laguna

University of Washington Press
SEATTLE AND LONDON

979.8
D 37 c
7 3641
March, 1971

Kaj Birket-Smith
Tak for Rejse
til
Guld og Grønne Skove

Preface

THIS REPORT is based upon research in Prince William Sound, Alaska, during the summers of 1930 and 1933. In 1930 the author and her brother, Wallace de Laguna, made an archaeological reconnaissance of Prince William Sound (June 27 to August 20) and Cook Inlet for the University of Pennsylvania Museum. A small collection of specimens, numbering a little over 100, was made, reports of most of the sites described in Chapter II were obtained from the natives, and about half of these places were visited. A brief summary of the results of this exploration has already been published.[1]

In 1933 an expedition to Prince William Sound, sponsored jointly by the National Museum of Denmark and by the University of Pennsylvania Museum, was organized under the co-leadership of Dr. Kaj Birket-Smith and the author. Mr. Norman Reynolds, then a student of anthropology at the University of Washington, Seattle, and Dr. Wallace de Laguna, then a student of geology at Harvard University, accompanied the expedition as assistants. Professor Grace A. de Laguna of Bryn Mawr College, although an unofficial member of the party, rendered valuable help in the field. The expedition landed at Cordova in Prince William Sound on April 26, 1933. From that date until May 14, ethnological data were gathered which were published in

[1] De Laguna, 1934, Chap. VI.

Copenhagen, 1938, with the title *The Eyak Indians of the Copper River Delta, Alaska,* under the joint authorship of the 2 leaders of the party. From May 14 until July 25, excavations were made at Palugvik, an ancient Eskimo village site on Hawkins Island, about 15 miles southwest of Cordova. During the first weeks at this site, the party was accompanied by Chief Makari Chimowitski, the oldest living Eskimo in the Sound, and by his daughter, Matrona (Mrs. August Tiedmann), who acted as interpreter. Both have since died. From them information was secured which has been incorporated in Dr. Birket-Smith's ethnological report, *The Chugach Eskimo,* published by the Danish National Museum in 1953. From July 25 to August 9, the U.S. Forest Service took the party on an exploratory tour to the southern and western parts of the Sound in the launch *Chugach.* During this trip the party visited Chenega Village as the guests of Mr. and Mrs. Larry Nonini, the superintendent and teacher at the Indian Service School. While Dr. Birket-Smith and Norman Reynolds remained at Chenega to make ethnological investigations, the author and Wallace de Laguna chartered a boat owned by Mr. William Paye of Latouche and explored archaeological sites on Glacier Island and Long Bay in the northern part of the Sound. The party returned together to Latouche, where the U. S. Forest Service launch brought them back to Cordova. From this town Dr. Birket-Smith made a trip to Chitna on the Copper River as a guest of the Copper River and Northwestern Railroad. He had to sail on August 16, but the rest of the party continued the excavations at Palugvik until August 25. From this date until September 9, additional ethnological material was obtained from the Eyak Indians, and the author and Norman Reynolds made a week's trip in the motor boat belonging to Mr. and Mrs. August Tiedmann along the eastern shore of the Sound as far as Port Gravina, exploring several sites and collecting Eskimo and Eyak folk tales, while Wallace de Laguna packed the collections.

Half of the expenses for the season of 1930 were defrayed by the University of Pennsylvania Museum, and half through the generosity of Mr. Percy C. Madeira, Jr., Mrs. William Carter Dickerman, Mrs. Alexander Gordon, and the author's father, the late Theodore de Laguna. Expenses for the expedition of 1933 were met in part by the Rask-Ørsted Foundation of the Danish government, supplemented by a smaller grant from the Julius Skrike Institution of Denmark and in part by the University of Pennsylvania Museum. The collections obtained in 1933 were divided equally between the 2 museums collaborating, and in addition a small group, illustrating the principal types, was presented to the Washington State Museum in Seattle, in acknowledgment of Norman Reynolds' valuable services.

In the text and plate legends, specimens are designated by the following catalogue numbers. Those in the Danish National Museum are catalogued P. 548 to P. 1331. Those in the University of Pennsylvania Museum have accession numbers 33-37- and 30-25-, except for those marked D30-25- which are on permanent loan to the Danish National Museum. A single specimen acquired by the University of Pennsylvania Museum in 1935 has the number 35-26-1. The original field numbers, prefixed by WSM, indicate specimens given to the Washington State Museum in Seattle. Field numbers are used for a few specimens that were catalogued in the field and subsequently lost.

Measurements in parentheses are given when the specimen is broken and the original dimension cannot be estimated.

* * *

The members of the expedition desire to express their thanks to the following persons for their generous help: Mr. Harold E. Smith, Mr. W. J. MacDonald, and Mr. Earl Jacobsen of the U. S. Forest Service; Mr. Peter Buhl of the Copper River and Northwestern Railroad; Mr. Joseph Isom and Mr. Emmanuel Isom, owners of the Northern Sea Food Cannery at Cordova; Mr. and Mrs. Larry Nonini of the U. S. Indian Service at Chenega. In addition, the late Mr. Lee Pratt and Mr. H. J. Lutz, both formerly attached to the U. S. Forest Service at Cordova, were most generous in furnishing information about sites. Mr. Pratt initiated Wallace de Laguna and the author in the art of camping in Alaskan storms and took us to the important site of Palugvik; Mr. Lutz loaned for study his interesting archaeological collection, some specimens from which are illustrated in this report. Dr. E. W. Gifford and Dr. Robert Heizer of the Department of Anthropology at the University of California have been most helpful in furnishing data about the elusive mummies said to have been found in Prince William Sound. Dr. Neil Judd of the U. S. National Museum made it possible for me to examine the late Dr. Hrdlička's collections from Kodiak Island for comparative purposes. Dr. Seton H. Thompson, Chief of the Branch of Alaska Fisheries of the U. S. Fish and Wildlife Service, has furnished valuable information about the marine life in Prince William Sound. Drs. Philip Smith, John C. Reed, Stephen Capps, and other members of the Alaskan Branch of the U. S. Geological Survey have also supplied wise counsel.

The stones used for tools in the collections acquired by the University of Pennsylvania Museum have been identified by

Dr. Edward H. Watson of Bryn Mawr College. Dr. George Goodwin of the American Museum of Natural History in New York has identified some of the worked animal bones. The remainder, as well as the large collection of unworked bones from the various sites, were identified by Dr. Magnus Degerbøl of the Zoological Museum of the University of Copenhagen. Wallace de Laguna mapped the sites of Palutat and Palugvik. The cross sections, sketch maps, and pictures of skeletons were redrawn by Miss Jean Franksen, then artist at the University of Pennsylvania Museum, from field sketches. The photographs of specimens were made by Mr. Reuben Goldberg of the University of Pennsylvania Museum and by the late Mr. S. Bengtsson of the Danish National Museum. I am indebted to Miss Helen Fernald, then Curator of the Chinese Section at the University of Pennsylvania Museum, and to Mr. Victor Castillo, then a student at the University of Washington, for additional text figures. The skeletal material obtained in Prince William Sound has been studied by Dr. Bruno Oetteking of the Museum of the American Indian, Heye Foundation, and has been published by him under the title of "Skeletal Remains from Prince William Sound, Alaska," in the *American Journal of Physical Anthropology*, Volume III, numbers 1, 2, and 3, 1945.

In the preparation of this report the author has enjoyed the encouragement and friendly criticism of Dr. J. Alden Mason, Curator of the American Section of the University of Pennsylvania Museum, and of her comrade in the field, Dr. Kaj Birket-Smith. Although work on it was in one sense begun in 1930, a major portion was written during 1945-46 when the author held a postwar fellowship of the Rockefeller Foundation, to which institution she wishes to make grateful acknowledgment.

The author appreciates the interest which Dr. Ralph Linton, Dr. Irving Rouse, and the late Dr. D. S. Davidson have shown in this report.

It had been hoped that the ethnological and archaeological studies of the Chugach could appear simultaneously as companion volumes. The manuscript for this book was finished first and submitted to Dr. Birket-Smith, who has included references to it in *The Chugach Eskimo*, 1953. Although publication of the present work has been long delayed, the author regrets that circumstances have prevented her from including references to Dr. Birket-Smith's monograph, which would have been so valuable.

FREDERICA DE LAGUNA

Bryn Mawr College

Contents

Illustrations

PLATES

Transliteration of Native Words

The symbols used in transliterating Chugach words have approximately the following values:

Vowels

a as in father
e as in French été
ɛ as in bet
i as in French finir
ɩ as in hit
o as in French pose
ɔ as in French octobre
ʋ as in put
u as in boot
ɑ as in but

Vowels preceding velar consonants are velarized. It is unnecessary to indicate this except in the case of the third a in kaɫaaq (spirit).

Consonants

These are as in English with the following exceptions:

The surds, p, t, k, are not aspirated
q is the velar k
c is used for sh as in she; and η for ng as in sing
ɫ is the surd l
ț is palatalized as in tune, often sounding like ch as in chew
γ is the continuant g; γ is the velar form (rather like French r)
x is the consonant in German ich; x̣ is the velar form as in German ach
v is bilabial as in Havana (Habana)

The raised period (·) indicates that the preceding vowel or consonant is doubled in duration; otherwise all sounds are short.

CHUGACH PREHISTORY
The Archaeology of Prince William Sound, Alaska

CHAPTER I

Prince William Sound

1. GEOGRAPHY

PRINCE WILLIAM SOUND, also known as the Gulf of Chugach, is a great embayment, embraced in the arc of the Chugach Mountains, between the Copper River and Kenai Peninsula (west longitude 145° 37' to 148° 43', north latitude 59° 46' to 61° 61'). The crow must fly 105 miles from the head of Cordova Bay on the east to the head of Port Nellie Juan in the west; from the southern tip of Montague Island it is 104 miles to the glaciers at the head of College Fiord in the north. The coast line is rocky and irregular. There are few sandy beaches, except where the Pacific surf pounds on the more exposed shores of Montague and Hinchinbrook islands that guard the entrance to the sound. Travel by land is almost impossible. Attempting to follow the shore, one may be able to walk only half a mile or so along the shingle before coming to an impassable headland. Turning inland, even on one of the islands, one faces an almost impenetrable forest of spruce and hemlock, fringed with a tangle of alders, devilclubs, and salmonberry bushes. There are few trails, so that the easiest access to the uplands above the timber line is up a stream bed or a talus slope, or across an open swampy meadow where the layers of moss and peat quake under the foot and apparently shallow pools conceal bottomless quagmires. The land in some places rises abruptly from the water's edge to tree-less summits 1,000 to 3,000 feet high, while only a few miles inland the snowy peaks of the Chugach Range tower to altitudes of 10,000 feet. In other areas, a low plain must be crossed before reaching the hills. But for the traveler by boat, the sound offers innumerable fiords, inlets, and passages, The coast line is over 2,000 miles long, if the islands are included, and is varied by streams, waterfalls, lagoons, salt swamps, mud flats, gravel beaches, cliffs, and skerries.[1]

2. GLACIAL HISTORY

During the Pleistocene the whole sound was covered by an enormous sheet of ice that floated out beyond the farther shores of the sound, probably as far as Middleton Island, some sixty miles out in the Gulf of Alaska, and that rose high up on the flanks of the mountains. This was only part of the great ice mass that covered all of southeastern and southwestern Alaska, from Dixon Entrance to Unimak Island, including all the mountainous hinterland. This whole area was then, of course, uninhabitable. The ice sheet in the sound lasted long after the end of the Pleistocene in other areas of North America, for geologists have found traces of glaciation hardly yet touched by erosion. There still remain many snowfields in the mountains, and from these descend innumerable glacial tongues, which reach tidewater in the northern and

[1] Data from Grant and Higgins, 1910, p. 9.

1

western part of the sound (Pl. 4, *4*). Conditions in this part of Alaska are not so much postglacial as interglacial.[2]

Native traditions recall a time when some of these glaciers were more extensive than they are today. Thus, Fred Allen, a former Eskimo shaman of Nuchek, told Lee Pratt that in ancient days the climate was much colder and there was no wind. Icy and Whale bays (see Map 1) were then filled with glaciers; Columbia Glacier covered Columbia Bay and the islands in it nearly to Glacier Island. The glaciers in College Fiord came to within three miles of Coghill Point. There were big glaciers on Montague Island; one of these was above Port Chalmers, opposite Green Island. There was also ice in Port Etches and at Hook Point, Hinchinbrook Island. When telling us the story of the Sea-Lion Rock, our Eskimo informant, Makari, explained that Chenega Glacier in Icy Bay once extended so far out into the sound that it covered the present site of Chenega Village and the Pleiades Islands (Map 6). At that time, the only village in that part of the sound was at Point Helen on Knight Island (Site 57). Later, as the ice retreated, the Pleiades were uncovered, and the people finally moved to Chenega Island and founded Chenega Village.

These stories receive some confirmation from the geologists. The studies made by Tarr and Martin and by Grant and Higgins[3] show that formerly the Chenega and Princeton glaciers filled Nassau Fiord in Icy Bay. These writers understood the natives to claim that the glaciers filled Icy Bay itself only 150 years ago, whereas the large trees growing about the bay and even part way up Nassau Fiord preclude this dating. The native tradition, however, does not refer to the last century but to some period before the coming of the whites. In 1794 Vancouver reported that Icy Bay was blocked by a wall of ice.[4] Grant and Higgins

believe that at this time the 2 glaciers extended out into the bay but not across it. Historical records indicate that Chenega and Princeton glaciers maintained a fairly constant position between 1787 and 1898, then retreated about 6½ miles between 1898 and 1908. Even in 1886 the glacier was still visible from Chenega Village. Thus, the rapid retreat of the ice at the turn of the last century may have been preceded by an equally dramatic egression in prehistoric times which has been recorded in the native legend.

Other recessions of the ice seem to have favored native travel in historic times. Thus, Miles and Child glaciers on the Copper River, east of the sound, have retreated since they were first observed. The Russians reported the native tradition that prior to the coming of the white man these 2 glaciers met to form a solid barrier across the canyon, under which the Copper River flowed. Tarr and Martin believe this tradition to be not improbable, but unverifiable.[5] In any case, the observed retreat of the ice in recent times has greatly favored communication up and down the river, a dangerous route at best, and has probably made possible the construction of the Copper River and Northwestern Railroad (abandoned since our visit in 1933). Certainly in the latter part of the eighteenth century there was native traffic along the river, by means of which the Chugach obtained copper.[6] Although Delarof's and Sauer's Eskimo informants spoke of traveling up the river for 14 days to the territory of what must be the Atna (Copper River Athabaskans), it is not at all certain that the Eskimo themselves commonly made the trip. Sauer's account fails to mention the Eyak living at the mouth of the Copper River. These Indians did not attempt the dangerous trip themselves, according to our Eyak informant, but it is more likely that the Atna descended the river to Eyak terri-

---

[2] *Ibid.*, pp. 18 f.; 1913; Capps, 1931, pp. 2, 4, 8.
[3] Tarr and Martin, 1914, pp. 376-79; Grant and Higgins, 1913, pp. 47-49.
[4] Vancouver, 1801, V, 304

[5] Tarr and Martin, 1914, p. 416.
[6] See reports made by the Eskimo to Delarof in 1783-84 and to Sauer in 1790 (Sauer, 1802, pp. 195 f., note on p. 197).

tory and that the Eyak acted as middlemen between the Atna and the Eskimo. In early Russian days, perhaps because the Copper River route was so dangerous, the Atna used to cross the divide into the valley of the Lowe River, which empties into Valdez Arm, and carried their wares to Nuchek, paying tribute to the Eskimo at Ellamar for the privilege of passing through their territory. Later, when a quarrel disrupted this arrangement, or because of fears arising from the measles epidemic of 1868, trade was carried on through the Eyak, and the Atna themselves also visited the Eskimo at Nuchek.[7]

While most of the glacial movement in the Prince William Sound area has undoubtedly been a regression, there is also evidence of recent glacial advance in at least one locality. During the Russian occupation, and even earlier, to judge by stories told me by Indians on Cook Inlet, travel was common between the inlet and Prince William Sound over the portage between Turnagain Arm and Passage Canal. The Russians whom Vancouver met in 1794 on Cook Inlet told him about this narrow isthmus, "across which isthmus is the route, by which they stated that all their intercourse between the Russian settlements, in this and that extensive inlet [Cook Inlet and Prince William Sound], was now carried on."[8] Near Hawkins Island in Prince William Sound one of Vancouver's exploring parties actually encountered a group of about 40 natives in 2 umiaks who had come with their boats from Cook Inlet via Turnagain Arm and Passage Canal. Another party sent out by Vancouver later visited this fiord and gave it its present name.[9] The portage is between 12 and 13 miles long, although the direct distance from tidewater to tidewater is only about 10½ miles. Tarr and Martin are confident that in 1794 there was no Portage Glacier of anything like its size in 1910, and that the valley was then

free of ice.[10] An advance of the glacier since that period may be one reason why this route was seldom used until World War II.

3. Sinking of the Land; Tidal Range

In addition to movements of the ice, there is evidence that the land has recently sunk in various parts of the sound. According to the evidence discussed in the next chapter, the land has sunk at Palugvik and at a near-by site (Sites 14 and 13, Map 3) as much as 4 feet or more, and evidence of subsidence was observed at a number of other localities. These are Sites 3 and 4 (?) on the western end of Hinchinbrook Island (Map 2); Site 8 on the eastern end of the island (Map 3), and the 2 sites on the opposite shore of Hawkins Island already mentioned; Site 56 on Chenega Island; Site 62 on Evans Island (Map 6); and Sites 64 and 65A and B at Stockdale Harbor on Montague Island (Map 7). No midden was found at Site 65B; it had presumably been washed away, as had most of the shell heap at Site 65A. The bottom of the remaining midden at the latter place is now 9 inches below the level of the beach gravel. This destruction was obviously caused by actual subsidence and not by storm waves, for the sites in Stockdale Harbor are on a protected lagoon. Grant and Higgins[11] found evidence that the land between Sheep and Simpson bays (Map 3) had sunk at least 4 feet, because the tundra, containing the roots of now dead trees, is actually below the high tide level. This would account for our failure to find traces in Sheep Bay of some of the ancient villages reported by the natives. In Port Gravina, Grant and Higgins found similar evidence of trees killed by salt water and of tundra with tree roots extending down almost to the low tide level, which indicated a depression of at least 10 feet. This tends to corroborate the account we received of a site buried under the beach in Port Gravina. The geologists

[7] De Laguna, 1934, p. 118; Birket-Smith and de Laguna, 1938, pp. 150 f.
[8] Vancouver, 1801, V, 195.
[9] *Ibid.*, pp. 288, 308-10.

[10] Tarr and Martin, 1914, pp. 362-64. Vancouver (1801, V, 308) says it was "very free from snow, and appeared to be perfectly easy of access."
[11] Grant and Higgins, 1910, pp. 16-18.

suggest an even more extensive subsidence in the western part of the sound, responsible for the complete submergence of a lowland which in the eastern part of the sound is 20 to 60 feet above sea level. The shallow water known as Dangerous Passage, between Chenega Island and the mainland, might possibly represent this submerged surface. In any case, they found trees killed by salt water in a cove one mile west of Point Helen on Knight Island, a locality where we searched but failed to find the ancient village site already mentioned (Site 57, Map 6). They noted a similar phenomenon on the west side of Latouche Island (i.e., not far from Site 62 on Evans Island, where there was evidently a midden which the sea has washed away). We ourselves noticed a sunken beach and trees killed by the sea at Port Chalmers, Montague Island (Pl. 4, 3), near a place where the natives told us there had once been a settlement (Site 66, Map 7).

The most interesting observations were made by Vancouver, who anchored in Port Chalmers from May 25 to June 17, 1794.

> The shores [of Port Chalmers] are in general low, and as has been already observed, very swampy in many places, on which the sea appears to be making more rapid incroachments than I ever before saw or heard of. Many trees have been cut down since these regions had been first visited by Europeans; this was evident by the visible effects of the axe and saw; which we concluded had been produced whilst Messrs. Portlock and Dixon were here, seven years before our arrival; as the stumps of the trees were still remaining on the earth where they had originally grown, but were even now many feet below the high water mark, even of neap tides. A low projecting point of land behind which we rode, had not long since afforded support to some of the largest pine trees in the neighbourhood, but it was now overflowed by every tide; and excepting two of the trees, which still put forth a few leaves, the whole were reduced to naked, dead white stumps, by the incroachment of the sea water to their roots; and some stumps of trees, with their roots still fast in the ground, were also found in no very advanced state of decay nearly as low down as the low water of spring tides.[12]

At the spring tides Vancouver observed a

maximum rise of 13 feet 4 inches.[13] [The land must, therefore, have sunk at least 10 feet. Some of this subsidence certainly took place between 1787 and 1794, and part of it may have occurred earlier. Our own observations in this same area would indicate that further subsidence probably occurred here after 1794.

The sinking of the land in Prince William Sound was evidently widespread and is paralleled by a similar subsidence in Kachemak Bay which occurred during or after the Third Period of the Kachemak Bay culture. Yet we must not assume that all of these areas were affected at the same time, for we are probably dealing with a series of local movements, only some of which may have been contemporaneous, and the movements in any one place may have been repeated over a long period of time. Certainly the submergence of the lowland shelf in the western part of the sound was much greater and more ancient than the subsidences which killed trees, the remains of which were still preserved or even still standing when seen by Vancouver in 1794, by Grant and Higgins in 1905 and 1908, and by ourselves in 1933. Moreover, we were told by members of the U. S. Forest Service that they had witnessed a local subsidence of about 2 or 3 feet which affected only a gravel spit in Zaikoff Bay, Montague Island. This was accompanied by a tremor, the full strength of which they did not feel, since they were aboard a launch at the time. Unfortunately, therefore, most or all of the subsidences which have affected the sites in Prince William Sound are probably too recent to serve as a guide in dating them, even though these sites range in age from prehistoric (Palugvik, etc.) to presumably modern (Site 64).

Grant and Higgins also noticed evidence of recent uplift of the land on the eastern shore of Columbia Bay.[14] If similar movements occurred in other parts of the sound they would serve to complicate the picture.

There is a considerable tidal range in

---

[12] Vancouver, 1801, V, 335 f.
[13] Ibid., p. 322.

[14] Grant and Higgins, 1910, p. 18.

the sound, in most parts from an extreme low of minus 3 feet to an extreme high of 16 feet 4 inches, as measured from mean lower low water, with marked differences between the 2 high and the 2 low tides of the same day. Most shellfish are obtainable only at the lower of the 2 low tides, especially during the minus runoffs at the spring tides.

4. GEOLOGY AND MINERALOGY

Prince William Sound has a complex geology, only the outlines of which need to be given here.[15] There are 2 main groups of sedimentary rocks. The older division, known as the Valdez, outcrops on the northern and western part of the sound and consists of slates and graywackes, in places altered to schists. The younger formations of the Orca group form the southern, eastern, and central parts of the sound and are composed also of slates and graywackes, together with greenstones (altered diabase and gabbro), conglomerates, and limestones. The graywackes include arkoses, sandstones, and quartzites. There are also basic and granitic dikes in various parts of the sound. Greenstone, which the natives used extensively for adzes, forms Bainbridge, Hoodoo, Elrington, Knight, and Glacier islands and the mainland from Valdez Arm to Landlocked Bay on the north shore of Port Fidalgo. The best quality of slate is also found in the Orca formation, especially in the younger layers which lie south and east of the greenstone belt.

Chalcopyrite is the most important copper-bearing ore in Prince William Sound,[16] and for a time there was considerable prospecting and some mining, notably at the now abandoned workings at Ellamar and Latouche. Native copper also occurs, however, and was utilized by the natives in late prehistoric times. It has been found at the following localities: at the head of Landlocked Bay in Port Fidalgo; between Cordova and the now abandoned town of Orca; 10 miles northeast of Orca near the

Scott Glacier (i.e., presumably in Eyak territory); and at the Bonanza Mine on Latouche Island. Billy Paye of Latouche told us that when this mine was opened Eskimo stone mining tools (probably the heads for mauls or splitting adzes) were found at the foot of the cliff, where the "Glory Hole" is now. Fred Allen told Lee Pratt that the natives formerly mined copper behind a big waterfall near Garden Cove in Port Etches (see Map 2), but that they did not reveal the locality to the Russians, although the latter were prospecting for copper on the western end of Hinchinbrook Island. It is interesting that the Eskimo name for Garden Cove is kan·ualₜk, "copper place."[17] In 1778 Captain Cook noted that many of the natives' arrow and lance points were made of copper, which he concluded was locally procurable or at least obtained from neighboring tribes, since the natives seemed to have so much of it that they refused to accept it in trade.[18] Another member of Cook's expedition speaks of copper ear and nose ornaments.[19]

Among other ores found in the sound are pyrite and hematite.[20] The former was apparently sometimes used by the natives for making fire. Pyrite crystals nearly an inch in diameter were common at the Bonanza Mine on Latouche Island and rare at Ellamar. Hematite was used for red paint and was obtained especially at a bluff called qₐtaq, "red paint," which Makari said was inside the lagoon just south of Johnstone Point, Hinchinbrook Island (Map 2). Grant and Higgins report thin layers of hematite on the slate or shale cliffs near this locality (about 1½ miles southwest of the point), and also a 2-foot vein of hematite between the south shore of Port Etches and Signal Mountain above

[15] *Ibid.,* pp. 11-50.
[16] *Ibid.,* pp. 52, 54, 62, 70.

[17] For explanation of transliterations of native words, see p. xix.
[18] Cook, 1785, II, 379, 380.
[19] Forster, 1781, p. 236. The mention of tin (*Blech*) ornaments is certainly a mistake, either of the observer or of the translator, since Cook did not speak of tin in his longer and much more carefully prepared account.
[20] Grant and Higgins, 1910, esp. pp. 53 f., 79.

English Bay. Makari also told us that the Chugach made paints of copper ore and of black, yellow, gray, brown, and blue rocks and earths.

The following rocks and minerals used by the natives for tools, paints, etc., were represented by specimens obtained from various archaeological sites. Those in the University of Pennsylvania were identified by Dr. Edward H. Watson, Department of Geology, Bryn Mawr College. The list includes slate (black or gray, some fine-grained, and some coarse with secondary mineral developments), sandstone (usually fine-grained, some of it arkosic), quartzite, soft altered tuff, pumice, greenstone (some with dark mineral inclusions, some of a slaty texture, and some altered to green chert), gray and black chert of unknown origin, basic schist (sometimes coarse and micaceous), altered basic rock, altered gabbro, dolerite, serpentine, syenite, granite, granite gneiss, hematite, pyrite, and native copper.

The natives also informed us that amber, which was prized for ear ornaments, was found on the beaches of Kayak Island in Controller Bay, east of the Copper River. Cook also observed beads made of "a substance like amber," worn as bracelets or as ornaments for the ears and nose.[21]

5. Fauna and Flora

Prince William Sound was formerly rich in game which supplied the Chugach with food and furs, skins, bones, horns, teeth, etc., which were used for clothing, tools and weapons, ornaments, and other manufactures. In hunting they turned more naturally to the salt water than to land, for in the sound were harbor seal, harbor porpoise, fur seal, and probably other varieties of seal, sea otter, sea lion, beluga or white whale, blackfish whale, killer whale, and larger baleen whales. Walrus were rare, and the walrus ivory found may represent trade extending to the Alaska Peninsula or beyond, for the Chugach knew about the Eskimo of Bristol Bay, even though they

[21] Cook, 1785, II, 370.

denied that walrus tusks were received in trade. Fish included halibut, cod, herring, bass, eulachon, shark, octopus or devil-fish. Whitefish and various kinds of trout could be caught in fresh water. The most important fish of all was of course the salmon. There were relatively few kings, reds, or silvers, but multitudes of pink (or humpbacked) and dog (or chum) salmon crowded the streams during the spawning season.[22]

In the late winter and early spring, when bad weather sometimes prevented hunting and the supplies of dried salmon were running low, the natives relied upon shellfish. That these also formed an important addition to the diet at all times is suggested by the accumulations of shells that mark almost every village site or camping spot. These middens contained several kinds of clams (especially butter clams and horse clams), large cockles, and blue mussels, as well as lesser numbers of whelk, sea urchins, and amphineura (or chiton).[23] Razor clams, crabs, and shrimps are common in the sound but do not seem to have been used by the natives. We found no crab or shrimp shells in the middens, and only a few razor clam shells at one or 2 late sites. The latter would be very hard to secure without modern steel-bladed clam shovels, and we were in fact told that the only method the natives had to dig the fast-burrowing razor clam was to skewer its neck with an 8-inch peg and so force it to dig itself up to the surface. Only a few clams were obtained by this method, and, since they were usually opened and cleaned on the mud flats, no shells would be found around the older villages. During the spring of the year the natives speared and ate a large sea slug.

It is well known that at certain seasons and at certain localities shellfish and especially mussels, are poisonous. The symptoms are severe and come on quickly, apparently

[22] Birket-Smith and de Laguna, 1938, p. 114.
[23] For the Kodiak Eskimo also, blue mussels were a common and favorite food (Holmberg, 1855, p. 94), while shellfish in general constituted their main resources in early spring (Lisiansky, 1814, p. 173).

attacking the nervous system and causing paralysis, in some cases bringing death within a few minutes. Thus Makari would not eat mussels at all because in his youth he had been poisoned by some he had eaten when stormbound during a sea otter hunt on the outer shore on Montague Island. Holmberg tells of a party of Kodiak hunters on Peril Strait near Sitka, many of whom died from eating mussels under similar circumstances.[24] Davydof also gives an account of the same incident, which apparently occurred in 1797.[25] Mussels and clams were scarce in the Aleutian Islands, and according to Veniaminof were sometimes poisonous from May to September.[26]

Dr. Seton H. Thompson, Chief of the Branch of Alaska Fisheries, U.S. Fish and Wildlife Service, informs me that mussels and some species of clams may be highly toxic during the summer months and at certain beaches at all times, because of the ingestion of the dynoflagellate *Gonyaulax catenella,* which occurs in coastal waters from California north to western Alaska. At times, especially during the summer, this organism or "bloom" increases in numbers to such an extent that the water has a reddish cast. It is not the same organism as that which caused the red tide on the west coast of Florida in 1947 but is closely related to it. Dr. Thompson further informs me that there have been a number of cases of mussel poisoning in Alaska in recent years; during the late 1930's a number of persons died on a picnic on Douglas Island from that cause, although they were within a short distance of medical help at Juneau. The U.S. Food and Drug Administration in 1946 seized most of the pack of southeastern Alaskan butter clams because of toxicity, and since that time the U.S. Fish and Wildlife Service has been conducting research on the problem.

Land animals found on the islands and mainland include the black bear, the brown or Kodiak grizzly, mountain goat, fox, mink, marten, beaver, muskrat, wolf, wolverine, lynx, groundhog, porcupine, marmot, weasel, squirrel, and land otter. Many of these were useful chiefly for their furs. The red deer, now common on Hawkins and Hinchinbrook islands, was introduced recently from southeastern Alaska. The natives told us that they used to get caribou skins from the Atna and from the Port Graham Eskimo.[27] Cook obtained the skins of white (polar) bear cubs and pieces of those of adult bears. These had obviously been traded, probably from the Bering Strait area, since the polar bear is rarely encountered south of the Alaska Peninsula.[28]

Bird life was also rich and included several varieties of ducks, geese, and gulls, as well as swan, crane, grouse, ptarmigan, eagle, cormorant (shag), puffin (sea parrot), coot, awk, loon, kittiwake, snipe, plover, tern, owl, raven, jay, sparrow, hummingbird, and a number of small songsters. Some of these were eaten; others were valued for their feathers or beaks. A number were associated with shamanism, •or, like such economically unimportant animals as the frog and red-backed mouse, are of interest chiefly as characters in mythology.

The forests are predominantly of spruce and hemlock, with some cedar, birch, willow, and alder. Wood was used for a variety of manufactures, including vessels and boxes with the sides made of a bent plank. Spruce roots were used for twined baskets, grass and shredded bark (?) for matting and cords, and some baskets seem to have been made of birch bark. In the vicinity of Chenega Village and some of the former settlements the hemlock is absent, ap-

24 Holmberg, 1855, pp. 94 ff. He also mentions a kind of sea urchin so poisonous that it is avoided even by the gulls (p. 135).
25 Quoted by Hrdlička, 1945, pp. 84 f.; cf. Bancroft, 1886, p. 300.
26 Quoted by Hrdlička, 1945, p. 94.

27 Merck, who was with Billings in 1790, said that caribou hides were used by the Chugach for their outer frock (Jacobi, 1937, p. 133). Some caribou bones, found at one of the sites, show that the animal was hunted by the Chugach.
28 Cook, 1785, II, 377. Strange apparently saw polar bear skins in Prince William Sound in 1786, for his vocabulary contains a word for "a white Bears Skin" (1928, p. 55). A few polar bear bones were found in the layers of Kachemak Bay II (de Laguna, 1934, p. 31).

parently because the natives killed the neighboring trees in getting the inner bark, which was relished for its sweet taste. None of the timber in the sound attains the great size found in southeastern Alaska, yet it was able to furnish logs big enough for house posts (Plates 58 and 59) and planks, coffins (Plates 7 to 9), and small dugouts (Plate 56). The natives also appreciated the many salmonberries and cloudberries (both varieties of raspberry), high and low bush cranberries, currants, blueberries, huckleberries, and strawberries. Other edible plants were the Kamchatka lily which furnished "rice," wild celery, fern roots, and other unidentified roots and greens. There were also seaweeds that were boiled and eaten. Skunk cabbage was used to wrap foods for baking; kelp furnished materials for fishing lines. Even the terrible spiked devilclub was useful as a magical prophylaxis.

6. CLIMATE

Prince William Sound enjoys a temperate climate,[29] thanks to the Japanese current, although it is lashed by the cyclonic storms which breed during fall and winter in the Gulf of Alaska and over the Aleutian Islands. Rainfall is heavy, especially along the southern edge of the sound where the total annual precipitation averages 131 inches at Cordova and 147 inches at Latouche, as against only 52 inches at Valdez. On the other hand, Valdez has an average of 269 inches of snow a year, whereas the average for Cordova is 150 inches. The amount of snow varies greatly from year to year. The first appreciable fall at sea level generally occurs in October and the last at the end of April, but there have been seasons when no snow has come before December and none has fallen after Febru-

ary. In the southern part of the sound, the accumulated winter snows generally melt at sea level sometime between the first of March and the middle of May. In 1933 planes were still able to land on the ice of Eyak Lake near Cordova at the end of April, and there was still a patch of frozen soil at Palugvik in the middle of May. The wettest months are September, October, and November; the drier season is in spring and early summer.

The mean temperature at Cordova ranges from 26.2° Fahrenheit in January to 54.4° in July, with a record high of 87° and a record low of 7° below zero. At Valdez the mean monthly range is from 17.5° in January to 53.6° in July, with records of 83° above and 14° below zero. In general, the first frosts may be expected in September or early October, the last in May. It is very rare that ice interferes with navigation in the sound. Still, native tradition tells of a terrible period of starvation when ice in the bays around Hawkins Island prevented hunting for a long time. Fred Allen told Lee Pratt that the Copper River Indians who came to trade with the Eskimo at Nuchek used to be able to cross the ice on snowshoes from Point Whitshed to Dan Bay, Hinchinbrook Island, at the angle of Hawkins Cut Off. This last report is scarcely credible, however.

The chief disadvantages of the climate are violent storms, brooding fog, or days and even weeks of steady drizzle. That storms, wind, and rain were felt as hardships by the natives, in spite of their waterproof gutskin clothing and seaworthy skin boats, is shown by the number of magic rites and spells which they practiced in order to bring good weather. There were also various folk methods of forecasting the weather; some men were especially skilled as weather prophets, and some shamans claimed the power of controlling the weather.

[29] The following is based upon a *Summary of Climatological Data of Alaska*, Section 1, published by the U.S. Weather Bureau, 1922 (?).

CHAPTER II

Archaeological Sites on Prince William Sound

1. INTRODUCTION

PRINCE WILLIAM SOUND is the home of the Chugach Eskimo, or cuaṭit, as they call themselves.[1] At present, their nearest Eskimo neighbors are the small group living at Port Graham on the southeastern shores of Cook Inlet. There were once Eskimo settlements along the southern coast of Kenai Peninsula, but the inhabitants were not considered as fellow tribesmen by the Chugach. The Chugach Range and the mountains of Kenai Peninsula form natural boundaries between the Chugach and the Tanaina Athabaskans of Cook Inlet and other Athabaskan groups in the interior. At the extreme southeastern edge of the sound the Chugach were in contact with the Eyak Indians, whose territory embraced the narrow coastal strip along the delta of the Copper River from Cape Martin on the east to the present site of Cordova in Prince William Sound. During the Russian occupation the Eyak expanded northward into the sound as far as Port Gravina. The Eyak acted as middlemen in trade between the Chugach and the Atna Athabaskans of the Copper River. More recently, the Atna Athabaskans came down the river and traded directly with the Chugach. Tanaina legends tell of a Chugach raiding party that crossed the narrow peninsula between Portage Canal and Turnagain Arm only

to be defeated in Cook Inlet. Chugach stories deal with wars between themselves and the Koniag, and of raids made by the Tlingit during historic times. Some of these enmities seem to have been forgotten in later years, for in 1783 the Tanaina and Koniag assisted the Chugach in an attack on the Russian explorers under Potap Zaikof who had been committing outrages in Prince William Sound. Two years later the Tanaina and Chugach joined with the Koniag of Shuyak Island (the northernmost of the Kodiak group) in raiding the Russian fort at Kodiak.[2]

In the eighteenth century the Chugach also claimed the Controller Bay area, including Kayak and Wingham islands, although to reach this eastern hunting territory they had to traverse Eyak waters at the mouth of the Copper River.[3] This may well represent an Eskimo seizure of a more ancient Indian area, for the Eyak had settlements all along the Gulf of Alaska nearly to the mouth of the Alsek River. Yakutat traditions recount ancient Eyak and Athabaskan migrations eastward from the Copper River, and a northward movement of Tlingit who intermarried with the Eyak, thereby introducing the Tlingit language and clan system at Yakutat in late

[1] See p. xix.

[2] Bancroft, 1886, pp. 186-91, 228. Zaikof himself seems to have been fairly decent; the worst of his expedition was Polutof.
[3] Birket-Smith and de Laguna, 1938, pp. 343-53 and authorities cited.

prehistoric or protohistoric times.[4] In any case, the Chugach were driven out of Controller Bay by the Tlingit (or mixed Eyak-Tlingit), who continued to expand northward and westward during the Russian period. For a time (in 1805) they even seized the village of tauxtvik (Site 16) on Hawkins Island, but were soon defeated. During the nineteenth century, the Tlingit from Yakutat used to visit the trading post at Nuchek.

Middleton Island in the Gulf of Alaska was also part of Chugach hunting territory. In 1788 the explorer Ismailof was taken there by guides from the sound. The Russians traded with the natives on the island and were later attacked by them. There seem to have been several houses there and a chief, but it is not clear whether this was more than a summer settlement.[5]

It is possible that the Chugach sometimes penetrated as far east as Tlingit territory at Lituya Bay, for here La Pérouse in 1786 found a large skin umiak and was told that, of 8 umiaks that had visited the bay, 7 had been wrecked in the tide rips. The boat seen by the French explorer was set on a stand beside a group of grave boxes which he assumed held the remains of the drowned natives.[6] Since the Eyak and Yakutat made skin canoes like the Chugach, the identity of the party is uncertain. Indian informants in Yakutat (1952) maintained that not only were a number of place names in that area in the Eyak language but that others were in "Aleut" (i.e., Chugach Eskimo), although they were unable to say whether the "Aleut" ever lived near Yakutat or only visited the bay, and different informants mentioned conflicting traditions.

Chugach territory was first visited in 1741 by Vitus Bering, whose expedition saw Eskimo hunting camps on Kayak Island (Cape St. Elias) and Wingham Island, although the inhabitants fled at their approach. The first European to meet the Chugach was Captain James Cook, who discovered Prince William Sound in the summer of 1778. He told the Russian, Ismailof, whom he met on Unalaska Island later that summer, about his discovery, and the publication of his journals in 1781 informed the world, so that Cook was followed by a procession of explorers, traders, and hunters. The most important of these visitors were: (1779) Zaikof's men in a skin bidar (umiak) from Cook Inlet, Arteaga in the *Princesa* with Bodega y Quadra in the *Favorita;* (1783-84) Zaikof in the *Alexandr Nevski,* with Delarof in the *Sv Alexei* and Polutof in the *Sv Mikhail;* (1785) Shelikof and a party in 4 bidars from Kodiak Island; (1786) Strange with Laurie in the *Captain Cook* and Guise in the *Experiment,* Tipping in the *Sea Otter;* (1786-87) Meares in the *Nootka;* (1787) Portlock in the *King George* and Dixon in the *Queen Charlotte;* (1788) Martinez in the *Princesa* and de Haro in the *San Carlos* (or *"Filipino"*), Colnett and Hutchins in the *Prince of Wales,* Douglas in the *Iphigenia,* Ismailof and Bocharof in the *Trekh Sviatiteli,* Portlock in the *King George;* (1790) Billings, with Merck, Sauer, and Sarychef in the *Slava Rossie,* Fidalgo in the *San Carlos;* (1791) Malaspina in the *Descubierta* with Bustamante in the *Atrevida* (off shore only) ; (1792) Moore in the *Phoenix,* Ismailof in the *Sv Simeon,* Bananof with 2 bidars from Kodiak, as well as rival Russian hunters and traders; (1794) Vancouver in the *Discovery* with Broughton in the *Chatham.*

From 1792 until 1799 when an Imperial ukase granted a monopoly to the Russian American Company (formerly the Shelikof Company), Prince William Sound had been one of the fur trade areas over which the Shelikof-Golikof, the Lebedef-Lastochkin, the Orekhof, and several other rival Russian companies had contested bitterly. The first Russian post was founded in 1793 by the Lebedef-Lastochkin Company at or near Nuchek on Hinchinbrook Island, where it was visited by one of Vancouver's exploring parties the following year. According to

[4] De Laguna, 1953, pp. 55 f.
[5] Coxe, 1803, II. 314 f.
[6] La Pérouse, 1798, II, 205-7, 234.

Dall the post at Nuchek was not founded until 1798, but Bancroft explains that the post was merely shifted to a new site in 1799 or 1800.[7] It was named Fort St. Constantine and Helen. In any case, Russian domination of the Chugach was well established by the turn of the century.

In former days the Chugach were divided into 8 tribes: the Nuchek, Shallow Water, Sheep Bay, Gravina Bay, Tatitlek, Kiniklik, Chenega, and Montague Island peoples. These tribes or geographical groups shared the same culture, spoke the same language, entertained each other at feasts, but were politically independent. Each group appears to have had its own chief or leader and its principal village. The tribes sometimes raided each other but on other occasions might unite against common enemies such as the Tlingit, Tanaina, or Koniag.

The Chugach have a keen awareness of geography and history. Every bay, island, rocky point, or beach has its name, and many of these were the scenes of historical or legendary events. We collected a number of such stories and myths, chiefly those dealing with the southeastern part of the sound where most of our archaeological work was done. We were able to visit a number of the villages mentioned in these stories, and in many cases were able to discover the site. The myths also referred to other localities as the "villages" inhabited by the "souls" of animals or plants, but these places usually failed to reveal any trace of human habitation.

Village sites were invariably on the shore, usually on protected waters, for travel in this area is practically restricted to boats. The village was frequently so placed that it commanded a view of the approaches, and a strategic position seems to have been a much more important consideration than the neighborhood of a salmon stream or a particularly rich bed of shellfish. Thus no permanent villages were located at the heads of bays, in spite of the tempting presence of some of the best salmon streams, because these were "dead ends" from which no escape by water would be possible in the event of an attack. Temporary camps were, however, made at fish streams during the salmon runs. There are few beaches or rocks without shellfish, and the natives did not have to worry about fresh water since almost every mile of shore has a small creek or a trickle of water over the rocks. Small rocky islands or skerries which were difficult to climb were used as refuge places or natural forts in time of war. The women, children, and aged would sometimes be put there when their men were away on a raid to protect them from possible retaliation.[8]

Sea otter hunters made temporary camps on the exposed outer shores of Montague and Hinchinbrook islands, but there were no permanent villages in these places because of the dangers of access. It would seem probable that the houses on Kayak, Wingham, and Middleton islands were used only by hunting parties in summer. Our informants sometimes made a distinction between winter and summer villages and in other cases told us that certain settlements were inhabited throughout the year, but we could discover no obvious differences among the archaeological remains at these various types of sites except that at some places the middens were so scanty as to suggest only a short occupation (perhaps for only one or 2 seasons). There were no settlements in the interior, for the rocky hinterland of the larger islands and the mainland was frequented only by hunters. Rock shelters and caves near the shore might be used both as camping places and as burial grounds, and the rock walls of such shelters were sometimes utilized for pictographs.

In the following pages are descriptions of sites explored in 1930 and 1933 and information about sites reported but not visited. Some of the reports may be misleading, and some of the alleged sites for which

---

[7] Dall, 1870, p. 318; Bancroft, 1886, pp. 294, 339, 395, 414 n. 9.

[8] Cf. Meares, 1791, p. xlix. Similar refuge islands were used by the Kachemak Bay Eskimo, the Koniag, and the Aleut (de Laguna, 1934, p. 163; Hrdlička, 1944, pp. 82 f.; 1945, pp. 146 ff.; and sources cited).

we searched in vain may not exist. Numbers have been assigned, however, to all or almost all the places mentioned, for convenience in locating them on the accompanying maps. The order is roughly counterclockwise around the sound, beginning with Hinchinbrook Entrance. The sites are thus grouped according to the territories of the 8 Chugach tribes, although the archaeological evidence failed to reveal any significant cultural differences among them.

The original draft of this report listed by catalogue number all specimens obtained from the various sites. For reasons of economy these numbers are omitted from this chapter and from Chapter III on burials, but will be found in the appropriate sections of Chapter V where the specimens are described.

2. TERRITORY OF THE NUCHEK PEOPLE: SITES 1 TO 6

Hinchinbrook Island: Western End

The western end of Hinchinbrook Island from Cape Hinchinbrook in the southwest around to the northern end of Hawkins Cut Off belonged to the Nuchek People (nuṭiɣmiut) (Map 2, Sites 1 to 6).

Nuchek. The principal village of these people in historic times, and indeed the most important in the whole sound, was Nuchek (nuṭʋk), formerly called iɣaqṭi. The natives all agreed that it was not settled until after the Russian trading post was founded. In 1794 Vancouver found only a few natives at the post of the Lebedef-Lastochkin Company at or near the present site of Nuchek, but understood that there was a large native village near the head of Port Etches.[9] Possibly the permanent fort of the Russian American Company was not established at Nuchek until the end of the century. The village was finally abandoned in the winter of 1929-30, when old Chief Chimowitski died and his family moved to Cordova. In 1930 we excavated at 5 different spots in the village and found nothing but

a few feet of swampy turf with bricks, glass beads, china, and hand-wrought iron implements. In 1937 Hrdlička visited Nuchek for a day, exploring graves near the Russian Church and in a graveyard south of a small lake, where the sea is washing out the coffins. These burials are all historic. Although Hrdlička found a stone lamp, "two damaged stone chisels," and a bone object in the village middens, which are from 1 to 3 feet deep, he reports these deposits full of Russian beads and other white men's goods.[10] There are said to be burial caves in the hills above Nuchek.

Site 1. At the base of the sandspit which juts out into Constantine Harbor from the north is reported to be the site of nunaɫʋq, the oldest village in the sound according to Makarı, our Chugach informant. It was inhabited for a short time after the Russians came. The last inhabitant was a man named vakaŋ. When the other people died, he moved to Nuchek and founded that village. We did not learn of this site until too late to visit it.

Site 2. On the northeastern side of the channel (paɪŋ·uacaq) from Port Etches to Constantine Harbor is a gravel bar with an abandoned smokehouse belonging to the last chief of Nuchek. A higher ridge of gravel, on the Constantine Harbor side of the point, is marked with several depressions, some opening into each other, which may have been house pits. Fire-cracked rocks were found in the bottom of two. North of these pits is a small midden of shells and animal bones, about 24 feet long and 3 or 4 feet deep. The shells seem to be as much decayed as those at Palugvik (see Section 12). The site is that of nujɪŋ·uacaq, "Little Nuchek," according to Makarı. The following specimens were collected here: a splitting adz (Pl. 10, 6), a fragment of a slate chisel, the butt end of a chipped stone pick, a hammerstone, and a maul head. The head of a human right femur was found below undisturbed layers of earth and shell; there were no other human bones.

---

[9] Vancouver, 1801, V, 292.

[10] Hrdlička, 1945, pp. 257 f.

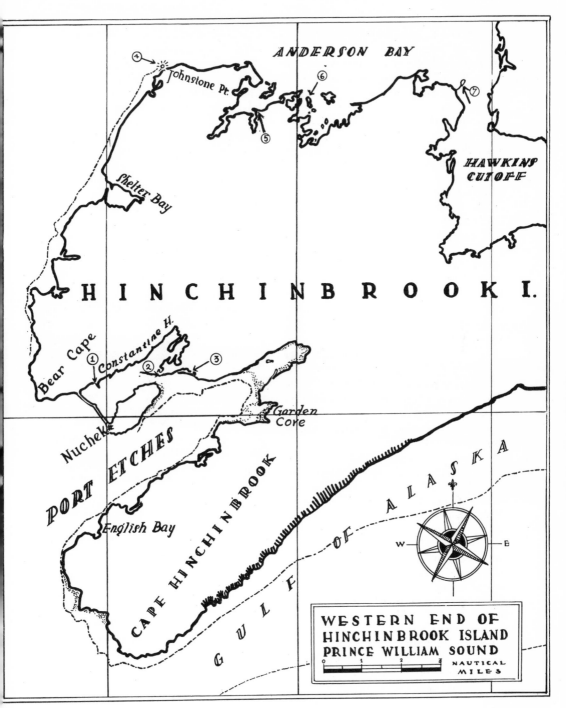

ANDERSON BAY

④ Johnstone Pt.

⑥

⑤

⑦

HAWKINS CUTOFF

Shelter Bay

H I N C H I N B R O O K I.

Bear Cape

① Constantine H.

② ③

Garden Cove

Nuchek

PORT ETCHES

English Bay

CAPE HINCHINBROOK

GULF OF ALASKA

W ——— E

WESTERN END OF
HINCHINBROOK ISLAND
PRINCE WILLIAM SOUND

0   1   2   3

NAUTICAL MILES

Map 2

PLATE 1. Sites of the Nuchek and Shallow Water Peoples

1, Site 4, qil·a·ŋ·al·ɩk, Johnstone Point, Hinchinbrook Island; the small grassy island, close to the point, typical of those selected as refuge islands; 2, Site 7, nunakṭʋq, Hawkins Cut Off, taken from Hinchinbrook Island, the site at the clearing overlooking the bar; 3, Site 10, tu·tɬiɣalɩk, Boswell Bay, Hinchinbrook Island, typical of the burial caves in Prince William Sound; 4, section of midden exposed at Site 7

Site 3. A settlement called uqciⱡɩŋuacaq is said to have been in Port Etches, east of the entrance to Constantine Harbor. The name suggests that it was a winter village, for uqcɔq means "winter" or "year." We searched in vain for this site in 1930. The beach is being washed away in this area.

Site 4. There is said to have been a village (probably a fort), qil·a·ŋ·al·ɩk, on the refuge island off Johnstone Point (Pl. 1, *1*). The sea here is attacking the land, and if any midden is left it can only be on the small skerry where the light is placed. We did not visit it.

Site 5. A village called x̣i·ɣdliaq, "Shining Bluffs," is reported on an island in the western half of Anderson or Double Bay on the north shore of Hinchinbrook Island. We did not explore it.

Site 6. On the west side of the westernmost island in Anderson Bay, facing south, was the village of aŋ·iⱡʋq. A few yards north of the site are several native huts belonging to Makari's brother, Fred Chimowitski, who died in 1930. The midden seems to be only 15 feet long and a few yards wide, and is on a cliff 4 or 5 feet above the beach. Most of the site has undoubtedly been washed away. Here we obtained 2 splitting adzes (Pl. 10, *4*), a planing adz (Pl. 12, 2), a grooved stone, a hammerstone (Pl. 20, *9*), a fragment of a lamp (?), an unfinished hunter's lamp (Pl. 20, *12*), and a cut animal articulation.

Although a stone lamp is said to have been found in the woods near the northern point of Hinchinbrook Island just west of Hawkins Cut Off, both Makari and Fred

Chimowitski denied the existence here of any settlement.

√ 3. TERRITORY OF THE SHALLOW WATER PEOPLE: SITES 7 TO 28

The eastern half of Hinchinbrook Island belonged to the Shallow Water People, txa·łaɣmiut, who also had villages on Hawkins Island, Mummy Island, and Point Whitshed at the southeastern edge of the sound (Map 2, Site 7; Map 3, Sites 8 to 28). In former times they also had hunting camps on Kayak and Wingham islands and at the mouth of Bering River in Controller Bay. Their principal village was Palugvik on Hawkins Island. A number of place names in the Controller Bay area, which were recorded at Yakutat in 1952, are clearly in Eskimo.

Hinchinbrook Island: Eastern End

Site 7 (Map 2). On a small island in the northern end of Hawkins Cut Off, facing the bar which joins the island to Hinchinbrook Island at half tide, was nunakṭuq, "Big Village" (Pl. 1, *2, 4*). The midden, about 50 by 50 or 75 feet in extent, is overgrown with high grass, ferns, wild celery, and salmonberry bushes. It has a maximum depth of 3 feet and is composed of shells, bones, and fire-cracked rocks, although the uppermost 6 inches are dark humus with few shells. The shells in the midden appear to be as much decayed as those at Sites 16 and 17 on Hawkins Island but not as old as those at Site 2 and at Palugvik.

From our excavations we obtained 2 splitting adzes (Pl. 11, *7*) and a fragment, 3 planing adzes (Pl. 13, *8*) and an unfinished specimen, 1 whetstone, 3 combination hammerstones and whetstones, a stone pick (Pl. 12, *11*) and 2 fragments, 3 lamps, a man's knife like an ulo (Pl. 27, *9*), a double-edged slate blade (Pl. 28, *6*), a socket piece for dart or arrow (Pl. 35, *12*) and an unfinished specimen, a halibut vertebra ring, and a cut bone.

In the turf above the midden was a Chinese coin (Fig. 33), identified by Miss Helen Fernald, then curator of the Chinese section at the University of Pennsylvania Museum, as belonging to the K'ang Hsi period, A.D. 1662-1723. We also purchased from Makari a bone mortar for snuff (Pl. 22, *3*), which he said had been found at the site.

Site 8. On Shorttail Point, the easternmost point of Hinchinbrook Island, just south of Hawkins Cut Off, was the village called aqłatuli, "Windy Place," because of its exposed situation. In 1930 Makari sold us 9 splitting adzes and a planing adz (Pl. 12, *7*) which he had found there, and on a visit with him to the site in 1933 we found a splitting and a planing adz blade on the beach, just inside the shelter of the point. Whatever midden there may have been was entirely washed away.

Boswell Bay Pinnacle Rocks. Matrona Tiedmann told us that a skeleton in a coffin, accompanied by native beads, had been found on top of Pinnacle Rock, napalaɣeaq, the largest gull rock at the entrance to Boswell Bay (Pl. 2, *4*). However, when we visited the rocks with her, she was uncertain of the location. We were also informed that a skeleton had been found on top of the second largest rock, napalaɣeaqṭaq. This report may or may not refer to the same burial. Wallace de Laguna in 1930 and Norman Reynolds in 1933 explored the smaller rock, but found nothing. It would have been very difficult to hoist a body to the top of any of these bird rocks.

Site 9. There were several camping places in Boswell Bay but no permanent villages. One of these camp sites is qaɣuaviɣat, on a beach on the north side of the bay, just inside the mouth. There is an abandoned cannery here, but no trace of a midden. On the rocky cliff (Site 9) at the eastern side of the beach are red pictographs (Fig. 21). The tide reaches the foot of the cliff below the paintings, but 4 or 5 yards farther up the bight there is a dry shelter under the cliff. We found nothing in it, however.

Site 10. On the north side of the bay, a little over half a mile west of the abandoned cannery, there is a large cave, tu·ṭłiɣalɪk,

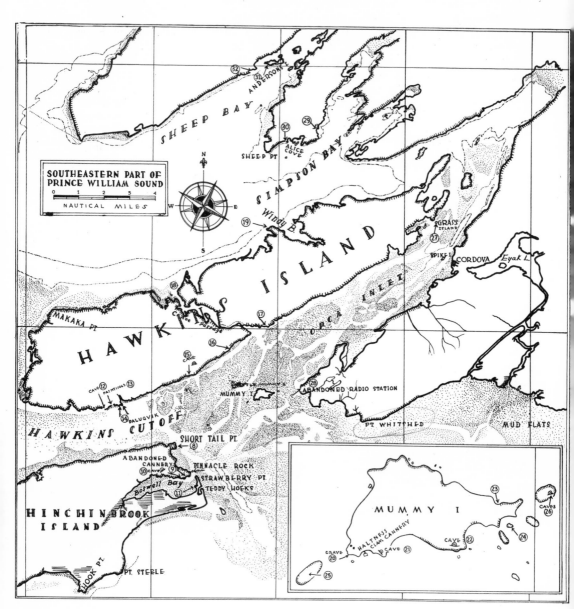

MAP 3

about 75 feet wide, 30 feet deep, and 20 feet above the beach (Pl. 1, *3*). In it we found numerous remains of fires, many animal and bird bones, and part of a torsion trap (klιpcaq or "klipski"). At the back of the cave under some stones, evidently the remains of a grave set about and possibly covered with large rocks, were 3 human vertebrae.

Site 11. On the south side of Boswell Bay, just inside Strawberry Point, where Teddy Hoek had a cabin and garden in 1930, was the summer camp site, ţιkνχtaγuaq. A very scanty midden contained fragments of flowered china, the stem of a clay pipe, animal bones cut with a steel knife, and a barbed bone arrowhead (Pl. 36, *1*). The site cannot be old, certainly not earlier than the first contact with the Russians.

Other summer camping places in Boswell Bay were not visited. Some are by streams where the Eskimo used to put up salmon; others are at the beginning of 2 portages leading to the sea otter camps along Point Hook and Point Steel on the outer shore of Hinchinbrook Island.

Hawkins Island √

This island lies entirely within the territory of the Shallow Water People, and on it were their most important villages.

Site 12. On the south shore of the island, about 3¼ miles east of the southwest point (opposite Rip Rock) and ¾ mile west of Palugvik, is a burial cave called qucuγνli, "High Place." The cave is about 24 feet long and 15 feet above the beach. The floor is covered by a shell heap, 2½ feet thick, on top of which are 3 inches of earth and fallen stones. In a recess at the back, we found the remains of an adult and 2 infants which had probably been placed under stones or within a ring of stones, although the grave (graves?) had been disturbed by modern looters. On the face of the rock were several paintings, one of which (Fig. 22C) was directly above the grave but may have had no connection with it. These pictures are described in Chapter IV. A barbed

slate blade (Pl. 29, *14*) was the only object found in the cave.

Site 13. About ¼ mile west of Palugvik, beyond a stream which flows into a small bight, is an overhanging cliff running obliquely across the beach (Pl. 2, *3*). This place is called νη·ιlιη·uaq or aηιlιηuaγuaq, "Like a Cave," and was originally a rock shelter, although the land has evidently sunk so that the original floor is now covered by beach gravel and the base of the cliff is washed by the tide. There are a good many paintings scattered along the face of the cliff for a distance of 15 feet (Fig. 23). The lower group is only 6 inches to 3 feet above the beach; the upper is about 4 feet above a narrow ledge which is some 8 feet above the gravel. This ledge may have been wide enough to stand on when the pictures were made, or else the painter used a scaffold, as I did in tracing the pictographs. They are described in Chapter IV.

√ *Site 14, Palugvik.* Palugvik (paluγvιk), the chief village of the Shallow Water People, is the most important site excavated and will be described in sections 11 to 13 of this chapter. It was found by Lee Pratt of the U.S. Forest Service, who took us to it as well as to Sites 16 and 17.

Site 15. About halfway between Palugvik and Canoe Pass is a burial cave about 15 feet wide and 25 or 30 feet above the water. The cave is unnamed, but the beach below is tuluγlιη·uacaq, "Camping Place." Makari was with a party of natives that found a skeleton here many years ago. There were no remains of clothing, but Makari claimed he could tell the body was that of a man from the dried flesh still adhering to the bones. A second priest, or lay leader, with the party baptized the skeleton "Michael" and buried the bones in a child's dress. Makari took us to the cave in 1933, and we secured the skeleton. Dr. Oetteking has identified it as that of an adult, probably a woman. Nothing else was found here.

Site 16. The site of tauχtvιk, "Cockle Place (?)," is in a shallow bight, facing southeast, about one mile west of Canoe

PLATE 2. Sites of the Shallow Water People

1, Site 28, Point Whitshed Radio Station, from Mummy Island; the larger island in the extreme left, naŋın·a with Site 26; the small island with Site 24, directly below the little island to the right of Site 26; 2, Cordova Bay, taken from Mount Eyak above Cordova; the mainland from the former Eyak camping place at Old Town, Cordova, down to Point Whitshed seen on the left; Hawkins Island on the right; and the Mummy Island group in the left center, with the entrance to Boswell Bay, Hinchinbrook Island in the far distance; 3, copying the pictographs at Site 13, vŋ·ɪlıŋ·uaq, Hawkins Island, the pictures extending from the extreme right of the photograph to just beyond the scaffold on the left (see Fig. 23); 4, Pinnacle Rock, Boswell Bay, Hinchinbrook Island; a burial was reported on top of the smaller rock to the right (*Photograph by Kaj Birket-Smith*)

Pass. A pyramidal rock in the bight serves as a landmark. The village was on top of a cliff, about 250 feet long and from 20 to 30 feet high, which is interrupted in the middle by a sloping bank where the path must have been. The clearing, overgrown by salmonberry bushes, devilclubs, and alders, suggests that the site extends about 150 to 200 feet back from the cliff. Lee Pratt found some lamps in the bank, where the midden is 1 to 2 feet thick, and there we also excavated 3 slate chisels (Pl. 14, *10. 11*), a hammerstone, and 2 wooden pegs. The shells and animal bones do not appear

to be as much decayed as those at Palugvik. A lump of weathered granite with a groove (for sharpening points?) was found on the beach, and a fine pestle (Pl. 22, *1*) was found near the site by the Tiedmanns.

According to Makari, this village was captured by a war party of "Blackfish" (Killer Whales) Tlingit from Yakutat. The tauxt-vɪk natives sent word of their plight and were aided by avenging parties dispatched by all the 8 tribes in the sound. All of the Tlingit were killed, except for one man who eventually made his escape to the mainland. This took place during the Russian occupation of Nuchek, and the story evidently refers to an incident which occurred during the fall of 1805.[11]

Several hundred feet northeast of the clearing is a cliff with a burial cave, facing south. The mouth of the cave had once (purposely?) been blocked by earth and boulders, already partially removed by looters who had rifled the cave before our first visit in 1930. The cave is about 12 feet wide, 5 or 6 feet deep, and so low that we had to lie down to excavate. In it we found the remains of 4 individuals, some stone implements, and blue and white glass beads, suggesting that the cave had been used for burials in both precontact and historic times. The contents are described in Chapter III, section 6.

A few yards from the extreme western end of the village midden is a small overhanging rock, facing southeast and sheltering a space about 6 feet long. Here were a few shells, fire-cracked rocks, and the skeleton of a man (see Chapter III, section 6), with whom had been buried a splitting adz (Pl. 10, 9) and a stone saw.

Site 17. In a small bight about ¼ mile northeast of Canoe Pass was the village of qι·aɣvιk, "Where Someone Cries." The site is on top of a very steep bank, about 25 feet high, and probably extended for the whole length of the beach, about 160 feet, and inland for 40 or 50 feet. The midden of black earth, shells, fire-cracked rocks, and animal bones is only 6 inches thick at the bottom of the bank but 3 feet thick some 12 feet above the beach. On top of the bank are 2 rows of shallow depressions, probably house pits. They are so indefinite, and the site is so thickly overgrown with bushes, that it was impossible to count the pits or trace their outlines. We dug in the most clearly marked pit for a depth of 3 feet without reaching the bottom of the midden. Here we found a slate chisel (Pl. 14, 16), a broken hammerstone, and 2 pieces of cut whale bone, all at a depth of 3 feet. In the midden on the face of the bank was

a bone arrowhead (Pl. 36, 20). Lee Pratt has a slate chisel and several splitting adzes from this site.

We had hoped to excavate here at the conclusion of our work at Palugvik, but bad weather so delayed us that this project had to be abandoned.

Makaka Point. In 1933, Makari was still living in one of the huts at aŋ·ik, on the north shore of Hawkins Island, just inside the slough southwest of Makaka Point. There is no sign here of ancient occupation, and both Makari and his brother told us that the camp was modern.

Site 18. Devil's Rock, naɣa·ulιk, at the north end of Canoe Pass, was reported as a former refuge island.

Site 19. We were also unable to visit a camp or village site, nun·aq, on an island off the west point of Windy Bay.

Mummy Island ✓

Mummy Island, Little Mummy Island, and the smaller islands and skerries of the group (Pl. 2, 2) lie in the middle of the extensive mud flats for which the Shallow Water People were named. While channels permit travel by small boat down the shore of Hawkins Island from Cordova Bay to Hawkins Cut Off and even to the mouth of Boswell Bay at all stages of the tide, the Mummy Island group is completely isolated by mud flats at low water. The position of the flats and of the small channels that traverse them changes from year to year, so we do not know if there was once a channel to Mummy Island.

Site 20. The village site, ictam uqciⱡa or aixax̱talⱡt, is above a cliff, 15 to 20 feet high, on the southwestern point of Mummy Island. The land is now occupied by the Haltness Clam Cannery, and the midden was so overgrown with bushes that we did not attempt to dig, although we found a hammerstone on the beach. The village of 200 natives, reported by Vancouver in 1794, was probably located here.[12]

Just west of the point, under an over-

11 Bancroft, 1886, 451 f.

12 Vancouver, 1801, V, 286.

hanging rock some 20 to 30 feet above the water, we found the skeleton of an elderly man who had suffered from tuberculosis of the spine, the skeleton of a mature arthritic woman, and two "Cook type" blue glass beads, but it was impossible to say with which body the beads had been originally associated (see Chapter III, section 6).

Site 21. In the small bight on the south side of the island, just east of the cannery dock, is a small cave about 50 feet above the water, where we were informed that several skeletons had been found in coffins made of adzed planks nailed with wooden pins. We found nothing in the cave but picked up a planing adz blade and a maul head (Pl. 20, *16*) on the beach below.

Site 22. On the south shore, some 25 feet above the beach and directly below the highest point of the island, is the large cave, about 100 feet wide, for which Mummy Island is famous. Huge blocks, fallen from the overhanging rock, form the roofs for 3 separate chambers. There is a fourth hole, extending below tide level, which cannot be entered except by a ladder. In 1930 the caves contained only a few bones which someone had gathered into a pile. Galucia Nelson, our Eyak informant, who had seen the cave before it was rifled, reported that it contained several mummies, wrapped in sea otter skins, sitting doubled up against the wall. Captain Rude of the U.S. Coast and Geodetic Survey is said to have taken some of them. We found a splitting adz on the beach below the cave.

Site 23. In a thin midden at the northern end of the narrow isthmus across the easternmost point of Mummy Island, we found a stone ax. On the beach at the south end of the isthmus were found a lamp (the gift of Dan Nelson, Pl. 25, *5*), 2 broken splitting adzes, and a planing adz.

Site 24. On the north side of the tiny grassy islet, u·m·ilɯɔq, (Pl. 2, *1*), opposite the southern end of the isthmus, is a midden about 10 inches thick, containing mussel and cockle shells and a bear skull.

Site 25. Makari denied that anyone had

lived on the little island, vi·va·kɬk, off the southern point of Mummy Island, although we found a shallow midden and some indefinite depressions (house pits?, caches?) in the grassy saddle on the island.

Site 26. There are several caves and rock shelters on the eastern end of naɳn·a, the largest and most northerly island off the eastern end of Mummy Island (Pl. 2, *1*). At the lowest cave were many scattered human bones, of which we secured only one jaw. The middle cave was empty, but outside was a stone lamp (Pl. 24, *1*). In an upper shelter was a grave, set about with boulders, which had already been robbed, and all that we saw there were a few fragments of boards and a blue glass bead.

From this upper shelter we could look through a hole into a small cave containing a wooden coffin. After attempting to enter the cave through this hole, Wallace de Laguna discovered what must have been the original entrance, later blocked by boulders. The cave is about 50 feet above the water, 12 feet long, 3 feet wide, and 4 feet high. The mummy in the coffin (Fig. 20) and the associated objects are described in Chapter III, section 6.

Grass Island, Site 27

In 1930 we excavated a small shell heap on the south end of Grass Island, axilɯa·γuaq, off the south shore of Hawkins Island almost due north of Cordova, but found only a piece of cut whale bone. Although the midden reached a maximum depth of 2 feet, it seems to have been only a few yards in extent. Since the sides of the island are too low to afford protection from enemies, and the island lacks water, it could have been only a temporary camping place. On the beach was a splitting adz.

Point Whitshed Radio Station, Site 28

This place, called txałam qidl·ua, "Behind Mummy Island (Flats?)" by the Eskimo, may have been either a Chugach or an Eyak site (Pl. 2, *1*). Thus, Gus Nelson, an Eyak, said it was in Eskimo territory;

Makari said that the Eyak used to come here to dig clams; and Galucia, Gus's brother, said the Eyak even had a summer camp here. The midden, 75 feet long and 6 inches deep, lies between a cannery and the nearest cabin on the east and is one of the few deposits where razor clam shells were found. In the midden is the stump of a tree which was burned during the occupation, for the charred roots are covered by deposit containing fire-cracked rocks and shells. From the midden we obtained a planing adz, an ax (Pl. 12, 9), a slate "awl," and 2 pieces of cut bone. On the beach was the greenstone blade for a man's knife like an ulo. Northeast of the point is supposed to be a burial cave.

Pictographs on Cordova Bay, Orca Inlet

Makari and Old Man Dude, an Eyak, both reported red paintings, representing men, on the cliff along the north shore of the narrows that open into Cordova Bay around the north point of Hawkins Island, that is, on the mainland opposite Channel Island. The pictures are said to be visible from a boat and to become more brilliant when wet by rain, from which we judge that they are on an exposed cliff, not in a rock shelter. In 1933 we explored the 6-mile stretch from opposite North Island to well beyond Channel Island but could not find them (see also Chapter IV, section 1).

4. TERRITORY OF THE SHEEP BAY PEOPLE: SITES 29 TO 32

The Sheep Bay People, alukaɣmiut or kaŋiɣmiut, were a small group, claiming only Sheep and Simpson bays, on the mainland between Cordova Bay on the southeast and Port Gravina on the northwest (Map 3).

Simpson Bay

Both Makari and his brother Fred told us there were no old sites in Simpson Bay, as did Old Man Dude, the Eyak shaman who lived on the point between the 2 arms of the bay. However, Makari told us myths referring to 2 villages in the bay. On the beach in front of Dude's cabin we found a slab of slate with a drilled hole, but it was impossible to determine whether it was of native manufacture.

Site 29. On a gravel bar that forms a small lagoon on the west shore of Simpson Bay, about 1¼ miles northeast of Alice Cove, we found a midden 4 inches thick, consisting of a few shells, animal bones, fire-cracked rocks, and a few fragments of wood. It does not seem to be very old, although I believe it to be the site of a village called nu·n·aq in one of the myths told by Makari.

Site 30. About ½ mile west of the Tiedmanns' former home in Alice Cove, on the west side of a point, is a place where Matrona Tiedmann told us she had found some Russian pottery. She identified the site as that of nuna-ɣam vaqⁱia, a village mentioned in one of the myths. Here we found only a 12-inch layer of humus with some fire-cracked rocks, but very few shells and animal bones.

Sheep Bay

Site 31. The main village of the Sheep Bay People was on Anderson Island and was called alu·kaq, "Namesake." In 1933 we purchased a number of specimens from Mrs. Martin Anderson, including a planing adz (Pl. 13, 5) and a double-pointed war pick (Pl. 12, 6), which had been found on the island. There were also a splitting adz, from the small island north of Anderson Island, and 2 planing adz blades (Pl. 12, 4) from Dooly's Island, northeast of Anderson Island. We were not able to explore any of these islands.

Site 32 and others. A village (winter settlement?) called uqciɫoq was reported on the northwest shore of the bay, inside or near a lagoon just southwest of the point opposite Anderson Island. Although we failed to discover the site, we found 2 splitting adzes and a green chert chisel (Pl. 12, 8) on the beach of the gravel bar which forms the lagoon. It is possible that the village was on the bar and has since been washed away.

PLATE 3. Sites of the Port Gravina, Tatitlek, and Chenega Peoples

1, Site 33, aṭiat, Port Gravina, on the spit with the single tree; Site 34, nua, in Olsen Bay, just to the right, behind the spit; Site 35, kayakɫɪk, on the beach to the extreme right; 2, Site 42, "Indian Village," Galena Bay; 3, Site 54, refuge island at entrance to Jackpot Bay; 4, Site 55, Chenega Village

In a tiny bight about ¼ mile west of the lagoon, J. B. Harris of the U.S. Bureau of Fisheries is said to have found a stone dish or lamp decorated with an encircling groove, but we found nothing here.

The beach northeast of the point opposite Anderson Island was called uɣumeqtuli or uɣʋmiɛ̱xtuli, and seems to be the site of the village to which Raven is supposed to have brought fire. Men logging here in 1930 reported that the natives also told them it was an old site, but we failed to discover any trace of former occupation.

5. TERRITORY OF THE PORT GRAVINA PEOPLE:
SITES 33 TO 36

The Port Gravina People, aṭiaɣ·miut or ic·aɣmiut, claimed the mainland between Gravina Point and Porcupine Point at the entrance to Port Fidalgo (Map 4).

Port Gravina

Site 33. The main village of this tribe was aṭiat, "Underneath," on a gravel bar which encloses a small lagoon on the west side of the mouth of Olsen Bay (Pl. 3, *1*). In 1933 we visited the place in company with Paul Elie, a local native, but found only a few fire-cracked rocks under the turf at the south end of the bar. Makari also mentioned aṭiat but located it on a spit west of Hell's Hole (see below, "Reported Sites").

Site 34. Paul Elie told us there was a mummy under an overhanging rock on the west side of the small island in Olsen Bay (Pl. 3, *1*) called nua, "Cache," because the people of aṭiat used to hide their weapons on it. We visited the spot with Paul as a guide but were unable to find the body. A tree here had recently blown over into the

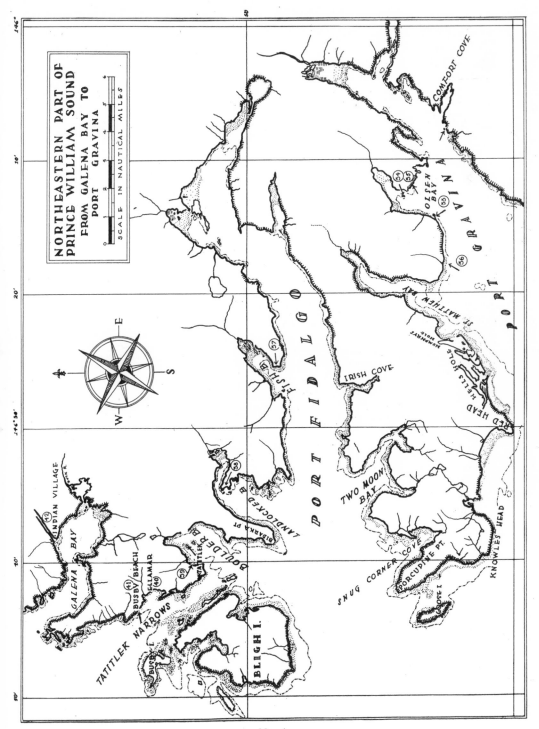

NORTHEASTERN PART OF
PRINCE WILLIAM SOUND
FROM GALENA BAY TO
PORT GRAVINA

SCALE IN NAUTICAL MILES

0   1   2   3   4   5   6

COMFORT COVE

PORT GRAVINA

OLSEN BAY

ST MATTHEW BAY

HELL'S HOLE MUMMERY'S HOLE

RED HEAD

IRISH COVE

PORT FIDALGO

FISH B.

TWO MOON BAY

KNOWLES HEAD

GOOSE I.

SNUG CORNER COVE

PORCUPINE PT.

LANDLOCKED B.

BIDARKA PT.

BOULDER B.

INDIAN VILLAGE

GALENA BAY

TATITLEK NARROWS

BUSBY BEACH

ELLAMAR

TATITLEK

BUSBY I.

BLIGH I.

MAP 4

water and may have carried with it some of the rock and the body. Paul suggested, however, that the Tatitlek natives had taken the body to their village for Christian burial, as the second priest there had urged them to do. (See Chapter III, section 6.)

Site 35. On top of a 6-foot gravel bank, above a beach ¼ mile long, just east of the mouth of Olsen Bay, we found traces of a former camping place called kayaktɩk, "Kayak Place," by Paul (Pl. 3, *1*). The soil is rich and black, but the site was too overgrown with bushes for us to determine its extent. Although the midden is 2 feet deep, it is not very old, for the shell and bone material is not much decomposed, and the midden is exposed in some places. Here we found 2 splitting adzes, a stone saw, a stone pick, a paddle-shaped stone scraper (Pl. 18, *5*), a lamp, a slate "awl," a scraper of split animal bone, and a piece of cut whale bone.

Site 36. Although Makari reported the village of maṭaŋkanɩk, "Sunshine Place," on a gravel bar between Olsen Bay and St. Matthew Bay, and Willie Totemof, a Tatitlek native, located the village of taniɣam nuɣuɩk at the same place, we were unable to find any trace of habitation.

Island near Comfort Cove. With Paul we visited the small island in the second cove south of Comfort Cove on the east shore of Port Gravina. This island is called iqaɫʋq, after the man who is supposed to have been buried on it. Here we found nothing except a fine lamp (Pl. 24, *4*) among the rocks at the high tide line.

Reported Sites. Other sites in Port Gravina were too vaguely described for us to locate. One of these was the village of cala·ɫʋq, which Makari said was on a little island shaped like a house, in the northern part of Port Gravina. Willie Totemof spoke of a small island in the bay south of Bear Trap Bay which may be the same one, although he called it tumʋŋialʋq.

On the northwestern shore of Port Gravina, between St. Matthew Bay and Red Head, is a complex of lagoons called Hell's Hole. Makari located the site of aṭiat on a

sandspit just west of these, and an old settlement, ɣioɣolʋq, in one of the lagoons. His daughter mentioned the site of iɣamʋn in Humphry's Hole, the northeasternmost lagoon. We were able to make only a hurried exploration of this lagoon, and found nothing. It is unlikely that there were settlements in this area, unless the land has subsided, for the shore is now very low and swampy.

August Juntumen, a prospector whom we met on Cook Inlet, told us that he had found a site in Port Gravina where specimens were washed out on the beach, although he would not reveal the location. He claims to have found 14 or 15 stone objects, including a green "agate" needle 3 inches long, with a groove around the end instead of an eye. There were also 5 lamps, some chisels, adzes, and several stone dishes ornamented with "flowers" on the outside.

Goose Island

From what we could observe while passing in a boat, there are several possible sites on Goose Island and on the mainland opposite.

6. TERRITORY OF THE TATITLEK PEOPLE: SITES 37 TO 42

All the northeastern part of the sound, beyond Porcupine Point at the entrance to Port Fidalgo, belonged to the Tatitlek People (tatiɫaɣmiut). Tatitlek (tatiɫaq) for which they are named is not, however, an old village, although in 1933 it was one of the few native settlements left in the sound. Makari said that it was formerly called mam·taq, "Smokehouse," but his information about this area is not very detailed (Map 4).

Port Fidalgo

Although we have no information about sites in Snug Corner Cove, there may have been a village or summer camp in the vicinity, for here Captain Cook met an umiak with 20 women, one man, and several children, as well as several one-man and

2-man bidarkas.[13] It became a favorite anchorage for the fur traders that followed Cook.

Black Stepan of Chenega said that the people whose bodies were found in Palutat Cave came from a village in Two Moon Bay (see section 14). Paul Elie told a story about a village in Irish Cove (aimqiaq).

Site 37. A village called axtuqackcu·miq, "Anybody Could Touch Me," mentioned in one of Paul Elie's stories, is located on Fish Point, a sandspit at the mouth of Fish Bay. Here H. J. Lutz found a splitting and a planing adz.

Mrs. Anderson of Sheep Bay said that several mummies had been found on one of the islands at the mouth of Fish Bay.

Site 38. Makari reported a village, il·u·ti, on the large point which runs out toward the northwest into Landlocked Bay.

Site 39. There was a village, called kaŋi-γaɔγulʋq by Makari and nanuɔγnalʋq by Willie Totemof of Tatitlek, just east of the mouth of a salmon stream on the west side of Boulder Bay, less than ½ mile north of the point below Tatitlek. Here we found only a few fire-cracked rocks, shells, and animal bones.

Islands in Boulder Bay. Nikolai Gromof of Valdez reported a former settlement on the smaller of the 2 islands in Boulder Bay which he called qɪktaγua, "Island (?)," while Makari called it ʈuluxtaɬʋq, "Camping Place." We found nothing here.

Mrs. Anderson told us that 2 mummies had been found on the larger island and exhibited in a saloon.

Tatitlek Narrows

Although the present village of Tatitlek is modern, the Washington State Museum in Seattle obtained on loan a small collection said to come from Tatitlek. It is probably from Site 39 on Boulder Bay or Site 40 at Ellamar. It consists of 2 splitting adzes, an "intermediate type" adz, a combination adz and ax, and a nicely finished slate bar whetstone.

[13] Cook, 1785, II, 357, 361.

Site 40, Ellamar. According to natives at Tatitlek there was an old village called palu·taq at the southwestern end of the bay on which the mining town of Ellamar is located. The site is apparently hidden under modern buildings. Bill Buyer of Valdez told us he found some adzes when digging the cellar of his house at Ellamar. On the beach just north of the mine we found a splitting adz reshaped as a planing adz, and a hammerstone. Just inside the point at the north end of the bay we found a splitting adz and an unfinished hunter's lamp. Ross Padin, the mine watchman, and Louie Falk gave us 2 lamps (Pl. 25, *1, 3*) which presumably came from the old site. In the collection purchased from Mrs. Anderson were 3 splitting adzes (Pl. 10, *2*), 2 lamps, and a mortar (Pl. 22, *2*), reportedly from Ellamar.

Site 41. According to tradition, the people who settled at palu·taq had formerly lived at kɪni·n, or Busby Beach, on the mainland about a mile north of Ellamar, opposite Busby Island. The site is on top of a gravel bank about 400 feet long and from 6 to 20 feet high and, to judge by the clearing, runs back about 400 feet. The timber near the site is all spruce; the natives evidently killed the hemlock in getting bark. The midden is composed of earth, beach gravel, and fire-cracked rocks. We found no animal bones or shells, but may not have located the main part of the site. We found a slate blade 1½ feet below the surface near the north end of the site, and near the south end a stone ṣaw (Pl. 16, *2*).

Mummies are said to have been found on Bligh Island, and stone lamps on the small island between Busby and Bligh islands. Fred Dedishof of Tatitlek called this island kɔŋoqila (should this be kaŋiam qidlua?).

Galena Bay

Several places near the mouth of the bay looked worth exploring, although we had no opportunity to do so.

Site 42, "Indian Village." The "Indian Village" of the U. S. Coast and Geodetic

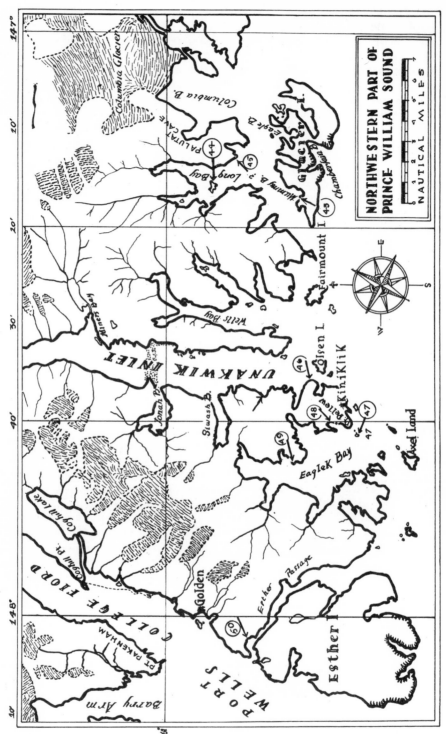

NORTHWESTERN PART OF
PRINCE WILLIAM SOUND

NAUTICAL MILES

MAP 5

Survey charts (Pl. 3, 2) was occupied during the summer of 1930 by 2 men from Tatitlek, Fred Dedishof and Joe Ivanof. They called the village kɔŋoqɬi, "Where They Catch Fish for Winter," and reported the former remains of 2 "barabaras" (semi-subterranean houses), since washed away. The only trace of early occupation that we found was a 2-foot layer of humus and fire-cracked rocks at a sand beach a few hundred yards southwest of the present cabins. A splitting adz, a broken pestle, and an unfinished hunter's lamp (Pl. 23, 6) came from the right bank of the stream west of Joe's cabin.

7. Territory of the Kiniklik People: Sites 43 to 50

From Glacier Island and Long Bay west to Port Wells, all the northern part of the sound belonged to the Kiniklik People (kaŋixlʋɣmiut?) (Map 5). It is in this area that the greatest number of valley glaciers reach tidewater, of which the most famous is Columbia Glacier (Pl. 4, 4). Which was the chief village here in former times we could not determine, for Kiniklik itself seems to have been modern, although it had already been abandoned in 1930.

Glacier Island

No village sites were reported on the island, although mummies are said to have been found in a cave just inside the western point of Eagle Bay, an area we did not explore.

Site 43. In 1933 we found a burial ledge on the north shore of Glacier Island on the west side of "Mummy Bay," the second bay east of the extreme western point of the island. The ledge has 2 levels; the upper, on which Skeleton I (Fig. 18) was found, is about 6 feet above the lower, or some 30 feet above the water. This upper ledge was just large enough for the grave. The lower ledge, containing Skeleton II (Fig. 19), is 15 to 20 feet long and 10 to 12 feet wide. These burials and the glass beads and shell pendants (Pl. 45) found with them are described in Chapter III, section 5.

The late Professor Edmond S. Meany of the University of Washington found a very similar burial in a near-by rock shelter. His account is quoted in Chapter III, section 5.

Long Bay

A village called qaɣaɣdlua, "Cheeks," mentioned in one of the myths, is described as being on the mainland, across from Columbia Glacier and opposite Glacier Island. It is near "Billy's Hole," a salmon stream in Long Bay, found by William Ripstein in the 1880's or 1890's.[14] The name "Billy's Hole" has also been applied to Long Bay or to Palutat Cave, Site 44.

Site 44, Palutat Cave. This important burial cave, on an island in Long Bay, will be described in section 14 of this chapter.

Site 45. A village site, ṭɨktaɣuɨk (Makari, Willie Totemof) or ṭɨktaɣua (Nikolai Gromof), was reported on high rocks on the east shore of Long Bay, 1 or 1½ miles above the mouth of the bay, and behind a small island. Willie Totemof, who had a smokehouse here in 1930, sold us 7 splitting adzes (Pl. 10, 5, 7, 12), which he had found on the beach. Makari said the place was not occupied very long. We explored this part of the shore for a distance of 2½ miles but were unable to locate the site.

Unakwik Inlet

Paul Elie reported red paintings in Siwash Bay. In a story told by Black Stepan, mention is made of a small village, makeli, somewhere in the inlet.

Site 46. Steve Vlassof of Chenega said that an old village, nanuɔɣnalʋq, was on the west shore of the inlet, opposite the largest of the small islands behind Olsen Island.

Wells Bay

The story of puki·tʋq, who turned into all different kinds of animals, refers to a village, kaŋixɬʋq, "Corner," at a bend near the mouth of Wells Bay. The island in front of the village was called pukitʋm qu·ŋ·ua, "puki·tʋq's Grave."

[14] Meany, 1906, p. 465.

Kiniklik

This village, deserted when we visited it in 1930, is called kaŋi·xɬʋq, and is possibly the village of the puki·tʋq story. The location—at a bend, with an island in front—fits that of the village which Makari placed in Wells Bay. Or, since we failed to find any indication of an old site at Kiniklik, the name for an older village may have been applied to this modern settlement.

Eaglek Bay

Site 47. The Chenega natives reported a former village on the largest of the islands, napalaɣeaq, off Point Pellew. It was probably a refuge island.

Site 48. A summer camp, aɣatiut, "Cormorants," is said to have been on the east side of the bay about ½ mile above Point Pellew.

Site 49. Steve Vlassof located another summer camp, nuaɣuaq, on the point 5 miles north of Point Pellew.

Esther Passage, Site 50

A village, uqciuvit, from the name probably a winter settlement, was on the north side of Esther Passage, about a mile from the western end and so placed that it commanded a view of the entrance. We passed this site, marked in 1930 by a salmonberry patch about 100 to 200 feet long, but were unable to explore it. Mrs. Nick Saski of Chenega said there were "three places at that one place," but we were unable to get a clearer explanation.

Port Wells

Mrs. Anderson said there had been red paintings, now defaced by prospectors, on the rocks on the east side of Port Wells between Esther Passage and Golden.

A village, nanuɔɣnasaq, was reported just inside Harrison Lagoon, on the north side of the entrance. We examined the place but could find no trace of the settlement. Vancouver describes a cremated burial here (see Chapter III, section 7).

Passage Canal was used by natives going over the portage into Turnagain Arm of Cook Inlet. About 500 yards from the head of the bay there is said to have been a camping place. Steve Vlassof called the camp oɣotu and gave the name tuxtiaq to Passage Canal, but Makari called the camp tuxtaq. Vancouver's men found a hut at the head of the canal (see section 15 of this chapter).

8. TERRITORY OF THE CHENEGA PEOPLE: SITES 51 TO 62

The Chenega People, taniɣmiut, claimed all of the western part of the sound below Port Wells (Map 1, Sites 51, 52; Map 6). Their principal village, Chenega, is still inhabited and is the most important native settlement in the sound.

Culross Island

Makari doubtfully placed a village, ica, in Hidden Bay. Nikolai Gromof of Valdez corrected the name to ica paɯani, and located it on a fox island, near a big lagoon. We were unable to find it.

In 1911 there were still some barabara ruins on the southern end of Culross Island, on the mainland opposite, and also on Applegate Island.

Site 51 (Map 1). Mr. Carlsen of Latouche is reported to have taken 2 mummies from some caves on the northernmost point of Culross Island.

Eshamy Bay, Site 52 (Map 1)

We located traces of a former settlement on the north shore of the lagoon behind a small island, about a mile from the head of the bay. There is a 2-foot midden of shells and animal bones, but it does not seem to be very old. Across the cove was an abandoned native camp consisting of 3 buildings and a sweat house.

Ewan Bay, Site 53 (Map 6)

The Chenega natives reported a site, naxquałaq, now covered with salmonberry bushes, on an island at the mouth of Ewan Bay.

Jackpot Bay

A settlement, ajeɣqulɩk, "Good Weather

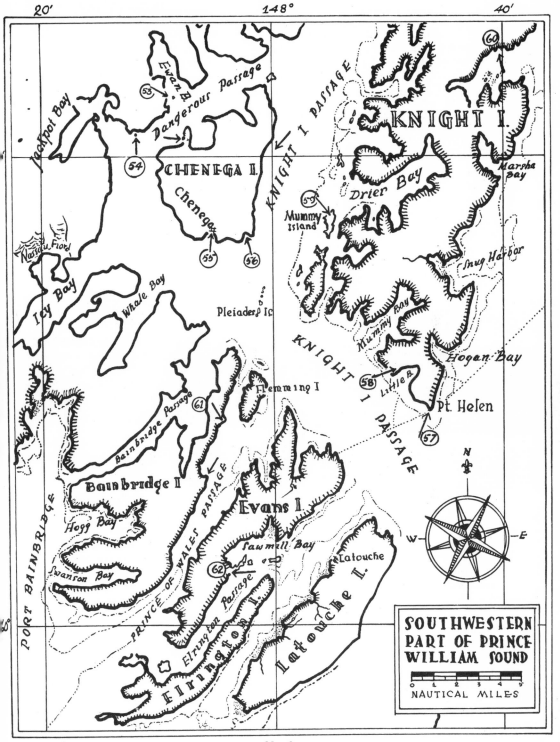

Jackpot Bay

Evan B.

⑤③

Dangerous Passage

⑤④ CHENEGA I.

Chenega

Nassau Fiord

Icy Bay

Whale Bay

⑤⑤   ⑤⑥

Pleiades I?

KNIGHT I PASSAGE

KNIGHT I.

Drier Bay

Marsha Bay

⑤⑨

Mummy Island

Snug Harbor

Mummy Bay

Hogan Bay

Little B.

⑤⑧

Pt. Helen

⑤⑦

KNIGHT I PASSAGE

Flemming I

⑥①

Bainbridge Passage

Bainbridge I.

Hogg Bay

PORT BAINBRIDGE

Swanson Bay

PRINCE OF WALES PASSAGE

Evans I.

Sawmill Bay

⑥②

Elrington Passage

Elrington I.

Latouche

Latouche I.

N

W   E

S

SOUTHWESTERN PART OF PRINCE WILLIAM SOUND

0 1 2 3 4 5
NAUTICAL MILES

MAP 6

Place (?)," probably a summer camp, was reported about 300 feet from the head of the bay, and Steve Vlassof said there was a cave full of bones somewhere in the bay.

Site 54. The site of napalaɣeaxqʋn is on a very small island off the point east of the mouth of Jackpot Bay. The midden here is only 12 inches deep. Among the objects purchased from the Chenega Church is a pestle (Pl. 20, *10*), which Steve Vlassof found on the island. A slate pendant (Pl. 43, *23*) was also found somewhere in Jackpot Bay.

Chenega Island

Site 55, Chenega Village. Chenega, called i·η·im aṭ·ia, "Under the Mountain," is the only ancient settlement on the sound which is still inhabited (Pl. 3, *4*). Although we visited the village in 1930 and 1933, we were unable to locate the spot where the ancient houses once stood. Excavation was impossible because of the modern graves and houses. The old midden may, of course, have been washed away. In the stream which supplies water for the village we found a splitting adz, and on the beach a crude hunter's lamp (Pl. 24, *5*). A barbed slate blade (Pl. 28, *1*), also found on the beach, was among the objects purchased from the Chenega Church.

Site 56. A summer camp, qɩ·aɣvɩk, was on the west shore of the easternmost of the 3 bays on the south side of the island. No midden remains, for the sea has washed it all away, but on the beach were found 9 splitting adzes (Pls. 10, *10;* 11, *3*), a grooved stone, 3 lamps, and a slate bead (Pl. 43, *27*).

Other Sites. A story told by Makari mentions a summer camp, aki·ɣqaq, on the east side of Chenega Island. I judge it to have been on the flats at the mouth of a stream a little north of the middle of the island, although we were unable to land here. In the same story reference is made to another camp, ɬudyun, on the west shore of the island. This Makari located on the western

side of the large point west of the bay opposite Ewan Bay.

Jacobsen's description of 3 burial caves on Chenega Island is quoted in Chapter III, section 8.

Knight Island

Makari said that Knight Island was used as hunting territory by both the Chenega People and the Montague Island People, the former frequenting the west coast and the latter the east.

Site 57, Point Helen. In the story about the man who visited the sea lions it is related that people lived at Point Helen before they moved to Chenega Village. Makari at first called the village uqciɬɩηuacaq but later spoke of it as ṭayɣu·lɩk. From the story, however, we gather that these were distinct settlements. The first is "The Village Where They Used to Spend the Winter," and is probably the site at or near Point Helen. The second, "Silver Salmon Place," is obviously a summer camp which Makari later placed at the mouth of "Chenega Bay" (Icy Bay on the mainland, or the small bay at Chenega Village ?). We visited Point Helen in 1930 and 1933, but could not find any midden. The most obvious place for a village is on the lagoon west of the light, although Lee Pratt found some stone adzes just east of the light. There is no midden at this last place, so we may assume that the site has been washed away.

Site 58, Little Bay. Mr. Lutz located an ancient site in the small bight west of Little Bay. He writes, "This bight is small, well protected, has an excellent gravel beach, and affords a good view of the outside waters." On the beach he found several splitting adzes, planing adzes, an ax (Pl. 12, *10*), a broken lamp, 2 fragments of copper blades, and "a flat piece of shale with a long groove in it,"

Mummy Bay. The mummies said to have been found in a deep cave on Mummy Bay are described in Chapter III, section 8. Here will also be found Jacobsen's account of a mummy cave which he visited on

Knight Island, although he fails to indicate its location.

Site 59, Mummy Island. There is a burial shelter on the west side of the north point of Mummy Island in Drier Bay. The floor is about 15 feet above the water, and the open cave is 20 feet long and 12 feet wide. Seven mummies are said to have been found here, sitting with their backs against the cliff. Nothing remained in 1930 but some adzed planks and scattered bones. We revisited the site in 1933 and discovered some pictures painted in red on the overhanging rock, 5 feet or more above the floor of the shelter (Pl. 7, *1;* Fig. 24). They are described in Chapter IV.

Site 60. Makari reported an old village, vaɣʋɳayɩk, on the north shore of the Bay of Isles, just inside the point.

Bainbridge Island

Steve Vlassof reported a burial cave at the north end of the island, on the west side facing Bainbridge Passage.

Site 61. There is a site on the point opposite the south tip of Flemming Island. The midden, 2½ feet thick, is exposed on both beaches. Here we found 2 splitting adzes, 2 hammerstones, and a scraper (Pl. 16, *14*). On the Coast and Geodetic Survey Chart this point is called Panhat. Steve Vlassof, however, called the place Rhubarb Point and the site aɳiaxtunit, and located the site of panxat on another point 2 miles farther south, which we did not visit.

Evans Island

Site 62. There was formerly a site on the isthmus at the base of the south point of Sawmill Bay. It was on the outer beach, facing Elrington Passage. Mr. Lutz writes: "The old village site is just below Sawmill Bay and at present is marked by a dilapidated old native hut of comparatively recent origin and by a frame building used by the San Juan Cannery as a web house. . . . The site is protected from storms and has an excellent gravel beach." Here he found 2 splitting adzes, a broken lamp, a copper arrowhead, and many animal bones. We

found no midden here. Evidently the land has sunk and the former shell heap has been washed away, for the beach is strewn with fire-cracked rocks, among which we picked up 2 splitting adzes (Pl. 11, *1*) and several fragments (not saved), 2 hammerstones, an unfinished greenstone scraper (?), a mortar, a chipped slate ulo or scraper (Pl. 18, *12*), and a slate "awl."

Elrington Island

In Mr. Lutz's collection there are a fine copper arrowhead (Pl. 36, *19*) and 2 splitting adzes which are catalogued as coming from a site on the north end of Elrington Island.

Latouche Island

Eskimo copper mining at the site of the Bonanza mine has already been mentioned in Chapter I, section 4.

9. Territory of the Montague Island People: Sites 63 to 67

As their name, cuqluɣmiut, implies, the home of these people was Montague Island, cuqlɪq, the largest island in the sound and that which forms the greater part of the barrier between the sound and the open Gulf of Alaska. If they went to Knight Island to hunt, they may also have frequented the southwestern islands—Bainbridge, Evans, Elrington, and Latouche—and they almost certainly went to near-by Green Island.

Montague Island

Makari enumerated 13 sea otter camps on the outer shore of Montague Island, but the locations are vague, and we do not know the age. He also listed 5 permanent villages on the more sheltered shores: one in Zaikoff Bay, 2 in Stockdale Harbor, the fourth in Port Chalmers, and the fifth in San Juan Bay (Map 7, Sites 63 to 66; Map 1, Site 67).

Site 63. The first of these villages, mentioned also in one of the legends told by Makari, was maţaɳ·kanat, "Sunshine ——?" (from maţak, "sunshine"), on the north shore of Zaikoff Bay at the north-

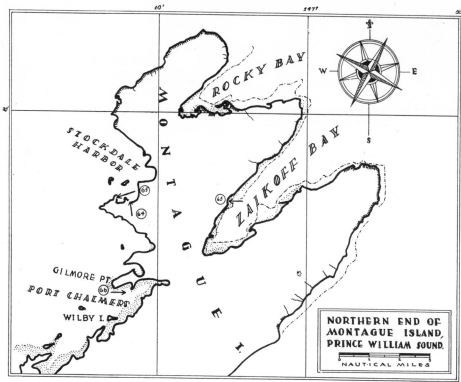

MAP 7

eastern end of the island. We did not visit it.

Site 64. In 1933 we found 3 sites on the lagoon at the south side of Stockdale Harbor, but we do not know whether these represent the villages listed by Makari.

The first site is on a small gravel spit about 200 feet long, on the east side of the lagoon, a few hundred feet from the entrance. The midden, containing a great many fire-cracked rocks, is 2½ feet thick and is overgrown with salmonberry bushes. It is being washed away, and in consequence is mixed with fresh beach gravel. The site does not seem old, for here we found a beluga rib which appeared to have been cut with a steel knife. This is possibly the village called ṭaɣuanaq by Makari or nanuɔ-ɣanaq by Steve Vlassof. The latter specified that the place to which he referred was on the left side of the entrance to a lagoon on

the south shore of Stockdale Harbor, half a mile from the south point of the harbor, which fits the locality we visited.

Sites 65A and B. The 2 other sites in Stockdale Harbor are both on the inner shore of the small island which forms the northern side of the lagoon (Pl. 4, 2). This island is attached by a chain of sandbars to 2 other small islands, and these in turn to the south point of the harbor. Site A is at the eastern end of the island, just inside the lagoon entrance. Site B is a few hundred feet southwest, at the base of the spit connecting this island with the next. These 2 sites probably represent one settlement, perhaps that called uqciłɔq by Makari.

All of the midden at Site B (Plate 4, *1*) and almost all of that at Site A have been washed away, and the beach is strewn with fire-cracked rocks. Every specimen found was picked up on the beach except the

PLATE 4. Sites of the Montague Island People; Columbia Glacier

1, Site 65B, Stockdale Harbor, Montague Island, the party collecting specimens from the beach *(photograph by Wallace de Laguna)*; 2, Sites 65A and B from Site 64, Stockdale Harbor, Montague Island, Site A on the point, Site B on the beach to the left; 3, sunken land at Port Chalmers, Montague Island; 4, Columbia Glacier

copper arrowhead from the midden at Site A. This shell deposit, 2½ to 3 feet thick, extends down for 9 inches below the beach gravel, showing that the destruction of these sites has been caused by a relative subsidence of the land.

At Site A the following were found: 6 splitting adzes (Pl. 10, *8, 11*), a splitting adz reshaped as a planing adz, a splitting adz or pick reshaped as an ax (Pl. 11, *4*), 2 planing adzes (Pl. 12, *5*), 3 hammerstones, 3 maul heads (Pls. 20, *13*; 21, *5, 10*), 2 lamps (Pl. 25, *2*), 2 ulo blades, 2 double-edged slate blades (Pl. 29, *6*), and the copper arrowhead (Pl. 28, *3*).

The following specimens are from Site B: 9 splitting adzes (Pls. 10, *3*; 11, *5, 10*), a splitting adz reshaped as an ax (Pl. 11, *8*),

a fragment of an adz or pick, a planing adz, a combination ax and adz (Pl. 12, *1*), 4 slate chisels (Pls. 14, *13*; 15, *8*), 4 hammerstones (Pls. 20, *4*; 21, *2*), a maul head (?) (Pl. 20, *15*), 2 lamps, an ulo blade (Pl. 27, *8*), and 4 double-edged slate blades (Pl. 20, *1*).

Black Stepan of Chenega told us that his grandmother had lived in a village in Stockdale Harbor called atχaq but did not explain the location further. According to Fred Allen, Lee Pratt's informant, the Russians had a penal colony in Stockdale Harbor, but we found no trace of it.

Site 66. Both Makari and Steve Vlassof mentioned a village called nunaχ̣vη̣aq, near the end of Gilmour Point in Port Chalmers. Steve located it on a little island, although no such island is marked on the chart. Makari also indicated a village, puyuɣɔnit, at the end of the small point just inside (south) of Point Gilmour, but since he also applied the same name to Port Chalmers itself, this settlement may be the same as nunaṭʋŋaq. We explored the north shore of Port Chalmers but were unable to find any signs of ancient habitation. Since the tide was high, it was impossible to explore the beach for traces of a destroyed midden, although we noted evidence that the land had recently sunk (Pl. 4, 3). On the bar north of the entrance into the lagoon at the head of Port Chalmers we found a few fire-cracked rocks, but no midden; it is possible that there was once a site here. We also explored the inner shore of Wilby Island without result. Portlock (1787) was also surprised to find no trace of habitation in this bay.[15]

Site 67. Makari's fifth village is supposed to have been qauɣuia, "Gravel," on San Juan Bay. We tramped the entire shore of the bay on both the inner and outer sides of the high gravel bar which dams up a lake behind the beach, but found no indications of a site. The village may have been on either of the rugged headlands north and south of the bay, or on the bar. If it was on the bar, it must now be obscured by gravel and sand or else have been washed away. The beach below the bar is composed of fine, surf-pounded sand and is without any shellfish, as far as we could tell, and the bay seems unsuitable for a permanent village.

Wooded Island

Black Stepan's grandmother's father was supposed to have lived on Wooded Island, the largest island off the outer shore of Montague Island (opposite Mcleod Harbor). Makari did not mention any villages in this group of islands, but said there had been a sea otter camp on the westernmost island. The name for the island, uqci·uvɪt, "Winter Place," suggests, however, a more permanent settlement.

[15] Portlock, 1789, p. 214.

10. THE ESKIMO OF KENAI PENINSULA

There were Eskimo settlements on the south shore of Kenai Peninsula in former times, although the inhabitants were not considered to be Chugach and were called by the latter the unixkuɣmiut. The territory of this group seems to have extended from somewhere in the vicinity of Puget Bay (Map 1) to Cook Inlet, including Kachemak Bay. These Eskimo had probably occupied most or all of Cook Inlet during the Third Period of the Kachemak Bay culture, and possibly earlier, to judge by the scanty archaeological evidence from the Inlet above Kachemak Bay.[16] At present, however, all of the inlet, from Kachemak Bay on the east to Kamishak Bay on the west (and inland to Lakes Clark and Iliamna) belongs to the Tanaina Athabaskans.[17] In 1778 Cook encountered Tanaina Indians at Point Possession on the eastern shore of Cook Inlet at the entrance to Turnagain Arm,[18] but it is uncertain who were the natives that he met near North Foreland on the western side of the inlet. Of the latter he writes: "I could observe no difference between the persons, dress, ornaments, and boats of these people, and those of Prince William's Sound, except that the small canoes were rather of a less size, and carried only one man. . . . They evidently spoke the same language."[19] They may have been a party of Chugach who had ventured into Tanaina territory, or Eskimo from the lower inlet, or even from Kodiak, since my Tanaina informants had many stories about Koniag raids up the inlet. Yet it seems unlikely that they could have been visitors, since "they all retired to the Western shore," as if they lived there; and in that vicinity, certainly in later times, were the settlements of the Tyonek Tanaina, who would have been their enemies. Bancroft suggests that they were Aleut sea otter hunters, dispatched by

[16] De Laguna, 1934, p. 148. Most of this report deals with Eskimo archaeological material from Kachemak Bay.
[17] Cf. Osgood, 1937.
[18] Cook, 1785, II, 397-401.
[19] *Ibid.*, p. 392.

the Russians, and they evidently used the Russian word for iron;[20] yet this seems even less likely if the Tanaina lived in the vicinity, for the Aleut were more timid than their warlike Eskimo neighbors, and it is also doubtful if they could have expected to find any sea otter so far up the inlet. We do not have to assume that these people were Eskimo, for we know that the Tanaina adopted a great deal of Eskimo culture, including the kayak,[21] and, like many Athabaskans in contact with the Eskimo, they may have learned some Eskimo words for purposes of trade. It is, therefore, impossible to tell from Cook's account how far up the inlet Eskimo territory extended in 1778.

The abandonment of Kachemak Bay to the Tanaina probably took place only shortly before the Russian occupation of Cook Inlet in the last decades of the eighteenth century.[22] In 1890 there were still Eskimo at Seldovia, near the southwest corner of the bay.[23] The last settlement on the south coast of Kenai Peninsula was abandoned about 1880, for Porter writes in 1893: "10 years ago a settlement of Chugachigmiut existed in Ayalik bay, a few miles west of Blying sound, but upon the advice of the monk in charge of the Russian mission on Cook inlet they migrated to the settlement of Alexandrovsk, on English bay, beyond Cape Elizabeth." In 1890 the only residents on the whole coast of 120 miles from Cape Puget at the entrance to Prince William Sound to Cape Elizabeth at the entrance to Cook Inlet were a white man and his half-breed wife who had settled in Resurrection Bay (near the present site of Seward).[24] At present the only Eskimo settlements in all this former Eskimo area are those of Port Graham, English

[20] Bancroft, 1886, p. 207 notes 21 and 25.
[21] Osgood, 1937, pp. 67 ff.
[22] De Laguna, 1934, p. 15.
[23] Porter, 1893, p. 69, erroneously listed as Kodiak Eskimo, although the population may well have been mixed.
[24] *Ibid.*, p. 68. The settlement which was abandoned may possibly have been Yalik in Nuka Bay, since this is listed in the Tenth Census (Petroff, 1884, p. 29), whereas there is no mention of a village in Ayalik Bay.

Bay, and Koyoktolik (Dogfish Bay), on the east coast of Cook Inlet, below Kachemak Bay. I am uncertain whether any Eskimo still live in Port Chatham, just above the mouth of the inlet.

The Port Graham Eskimo, by which name we may designate the remnants of the once larger group of Kenai Peninsula Eskimo, seem to be more closely allied to the Chugach than to the Koniag, for a Kodiak Eskimo whom I met near Seldovia told me that he had traveled in Prince William Sound and had found that the Port Graham dialect resembled Chugach speech more closely than that of Kodiak. Stories told by Chugach informants indicate that the Prince William Sound and Kenai Peninsula Eskimo sometimes fought each other and sometimes were allied in raids on the Tanaina, and that visits and even intermarriages between the 2 Eskimo groups were not infrequent. We do not know into how many independent tribes the Kenai Peninsula Eskimo were divided.

Information about Eskimo sites on Kenai Peninsula is scanty, and I have not visited any between Prince William Sound and Port Graham. Such former villages as have been reported are here mentioned in order from east to west.

There were villages in Day Harbor (east of Resurrection Bay), belonging to a local group known as the kaŋiaɣmiut, "Bay People." In one story a small village at or near the present town of Seward is called kuta·ɬʋq. A double village somewhere in the vicinity was called kaŋi·lik, "Two Bays," because there were settlements on 2 adjacent bays. A former village in Ayalik Bay was reported by the Port Graham Eskimo. A white man, whose name I have unfortunately forgotten, indicated on a map places which he thought might have been former sites. One of these is still farther west, in Two Arm Bay, the name of which suggests the unlocated village called "Two Bays." He marked another possible site on the north side of McArthur Pass, which leads between the Pye Islands and the mainland into Nuka Bay, and 2 others on the mainland shore of Nuka Island Passage, a similar channel on the western side of the bay. One is opposite the north end of Nuka Island, the second opposite its southwestern point. Port Graham and Chugach informants spoke of a village called yaliq in Yalik Bay, a western arm of Nuka Bay. The inhabitants, yaleᵧmiut, were an independent tribe with their own chief. Off the entrance to Nuka Bay, the Billings expedition in 1790 met a party in one-man kayaks, who indicated that "their habitations lay in one of these havens."[25] Petroff reports 32 Eskimo at Yalik in 1880, evidently just before the village was abandoned. In Port Dick, still farther west, Vancouver in 1794 met not less than 400 natives in 2-man bidarkas. After trading with the whites, most of them retired to the northwestern part of the bay, but we do not know whether there was a settlement here.[26] The party seems to have been much too large to represent one community, and was probably a fleet of sea otter hunters rounded up and sent off by the Russians. Our informants also spoke of a village called nuna·ṭuŋaq in Rocky Bay, near the southwestern point of Kenai Peninsula.

Turning northward into Cook Inlet,[27] we should note that Vancouver reported a village in Port Chatham, near a cove on the north side.[28] This may be the village (still inhabited?) called axu·layₗk. The (modern?) settlement of Chrome at the entrance to the bay is known to the Port Graham Eskimo as tɔ·qakvₗk. The Eskimo village in Koyoktolik or Dogfish Bay is called koᵧɯ·xtolₗk. Alexandrovsk on English Bay, where the Russians established a trading post and fort about the end of the eighteenth century, is called nanu·alᵥq (should be nanu·alₗk?). In 1880 there were 75 Eskimo, 12 half-breeds, and one white man

here, while in 1890 the settlement boasted 100 Eskimo, a few whites and "creoles" (half-breeds), evidently including the recent immigrants from the south coast of Kenai Peninsula.[29] This village is still inhabited. The native village, Port Graham, in the bay of the same name, is called palu·vik (should be paluᵧvik?), like our site on Hawkins Island. Across the bay is the now abandoned site of i·ŋulumᵥq. In 1932 I found 2 sites on Passage Island at the entrance to Port Graham. Portlock in 1786 saw no village in Port Graham, but while surveying the bay noticed "a number of huts scattered here and there, some of them very large, and several appeared to have been but lately deserted."[30] The sites in Port Graham, at least the main site on Passage Island, seem to date from late prehistoric times and "may represent the last stage of the Kachemak Bay culture when Kachemak Bay itself was already in possession of the present Indian inhabitants."[31] My failure to find anything older does not prove that more ancient sites do not exist in this area.

11. PALUGVIK: THE EAST POINT

Palugvik (paluᵧvₗk, "Where the People Are Sad"), Site 14 on Hawkins Island, was the most important village of the Shallow Water People (Fig. 1). It is on the south shore of Hawkins Island, approximately 3¾ miles from the southwestern point of the island (at Rip Rock), and 5¾ miles from the southern end of Canoe Pass, which cuts the island in two. The 2 nearest villages, Site 8 on Hinchinbrook Island and Site 16 on Hawkins Island, are about 3¾ and 4¾ miles distant, respectively.

Palugvik seems to have been a double village, with dwellings on the 2 bars that connect 2 small islets with Hawkins Island. These bars are separated by a small bight, about 630 feet wide, which drains dry at extreme low water, exposing fine beds of clams, cockles, and mussels which supplied

25 Sarytschew, 1807, Part II, p. 20.
26 Vancouver, 1801, V, 255-57, Pl. XIII.
27 Information on these sites is expanded from de Laguna, 1934, pp. 15 f., where an account of my exploratory excavations in Port Graham will be found.
28 Vancouver, 1801, V, 224.

29 Petroff, 1884, p. 29; Porter, 1893, p. 69.
30 Portlock, 1789, pp. 105, 107.
31 De Laguna, 1934, p. 16.

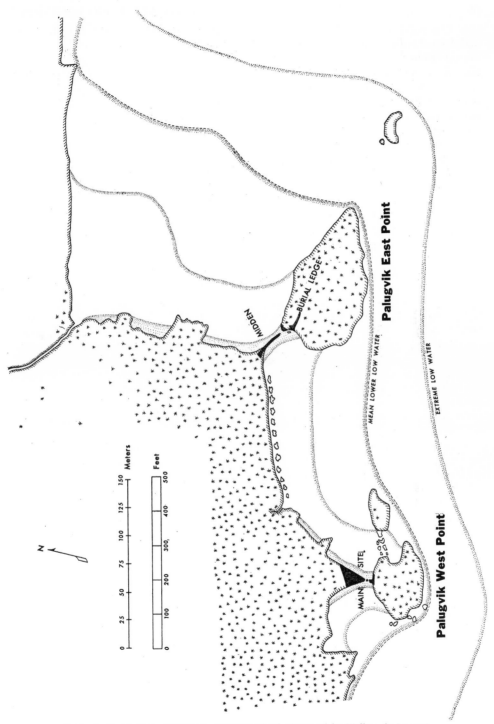

FIGURE 1. Sketch map of Palugvik, Hawkins Island (*Surveyed by Wallace de Laguna*)

PLATE 5. Palugvik

1, Palugvik East Point taken from the West Point, the burial ledge visible just to the left of the
dead tree in the foreground, the midden on the spit to the left; 2, Palugvik (West Point) taken
from the East Point, the midden on the spit partly excavated; 3, back wall of Palugvik midden
after excavation, the layers indicated by numbers (see Fig. 3)

the inhabitants with food. Water is obtainable from a small stream in the bight and
from larger creeks in the coves east and
west of the settlements. The shell heap on
the western point is much larger than that
on the eastern, and it is from this midden
than most of our specimens were obtained
in 1930 and 1933. It will be designated
simply as "Palugvik."

The midden on the eastern bar, "Palugvik East Point," is about 2 feet thick and
100 feet long, extending onto the rocky
point, or former island, where 2 large trees
are growing in the shells. Under one of
these trees the midden is 3 feet deep. The
sea has cut through the spit near its junction with the island, and since 1930 has
washed away a great deal of midden material from the eastern side. The following

specimens were found in the Palugvik East
Point midden: a whetstone (Pl. 16, 12), a
large oval grinding slab, a stone saw, a
man's knife like an ulo, 2 double-edged slate
blades (Pl. 29, 12), 2 slate "awls," a detachable barbed head, and a decorated slate
plaque (Fig. 32).

A tubular bead of walrus ivory (Pl. 43,
24), found on the beach, was probably
derived from the midden.

On the northern or landward side of the
rocky islet forming the point is a narrow
ledge, running east and west, sheltered by
an overhanging rock. It is about 20 feet
long and 4 feet wide. At its western end,
the shelf of rock which forms the floor of
the ledge slopes abruptly down to the
beach, some 15 feet below, and down this
steep crack have slipped earth, ashes, arti-

facts, and human bones from the midden deposit on the ledge, which is about 4 feet wide and 2½ feet deep. Systematic excavation in the undisturbed deposit on the ledge revealed 3 skeletons that had apparently been interred in a common grave. This triple burial (Fig. 12) and the objects found with it (Pls. 46 to 48), as well as the human bones and artifacts from the fallen portion of the deposit, are described in Chapter III, section 3.

Beyond the burials, at the eastern end of the ledge, was a deposit of charcoal around which were scattered a number of objects, suggesting that the rock shelter had been used as a camping place before the burials were made. From this place, not associated with the graves, were obtained the following artifacts, which we have designated as from "Palugvik East Point burial ledge": a planing adz fragment, 2 stone saws (Pl. 17, 6), a stone dish (Pl. 23, 3), 4 ulo blades (Pls. 26, 2; 27, 7), a single-edged slate knife (Pl. 14, 7), a green chert knife (Pl. 20, 3), a slate lance blade (Pl. 28, 17), a slate "awl," a slate blade fragment (see Chapter V, section 29), and a broken slate plaque with hole (Pl. 19, 5).

We are not able to correlate chronologically the material from the ledge with the culture represented by any particular layer of the large midden on the west point, although the broken slate plaque with hole may possibly fit a broken specimen from the lowest layer of the west site (cf. Pl. 19, 8). The decorated slate plaque from the midden on the east spit, however, suggests a relationship to the 2 oldest layers of the main midden on the west point.

√ 12. PALUGVIK: THE MAIN SITE

The large midden on the western spit we have designated simply as "Palugvik" (Pls. 5, 2; 6, 1). When we visited the site in 1930, the shell heap extended 106 feet from Hawkins Island onto the rocky island or point. On the point it has a maximum depth of only 2 feet, and 2 large trees are growing in it. On the spit, the midden is covered with grass, salmonberries, and alders. At the northern or landward base of the spit, the end of the midden is marked by the edge of the forest. In the immediate vicinity of the site there are only spruce trees, although the forest on Hawkins Island everywhere else contains both spruce and hemlock. Evidently the inhabitants of Palugvik, like those of Chenega and "Indian Village" (Site 42, Galena Bay), killed off the near-by hemlock trees by gathering the sweet inner bark.

In 1930 the maximum width of the midden at the base of the spit was 52 feet; the narrowest part, at the junction of the spit and rocky point, was 11 feet; the maximum thickness (at a spot south of what we termed Section SA, which had already washed away by 1933) was 9 feet. Yet even in 1930 a great part of the original deposit must have been destroyed by the sea. Our explorations at that time were confined to the narrowest part of the midden, where the upper layer of the deposit had already sloughed off and the lower half of the midden was about 3 feet thick. During the interval between 1930 and 1933 the sea attacked this part, enlarging the gap, until on the landward side a spit of midden only 70 feet long remained. Attached to the rocky islet was a short spit of midden 14 feet long. In the middle of the gap of bare beach between these 2 shell deposits there was left only a hump of much disturbed midden about 10 feet long, 6 feet wide, and 4 feet high. This hump seems to represent the lowest layer and perhaps the bottom portion of the second layer. Our excavations of 1930 were in the section between this hump and the main part of the spit.

Before excavation began in 1933, the main portion of the midden was a triangular deposit, its base against the mainland of Hawkins Island. The midden measured 70 feet on the east side, 58 feet on the west side, and 51 feet across the base. The surface of the midden was arbitrarily divided into 6-foot sections, in rows parallel to the eastern beach. The arrangement of these is shown in Figures 4 to 7. The midden was removed in 6-inch levels, but the specimens obtained were segregated according to the true stratification of the deposits, as accurately as these could be determined (Figs. 2, 3; Pl. 5, 3).

Before excavation was begun the height of the midden was measured at the corners of the sections, and the height of the bottom of the midden was similarly measured after excavation. Mean lower low water was taken as the point of reference. The maximum tidal range in this part of Prince William Sound, as measured at Gravel Point just above Point Whitshed Radio Station, is from an extreme low of 3½ feet below mean lower low water to an extreme high of 16 feet 4 inches above the same level. Naturally during southeasterly storms the waves wash up much higher. The bottom of the midden ranges in height from only 15 feet 1½ inches above mean lower low water (northern part exposed on west beach) to 18 feet 4 inches above mean lower low water (northeast corner of Section I), while the average height is about 17 feet. In other words, the lowest part of the midden is over one foot below the level of high water, and all of the bottom of the. midden is below the level of storm waves. The top of the midden was also fairly level, ranging from 22 feet 8½ inches (between Sections 5D and 5E) to about 25 feet above mean lower low water (northwest corner of Section 2I and at Section SA). The thickness of the midden varied from 6 feet 3 inches to 8 feet 2 inches, but it will be remembered that the thickest part (south of Section SA) was destroyed between 1930 and 1933.

Cross sections, or diagrammatic sketches of the stratification, were made of the midden as exposed along the east beach before excavation (Fig. 2) and of the wall of midden remaining after our work was finished (Fig. 3; Pl. 5, 3). These give some notion of the character and relationship of the 4 main layers or strata of which the shell heap is composed. Other features are illustrated in the plans of the midden at different stages of excavation (Figs. 4 to 7).

Bottom of Midden (Fig. 4; Pl. 6, 3)

The midden rests upon a deposit of sour swamp soil or peat, composed of very compact layers of moss, etc., which is the characteristic soil in the Prince William Sound area. It is termed "tundra" on the U.S. Coast and Geodetic Survey charts, although it is not permanently frozen, as the name might suggest. In the bottom of Section 1C a test pit was sunk in an attempt to reach the bottom of the peat. At a depth of 3 feet rock was encountered, but we are not able to say whether this was bedrock or an isolated boulder. In any case the bottom of the peat is at least 2 feet below the present level of extreme high water, clearly indicating a relative subsidence of the land since the peat was formed. Furthermore, we can be fairly certain that subsidence has taken place since the first occupation of the site, because the lowest part of the midden is below the level of the spring tides. The land probably stood at least 4 feet higher than it does now when the first natives built their houses at Palugvik; otherwise these would have been lashed by the sea during equinoctial storms. It was into the swampy soil that the post holes for House 1 were dug (see below).

Layer 1

Layer 1 (originally called Stratum IV in our field notes) consists of very disintegrated shells, chiefly blue mussels in the upper part, and in the lower part of shells stained yellow by seepage from the northern end of the midden. This band of yellow shells is thickest at the northern end of Section I, and it is into the upper portion of this band, which is here separated from Layer 2 by a thin deposit of pebbles, that the bottom of the double grave (Skeletons I and II, Figs. 5 and 9) was dug. The yellow shells narrow to a very thin strip in Sections F to D, and are here overlaid by a floor of mud and gravel. This floor is 17½ feet above mean lower low water, or about 6 to 12 inches above the uneven bottom of

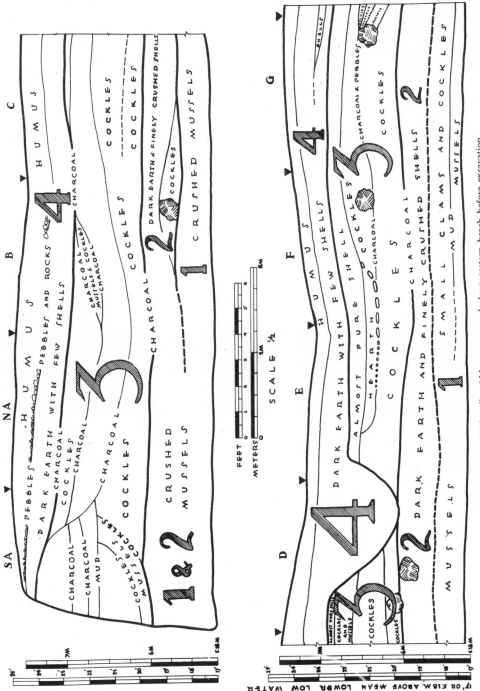

FIGURE 2. Cross section of Palugvik midden as exposed along eastern beach before excavation

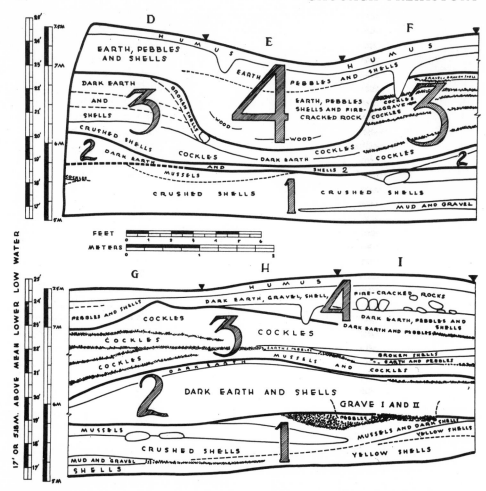

FIGURE 3. Cross section of Palugvik midden as exposed after excavation. See Plate 5, 3

the midden, and is associated with Hearth 1 (Pl. 6, 3) and perhaps also with the house posts at the bottom of the midden. At the very bottom of Layer 1 in Section 3C, parallel to the line between 2 of the house posts, was found a wooden coffin containing the skeleton of an elderly woman (Skeleton III). This coffin is not a box, but a hole lined with planks, and therefore could not have been made until a depth of midden sufficient to cover and support the wooden sides had accumulated (Pl. 9, 4; Fig. 10). If, as seems probable, the house (House I) represented by the posts dates

from the very first settlement of Palugvik, the grave must be somewhat younger. It is, however, also from the period represented by Layer 1, since the upper part of this layer above the grave was undisturbed. At the 17½-foot level in this same section we found part of a circle of boulders, directly above the coffin but separated from it by a foot of midden deposit. The center of the circle was probably in Section 3D (unexcavated), and it may have been from 6 to 10 feet in diameter. The fill of shells inside the ring was lighter in color than the midden outside; that is, the fill contained a

PLATE 6. Palugvik

1, Palugvik (West Point) taken from a tree top on the island at the end of the spit, the excavation of the midden almost completed *(photograph by Wallace de Laguna)*; 2, Hearth 3, Section I, 20-foot-6-inch level, graves I and II under boards at the right (see Fig. 6); 3, Hearth 1, Sections 1F and 2F, 17-foot level (see Fig. 4); 4, Hearth 4, Section 2D, 20-foot-6-inch level (see Fig. 6)

smaller proportion of earth. Nothing was found in the segment of the ring which we excavated, and we do not understand its significance. Under the outer edge of the stone circle was found the skeleton of an infant (Skeleton V, Fig. 11). At the very bottom of the midden in Section 1C were the skeletons of 2 small puppies about 2 weeks old.

Four large posts and several stakes, found in the soil under Layer 1, probably represented a single structure which we have called House I. These posts and stakes are described in Chapter V, section 92. Three posts were on a line about 30 feet long: the first post in the northern part of Section H; the second (Pl. 58, *3*) near the northwest corner of Section 1G; the third in the extreme southwest corner of Section 2D. The fourth post (Pl. 59, *5*), in the extreme

northwest corner of Section 3C, was placed a little south of a line at right angles to the line formed by the other posts; that is, the 4 posts form a somewhat obtuse angle. If we assume that this angle was at one corner of the house, the interior of that structure lay west and north of that corner, most of it in the unexcavated portion of the midden. In that case, the coffin of Skeleton III also lay outside the house. Although the grave for Skeleton III must have been dug some time after the building of the house, the coffin lay parallel to the line of the wall, suggesting that the wall was still standing when the burial was made.[32] Since the circle of stones in Section 3C crosses the

[32] A similar orientation of a grave with reference to the wall of a house was observed at Cottonwood Creek, a site of the Third Period in Kachemak Bay (de Laguna, 1934, p. 39, Pl. 6).

line of the wall, it must have been made after the house had fallen into ruins.

However, the angle formed by the lines of posts may have been a re-entering corner, perhaps the corner between the main room of the house and a smaller room.[33] In that case, the interior of the house lay in the excavated portion of the midden, although the farther walls were not found. This interpretation would place Hearth 1 inside the main room of the house, and the layer of mud and gravel about it, in which were traces of wood, must have been the floor. It would have been natural to use gravel for flooring, since the underlying soil is so swampy. In this case also, the coffin of Skeleton III would have been inside the house, presumably inside the smaller room. The house may, of course, have been abandoned when the burial was made, unless the inhabitants followed the Aleut custom of sometimes interring the dead in a compartment of a house which was then sealed off from the inhabited portion.[34] It is also possible that these posts did not stand at corners of the house, but that some may have been placed in the middle of a large structure as supports for the roof. In any case, there is no evidence that the house was semisubterranean. In this respect it fits our informants' description of the large plank house ("smokehouse" or mam·taq), of which the floor was not excavated and which had a large central room with fireplace for cooking, and small annexes at the ends for sleeping and sweat bathing.

Layer 2

The line of division between Layers 1 and 2 is not at all clear, and perhaps they should be considered as parts of the same stratum. Certainly the cultural material is the same from both. Layer 2 (originally called Stratum III) is characterized by dark earth and finely crushed shells. There

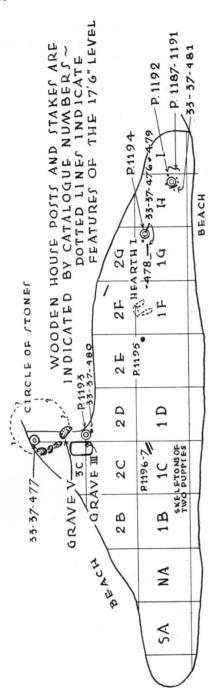

FIGURE 4. Plan of Palugvik midden after excavation, at 17-foot level above mean lower low water

[33] A similar arrangement of rooms was observed in the same house at Cottonwood Creek, in which the angle between the 2 walls was also not a true right angle (ibid.).
[34] Dall, 1878, p. 7; Jochelson, 1925, p. 49.

is some admixture of gravel, especially in Sections D and E where there is also charcoal, and in Sections H and I where the line of fine pebbles at the bottom of the layer seems to be cemented together with fat. The fat was probably derived from the stone fireplace, Hearth 3, at the north end of Section I at the 20½-foot level (Fig. 6). This pebble layer runs below the bottom of the double grave (Skeletons I and II, Fig. 9; Pl. 9, 2) at the north end, but at the south end the pebble layer was removed in digging the foot of the grave. The bottom of the grave is roughly at the 19-foot level (Fig. 5). Also at the same level is a line of large rocks, running in a curve across Sections 1E and 2F, associated with which is a deposit of charcoal. These seem to be a disturbed fireplace, Hearth 2. Another stone fireplace, Hearth 3, is in Section I, at the top of Layer 2, at the 20½-foot level (Fig. 6). Several scattered boulders extend from this hearth across the western side of Section H (Pl. 6, 2). The charcoal scattered from this hearth overlies the grave near by, showing that the hearth was built after Skeletons I and II were buried. The double burial dates, therefore, from within the period represented by Layer 2. The skeletons of 3 infants were also found at the bottom of Layer 2: Skeleton IV in Section 2C, VI in 3C, and VII in 1B. These all date from the beginning of the period.

Layer 3

The break between Layers 2 and 3 is more clearly marked than are the divisions between other layers, and this separation is also more significant from the point of view of the cultural materials. The top of Layer 2 is very uneven, in part because of excavations carried out during the period represented by Layer 3. Thus, in Section H, at about the 21-foot level, was a shallow oval depression dug into the top of Layer 2 and filled with the cockle shells of Layer 3. It is about 5½ feet long (northeast to southwest), 3 feet wide, and 9 inches deep. In Sections 2D, 2E, and 2F the top

of Layer 2 has also been removed for a depth of about 15 inches, making a fairly level floor which is about 7 feet wide in a north-south direction (Fig. 3). The edge of the pit extends almost to the line of

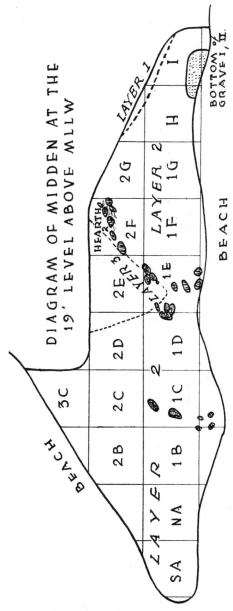

FIGURE 5. Plan of Palugvik midden at 19-foot level above mean lower low water

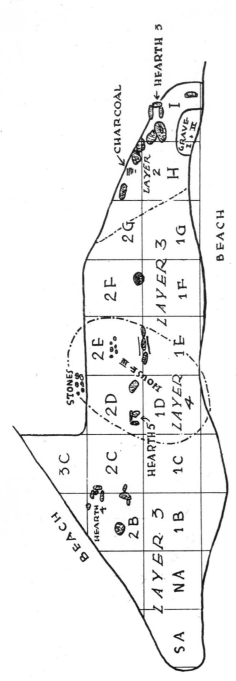

stones associated with Hearth 2 (Fig. 5),
and the bottom is about at the 19-foot
level. The thin stratum of Layer 2 under
this excavation contains charcoal and
gravel, and it may, therefore, represent the
floor of a small structure, which we have
tentatively designated as House II. It is
possible that the line of stones in Sections
1E and 2F is in some way associated with it.

Layer 3 (originally called Stratum II) is
composed of large numbers of cockle shells
lying in several bands separated by layers
of beach gravel and broken beach shells,
evidently brought into the midden by
human agency. At the southern end of the
midden, the various bands of Layer 3 are
separated by thin lenses of charcoal. At
the northern end the cockles give way to
deposits of blue mussel shells. A sampling
of unbroken cockle shells from Section 1B
included 83 right-hand shells and only
11 left-hand examples, showing that the
ancient inhabitants were accustomed to
breaking the left half of the cockle when
opening it. Hearth 3 lies so close to the
top of Layer 2 that it may actually belong
to Layer 3. In addition, Hearth 4 (Pl. 6,
4) was found in Layer 3 at the 20½-foot
level. The only baking hearth was found
in Sections 1E and 1F (Fig. 2). It is 7 feet
long (in diameter?), 9 to 12 inches deep,
and incompletely lined with stones. The
bottom is about at the 21-foot level. The
interior of the hearth is filled with sand
and charcoal.[35] Fire-cracked rocks were
scattered at various levels throughout this
layer and were more numerous than in the
2 lowest layers at the site.

Layer 4

The most interesting feature on the top
of Layer 3 is the large pit which was excavated in Sections 1D, 1E, 2D, and 2E and
which is filled with Layer 4. It can be seen
on both cross sections and also on Figures
6 and 7. The pit probably was for a house,
House III, excavated at the end of the

[35] Similar baking hearths were characteristic of
Kachemak Bay II and III (de Laguna, 1934, p. 34,
Pls. 13C, 14A). Hrdlička (1944, pp. 338 f., Fig.
175) reports 3 from his large site on Kodiak.

period represented by Layer 3, and was probably dug in this place because there were still the remains of the previous excavation, House II, not yet completely filled with the deposits of Layer 3, so that less work was required to make the second hole. House III is dug completely through Layer 3 in Section 1D but does not quite reach the bottom of the layer in Sections 2D and 2E. It is about 3 feet deep, the floor being at the 19½-foot level. To judge by the cross section shown in Figure 3, the pit was at least 9½ feet wide (north-south). The eastern end of the pit probably extended for a short distance into the part of the midden which had been washed away before our excavations began. After we had finished our excavations we dug into the remaining portion of the midden and found the western end of the pit about 2 feet beyond the western edge of Sections 2D and 2E. The pit must, therefore, have been from 14 to 16 feet long. There were traces of wood at the bottom of the refill in the pit, together with a large number of small greasy pebbles, probably used as cooking stones, which rested on a floor of brown mud or clay. At the 20½-foot level (Fig. 6) there was a stone fireplace, Hearth 5, in the fill, and at the same level a group of stones and particles of wood on a line between Sections 1E and 2E. A pile of fire-cracked rocks was in Section 2E. It is difficult to trace the outlines of the pit in the 22- and 22½-foot levels (Fig. 7). The southern edge seems to be marked by a line associated with 4 post holes in Sections 1D and 2D. Just north of this, inside the house fill, is a line of boulders which may have been placed originally on the roof and later have fallen into the pit when the house collapsed. At the 22½-foot level there is a distinct break in the character of the midden on a curving line which runs as far north as Section 2G (Fig. 7), suggesting an extension of the house in this area, which would make the total length at this level about 18 feet. The floor here evidently sloped, suggesting an entrance. Although

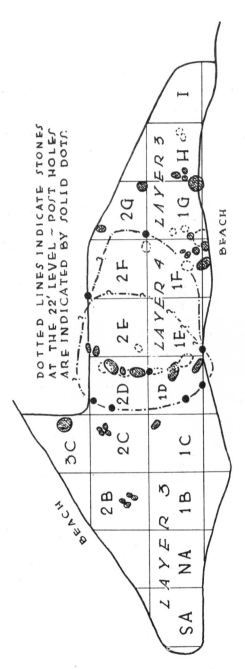

FIGURE 7. Plan of Palugvik midden at 22½-foot level above mean lower low water

our information about this structure is far
from clear, it does suggest that House III
was a semisubterranean building, perhaps
a small winter hut, such as was described
by our informants.

Layer 4 (originally called Stratum I) is
the uppermost deposit at Palugvik. A large
proportion of it consists of earth, pebbles,
and fire-cracked rocks. There is evidently
some beach gravel, mixed with material
which had washed out from an older part
of the midden and was later carried back
onto the site. Two slate blades from this
layer (Pl. 29, 1) are waterworn. Since the
whole terrain is wet, we can assume that
these layers of gravel were intended to pro-
vide a dry flooring for a structure or yard.
Similar layers of gravel were found at the
bottom of Layer 1 associated with House I,
and in the middle of Layer 3.[36] The upper
part of Layer 4 grades into humus, and
when we were stripping the turf we found
a number of specimens in the grass roots.
Nothing was found at Palugvik, however,
which indicated contact wih Europeans,
so we must assume that the village had
been abandoned before their coming. Several post holes are found in Layer 4, and
some of these are shown in Figure 3.

Layer 4 was also represented by the
midden on the rocky point, but it is not
clear whether the other layers were also
found here. Most of the specimens obtained
in a small test pit dug on the point were
from Layer 4 and are so designated.

Other Features

About 1,000 specimens were found in
the midden at Palugvik and are designated
according to layer. About 100 more were
found on the beach or in slumped portions
of the midden and so could not be assigned
to any layer, but are catalogued "Palugvik,
layer (?)." While the material from this
site is so homogeneous that we are not
justified in assuming more than one major
cultural stage, there are minor differences
which distinguish the upper half of the

midden (Layers 3 and 4) from the lower
layers. Thus, the few copper objects are
limited to the upper part, and the decorated
slate plaques are found only in Layers 1
and 2. Fire-cracked rocks are plentiful in
the 2 upper layers but not in the 2 lower,
and there are similar changes in the character of certain specimen types which will
be pointed out in Chapter V.

Excrement was found in several places
in the midden. A sample from Layer 2
(33-37-301), composed almost exclusively
of fish bone fragments, is probably that of
a large dog. Other samples came from
Layer 2 (P.1322), above the double burial
of Skeletons I and II, and from Layer 1
(P.1004). (See Preface for explanation of
catalogue numbers.)

Five stone fireplaces have been mentioned
in addition to the baking hearth. These
were in Layer 1 (Pl. 6, 3), Layer 2 (Pl. 6,
2 and Hearth 2, unillustrated), Layer 3
(Pl. 6, 4), and in Layer 4 in House III
(Hearth 5, unillustrated). These hearths
are small rectangular boxes, set about with
stone slabs or boulders, about 12 inches
long and 8 inches wide (30 x 20 cm.). One
end is open. The shape of these fireplaces
would suggest that some form of pot was
set over the fire, yet no cooking vessels of
pottery or stone were found, and we know
from the reports of the natives that they
cooked by means of hot rocks in wooden
boxes and spruce root baskets. We did not
find any flat slabs of rock which could have
served as roasting slabs or "frying pans."
The walls of these fireplaces were not intended, therefore, to support anything, but
rather to concentrate the heat of the fire
and conserve fuel which must have been
hard to obtain with stone adzes. No rectangular, vertically walled slab fireboxes
like these were found in Kachemak Bay, but
they were quite common in what Hrdlička
terms the "Pre-Koniag" layers of the large
site on Kodiak Island. He also reports a
few from Agattu, but notes that well-formed
fireplaces were lacking on the Aleutians.[37]

---

[36] Similar layers of beach gravel were found at
Kachemak Bay (de Laguna, 1934, p. 34).

[37] Hrdlička, 1944, pp. 338 f., Figs. 65, 67, 68, 139;
1945, pp. 310, 411.

As already suggested for the prehistoric Cook Inlet Eskimo, the comparative scarcity of fire-cracked rocks in the lower levels may indicate that the present type of steam bath was not known from earlier times—in Cook Inlet not until the end of the Eskimo occupation in Kachemak Bay.[38] Hrdlička also remarks on the abundance of fire-cracked rocks in the upper levels of the great site which he excavated on Kodiak Island, whereas they were rare in the lower, so-called "Pre-Koniag" deposits. He also believes that the rocks indicate the introduction of the steam bath.[39] I had suggested that the Pacific Eskimo adopted the steam bath from the Indians, and this theory gains support from the evidence in Prince William Sound, which would indicate that the steam bath was used here at an earlier time than in Kachemak Bay, presumably because of the closer contacts between the Northwest Coast Indians and the Chugach. Unfortunately Hrdlička's neglect of stratigraphy prevents us from knowing with any certainty when the steam bath appeared on Kodiak Island. Lack of fuel prevented its practice by the Aleut.[40]

13. ANIMAL REMAINS FROM PALUGVIK

I am deeply indebted to Dr. Magnus Degerbøl of the Zoological Museum of the University of Copenhagen for an identification of the faunal remains at Palugvik and Palutat Cave.

The most common shells composing the midden at Palugvik were those of clams (*Saxidomus nuttalli* [Conrad], *S. giganteus* [Deshayes], and *Paphia staminea*), cockles (*Cardium corbis* [Martyn]), and mussels (*Mytilus edulis*). In addition there were also some shells of whelks (*Thais lamellosa* [Gmelin]), marine snails (*Littorina sitchana* [Philippi]), and limpets (*Acmaea cassis* [Eschscholtz]). Mussel shells were most prominent in Layer 1, and cockles in Layer 3.

Sea mammal bones were almost 3 times

as numerous as those of land animals or birds. The sea otter (*Enhydris lutris*) was of outstanding importance, being represented by more than half of the mammalian bones. Other sea mammals were the seal, including the harbor seal (*Phoca vitulina*) and unidentified species, the porpoise (*Phocaena*), the sea lion (*Arctocephalus*), and unidentified species of whales (*Cetacea*).

Most important among the land mammals was the marmot (*Marmota caligata*), followed by the bear, represented by both the black bear (*Euarctos americanus*) and the Kodiak grizzly (*Ursus horribilis*), the beaver (*Castor canadensis*), and the land otter (*Lutra canadensis*). Other land animals were the porcupine (*Erithizon dorsatum*), mink (*Lutreola vison*), fox (*Vulpes*), and some ungulates, most of which were probably mountain goats, although the caribou was also represented.

There were about as many bird bones as bones of land mammals. The species represented were loon (*Gravia*), cormorant or shag (*Phalacrocorax*), albatross (*Diomeda*), scoter or coot (*Melanitta*), eider duck (*Somateria*), gull (*Larus*), auklet (*Aethia*), and eagle (*Haliaëtus*). This list is probably not exhaustive, however.

Fish bones, mostly jaw and skull fragments, were scanty in numbers, and the only species which could be identified were cod (*Gadus*) and spiny dogfish (*Squalus acanthias*). Curiously enough, no salmon bones were recognized, and most of the fish remains are unidentified. This scanty representation may be due to several factors: the fish bones may have rotted more readily than the more compact bones of mammals and birds; we may have failed to save all that we found; the natives may have believed that it was necessary to throw the bones back into the water to secure the reincarnation of the animals. This last explanation might apply perhaps with especial weight to the salmon. All these possible factors may have operated together.

It is quite evident that the sea furnished the bulk of the food secured by the inhabi-

[38] De Laguna, 1934, p. 162.
[39] Hrdlička, 1944, pp. 30, 133, 340, 394.
[40] Cf. Hrdlička, 1945, p. 51.

tants of Palugvik. The great importance of the sea otter is perhaps not too surprising since it was not far to the sea otter hunting grounds off the outer shores of Hinchinbrook Island. Dr. Degerbøl suggests that these animals were probably hunted more for the sake of their furs than for their meat, since the meat is generally said to be of rather poor quality. The bones are only slightly fragmented and have not been broken for the marrow. The brain case, however, has always been crushed. Many of the bones—as, indeed, is true of all species—have been gnawed by dogs, while only a few are charred. Dr. Degerbøl suggests that a breeding place must have been in the vicinity, because there are many bones and jaw fragments with milk teeth which belonged to quite young animals. The presence of these young individuals does not prove that the site was inhabited chiefly in the summer, however, for sea otter do not bear their young at any definite season of the year. At least 32 individuals (19 adults, 13 pups) are represented by the more than 632 bones. Of these, 147 bones can be assigned to Layers 3 and 4 of the upper half of the midden, while over 429 came from Layers 1 and 2, which constitute the lower half. Over 56 bones came from Layers 2 or 3 and could not be assigned to either large division of the midden.

Second in importance was the seal, but of this animal we have only something over 94 bones. Again, over half of these come from the 2 lowest layers of the midden. Porpoise and sea lion are far less important. Only a very few whale bones were found, chiefly parts of vertebrae, but it is to be remembered that one whale represents an impressive amount of food and that the bones were probably left on the beach, where the carcass was flensed, except for the pieces needed for tool material.

There are only about one third as many land animal bones as bones of sea mammals. Yet of the approximately 243 that were recovered, 118 come from the upper half of the midden and only 103 from the lower. This seems to be a reversal of the very marked trend shown by the sea mammal bones, and is because of the greater numbers of marmot and porcupine bones in Layers 3 and 4. The other land mammals are poorly represented.

It is significant that very few skulls were found in the midden. The only fairly complete skull is that of a large mink from Layer 3. While there were 37 skull fragments of sea otters, 21 of these were pieces containing portions of the bulla or tympanic bone. In addition there were 19 fragments of upper jaw and 39 mandibles or pieces of mandible. Even more striking is the lack of seal skulls. Of 11 seal skull fragments, 10 are bullae, while there are only 3 pieces of upper jaw and 2 fragments of the lower jaw. One fragment of whale skull and 2 fragments of bear skull complete the list. Although some 46 mandibles or parts of mandible of the marmot were found, there are only 3 pieces of upper jaw and no fragments of the brain case. It would appear that the marmot mandibles may have been purposely saved, perhaps because they were useful as tools. This absence of animal skulls is not peculiar to Palugvik; only on a small island (Site 24) off Mummy Island was a complete skull found, that of a bear. It would appear that the skulls (and possibly other bones) of certain species were either left where the animal was killed or were disposed of by burial or by throwing into the sea, presumably to permit the soul of the dead animal to become reincarnated in a new body. The skulls of sea otter and seal were apparently crushed. The bullae or tympanic bones were frequently made into beads (see Chapter V, section 73). Hrdlička also noted the absence of bear skulls in the midden at Uyak Bay, Kodiak Island, although bear bones were common in that site. In addition, he found the broken out bullae of seals here and in Aleutian sites, although sea mammal skulls were absent.[41] Animal skulls were also rare or absent at

41 Hrdlička, 1944, p. 479; 1945, p. 155.

Kachemak Bay sites, although a number of seal and porpoise tympanic bones were found, especially in layers assigned to Periods sub-III and early III. There is no doubt that certain bones of certain species had especial significance for the Chugach. Thus the humerus of the land otter was mentioned in one story as a die for gambling, or rather in this case for foretelling the future. The land otter itself was believed to be the transformed body of a human being who had drowned.

Of the 259 bird bones, 162 come from the upper part of the midden and only 89 can be ascribed to the lower 2 layers. Fish remains are too scanty to suggest any trend.

One has the impression that flesh was more important than shellfish in the earlier prehistoric period at Palugvik, since out of a total of 1,304 or more bones of edible animals, 723 and over can be assigned to Layers 1 and 2, while only something over 482 came surely from Layers 3 and 4, although the latter contained a greater bulk of shells. It should be remembered that no count of shells was even attempted, and that this impression is probably faulty since the shells in the lower layers were far more crushed and compacted than those in the upper part of the midden. It would also seem that there had been a relative shift from an overwhelming dependence on sea mammals to a somewhat greater emphasis on land mammals and birds. It is possible that this change indicates a change in the seasonal importance of the site or a shift in the interest of the inhabitants. It should be remembered, however, that a good deal of the site had been washed away before we explored it and that we did not excavate all that was left, so that our sample is really inadequate.

Of interest also are the dog bones found in the midden. These are described as belonging to medium-sized Eskimo dogs. One dog skull, minus the lower jaw, was found in the grave with Skeletons I and II, dated from the period represented by Layer 2 (see Chapter III, section 2). Dr. George G.

Goodwin, Department of Mammalogy, American Museum of Natural History in New York, who identified for me the dog bones found in Kachemak Bay,[42] examined this specimen and reported that it was much smaller than either the Eskimo or Indian type dogs from this area. I am uncertain whether or not it should be taken as typical of the general run of Palugvik dogs or whether it represents a slightly different breed. Dr. Goodwin felt, however, that it resembled very closely the dog photographed at Chenega Village (Pl. 9, 3), although the latter was probably a little smaller. These modern dogs are bred by the Chugach for hunting because their small size enables them to pursue small fur-bearing animals into their dens and burrows. They look like undersized and undernourished collies. Dogs may well have been used for hunting in prehistoric times also. In addition, they could have been used to carry packs, but travel by dog sled would certainly have been impracticable in the rocky terrain.

More than 170 dog bones were found in the midden, not counting the skull in the double burial or the almost complete skeletons of 2 pups about 2 weeks old that were found at the bottom of the midden. Of these bones, only 18 came from the upper half of the midden, while 138 came from the lower half. This illustrates the striking decline in the dog population at Palugvik, which may be correlated with a decrease in the amount of animal food available to feed them or a realization that they were economically of little value. Many of the animal bones at Palugvik, including those of the dogs themselves, had been gnawed, presumably by the dogs, and there were also pieces of dog excrement. At least 17 individual dogs were represented: the 2 very small pups, 2 other very young pups, 3 young animals with erupting and shedding teeth, and 10 young adults. What happened, one wonders, to the old dogs? The distribution of types of dog bones is

[42] De Laguna, 1934, pp. 28, 31 f.

probably what one might expect to find if the owners made no selection of bones for special disposal.

The decline in the number of dogs is paralleled by that noted on Kachemak Bay, where bones of the Eskimo dog were fairly common in the First Period, but were barely represented in the Third. At the very latest period of all, probably at the time of the Athabaskan advance, an Indian type of dog, with coyote characteristics, made its appearance.[43]

Although dogs were found throughout the period represented by the occupation of the site on Uyak Bay, Kodiak Island,

Hrdlička found that fox remains were much more common, and believes that these were kept as pets. One type of dog was like the Eskimo dog; the other was smaller with a shorter skull.[44]

The table below indicates the distribution of animal bones according to layer.

√ 14. PALUTAT CAVE

Palutat Cave, Site 44, is on the eastern side of the island in Long Bay, just south of the island's easternmost point. The wall of rock which overhangs to form the cave or rock shelter runs north and south and is about 100 feet from the shore. The cave

Animal Bones from the Paluguik Midden

Layers:	4	3 or 4	3	2 or 3	2	1 or 2	1	Total 3 & 4	Total 1 & 2	Total
Sea otter[a]	38	24	85	56	216	60	153	147	429	632
Seal	9	11	13[a]	8	25	5	23	33[a]	53	94[a]
Porpoise	3			1	12	1	9	3	22	26
Sea lion	1		1		1		4	2	5	7
Whale			1	2	2		2	1	4	7
Total of										
Sea Mammals[a]	51	35	100	67	256	66	191	186	513	766
Marmot	16	26	33	14[a]	24	8	28	75	60	149[a]
Porcupine	5	2	1	1				8		9
Beaver	4	1	2	2	2		3	7	5	14
Otter	1	3	3		6		2	7	8	15
Mink			1	2	3	1	1	1	5	8
Fox	1							1		1
Bear	8	3	3	3	7	3	12	14	22	39
Goat (?)	4		1		1		1	5	2	7
Caribou					1				1	1
Total of										
Land Mammals	39	35	44	22	44	12	47	118	103	243
Birds	62	47	53	8	30	9	50	162	89	259
Fish	5	4	7	2	7	1	10	16	18	36
Total of										
Food Animals[a]	157	121	204	99	337	88	298	482	723	1304
Dog	5	4	9	14	29[b]	11	98[c]	18	138	170
TOTAL	162	125	213	113	366	99	396	500	861	1474

[a] This does not include a number of fragmentary vertebrae and ribs.

[b] This does not include the dog skull from the double burial.

[c] This does not include the almost complete skeletons of 2 pups.

[43] *Ibid.*, pp. 31 f.   [44] Hrdlička, 1944, p. 479.

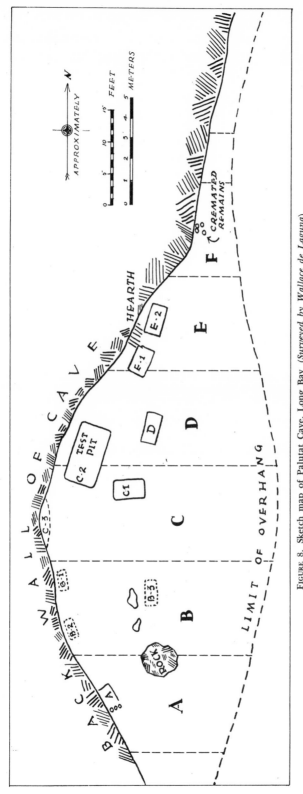

FIGURE 8. Sketch map of Palutat Cave, Long Bay (Surveyed by Wallace de Laguna)

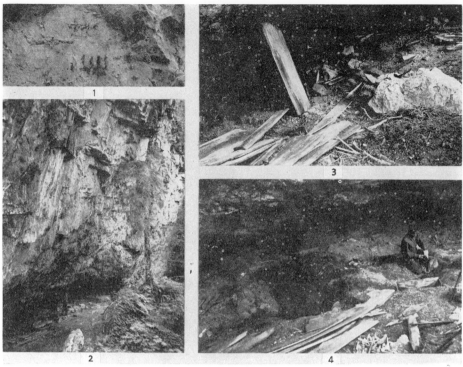

PLATE 7. Rock paintings at Knight Island; Palutat Cave

1, Painting of men in boats, Site 59, burial ledge, Mummy Island, Drier Bay, Knight Island (see Fig. 24) ; 2, Palutat Cave, Long Bay, taken from the south end of the cave; 3, coffin lids and canoe fragments in Sections A and B, Palutat Cave, Grave A under the cave wall to the left of the inclined coffin lid, Graves B2 and B1 in the dark recess to the right (see Fig. 8) ; 4, Grave C1 (center) and Grave D (right) , Palutat Cave

is about 100 feet long, 60 feet high at the front, and 40 feet wide at the widest part. Huge blocks of rock have fallen from the face of the cliff and have built up a natural wall along the front of the cave. This barrier has served to shelter the floor of the cave from driving rains. Although the cliff can be seen from the water, the cave itself is hidden by a stand of the largest timber seen in the sound. Plate 7, 2 shows the appearance of the cave as we first saw it.

Before excavating or removing any specimens, we divided the main part of the cave into 6 sections, each about 15 feet (5 paces) long, designated as A to F, inclusive, from south to north (Fig. 8). Sections C and B were the widest. We made no attempt to excavate north of Section F where there is

a narrow strip, 40 to 45 feet long, sheltered by the cliff. In this part we noted 5 piles of rock, probably denoting as many graves.

Burials in the cave were designated according to the section in which they were found. Thus there are graves A, B1, B2, B3, C1, C2, C3, D, E1, E2 (not excavated) , and F. These graves are described in detail in Chapter III, section 4. In addition to the burials which we found still more or less intact, there must have been many others, for the floor was literally strewn with human bones, which we made no attempt to save or identify since they were only the bones discarded by curio hunters who had taken the specimens of any scientific value. There were also many scattered planks which had been shaped with native tools and which were undoubtedly parts of rifled coffins (Pl. 7, 3). According to Professor Meany, from whose account we quote below, there were at least 23 burials in the cave, of which 3 had been removed prior to his visit. Our informants mentioned 6 (additional?) mummies which had been taken to Valdez. A thorough excavation of the cave would probably reveal many more undisturbed burials now hidden by surface accumulations. Before being plundered, Palutat Cave must have been one of the great archaeological treasures of southwestern Alaska.

Palutat Cave was mentioned to us several times before we were able to visit it. Thus, Mrs. Martin Anderson, a half-breed Eskimo living in Sheep Bay, said that the cave once contained many seated mummies wrapped in sea otter skins, their paddles beside them. When removed, the mummies and fur robes fell to pieces. The bodies were supposed to have been those of people who had been trapped by ice in the bay and had died of starvation. Makari also referred to the cave, which he located vaguely as being "this side [southeast] of Kiniklik, on the left-hand [north] side, going in to Valdez." The full name of the place is palu·tat ɲiləmʋq, "Hidden People in a Cave." In the cave, he said, were the mummies of 6 men, dressed in armor and ground-hog skins. Some wore masks representing human faces. They were ordinary people, not shamans. The mummies were taken to Valdez, a statement corroborated by the white men who also told us about the cave. Makari apparently did not know that the Eskimo formerly buried the dead in caves.[45] He thought that all mummies or skeletons found in caves were "palu·tat," people who had been lost or who had hidden from enemies, and so had starved to death, or that they might be "iɣiat," people who had been murdered and hidden. Makari ad-

mitted, however, that some of the bodies in the caves were so well dressed that they seemed to have been purposely buried there. He was very much confused in his explanation of the use of masks, especially as worn by the dead, although he also reported masked mummies from a cave on Knight Island. This problem will be discussed below.

Although Black Stepan of Chenega said that formerly all dead persons were buried in caves, he told us the following special legend about Palutat Cave:

How the Different Villages Started in Prince William Sound

There was an old village in Two Moon Bay, in Port Fidalgo. A man there had five nephews, twelve sons, and two wives. He was sick and ready to die. He had a fine spear with a throwing board which he gave to his youngest nephew. Then he died.

The nephews and sons all went into one house. The sons were dividing up the dead man's things among themselves and the nephews. They gave each some bows or arrows or spears—all the man's hunting tools. The nephews were talking about the hunting spear. The oldest son said that his father had wanted to give it to the youngest nephew. The oldest nephew said: "No, he gave it to me." They started to fight for the spear. They were hitting each other with the spear. The oldest son grabbed it and threw it into the fire. Then they all quarreled and left.

They went all over. Some of the sons went over to the Cordova side. Some went to Mummy Island, and to all the different places. Most of the nephews with their families went to Palutat in Long Bay. They went into a big dry cave there. They pulled their bidarkas up and piled all their hunting tools together. Then they sat up against the wall with their knees doubled up under their chins—everybody, men and women, and the women held the babies. They died that way and dried up. You could see them there long afterwards.

The sons and some of the nephews went to all different places in the Sound—I don't remember all the names. That is how the different villages started.

After our exploration of the cave, Norman Reynolds discovered the account of an earlier visit by the late Professor Edmond S. Meany, University of Washington, from which we quote pertinent passages.

In Long Bay

are four little islands, on the westernmost of which is a cliff of rock. At the base of this cliff is one of

---

[45] Meany (1906, p. 468) also reports that the Chugach "deny that the mummies are of their people, and they manifest a dread of them." Meany himself attempted to prove by measurements that the mummies were the remains of people having the same stature as the Eskimo at Tatitlek.

the mummy caves. . . . This burial cave was first made known to the whites about fifteen years ago. Agent Smith, of the Alaska Commercial Company at Nuchek, was piloted to the place by "Hans," an old Aleut, who died but a few months ago. Smith took the best mummies and shipped them to headquarters at San Francisco. They have since been presented to the University of California. Mr. Ripstein knew of the cave at that time, but he did not visit the place until the summer of 1901, when he found debris indicating that two mummies had been carried off. In July, 1902, two prospectors named Boswell and Gibbon visited the cave again and carried off the last specimen. It may be called a mummified skeleton. There are but few little patches of dried skin left on the form, but the ligaments have all dried, leaving the bones rigidly in place. Its doubled-up position shows that it was prepared for burial just as the better mummies. Thus from the cave in Billy's Hole[46] were taken two good mummies and this mummy-skeleton. There were bones to indicate that here had been buried twenty other bodies that had failed to become mummies.[47]

In describing his own explorations, Meany states:

Flashlights, ropes and candles were all useless, for the "cave" was shallow and open. The portion used for burials was the strip lying in the crevice next to the wall of rock. The dry floor extended from this wall to the drip about thirty-five feet at the widest place, and the protected wall of rock thus used for burials extended about seventy-five feet in length.

Every grave had been uncovered and all those that had contained mummies had been plundered, but those containing only wasted skeletons were left undisturbed except that the board covers had been removed and thrown on a pile at one side. These undisturbed graves helped us to reinstate the original appearance as well as possible. A photograph was obtained of the interior, showing the floor covered with scattered debris. Our shovels were then brought into use, as there was no indication that any one had explored the graves beyond lifting off the cover and removing the mummies.

The account goes on to describe the grave which Meany excavated, the coffin plank and the dugout which he secured for the Washington State Museum, and other specimens including a paddle, two paddle-

like shovels for carrying hot rocks for sweat baths, fragments of skin clothing, and matting. These descriptions will be quoted in the appropriate sections of Chapter V. Meany's account is illustrated. He continues:

Not one solitary thing was observed that would betray the natives who made these particular burials had up to that time come in contact with the whites. Every evidence indicated that they were still in the stone age. . . .

Before leaving the cave in Billy's Hole, I obtained the hand and forearm of a mummy. It was lying apart from the graves and in the crevices of a rock. It had evidently belonged to a mature woman. The nails still adhered to the fingers. Besides this specimen I obtained three crania and a number of other bones for comparative studies.

We found the cave in the same condition which Meany described. The floor is composed of stones which had fallen from the roof, earth which had washed in from the slope above and beyond Section A, twigs, spruce needles, animal and fish bones, fragments of wood, bark, matting, etc., and wind-blown dust. Scattered about were the coffin planks, already mentioned, and fragments of small dugout canoes. Most of the canoe fragments were in Sections B and C. From these fragments we were able to piece together 4 canoes, 3 of which we removed. One is now in the Danish National Museum (Pl. 56, 2), one in the University of Pennsylvania Museum (Pl. 56, 1), and the third (Canoe E) we gave to the Washington State Museum in Seattle. This last museum also has the canoe collected by Meany (Fig. 36). The coffin planks were large boards, about 6 feet long and 2 feet wide, which had been split by means of wedges or splitting adzes. Some of these were still in an excellent state of preservation.

About 280 specimens were obtained from Palutat Cave. Most of these were found on the surface or covered by only a few inches of dust. These are too numerous to mention in detail, but the following types were represented: double-edged slate blades (Pl. 29, 9, 16); detachable barbed head (Pl. 32,

---

[46] "Billy's Hole" was the name originally given to a salmon stream in Long Bay, after its discoverer, William Ripstein (ibid., 464). Meany here seems to be applying the name to Long Bay.
[47] This and the following quotations are from ibid., 464-67.

25); wooden harpoon head, model (?) (Pl. 34, *3*); wooden lance foreshaft (Pl. 34, *7*) and lance shaft (Pl. 57, *1*); bone arrowhead (Pl. 36, *21*); barbed bone arrowhead or slender barbed point (Pl. 37, *6*); toy arrow (Pl. 49, *9*) and arrow shaft fragments; fire drills (Pls. 40, *9; 49, 5*) and drill shaft (Pl. 50, *8*); wooden knife handles (Pl. 50, *5, 6*); meat sticks (?) (Pls. 49, *1, 10; 51, 17*); wooden teeth for comb (Pls. 50, *4; 51, 6, 7*); wooden nails (?) (Pls. 49, *3; 51, 11, 16*); stakes (Pl. 51, *18*), shafts or rods (Pl. 51, *15*); pale blue glass beads (Pl. 43, *26*); fragments of wooden slat armor (Pls. 50, *1; 51, 5*); parts of a trap: hook (Pl. 51, *14* and Fig. 35, *10*) and bar; sewn skins, including fragments of garments, a cap or bag (Pl. 54, *1*), and a boot (Pl. 55); fragments of matting and cord (Pls. 52, 53); knotted withes (Pls. 49, *2; 51, 1* to *3*); dugout canoes (Pl. 56); prow handle for dugout (Pl. 50, *2*) and toy specimen (Pl. 51, *13*); fragments of bidarka frame (Fig. 37; Pls. 50, *3, 9; 51, 9, 19; 57, 2*) and of skin cover; paddle (Pl. 57, *3*) and fragments (Pl. 57, *4, 5*).

Other types, not illustrated, include a broken splitting adz, a hammerstone, a stone scraper, an ulo blade, fragments of cut bone, and pieces of wood worked with stone tools. Specimens found in the graves are mentioned in Chapter III, section 4. While some specimens, such as the mats, skin garments, cords, and probably the armor, must originally have come from plundered graves, it is evident that some others were lost by natives who had camped in the cave. It was probably used alternately as a burial place and as a temporary camping place, perhaps by hunting parties. The whole deposit in the cave was like a midden, although it lacked the accumulation of shells characteristic of sites in the open.

In addition to gathering material from the surface of the cave and excavating the graves, we sank a test pit, about 5 by 10 feet, down to the bottom of the midden in Sections C and D. The lower part of the deposit seemed to be of the same composition as that seen at the surface, except that it was damp, so that wood, matting, skins, etc. were not preserved. Near the bottom was a layer of gravel, probably derived from the slope above Section A. About 3 feet below the surface were many large stones (fallen from the roof, or brought into the cave?). The bedrock at the bottom of the deposit was encountered at a depth of 5 feet below the surface toward the back of the cave, but sloped up to 4 feet 3 inches below the surface at the front end of the test pit. The following objects were found in this test pit: depth 1 foot—ulo blade fragment (Pl. 27, *5*); depth 1 to 1½ feet—bone knife or scraper (Pl. 40, *7*), side prong for bird dart (Pl. 36, *26*); depth 1½ to 2 feet—splitting adz (Pl. 11, *6*), hammerstone (Pl. 21, *1*), slate lance blade (Pl. 28, *4*), retouched slate flake (Pl. 14, *9*); depth 3 to 3½ feet—lamp (Pl. 23, *5*); depth 4 feet—barbed leister (?) prong (Pl. 36, *25*), bone shaft fragment, bone awl handle (Pl. 39, *26*), Skeleton C2, and with it a slate lance blade (Pl. 29, *11*); bottom—bone knife or scraper (Pl. 41, *6*), unfinished needle, ivory toggle (Pl. 43, *44*), tip of bear canine, cut in making ivory bead.

The following objects were also found in the same pit, between 1 and 4 feet in depth. It was so dark in the pit at the back of the cave that we did not see this material until after it had been shoveled out: wooden plug or stopper (Pl. 51, *10*), wooden pin with decoration (Pl. 50, *7*), meat stick (?) (Pl. 51, *12*), handle of wooden spoon (?) (Pl. 49, *8*), 2 fragments of bidarka rib, broken whale bone wedge (?), fragment of cut bone, stick showing cuts made by crooked knife. Presumably the wooden objects came from the upper, drier part of the deposit.

During the excavating around the coffin of Skeleton E1, before its removal (Pl. 8, *3*), a stone chisel and a chipped slate blade (Pl. 28, *10*) were found, but they do not seem to have been associated with the grave.

A needle (Pl. 39, 2) was found 12 to 18 inches below the surface in Section F.

Behind graves E1 and E2 (Pl. 8, 2) was a hearth containing burned bones, fire-cracked rocks, ashes, and mussel shells. A barbed slate blade (Pl. 28, 5) was found in the ashes of this hearth, 6 to 9 inches below the surface. A stone flake was also found here.

There had been other fires at various places in the cave, but, while none of them seemed to have been recent, we had no way of knowing whether they were prehistoric.

The graves and the few objects found with the bodies will be described in Chapter III, section 4. It is sufficient to say here that the incomplete skeleton C2 (in the test pit) was the oldest found in the cave, since it was 4 feet below the surface. The next in age is probably B2, found 3 feet below the surface. All the other burials, with the exception of F, are probably more recent and of about the same age. The coffins (C1, D, E1, and E2) were all sunk to approximately the same depth, a little over 18 inches, and the lids were covered by 6 inches of earth. Skeleton B1 was also covered by about 6 to 8 inches, and Skeleton B3 by about 12 inches, although the grave had been disturbed. Graves A and C3 had already been opened. Skeleton F was cremated; the bone fragments were found in a hearth under a pile of stones and lay some 6 to 12 inches below the surface.

The artifacts found in Palutat Cave belong to the same culture as the specimens from Palugvik. Unfortunately not enough stone and bone material was obtained from the cave to permit a very close correlation with the various layers at Palugvik. The bottom of the midden in the cave may well be as old as the lowest layers at Palugvik. The bulk of the material which came from the surface of the cave probably belongs to a later period, probably that represented by the upper half of the Palugvik midden and by many of the minor sites in the sound. The blue glass beads from the cave would indicate that some, at least, of the surface finds are actually younger than anything from Palugvik.

Dr. Degerbøl has identified the bones of the following species of animals found in Palutat Cave: seal, porpoise, bear, marmot, mink, ungulate, fish, bird, and dog. The specimens are too few in number to be very significant. Seal bones are the most numerous, as was to be expected from the location of the site in the far northern part of the sound, since we are told that "close vicinity to ice-discharging glaciers attracts the hair seal in large numbers.[48] By contrast, the sea otter was not represented at all, probably because this animal is seldom found far from the surf-fringed, kelp-wreathed reefs of the open coast.

15. Houses

Practically nothing can be found in written accounts concerning villages or houses of the Chugach. Meares, despite his winter in Prince William Sound, was able to report only that the Chugach "are a vagrant people, without any fixed place of abode." [49] Portlock makes a much fuller and more accurate statement about dwellings, yet gives us no information about villages. He writes:

During the summer season they lead a strange wandering life, and the shelter they live under in bad weather, when from home, is either their canoes or small sheds, made of a few sticks covered with a little bark; their winter habitations are also very ill made and inconvenient; those I have seen are not more than four to six feet high, about ten feet long, and about eight feet broad, built with thick plank, and the crevices filled up with dry moss; and in those houses they generally stow very thick. The methods they use in making plank is, to split the trees with wooden or stone wedges; and I have seen a plank twenty or twenty-four feet long, split from a tree by their method.[50]

In 1786 Strange reports, about 30 to 40 miles north of Snug Corner Cove, "two deserted Villages; which contained from ten to twelve Houses each . . . not only in-

[48] Porter, 1893, p. 66.
[49] Meares, 1791, pp. xxv f.
[50] Portlock, 1789, p. 253.

finitely better constructed to exclude the Inclemancy of the Climate, but also much more neatly finished than those of Nootka."[51]

Sarychef noted what seems to have been a summer camp in Shelter Bay, Hinchinbrook Island (Map 2). "Some of them lived in huts of boards fixed together; others under large leather bidars, placed in an inverted position." [52] Merck, who was also on Billings' expedition, states: "There are also large skin boats, with which they leave their homes during the good season, and go to hunt on scattered islands. They spend the night in little huts made of planks which they carry with them. In winter they live in wooden houses."[53]

The only house described by Vancouver was one seen at the head of Passage Canal. This was a

small house, about five feet high, and eight feet square, covered with bark, not built after the Indian, but evidently constructed after the Russian manner; formed by logs of timber, made tight by vacancies being filled up with moss and clay; the bottom was strewed over with clean dried grass, and appeared not only to have been recently inhabited, but to be a place of frequent resort.[54]

This house sounds rather like the winter log cabin which Makari described to us, but it is doubtful whether the Chugach made such houses before the Russians came. In any case, the cabin seen by Vancouver's party was probably built, or at least used, by the Russians when portaging from Cook Inlet to Prince William Sound.

Petroff says only:

The dwellings of the people are generally under ground, according to Innuit custom, but where the Thlinket or Kolosh race has mixed with them and gained supremacy the mode of architecture changed at once to substantial log structures, entirely above ground, generally with a plank platform running along the entire front, on which the inmates assemble in fine weather, and sit upon their haunches, wrapped in greasy blankets, smoking and staring stupidly into vacancy.[55]

The second part of the passage, which describes the log house, seems to refer to the Eyak, whom Petroff believed to have been Eskimo who had been absorbed by the Tlingit, so that only the underground dwelling can be ascribed to the Chugach, unless indeed the log house is actually the Chugach plank "smokehouse."

Typical of the lack of attention which the Chugach have received in comparison with the Koniag and Aleut is the following passage in the Eleventh Census:

Their language is almost identical with that of the Kaniagmute [Koniag], and in their habits, manners, and traditions there is an equal resemblance. Here, as well as among the Kaniagmute, we no longer find the kashega, or kashim [was it ever used by the Chugach?]; the dwellings are nearly always constructed of logs and planks, affording good shelter during the long, cold winter.[56]

The best descriptions of Chugach houses remain those in the reports of Bering's expedition.[57] The hut on Kayak Island, described by Steller, seems to have been completely underground, the roof made of bark laid on poles and weighted down with stones, and the whole covered (at ground level) with cut grass. This "cellar" was about 20 feet long and 14 feet wide and deep. The summer dwelling on Wingham Island was described by Steller and Khitrov as a small hut made of nicely smoothed wide boards, with a plank floor and a fireplace in the corner.

Fred Allen, Lee Pratt's informant, said that the barabaras or huts were more than half underground and were made of small sticks. Heavy or hewn timbers were seldom used (yet see Plates 58 and 59). Spruce bark or the bark of the yellow cedar was used for roofing. He also said that the bath house was known long before the Russians came.

Most of the information which we obtained from Makari concerned the plank house or "smokehouse," occupied in summer and fall. It had bath room annexes,

[51] Strange, 1928, p. 42.
[52] Sarytschew, 1807, II, 24 f.
[53] Jacobi, 1937, p. 133, my translation.
[54] Vancouver, 1801, V, 309.
[55] Petroff, 1884, p. 27.

[56] Porter, 1893, p. 145.
[57] Golder, 1925, I, 97, 99; II, 47 ff., 52 ff., summarized and discussed in Birket-Smith and de Laguna, 1938, pp. 346 ff.

partitioned sleeping rooms on the sides, and a central fireplace. Even the winter log house was not described as semisubterranean, but the form of this dwelling may well have been modern. Depressions in the surface of the middens at Sites 2 and 17 were, however, interpreted by us as evidence of pit houses, although unfortunately we were not able to test this by excavation. Evidences of houses obtained at Palugvik (see section 12) would suggest that both surface and subterranean dwellings had been built at this site.

√16. CHRONOLOGY

It will not be easy to determine the relative chronology of the sites in Prince William Sound. There was little difference between the culture of the oldest and that of the youngest layer at Palugvik other than changes in the relative proportions of certain types of artifacts, and material from the other sites was too scanty to permit of statistical comparisons. This was true even of Palutat Cave, where our short stay precluded more than a sampling of its deeper layers, and where the surface deposits offered chiefly perishable materials not preserved at other sites. There are, nevertheless, a few criteria on which we may attempt to base an estimate of relative chronology.

The most obvious clue is the presence of objects of foreign manufacture, such as cloth, glass beads, coins, china, and iron tools (or wood and bone showing marks of such tools), or the presence of objects, like the torsion trap, which were copied from foreign models introduced by the whites. Equally diagnostic are skeletal remains showing the lesions of syphilis or tuberculosis, diseases unknown in Alaska before contact with Europeans. Sites yielding such materials may be presumed to be younger than sites from which foreign objects are entirely absent and where instead we find abundant evidence of purely native manufactures, especially stone and bone tools and weapons, bone and wood worked by such aboriginal tools, and ornaments of bone, ivory, and shell.

We can perhaps make further distinctions among these prehistoric sites. Thus one criterion would be our impression of the degree of disintegration of shells and bones in the midden, although this impression is admittedly subjective, especially since it is not checked by tests for such factors as drainage, exposure, acidity of the soil, etc., which might affect the rate of decomposition. Another criterion, applicable in relatively few cases, would be the presence of trees which had grown since the abandonment of a site, since it seems to take much longer for trees to grow on the limy soil of a shell heap than for alders, salmonberry bushes, and devilclubs. Conversely, the preservation of the remains of a tree that had grown before the accumulation of a midden would argue lack of great age.

Since native copper tools were confined to the upper half of the midden at Palugvik (probably to the uppermost layer only), and since the upper half is also characterized by a relative abundance of fire-cracked rocks, splitting adzes (versus planing adzes), and barbed slate blades (versus unbarbed double-edged blades), we may take the presence or relative abundance of these types at other sites as suggesting approximate contemporaneity with the upper layers at Palugvik.

Objects of foreign manufacture may also, perhaps, fall into two groups, on the basis of which we may be able to distinguish between a protohistoric and a modern period. Thus Captain James Cook, who discovered Prince William Sound in 1778, writes of the natives encountered in Snug Corner Cove:

Amongst those who came on board, was a good-looking middle-aged man, whom we afterwards found to be the Chief. He was clothed in a dress of the sea-otter's skin . . . and had on his head such a cap as is worn by the people of King George's Sound,[58] ornamented with sky-blue glass beads,

[58] Cook is referring to the basketry hats, painted with whaling scenes, worn by the Indians of King George's or Nootka Sound, Vancouver Island. The Chugach hats he later specifies (p. 369) were "high truncated conic caps, made of straw," or else were painted wooden headgear carved to resemble a seal's head. Plate 46 of the album illustrating

about the size of a large pea. He seemed to set a much higher value upon these, than upon our white beads. Any sort of beads, however, appeared to be in high estimation with these people; and they readily gave whatever they had in exchange for them, even their fine sea-otter skins. . . .[59]

These people were also desirous of iron; but they wanted pieces eight or ten inches long at least, and the breadth of three of four fingers. For they absolutely rejected small pieces. Consequently, they got little from us; iron having, by this time, become rather a scarce article. The points of some of their spears or lances were of that metal, others were of copper, and a few of bone, of which the points of their darts, arrows, etc. were composed.[60]

After describing ear ornaments, nose pins, and labrets, Cook writes:

But we found many beads of European manufacture among them, chiefly of a pale blue colour, which they hang in their ears; about their caps; or join to their lip-ornament, which have a small hole drilled in each point to which they are fastened, and others to them, till they hang sometimes as low as the point of the chin.[61]

They have a great many iron knives; some of which are straight; others a little curved; and some very small ones, fixed in long handles, with the blade bent upward, like some of our shoemakers instruments. But they have still knives of another sort, which are sometimes near two feet long, shaped almost like a dagger, with a ridge in the middle. These they wear in sheaths of skins, hung by a thong round the neck, under their robe; and they are, probably, only used as weapons; the other knives being apparently applied to other purposes.[62]

The metals that we saw were copper and iron; both of which, particularly the latter, were in such plenty, as to constitute the points of most of the arrows and lances.[63]

An unknown member of Cook's expedition also remarked that the natives traded furs "for the smallest trifle made of iron." "They also had lances, the points of which

were mounted with iron and were of beautiful workmanship, like well-polished knives; these they refused to barter, although we offered them a great deal."[64]

Cook was confident that his expedition was the first with which the Chugach had ever come in direct contact. He believed that the iron and beads had come to them, via inland tribes, from Hudson Bay or from settlements on the Canadian lakes. This opinion was unshaken, even when he found that the natives on Cook Inlet were "in possession of large iron knives, and of sky-blue glass beads, such as we found amongst the natives of Prince William's Sound."[65]

I have already questioned Cook's explanation that these beads and the iron came from Canadian sources.[66] The most obvious assumption was that the Chugach obtained them indirectly from the Russians, via intertribal trade, since a number of Russian expeditions had already visited Kodiak Island and there was a Russian post on Unalaska. Bancroft explains that Cook refused to accept the beads and iron as evidence even of indirect contact with the Russians because he did not wish to acknowledge the presence of another foreign power in the neighborhood. Bancroft points out that the word for iron, "goone," used by the natives Cook met on Cook Inlet, is evidently the Russian "chugun" or "chugoon," meaning cast iron, but applied by ignorant Russians to all articles made of iron. Blue glass beads, furthermore, were among the few trade goods carried by the Russian *promyshleniki*.[67]

It is evident that beads and iron weapons are the first foreign objects to be expected in Chugach sites, but the earliest date at which they might appear is still uncertain. We found no iron knives or spear points, but we did obtain a number of blue glass beads, of the type described by Cook (Chapter V, section 73). Two beads of this kind

Cook's narrative shows a "Man of Prince William's Sound" wearing a basketry hat shaped like a truncated cone, painted with a conventionalized design suggestive of Northwest Coast art. Glass beads are sewn about the top and about the brim.

[59] Cook, 1785, II, 357 f. Strange in 1786 (1928, pp. 36, 37, 42) also noted the eagerness of the Chugach to obtain sky-blue glass beads and their rejection of beads of other colors, as well as their lack of skill in bargaining and great timidity in dealing with Europeans.
[60] Cook, 1785, II, 357 f.
[61] *Ibid.*, p. 370.
[62] *Ibid.*, p. 373.
[63] *Ibid.*, p. 379.

[64] Forster, 1781, pp. 236, 237, my translation.
[65] Cook, 1785, II, 379 ff., 392.
[66] De Laguna, 1947, p. 225.
[67] Bancroft, 1886, p. 205 n. 20, p. 207 n. 21 and n. 25, p. 258.

were found among the bones of the arthritic woman near Site 20, Mummy Island, possibly fallen from the grave of the tubercular man above and may or may not antedate direct contact with whites. Two beads of the same type were found on the surface of Palutat Cave (Pl. 45, 26), evidently derived from a disturbed grave in Section F, and were the only objects of civilized origin in the cave. (A chip of fresh wood cut with a steel ax must be discounted, for it evidently is more recent than the Eskimo occupancy of the cave.) A bead from Nuchek was found with china, bricks, and hand-wrought iron tools. Glass beads of the same kind were found at Indian sites on the Yukon, some of which were relatively recent, while others, like Palutat Cave, yielded no other foreign items. It is quite obvious, therefore, that while these "Cook type" glass beads were among the trade goods brought by the Russians, they also reached the Tena and the Chugach before the Russians themselves appeared. The beads may have been of Chinese manufacture.[68] We know that the Russians carried Chinese wares, at least on some occasions, for Bering's men in 1741 left some Chinese articles, including 20 strings of beads, in a Chugach semisubterranean house on Kayak Island.[69] It is even possible that Cook saw some of these, although the natives probably had other sources of supply.

There is also evidence, however, that iron, and possibly beads, actually reached southwestern Alaska even before Bering's expedition in 1741. Thus Steller observes of the Aleuts encountered on the Shumagin Islands:

Two had hanging on their belt, like the Russian peasants, a long iron knife in a sheath of very poor workmanship, which may have been their own and not a foreign [the MS reads "European"] invention. . . . From the distance I observed the nature of the knife very carefully as one of the Americans unsheathed it and cut a bladder in two with it. It was easy to see that it was of iron and, besides, that it was not like any European product.[70]

68 De Laguna, 1947, pp. 224 f.
69 Birket-Smith and de Laguna, 1938, p. 350 and note.
70 Steller in Golder, 1925, II, 97.

Steller discussed the possibility that the natives were acquainted with the art of smelting iron or that they had obtained the knives from the Chukchi at Bering Strait. Golder adds in a note:

A party of Russians who spent the years 1759 to 1763 among the Aleuts of Unimak and Unalaska reported that the inhabitants "made knives out of iron, which iron they obtain from the islands to the eastward, which islands are wooded, in exchange for furs and clothing." In 1767 the officers of the Krenitsin and Levashev expedition saw and sketched these knives. It is not likely that the natives to the eastward knew how to smelt iron. They probably obtained this metal in some indirect way either from the white men or from wrecked vessels. In a report of a Russian hunter (about 1765) a statement is made that the Aleuts told him a large ship had been driven ashore to the eastward.[71]

Holmberg reports that the Koniag became acquainted with iron long before the arrival of the Russians, because the sea used to cast it up on their shores. He believes that the iron was from wreckage of civilized vessels and that the natives could not have failed to discover for themselves its potentialities as a tool material. An old native told him that iron was quite often found on the shores of Chirikof Island, southwest of Kodiak.[72] Jochelson cites a similar report by Davydof that the Koniag, long before the coming of the Russians, used to find iron objects drifted in by the sea and appreciated them greatly.[73] Veniaminof and Holmberg both report an Aleut tradition that, long before the Russians appeared, white men came to Avatanak Island in a sailing ship from which the Aleuts obtained their first iron.[74] The Atka Aleuts used to find iron and copper among wreckage on the shore. Although such wreckage was supposed to be bewitched, certain daring individuals took these metals and secretly beat them into knives and lances.[75] Jochelson also adds a rather con-

71 Ibid., note 216.
72 Holmberg, 1855, pp. 101, 135.
73 Jochelson, 1933, p. 22.
74 Hrdlička, 1945, pp. 100 f.
75 Jochelson, 1933, p. 15 n. 4, 18 f., 22 f.; Hrdlička, 1945, p. 100.

fused account given in 1747 by an Aleut boy from Attu that

as he remembered, men dressed in long many-colored silk and cotton clothing came to the island Attu in small ships with one sail; their heads were shaved to the crown and the hair on the back was plaited into tresses. Evidently these were China-men (if the report is correct). The same boy told them, that in former years a ship used to come to Attu, the men giving them iron, needles, and leaf-tobacco [which they did not want] in exchange for sea-otters' skins.

The latter ship seems to have been Russian.

There are a number of possible explanations for the presence of iron in southwestern Alaska before Bering's expedition. The first is trade from Asia via Bering Strait. Small scraps of iron were used by the Ipiutak Eskimo of Point Hope in the tenth century and by the Eskimo of St. Lawrence Island in the Punuk period for engraving tools, the introduction of metal gravers producing a revolution in art style on St. Lawrence Island; and little pieces may even have been available in the earlier Old Bering Sea culture for the tiny blades of splitting knives.[76] Although designs incised by metal tools (lines, compass-drawn dot-and-circle), which appear in later prehistoric Aleut art, in Kachemak Bay III, and on Kodiak Island suggest diffusion of Punuk style and perhaps of iron engraving tools,[77] yet there is no evidence at this time of larger pieces of iron at Bering Strait or farther south. The earliest known iron knives are from protohistoric Eskimo sites on St. Lawrence Island and the upper Kobuk River that yielded tree-ring dates in the last decade of the seventeenth and first half

of the eighteenth century. This iron may have been available as early as 1649, when the Russians reached the Anadyr River in their eastward expansion across Siberia.[78] Such pieces may even have been traded to southwestern Alaska.

The second possibility is that the Aleut may have traded with the Kamchadal or Kurilian Ainu, or even directly with Chinese, Japanese, or Russian adventurers before Bering.[79] But iron was evidently rare in southwestern Alaska, for it was used only for knife and lance blades. Only after Russian trade was firmly established did the natives secure ax blades. If glass beads were traded, they also must have been rare, for the earliest Russian travelers do not report them.

The third possibility is that iron was obtained from wreckage in the form of bolts, spikes, etc., attached to floating wood, but tools and beads could be obtained only from wrecks that were still fairly intact. There is evidence that Japanese ships were often wrecked near Kamchatka and on the American shores from the Aleutians to California.[80] But if their cargoes were secured, why did not the early travelers observe manufactured articles in native hands?[81] If the metal came from flotsam, we must infer that the natives were able to adapt to iron the aboriginal methods of working copper. We are, in fact, told that the Aleut of Unalaska "shape the iron ingeniously by rubbing it between two stones, and wetting it frequently with sea-water."[82] The sources cited above also suggest native

[76] Larsen and Rainey, 1948, pp. 83, 135, 159, 182. Ipiutak ivory carvings appear to be copies of iron regalia (chains and swivels) worn by Siberian shamans.

[77] De Laguna, 1934, pp. 210 f. (metal-cut lines alone appear in Kachemak Bay II); Hrdlička, 1944, Figs. 50, 121, for example; Quimby, 1945, Pl. XIII, 4, p. 78. Collins (1951, p. 434) and I interpret such designs as later on the Aleutians than the style consisting only of stone-incised elements suggestive of Dorset and Old Bering Sea I (Okvik) art. However, Quimby (1948) and Laughlin and Marsh (1952, p. 81) believe the metal-cut dot-and-circle to be very ancient on the Aleutians. This problem is briefly discussed in Chapter VI. section 2.

[78] Geist and Rainey, 1936, pp. 61 f., 226 f.; Giddings, 1941, p. 82; 1944, pp. 118, 131.

[79] De Laguna, 1947, pp. 224 f.

[80] Jochelson, 1933, p. 223; an unsigned report quoted by Pallas, I, 312; and Rickard, 1939. The Tlingit also affirm that they obtained iron from driftwood before they met Europeans (field notes, 1949 and 1950). Rickard argues convincingly that iron was obtained from wrecks, and suggests that Japanese and European survivors may even have taught the natives how to work it.

[81] The only instance I have found is in the report of an expedition in 1754-57 to Ataku, Agataku (Attu and Agatu?), and Shemya Islands, where 3 copper plates were seen and were presumed to have come from a wreck (Coxe, 1803, p. 128).

[82] Korovin (1762) in ibid., p. 184; Pallas, I, 312.

methods of working iron prior to white contact, as does Cook's report that the Chugach wanted pieces of iron. Portlock, who visited Prince William Sound in 1787, only 9 years after Cook and 4 years after the first Russian trading expedition under Zaikof, also states that the Chugach wanted only green and red glass beads and pieces of unwrought iron nearly 2 feet long, rejecting manufactured articles, even though hatchets, adzes, saws, and metal cooking utensils were offered.[83] Meares (1786-87) also found that the natives most desired pieces of iron which "approached, in any degree, to the form of a spear."[84]

Even though we are unable to date the first appearance of beads and iron in Prince William Sound, both may have been present in 1741, or even before, and iron from driftwood was probably older than blue glass beads. The protohistoric period characterized by these objects was brought to a close by the expedition of Zaikof, Delarof, and Polutof to Prince William Sound in 1783-84 which initiated the historic period. Was it during the protohistoric period that the Chinese coin (dated 1662-1723) found its way to Site 7 in Hawkins Cut Off?[85]

Venereal disease was almost certainly introduced into Prince William Sound by Zaikof's expedition of 1783-84, for the Russians pursued the Eskimo women as eagerly as they did their furs, and, in fact, Polutof and several others were finally killed by the outraged natives whose women had been raped, children kidnaped, and villages looted. This expedition, the many trading expeditions which followed, and the establishment of the post at Nuchek in 1793 brought an increasing amount of manufactured goods to the Chugach. A careful exploration of the deposits at Nuchek would, I believe, document the trans-

formation of aboriginal material culture. Among the early importations of this historic period were steel axes (at first generally hafted as adzes), steel needles, knives, saws, iron and copper kettles, tobacco pipes, china and glassware, various items of Russian clothing, etc. Large seines and the Siberian torsion trap (klipski) were adopted; Greek Orthodoxy supplanted or supplemented native religious beliefs; and Christian burial practices became customary. I believe that small blue, white, and black glass beads, of the type found on Glacier Island (Pl. 45, *11* to *13*), are characteristic of this period.[86] Thus, Dixon reports of the Chugach in 1787: "The ears of these Indians [*sic*] were ornamented with plenty of small blue beads, but these, we had reason to suppose were procured from the Russians, as some knives and iron weapons which they shewed us, were evidently of Russian manufacture."[87]

We seem, therefore, to have in Prince William Sound evidence of 4 stages of native culture: (1) older prehistoric, characterized by incised slate plaques, by the absence or relative scarcity of types characteristic of later periods, and by considerably decomposed middens; (2) later prehistoric, marked especially by native copper, by a relative abundance of fire-cracked rocks, splitting adzes, and barbed slate blades, and by an absence of foreign manufactures; (3) protohistoric, with native types like those of the later prehistoric culture, but with the addition of "Cook type" beads— and theoretically by small amounts of iron, although we found none; (4) historic, marked by "Glacier Island type" beads, abundance of white man's goods, evidence of introduced disease, and Christian burial customs.

Since it is only the presence of "Cook type" beads which have been taken to distinguish the protohistoric from late prehis-

---

[83] Portlock, 1789, p. 115.

[84] Meares, 1791, lxv.

[85] Cf. also the Chinese coin or amulet, perhaps as old as the Ming Dynasty (1368-1644), found at the head of Cook Inlet with a lamp with human figure of the Kachemak Bay III culture (J. A. Mason, 1928, pp. 179 ff.); and 2 Chinese temple coins in a Tlingit mask that is dated on shaky evidence to 1680 (Bolles, 1893, p. 221, Pl. XXIV).

[86] De Laguna, 1947, pp. 138 f.

[87] Dixon, 1789, p. 147. Portlock (1789, pp. 113, 115) mentions that the Tanaina of Cook Inlet ornamented their ears and noses with small blue glass beads.

toric sites, I must admit that I may be in error if I assume that this distinction indicates a chronological difference. Such beads must have been rare, and it would be largely a matter of chance whether or not they were actually found at a given site. As precious personal ornaments they would be more likely to be preserved in graves.

In spite of this and other misgivings, I shall attempt to assign the Prince William Sound sites as far as possible to these 4 cultural stages or periods:

Older Prehistoric

Palugvik 1 and 2
Palugvik East Point midden (and probably burial ledge)
Palutat Cave, below 2 feet

Younger Prehistoric

Palugvik 3 and 4
Palutat Cave, material from upper layers, and most of the material from the surface
Site 2, Hinchinbrook Island
Site 6, Hinchinbrook Island
Site 7, Hawkins Cut Off, below turf
Site 8, Hinchinbrook Island
Site 17, Hawkins Island
Site 35, Port Gravina
Site 40 at Ellamar
Site 42, Galena Bay
Site 45, Long Bay
Site 54, Jackpot Bay
Site 55 at Chenega Village

Site 56, Chenega Island
Site 61, Bainbridge Island
Site 62, Evans Island
Site found by Lutz on Elrington Island
Site 65A and B, Montague Island

Protohistoric

Palutat Cave, latest grave or graves only (?)
Site 7, Hawkins Cut Off, turf only (?)
Older burial near Site 20, Mummy Island (?). Other burial caves on the island represent prehistoric to historic periods.

Historic

Nuchek, Tatitlek, Kiniklik, and Chenega villages
Site 10, Hinchinbrook Island (at least part of burial cave)
Site 11, Hinchinbrook Island
Site 16, Hawkins Island. The village was still inhabited in 1805, and the large burial cave contains some modern material, but part of the midden and part of the large cave, as well as the small shelter, evidently contain older material.
Tubercular burial near Site 20, Mummy Island
Glacier Island burials
Site 64, Montague Island
Too little is known about the remaining sites to permit even a tentative classification.

CHAPTER III

Disposal of the Dead

√ 1. INTRODUCTION: PHYSICAL TYPE

A NUMBER OF SKELETONS were obtained in Prince William Sound in 1930 and 1933. Those complete enough to possess anthropometrical value were studied by Dr. Bruno Oetteking, Museum of the American Indian, Heye Foundation, New York City.[1] The predominant physical type is basic Western Eskimo and is represented by Palutat C1, from one of the later burials in the cave. This male has a mesocephalic skull with a relatively high vault, characterized by the typically Eskimo sagittal keel (Palugvik I was the only individual lacking this keel), a fairly long or high face, but with prominently developed cheek bones. The nose is narrow. The long bones are massive and robust. In general, the Prince William Sound type is somewhat shorter than the Western Eskimo with which Dr. Oetteking compared it. The second type individual, Palutat B2, is from one of the older burials in the cave and has the lowest skull of the series. It is slightly dolichocephalic, with a weaker development of the sagittal keel. The nose is also narrow. The third type recognized by Dr. Oetteking is represented by Palutat C2, the oldest burial in the cave. The skull fell barely within the dolichocephalic range but was the highest of the three, relatively and by actual

measurement. The nose was medium, almost broad.

Although these 3 type specimens are of different antiquity, the evidence is insufficient to indicate whether there has been any general change in physical type in Prince William Sound comparable to those changes claimed by Hrdlička for Kodiak and the Aleutian Islands.[2] We should expect variations in the Prince William Sound population at any one time, for the natives told us that they used to buy slaves from the Eyak and the Yakutat Tlingit and also took as slaves Tanaina from Cook Inlet and Eskimo from Kodiak. Many of these slaves were women, whom their masters married. Furthermore, they were visited by the Yakutat, Eyak, Atna, Port Graham and Kenai Peninsula Eskimo, Tanaina, Aleut,[3] and Kodiak Eskimo, for trade or for war, and some of these visitors undoubtedly had access to Chugach women, even though our informants denied that they loaned their wives.

In the following pages the various burials found by ourselves or recorded by others are described. These were encountered in village midden deposits or in rock shelters. We did not find any on refuge islands, high cliffs, or in graveyards, although these were mentioned by our informants.

[1] Oetteking in de Laguna, 1934, pp. 221 f.; and Oetteking, 1945.

[2] Hrdlička, 1944, Part IV; 1945, Part V.
[3] Veniaminof in Hrdlička, 1945, p. 143.

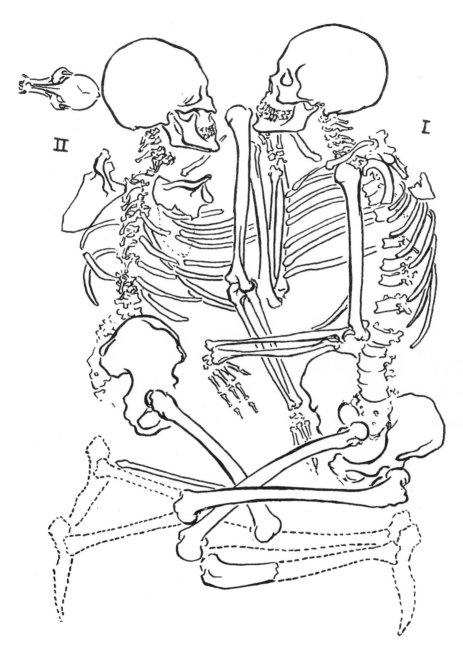

II   I

FIGURE 9. Skeletons I and II, Palugvik. See Plate 9, *2*

2. Palugvik Burials

In the main midden at Palugvik were found 7 skeletons, as well as some scattered human bones.

Skeletons I and II (Fig. 9; Pl. 9, 2)

Two skeletons were found together, interred in Layer 1 presumably during the period represented by the lower part of Layer 2. The stratigraphy has been discussed in Chapter II, section 12. The grave could not have been more than 2 or 2½ feet deep, for the line of charcoal at the top of Layer 2 was unbroken over the grave (see Fig. 3). Both bodies lay flexed on their sides, facing each other, their heads to the north. The woman (Skeleton II) must have been placed in the grave first, because the arms and legs of the man (Skeleton I) lie on top of hers. The woman's neck and the man's left wrist are sharply bent, as if broken, perhaps in forcing the stiffened corpses into the grave. The woman's skull has been crushed by the weight of the earth, and her left femur is missing. The bones of the lower legs and feet of both individuals are broken and incomplete because the man we hired to clear brush from the site unfortunately destroyed part of the grave before he noticed it. A few of the toe bones, however, were found below the level of the grave, apparently in the fill of a post hole which had been dug through the foot of the grave, presumably after its existence had been forgotten.

There was no trace of a coffin, and there were no objects in the grave except the cranium of a small dog placed just beyond the woman's skull. The mandible was not included. (For a discussion of dogs, see Chapter II, section 13.) Makari denied that dogs were ever killed at their master's funeral. Although 2 types of dogs were represented throughout Hrdlička's Kodiak site, fox remains were more common, and one or 2 skeletons of young foxes were frequently in close association with the skeleton of a child.[4]

[4] Hrdlička, 1944, p. 479.

Skeleton III (Fig. 10; Pl. 9, 4)

The oldest and most interesting burial at Palugvik was that of an almost senile woman, found at the very bottom of the midden. As already explained (Chapter II, section 12), the burial dates from the period represented by Layer 1. The wooden coffin, preserved by the excessive dampness, was parallel to the wall of House I, either in a small trash-filled side room or more likely in the midden accumulated outside the house. The coffin, like those of Palutat Cave, was simply the plank lining of a hole, originally 39 inches long, 21 inches wide, and at least 13 inches deep (100 by 53 by 33 cm.). Traces were preserved of a bottom board, a wooden pillow under the head, a plank on edge along each side, and head and foot boards, also on edge; there was no

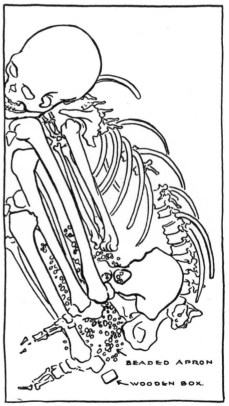

Figure 10. Skeleton III, Palugvik. See Plate 9, 4. For grave finds, see Plate 44

clear evidence of a cover. The body, tightly flexed on the right side, with head to the west facing north, was compressed within an area only 26 by 21 inches (66 by 53 cm.). At the feet lay a small box, carved from a single piece of wood, and among the leg bones were over 800 beads, evidently the decoration of a genital apron (Pl. 44). There were no other objects in the grave.

Skeleton IV

This child, not more than 9 or 10 months old, was in Section 2C at the bottom of Layer 2. It was tightly flexed on the left side, the head to the northwest. The scattered position of most of the vertebrae and ribs was probably due to the activities of dogs, for there was no evidence of deep burial.

Skeleton V (Fig. 11)

The skeleton of a child 2 or 3 months old was found in Section 3C, Layer 1, about one foot directly above the head of the coffin of Skeleton III. Here there seems to have been a circle of stones, arranged after the wall of House I had collapsed, and the body of the child had been forcibly thrust, head first (?), into the small space under the outer edge of one of the stones. The head was to the west.

Skeleton VI

This infant's skeleton was in Section 3C, at the bottom of Layer 2, near Skeleton IV and at the same depth. Comparatively few bones are missing, so we may infer that the body was complete at the time of burial, although we are unable to say anything about the position.

Skeleton VII

The remains of this infant were found in Section 1B, again at the bottom of Layer 2, and again unfortunately disturbed by our excavation before the grave was discovered.

These 4 infants, all less than a year old, were presumably covered with a little refuse, like the 2 puppies found at the very bottom of the midden in Section 1C, but

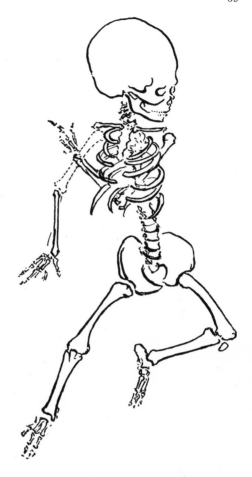

FIGURE 11. Skeleton V, Palugvik

there is no indication of real interment. This lack of care in burial does not clearly prove infanticide, for where unwanted children are killed they are almost always newborn babies, not infants as old as IV and V. On the other hand, infant mortality was probably high, and these are more likely to be children who died from natural causes. It is interesting that so many should have been found so close together. No skeletons as young as these were encountered in Kachemak Bay. Does this mean that, whereas adults might be buried anywhere in a midden, young children were always put into a special place, a place which I did not happen to find in previous excavations?

Scattered Bones

In addition to the regular burials, a number of isolated human bones were found scattered in the midden at various levels. These were: Layer 3 (or 4)—adult (male?) right femur in Section 1D; Layer 3—adult radius fragment in Section 2B; Layer 2 (or 3)—molar in Section 1C; Layer 2—3 infant vertebrae fragments, infant tooth, juvenile skull fragment, adult canine, all in Section 1G; 2 fragments of lumbar vertebrae, fragment of sacrum, fragment of skull, all in Section 2G; juvenile skull fragment in Section H; Layer 1 or 2—adult canine in Section 2D; Layer 1—adult phalange in Section A, adult vertebra in Section 3C, adult mandible at bottom of Section 1G, 2-year-old infant humerus and femur in Section 2G; adult metatarsal in Section H.

3. PALUGVIK EAST POINT BURIALS

The rock shelter on the north side of the islet which forms Palugvik East Point has already been described (Chapter II, section 11) as a burial ledge. Lee Pratt reported that 3 complete skeletons had once been found on the ledge, and in 1930 we recovered from the end of the rock a few bones, representing an adult and a child under 18 years of age. In our more extensive exploration of 1933 we found a few bones of an adult and of a child 10 to 12 years old (field numbers 221, 222), which had slid out of the deposit on the western end of the ledge and fallen onto the beach below. I do not know whether the bones found in 1930 and in 1933 represent the same 2 individuals, or whether any of them came from the 3 skeletons previously found. Mixed with the bones on the end of the ledge and on the beach below we found a grooved stone (Pl. 20, 7), slate "awl" (Pl. 30, 4), bone awl, a bone and a shell bead, and a lump of red hematite paint. These objects may or may not have been intentionally associated with the burials.

When systematic excavations were made of the midden on the ledge, 3 skeletons were found within a space of 8 by 4 feet (244 by 122 cm.), the latter dimension being the width of the sheltered ledge under the overhanging cliff. These bodies appeared to have been interred at the same time in a common grave, about 2 feet deep, and were covered by about 6 to 9 inches of midden and humus. Or they may represent the remains of mummies that had been simply placed in the shelter, over which midden material had accumulated. The middle skeleton of the group (II) seems to have been at a higher level than the others, i.e., the bottom of the grave was uneven. This triple burial is illustrated in Figure 12.

Skeleton I

The westernmost skeleton of the three, that of an adult (male?), lay flexed on the right side, the head toward the beach (west). Between the skull and hands was a lump of disintegrated iron pyrites.

Skeleton II

This was the skeleton of an adult (female?), lying flexed on the left side, the head to the northeast, the pelvis and feet close to the feet of Skeleton I, and the bent knees and hands near the feet of Skeleton III.

Skeleton III

The easternmost skeleton of the group is that of a mature male. He lay on his back, the head to the west, with the legs bent up close to the right side, the arms flexed across the body, and the hands crossed above the right breast. The skull was sunk forward on the chest.

Associated with this individual were a number of very interesting specimens. Two adz blades (Pl. 48, 1, 2) were near the left shoulder. Near the hands at the right shoulder were 2 pendants made from bear canines (Pl. 47, 8, 9), 2 ivory buckles or toggles carved in the shape of bears (Pl. 46, 18, 19), a decorated bird bone tube (Pl. 47, 1), a "shaman's tube" of bird bone (Pl.

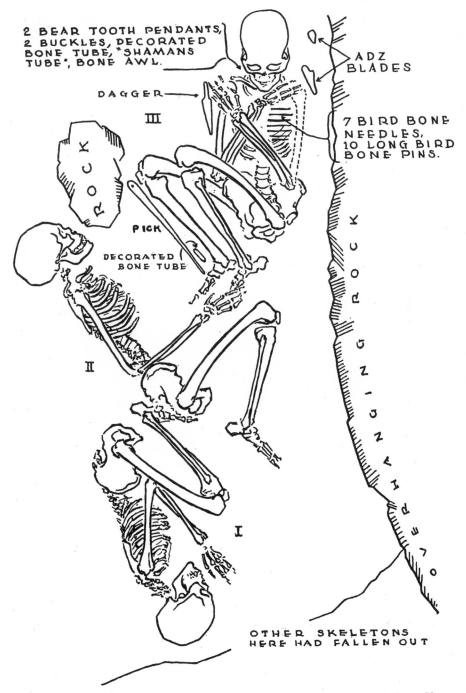

2 BEAR TOOTH PENDANTS,
2 BUCKLES, DECORATED
BONE TUBE, "SHAMANS
TUBE", BONE AWL.

ADZ
BLADES

DAGGER

III

7 BIRD BONE
NEEDLES,
10 LONG BIRD
BONE PINS.

ROCK

PICK

DECORATED
BONE TUBE

II

OVERHANGING ROCK

I

OTHER SKELETONS
HERE HAD FALLEN OUT

FIGURE 12. Skeletons I, II, and III, Palugvik East Point burial ledge. For grave finds, see Plates
46 to 48

47, *3*), and a crude bone awl (Pl. 47, *6*). Across the breast lay a bundle of bird bone needles, pins, and fragments (Pl. 46, *1* to *17*), probably representing 7 needles with eyes and 10 needles without eyes. By the right side was a whale bone dagger (Pl. 48, *4*), the handle at the shoulder and the point at the knees. Beside the right leg with the point at the ankle was a long whale bone pick or "bayonet" (Pl. 48, *7*), and a small decorated bird bone tube (Pl. 47, *2*) had been placed between the point of the pick and the ankle. There was also a shell bead which disintegrated when touched.

Beyond the head were additional objects which may or may not have been associated with the burial. There were a stone saw (Pl. 48, *3*), a whetstone (Pl. 48, *6*), the tang of a dart socket piece (Pl. 47, *7*), the point of a dagger like that found beside the body (Pl. 48, *5*), a whale bone knife handle or shaft fragment (Pl. 47, *4*), a marmot tibia originally drilled for suspension (as an amulet?) (Pl. 47, *5*), and 3 fragments of cut animal bone (Pl. 47, *10* to *12*). A lump of red hematite was possibly associated with the grave. Other objects found in the midden at the east end of the ledge, and enumerated in Chapter II, section 11, had no connection with the burials.

It is evident that this individual (Skeleton III) was an important person. The 2 others buried with him may have been members of his family or friends who died at the same time. On the other hand, it is possible that they were slaves killed at their master's death, even though our Chugach informants denied this practice.[5] The "shaman's tube" (Pl. 47, *3*) appears to be a degenerate copy of the larger, more beauti-

fully decorated bone tubes with split ends used by Tlingit shamans to hold imprisoned souls, so this personage may have been a shaman. We might also note that the apparent mixture of men's adzes and dagger with women's needles and awl suggests that he may have been a transvestite. Such persons, while not necessarily shamans, were considered "lucky" by the Chugach since they were supposedly endowed with the skills and abilities characteristic of both sexes, and a number of transvestites also seem to have been versed in magic. However, since hunters are said to have carried with them a skin sewing bag with needles, sinew thread, etc., for mending their bidarkas when on extended trips, we must remain uncertain about the status of this individual.

4. BURIALS IN PALUTAT CAVE

It will be remembered (Chapter II, section 14) that this cave was supposed at one time to have contained at least 6 seated mummies of men, dressed in armor and ground-hog skins (or wrapped in sea otter robes, according to another account), their paddles beside them. Some wore masks. According to another version the mummies were those of men, women, and children, with their skin boats and other possessions beside them. In any case, all of the best mummies, and presumably the most interesting grave goods, had been removed long before our visit, and even Meany, who explored the cave about 30 years earlier, found it already despoiled. He records that 3 mummies had been taken from it before his visit, that there were still 20 skeletons left, and that he himself removed 3 skulls and some other bones. We found evidence of about 11 burials and secured the bones of 9. These graves were designated according to the sections in which they were found (see Fig. 8).

Skeleton A

This was the skeleton of a mature man. The grave had already been opened when we found it (Plate 7, *3*), the skull removed,

---

[5] We might well be skeptical of this denial, since the Koniag and Aleut sometimes killed slaves to bury with a prominent person (Birket-Smith and de Laguna, 1938, p. 452; Hrdlička, 1944, pp. 87 f.; 1945, pp. 149 f., 178; Lantis, 1947, p. 9). However, group burials do not furnish proof to the contrary but, as Weyer suggests (1929, pp. 235 ff.), may indicate simultaneous but natural deaths, reuse of the grave, or the practice of saving bodies for common funerals. Multiple burials, in any case, are found in all areas of southwestern Alaska.

and the remaining bones somewhat disarranged. The body had been in a rough
cist, one side formed by the face of the cliff,
the other by a plank set on edge. The foot
was a row of 5 stones, one of which was
a partially shaped grinding block. The
plank or stones for the head of the coffin
had apparently been thrown aside by the
persons who took the skull. The cist was
about 4 feet long, 2 feet wide, and 18 inches
deep (122 by 61 by 46 cm.). A layer of bark

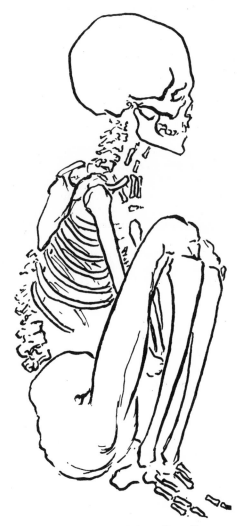

FIGURE 13. Skeleton B1, Palutat Cave. For grave
find, see Plate 52, 2

lined the bottom, and on it were fragments
of skins, the remains either of clothing or
of wrappings. The skeleton lay on the back,
the head toward the north. The arms were
crossed on the breast, and the legs, although
disarranged when we found the grave, had
doubtless been flexed, for the bones of the
feet were beside the pelvis. Besides bits of
skin, a detachable barbed head (Pl. 33, 1)
and a piece of stone like a paddle-shaped
scraper were found in the grave. It was
impossible to tell whether one of the many
scattered coffin planks' in the cave had
formerly covered this burial.

Skeleton B1 (Fig. 13)

The skeleton of a mature woman (?) was
at the back of the cave, lying tightly flexed
on the left side and parallel to the cliff,
with the head to the south (see Pl. 7, 3).
There was no evidence of a wooden coffin,
though fragments of bark were found above
and below the body. The bottom of the
grave was about 2 feet below the surface of
the deposit in the cave, and the bones were
covered by 6 to 9 inches of earth. The skin
on the right half of the pelvis and femur
was so well preserved that these bones were
still joined together. The body was wrapped
in coarse matting (a sample of which is
illustrated in Pl. 52, 2), and with it was a
fragment of grass cord. In the grave was
a whetstone. There were no other grave
goods, although a broken paddle blade
(Pl. 57, 4) and 2 wooden pins, possibly
teeth for a composite comb (Pl. 51, 7),
were found near by. A piece of the gunwale
of one of the dugouts (Pl. 56, 1) was half
buried in the dust above the grave, but its
position showed that it had been left there
recently, probably by modern looters.

Skeleton B2 (Fig. 14)

This is the skeleton of a mature man
with which the jaw and metacarpal of another mature man (B2x) had been buried.
The grave was against the back wall of the
cave, between A and B1 (Pl. 7, 3). Several
layers of boards covered the body, and the
grave was about 3½ feet long and 2 feet

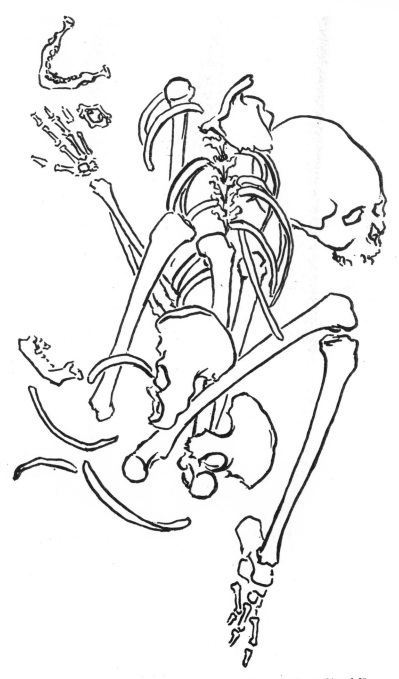

FIGURE 14. Skeleton B2, Palutat Cave. For grave finds, see Figures 34 and 35

wide (117 by 61 cm.). The bottom was about 3 feet below the surface, suggesting that this burial was older than B1. The skeleton lay face down, the head to the south. The bones were significantly disarranged (as can be seen in Fig. 14), and some (left scapula, right radius and ulna, most of bones of left foot) were missing. The extra mandible was at the distal end of the left tibia.

The disordered position of the bones suggests that the body was already beginning to decompose and fall apart at the time of burial. A somewhat similar burial was found in Kachemak Bay II, and perhaps the same explanation is valid for both.[6] It would seem that B2 had been a partially preserved mummy, secured in its wrappings, at the time it was removed from its original place and deposited in this grave, and that the handling of the remains was responsible for displacing the bones inside the bundle. Perhaps the extra mandible and metacarpal were thrown into the grave because they were supposed to be part of the same skeleton. The mummy may simply have been moved from another place in the cave to make room for a more important and more recent deceased, or the ancient Chugach, like the Aleut,[7] may have had the custom of keeping the mummies of beloved dead for as long as possible in the house, in which case this might represent a body that had been kept too long. Our informants said only that the corpse was kept in the house for a while, without specifying any definite period, but their accounts are not altogether satisfactory, for they knew nothing about mummification. Again, if the Chugach, like the Aleut,[8] ever suspended their mummies, the collapse of the bundle, after the body had begun to decompose, would be sufficient to displace the bones. We have no evidence, however, that Chugach mummies were suspended.

On top of the boards covering the grave,

6 De Laguna, 1934, p. 42.
7 Jochelson, 1925, pp. 41 f.
8 Veniaminof in Hrdlička, 1945, p. 184; Jochelson, 1925, pp. 44, 45, 49.

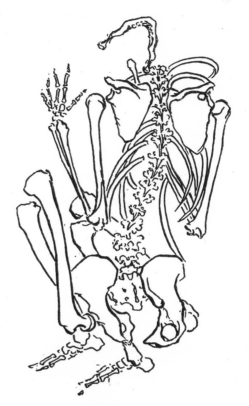

FIGURE 15. Skeleton B3, Palutat Cave

and directly above the skull, was found a pile of 12 wooden bars and 12 wooden hooks, probably parts of traps or snares (Figs. 34 and 35).

Skeleton B3 (Fig. 15)

The disturbed grave of an adult woman was found in Section B near the front of the cave. The skeleton was complete except for the skull, which had been recently removed. There was no trace of a coffin, though a few shreds of bark or wood were found above the bones. The grave was very shallow, the bottom being only 18 inches below the surface of the cave deposit. There were 12 inches of earth over some of the bones. Several scattered stones were near the skeleton, but it was impossible to say whether these represented a stone cist which the grave robbers had destroyed. The skeleton lay face down, but turned slightly to the left, with the right arm and leg folded under the body. The left arm and leg were also closely flexed; the head was to the south. An unfinished chipped slate blade for lance or knife was found in the grave, but its position may be only accidental.

Skeleton C1 (Fig. 16)

This skeleton was found in a wooden coffin, the lid of which was covered by 6 inches of earth (Pls. 7, *4*; 8, *1*). The remains are those of a mature man, who lay flexed on the left side, with the head to the east, resting on a wooden pillow. Aside from a mass of pupa cases of the blowfly larva and a few twigs and spruce needles (re-

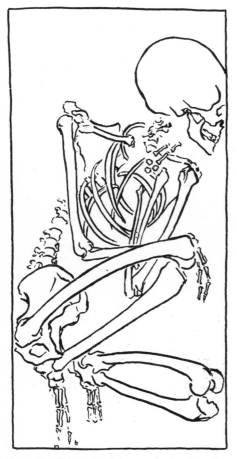

FIGURE 16. Skeleton C1, Palutat Cave. See Plate 8, *1*

mains of a bough bed? or of trash which had sifted in?), there was nothing else in the grave.

The wooden coffin was composed of separate planks which lined the grave. The largest of these, a slab measuring 5 feet by 2½ feet (153 by 75 cm), formed the lid. Two boards for the head and foot were set up on end, and the 2 side boards were placed on edge. The inside dimensions of the coffin were 3 feet 3 inches in length, 1 foot 5 inches in width, and 1 foot in depth (99 by 43 by 30 cm.). Lying flat in the dust along the left side of the coffin were several narrow boards or sticks on which the lid of the coffin rested. On the right side, at the foot, was a small stake driven into the ground outside the coffin, apparently to help prop up the side plank. There were also a plank at the bottom of the coffin and a wooden pillow propped up by 2 pieces of bark. The pillow was an old fire board (35 by 10 cm.), with 2 pits made by a fire drill. This was the only part of the coffin sufficiently well preserved to be removed.

Skeleton C2

When sinking the test pit near the back of the cave, we encountered human remains at a depth of 4 feet. Unfortunately it was too dark here to take a photograph or to make a drawing of the position of the bones. The remains are those of an adult male (?). The skeleton was incomplete and had been disarticulated at the time of burial. The skull lay on top of the pelvis, the 2 tibia were crossed, and the 2 fibulae lay side by side. A small double-edged slate blade (Pl. 29, *11*) was found among the bones, but the association may be accidental. It was impossible to tell whether these human remains had been interred, and, if so, what were the dimensions of the grave. This burial is the oldest in Palutat Cave and reminds us of the dismembered burials of Kachemak Bay III.[9]

[9] De Laguna, 1934, p. 164. Apparently Hrdlička found similar dismembered and incomplete burials of one or more individuals on Kodiak Island, in what he calls the "later Pre-Koniag" period (Hrdlička, 1944, Figs. 130, 131, p. 232).

Skeleton C3

In a small recess at the very back of the cave was an open grave from which all the bones except the vertebrae and a few ribs had been taken. The body had lain parallel to the rock wall.

Skeleton D (Fig. 17)

The skeleton of an adult woman was found about 6 feet from the grave of the adult man, C1. These 2 burials are very similar and seem to be of the same age (Pl. 7, *4*). The lid of the coffin was covered by about 6 inches of earth; the head was toward the south or southwest. The flexed body lay on the back, slightly turned to the right. The head was twisted so sharply to the left as to suggest a broken neck, but this may have resulted simply from disintegration of the tissues. There were a few other minor displacements of the bones—some of the ribs were scattered; the atlas and right patella lay to the right of the skull; the sternum and a cervical vertebra were beside the pelvis. These displacements may have been caused by mice, since remains of 2 dead mice were found in the coffin of E1 (see below). The coffin of D had certainly not been opened in modern times, and when found it was full of earth, dust, fir needles, and other rubbish from the cave floor, and the pupa cases of blowfly larvae.

The lid of the coffin, again the largest plank, was 53 inches long and 16 to 19 inches wide (136 by 43 to 50 cm.), with the widest part at the foot of the grave. The side boards were adzed smooth inside, but the outer surfaces were left rough, just as they had been split. They were about 39 inches long and 15 inches wide (101 by 40.5 cm. and 100 by 39 cm.), and as usual had been set on edge. The foot and the head of the coffin were each made of 3 small planks. The grave had a bottom board, 39 by 13 inches (100 by 33 cm.), and the skull was pillowed on a pile of 4 small pieces of wood, a little longer than the width of the bottom plank. Outside the

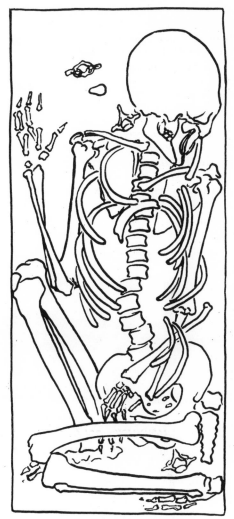

FIGURE 17. Skeleton D, Palutat Cave

coffin a narrow board lay along the left side. This coffin was in such an excellent state of preservation that it could be removed, and in 1938 the coffin and skeleton were installed in their original position in the Southwestern Alaskan Hall of the Danish National Museum.

Skeleton E1

The desiccated body of an adult woman was found in a coffin in Section E (Pls. 8, *2* to *4; 9, 1*). The lid was covered by

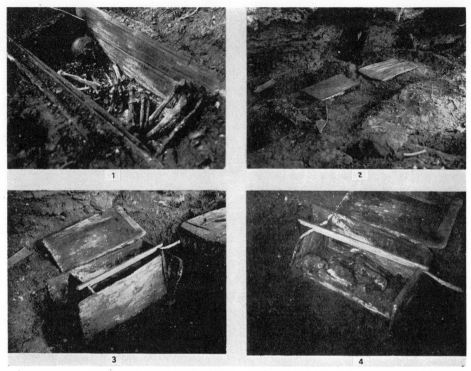

PLATE 8. Palutat Cave
1, Grave C1 after removal of coffin lid (see Fig. 16) ; 2, Graves E1 and E2, the test pit in Sections
C and D on the extreme left; 3, Grave E1, partially excavated, the notched sticks placed to
prevent the coffin from collapsing; 4, Grave E1 with lid and side board removed

about 6 inches of earth. After the interior had been opened and photographed, a large hole was dug around the coffin. The side and end boards were removed; the bottom board was tunneled under and, with the mummy in place on it, was slid out onto a firm plank. A box was built around it and packed with moss. The mummy survived the trip very well; there was almost no shifting of the bones or of the litter about them, although the skin cracked and peeled off to a large extent. The other boards of the coffin were shipped separately, and for a time the mummy in its reconstructed coffin was on exhibit in the Eskimo Hall of the University of Pennsylvania Museum.

The body lay on the back, the head to the south. The face was turned to the right, and the right arm was so flexed that the cheek was propped against the bent fingers of the right hand. The legs were both flexed to the left, the knees resting on top of the bent left arm. The toes of the right foot were cramped against the side of the coffin. Inside the coffin was a thin stake, lying along the right side; another stick lay across the foot. These may have served only to fill in the cracks between the side and bottom planks. There was no wooden pillow. The body had been wrapped in twined grass matting, fragments of which still adhered to the bones. In the space beyond the feet were shreds of skin, suggestive of the fringed edge of a garment. Extraneous material in the coffin included moss, bits of charred wood, twigs, pebbles, spruce cones and needles, small bits of bark, a few fish bones, and very small mussel shells. It is impossible to say whether these were

PLATE 9. Burials; Hunting dog

1. Grave E1, Palutat Cave, after removal of coffin lid, a fragment of matting across the legs and another fragment in the background; 2, skeletons I and II, Palugvik, layer 1 (see Fig. 9); 3, modern Prince William Sound hunting dog, Chenega, the breed probably the same as that of the dog found with skeleton II, Palugvik; 4, skeleton II, Palugvik, at bottom of midden, before removal of the wooden coffin (see Fig. 10)

purposely placed in the coffin, sifted in accidentally, or were brought in by mice. Near the head of the woman was found the skull of a mouse, and a completely mummified body of a mouse was in the rubbish near the feet. These mice were identified by Dr. Goodwin as belonging to the common Alaskan red-backed species.

The lid of the coffin is 3 feet 3 inches by 1 foot 8 inches (103 by 46 cm.). The ends are battered off, the inside surface adzed, and the split outer surface only slightly trimmed with an adz. The stains on the wood suggest that it was an old plank reshaped for its present use. The 2 side boards, 21 and 18 inches wide (54 and 47 cm.), were set on edge. The right-hand one is made of a crooked slab with knotholes, somewhat trimmed with an adz on the inner surface. The left side board is irregular in shape and beveled to fit the foot board in a mitered joint. The foot board was also set on edge. It is beveled along one end to fit the left side board and grooved across the other end to receive the right side board. A stake driven into the ground outside the coffin held this joint. The inner surface of the foot board was adzed, the outer surface simply split. It had evidently been used as a fire board, for there are 5 pits made by the fire drill in the outer surface. The head board was set on end between the projecting ends of the side boards and rested on the bottom plank. It was evidently an old piece of lumber, trimmed at the ends and adzed on both sides. The inside dimensions of the coffin are 36 by 16 inches, and the depth is about 18 inches (91 by 40 by 46 cm.). The fine adz marks on all the planks are those of a small stone tool.

Skeleton E2

Just north of grave E1 another coffin was discovered (Pl. 8, 2). Since the short time at our disposal and our lack of packing materials would have prevented proper excavation and preservation of the contents, this grave was not disturbed. The coffin was full of earth and moss, and just under the lid were 2 partially mummified birds (ducks?). Since the lid of the coffin was covered by about 6 inches of earth, the introduction of the birds must have been at an ancient time, even though it was probably after the burial had been made, to judge by the accumulation of earth inside the coffin. Was the dead person held in such esteem that offerings of food were made to him long after death? Are we also to interpret as offerings of food the fish bones and shells found in the coffins of Palutat E1 and of Glacier Island I (see below)? Our informants told us that the relatives used to take food and water to the grave of a dead person, even a poor one, for 40 days after the burial. When a dead chief was placed in a rock shelter, the people used to go to look at him "every day" and bring him a share of everything they had to eat. Sauer reports that the Kodiak Eskimo buried food with the mummy of a chief, while Davydof says that he never heard of the Koniag placing food or anything else with the dead.[10] Langsdorff reported that the Aleut used to include food among the grave goods.[11] It is possible that the birds in Palutat E2 do not represent food, but rather feathers.[12]

Skeleton F

At the back of the cave was a depression with stones about it, which we interpreted as an opened grave. Two blue glass beads of the "Cook type" (Pl. 43, 26) and the jaw of a mature woman(?) (Ex) were found near by and may have come from this grave. Just north of the depression was a pile of stones; presumably these had formed a cist and had been rolled aside by the grave robbers. A fragment of matting under the stones probably came from the grave.

[10] Quotations in Hrdlička, 1944, p. 87.
[11] Quoted by Hrdlička, 1945, p. 179.
[12] Compare the wooden dish filled with finch wings, found by Hrdlička in a mummy cave on Kagamil Island, Aleutian Islands (ibid., Fig. 172).

Cremation (?)

Under the pile of stones near the grave in Section F was a hearth, from 6 to 12 inches below the surface of the cave deposits. In the lens of charcoal and ashes we found fragments of burned human bones, probably of an adult man, consisting of portions of the skull, pelvis, femur, and humerus, as well as a fragment of burned animal (?) bone. This probably represents a cremation, even though our informants denied the practice, and the presence of the animal bone (if it actually is such) might suggest cannibalism.

Other Burials

As previously mentioned, there were piles of stones north of Section F which seemed to mark 5 (or possibly more) graves. These we left undisturbed.

Meany also excavated a grave in the cave. I quote from his account:

As far as could be determined the bodies were all buried with the head towards the east. Trinkets and weapons are nearly always buried near the head. Our excavations were therefore made carefully from the head toward the foot of the grave. Not a thing in the nature of an implement was found in the grave. Resting on the rock at the bottom of the grave was a layer of black earth containing many hemlock leaves that seemed almost carbonized [with age]. It was clear that the first part of this bed was made of hemlock boughs. Then came a layer of dust like that on the floor of the cave. On this floor was found a bed of spruce boughs, decayed and mouldy, but easily identified. On this bed was thrown more cave dust and the grave was ready for the dead. At the head and foot and outer side of the grave were placed protecting stones obtained from the cliff. Over these stones were placed the heavy plank cover which was held in place by weighting stones. These cover planks are themselves very interesting, as they plainly show what must be the marks of rude stone axes. A specimen board was secured, and is now deposited in the Historical Museum of the University of Washington [now known as the Washington State Museum]. It is fifty-two inches long, nineteen inches wide and one and a half inches thick. One side shows the cleavage marks of the original splitting. The other side was smoothed off with stone axes and the ends are apparently chopped off with similar implements. The wood seems to be spruce.[13]

[13] Meany, 1906, pp. 465-67.

This plank (catalogue number 3464) was, I believe, part of some structure, perhaps a house. Both ends and one edge are neatly trimmed and straight; the other edge is rotted. At the middle of the straight side edge has been cut a curved indentation, 3 inches wide. Since the edge of the plank is split away for some distance beyond this indentation its length cannot be measured, but it could not have been more than 15 inches long. This plank may have been at the edge of an opening into a house, perhaps a door or a window. Makari spoke of windows with gutskin panes. Meany continues:

The last grave at the edge of the cave was a poor one. There lay a skull, a scapula and the protecting grave stones. Alongside was the rotted bow of a canoe. It could not have been older than the better preserved graves, else it would not occupy the last place. It is possible that the custom of such elaborate preparation of the bodies had begun to decline when this burial was made. Its position was more exposed to the weather than the others.

In Palutat Cave, therefore, we have evidence of a number of seated mummies or of mummy bundles; 4 burials in wooden coffins (C1, D, E1, E2); at least 4 burials in stone or stone and plank cists, one of which at least was covered by a plank (A, F, Meany's 2 graves); 5 or more burials under piles of stones, 3 covered with bark or with boards (B1, B2, B3); a shallow inhumation about which nothing can be said (C3); evidence of cremation, or possibly of cannibalism (in F); and a partially disarticulated skeleton deep in the cave deposits (C2). Probably all of the bodies had originally been wrapped in matting and/or skins. Many of the artifacts found in the cave were probably grave goods. If the glass beads were associated with the stone cist burial in F, this was undoubtedly the most recent. The oldest burial was C2, the next in age B2. B3 may have been a little older than the remaining burials, which we can assume were of about the same period. The cremation in F may have been about the same age as B3. As far as we can tell, therefore, stone cists and plank coffins were in

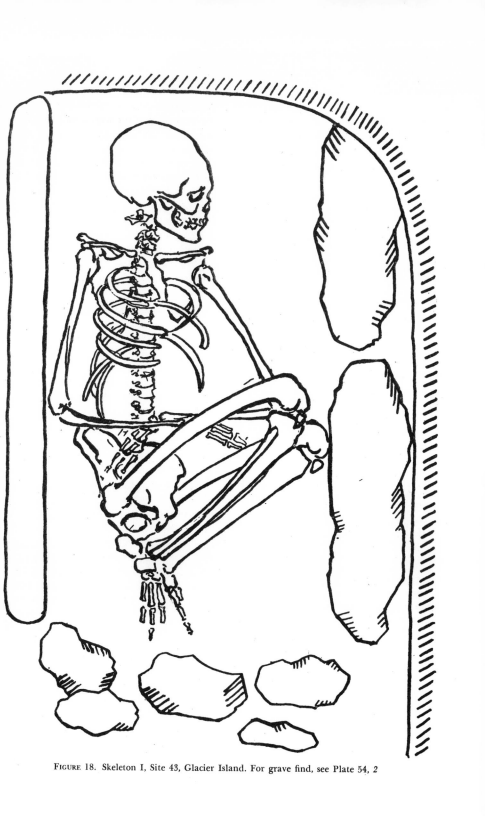

FIGURE 18. Skeleton I, Site 43, Glacier Island. For grave find, see Plate 54, *2*

use simultaneously, although the stone cist may have lasted in use later than the coffins, and rough coverings of bark or boards have antedated the coffins. On the whole, the differences in graves are more likely to reflect the varied social statuses of the deceased than changes in funeral styles.[14]

5. GLACIER ISLAND BURIALS

Makari told us that mummies had been found in a cave on a part of the island which we were unable to explore, and we learned no further details of this find.

Three skeletons were in small rock shelters in Mummy Bay, on the north side of the island, near the southwestern point. The name suggests that other finds had been made here, although we heard nothing about them. Two of the 3 skeletons were those which we found in a rock shelter, Site 43, and the third was recovered by Professor Meany from a near-by site.

Skeleton I (Fig. 18)

These remains are those of an adult, probably a man. They were on the small upper ledge in the shelter, in an open cist. The wall of rock at the end of the ledge formed the head of the cist, 2 large boulders that had fallen from the roof made the side next to the back of the cave, a large log formed the side next to the water, and a few rocks were piled across the foot. The only access to the shelf of rock was up the steep slope of the cave floor to the foot of the cist. The body was lying on the back, flexed and slightly turned to the left, with the head to the northwest. It had probably been clothed, for at the feet we found skin fragments which may have been from a boot. The head was enveloped in a heavy depilated skin, which Makari identified as a bidarka cover (Pl. 54, 2). The right side of the head was uppermost and was protected by this wrapping so that the skin of the face, including the right ear and right

eye, and some of the hair were preserved. Red paint adhered to the face and to the inner surface of the wrapping above it. This was evidently not an interment, for the skeleton was covered only by a little moss and decayed vegetable matter, nor was there any lid to the cist. Among the bones of the neck and under the skull we found a number of small blue glass beads. In the grave were many fish bones and opercula of marine gastropods. These may represent offerings of food, or they may have been brought in by the foxes that make their burrows in the lower part of the shelter.

Skeleton II (Fig. 19)

These are the remains of a young woman about 18 to 20 years old and were found in a rough coffin on the lower ledge in the rock shelter. She had apparently suffered from early hydrocephaly, for her brain case was expanded laterally to form an almost globular skull, which also exhibited a slight occipital flattening like that produced by a cradle board.[15]

The coffin was formed by 2 adzed planks set on edge along each side of the grave and another plank at the head. At the head there were also 3 or 4 large stones, and the foot of the coffin was formed by 3 boulders. The body had probably been covered with boards, for one was found partially protecting the skull, and other fragments of plank were lying close by. There were also traces of rotted wood (from a bottom board?) under the body. The coffin could not have been covered with earth, and when discovered the skull was visible above the very shallow depression. Again, we are not dealing with an inhumation. Samples of the coffin planks were saved, but it is not clear whether they were shaped with a steel or with a stone adz, although the former is more probable.

The skeleton was lying on the back, partially flexed, with the head to the northeast. A piece of skin, possibly part of a robe or wrapping, was in a corner of the coffin,

[14] Lantis, 1947, pp. 9 f., and the various original sources quoted by Hrdlička (1944, pp. 87 f.; 1945, pp. 178-95) show clearly that throughout southwestern Alaska the treatment of the dead varied according to economic and social position.

[15] Oetteking, 1945, pp. 59, 186-88, Pl. 6.

beyond the skull. About the skull and neck vertebrae were many small black, blue, and white glass beads, the blue ones exactly like those found with Skeleton I. Under the skull were a number of shell pendants which had undoubtedly been ear ornaments. Half of the beads and pendants are illustrated in Plate 45.

Meany's Skeleton

Professor Meany found a burial ledge on Glacier Island very near to that which we

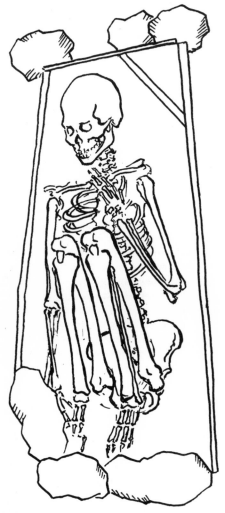

FIGURE 19. Skeleton II, Site 43, Glacier Island. For grave finds, see Plate 45

later visited. I quote his account:

On the southwest end of Glacier Island, fronting the fine Columbia Glacier, was a small overhanging cliff that proved important in my search. It was just large enough for one of these burials, and the little shelf was occupied by a lonely grave. Instead of the cover plank lying down flat, as in the larger cave [Palutat Cave], two planks were laid like the letter "A" over the grave, and were held in place by the usual large stones. After photographing the original form of the grave, I opened it and found the skeleton fallen apart with age, but showing unmistakably that the body had been doubled up and buried exactly like those in the mummy cave. There was no canoe by the side of the body, probably because there was no room on the narrow shelf. There were no implements in or about the grave. The covering boards showed what seemed to be the prints of stone axes on the faces, though the ends of the boards seem to have been cut with better tools. Thus far this little grave would seem like an outlying member of the colony in the larger cave, which was but five or six miles away. But there was one important difference. Across the brow of this corpse was the fragment of a decaying strap which had clasped the head like a crown. From this strap still dangled a few strands of Hudson Bay Company beads of blue, black and white glass. The other beads had fallen into the eye sockets and the mouth. Here was evidence which told us as plainly as possible that the burial custom which had produced the mummies had projected over into the time when the whites had come into contact with these people. This helps to verify the dates suggested by Mr. Dall.[16]

6. OTHER BURIALS

Site 2, Hinchinbrook Island

It will be remembered that miscellaneous human bones were found scattered in Layers 1 to 3 (or 4) at Palugvik. Similarly, the head of a human right femur was found in the shell heap at Site 2, at the entrance to Constantine Harbor, Hinchinbrook Island, but it was unassociated with any other skeletal remains. Scattered human bones have been found in midden deposits of Kachemak Bay II and III, at Port Möller on the Alaska Peninsula, in the intermediate or "later Pre-Koniag" deposits on Kodiak, and on the Aleutian Islands.[17] Hrdlička consistently interprets such finds as proof of

[16] Meany, 1906, pp. 467 f.
[17] De Laguna, 1934, pp. 48 ff., 166 f.; Hrdlička, 1944, p. 323; 1945, pp. 230, 298, 300, etc.

cannibalism, but they may merely indicate that the Aleut and Pacific Eskimo, like so many of their more northern relatives, were not concerned about breaking into old graves and scattering the bones.

Near Site 9, Hinchinbrook Island

We heard 2 conflicting reports about a burial or burials on the Pinnacle Rocks, just inside the entrance to Boswell Bay. A skeleton is said to have been found on a ledge halfway up the side of the second largest of these gull rocks. The body could not have been interred, for the white bones were visible from the water. Matrona Tiedmann reported that a skeleton was found in a wooden coffin on top of the largest rock, Pinnacle Rock proper. With the skeleton were many beads of native manufacture, some of baked (?) clay, according to her account. In view of the uncertainty as to whether we are dealing with one or 2 finds, nothing further need be said, except to point out that the Chugach, according to Makari, sometimes placed chiefs or rich people on top of high places so that others could not find the bodies and rob them. There was no need to hide poor people, because nothing was buried with them. Explorations of the smaller rock in Boswell Bay revealed no trace of any burial. Since we did not explore any other refuge islands or bird rocks, we do not know how common this type of burial might be among the Chugach. It was practiced by Tsimshian, Haida, and Tlingit for shamans, by the Tanaina in Kachemak Bay, by the Koniag for shamans (in a bidarka, placed on top of a cliff or sometimes in a cave), and by the Aleut, at least in the Unalaska area for distinguished persons.[18]

Site 10, Hinchinbrook Island

At the back of the large cave, Site 10, on the north shore of Boswell Bay, we found a few adult vertebrae and the pelvis of an

18 De Laguna, 1934, pp. 47, 165 f. See also Lantis, 1947, p. 11; Hrdlička, 1945, pp. 270 f., 183. Osgood (1937, p. 167) reports an Eskimo burial in a kayak covered with rocks in Kamishak Bay, southwestern Cook Inlet, but does not say whether it was on a high place.

infant. These were in a natural depression behind a large boulder and were covered with a few stones. The burial may have been originally in a stone cist, or under a pile of stones. Visitors to the cave had disturbed the grave when they removed the other bones. At one time there were supposed to have been other skeletons in the cave.

Site 12, Hawkins Island

At the back of this cave, in a recess formed by the downward sloping floor, we found the remains of 3 individuals—an adult (field no. 414) and 2 children about 6 or 7 years old (field nos. 415A and B). Most of the bones had been removed by recent curio hunters, and the remainder were so scattered that it was impossible to determine the original position of the bodies. We found these bones behind and under the rocks and earth piled across the front of the recess, and so we believe that the burial was originally under a pile of stones, or perhaps in a rough cist or circle of stones. Above the recess a complicated figure was painted on the wall of the cave (Fig. 22C).

Site 15, Hawkins Island

Nothing definite can be said about the original position of the skeleton obtained from this rock shelter (field no. 413), since it had been reburied by the Eskimo party that found it. Makari reports that there were no wrappings or clothing on it when he first saw it, so we can assume that it either was lying exposed on the surface or was covered very inadequately. Since there is little earth in the shelter, there could have been only a few rocks (or possibly planks) piled over or around the body.

Site 16, Hawkins Island

Two burial places were found near this site. The first is the cave northeast of the village. In this we found the remains of 4 individuals. Two of these were adult women, represented chiefly by the bones of the arms and legs. A number of other bones doubtless belonged to these individuals, but an identification was impossible. The 2 other persons were represented by such scanty remains that we can say nothing as to their age or sex. The skulls and most interesting bones had evidently been removed by curio hunters. We were told that 2 of the skulls had been sent to the U.S. National Museum, but that institution has no record of them.

Scattered among the bones in the cave were the following objects: 2 slate whetstones (Pl. 16, 8), a boulder chip (see Chapter V, section 12), the point of a slate "awl," 3 pieces of worked slate (see Chapter V, section 29), a greenstone drill point, a wooden peg, and some small blue and white glass beads. The latest burials in this cave are probably contemporary with those on Glacier Island, since the glass beads are identical, and the earliest may have been prehistoric. It will be remembered that the village was occupied in 1805.

The mouth of the cave was blocked with earth and boulders, but we do not know whether this was accidental. The bodies had not been interred, for the larger bones were exposed, and the smaller were covered by only a slight accumulation of dust and decayed matter.

In the scanty shelter of a small overhanging rock east of the village site we found the skeleton of a man (field no. 504) under a thin layer of shells, animal bones, and fire-cracked rocks. The body seems to have been placed on the back, with the head to the west or southwest, the arms extended at the sides. The skull and mandible were displaced; a portion of the pelvis lay beyond the head; the legs were represented by only one femur, tibia, and fibula, considerably disarranged. The body, if complete at the time of burial, could not have been covered by more than 6 inches of deposit, so we may attribute the condition of the skeleton to scavenging animals and to the dampness of the spot. A fine splitting adz (Pl. 10, 9) lay across the right humerus, evidently an intentional grave offering. A

stone saw (lost) was also found in the grave.

Site 20, Mummy Island

Two skeletons were found in the sheltered ledge just west of the southwesternmost point of Mummy Island. The lower skeleton is that of a mature woman. It was lying on the right side with the head to the east or southeast, the legs and arms tightly flexed. A number of bones showed arthritic lesions, a disease which was apparently common among both prehistoric and modern residents of the sound.

The upper skeleton, that of a mature to senile man, was on top of the lower skeleton, the head in the same direction. Although almost all the bones had recently been removed by curio hunters, it was evident from the small space in which the body had been confined that it must have been tightly flexed. Holding the skeleton in place against the back wall of the shelter was an adzed plank, set on edge on top of the skull of the lower skeleton. This burial had certainly been made in historic times, for the man had suffered from tuberculosis of the spine, a disease introduced by the whites.

Beside the woman's skull were 2 "Cook type" blue glass beads, but both burials were so disturbed that it was impossible to determine with which of them these beads had originally been placed. Nor was there any way of telling how long an interval had elapsed between the first and the second burial. A piece of skin, either from wrappings or from garments, was found among the bones. Neither of the burials could be called an interment, since the bones were but lightly covered with dust and rotted material.

Site 21, Mummy Island

Skeletons in wooden coffins made of adzed planks nailed together with wooden pegs were reported from a small cave on the south side of the island, although we found nothing in it. The use of pegs in making these coffins is a novel feature, and the report may be incorrect.

Site 22, Mummy Island

The large burial caves on the south side of the island are said to have contained a number of mummies wrapped in sea otter skins and squatting with their backs against the wall. There were only a few bones left in 1930.

Site 26, island east of Mummy Island

Several burial caves are on the largest island east of Mummy Island, called naŋιn·a.

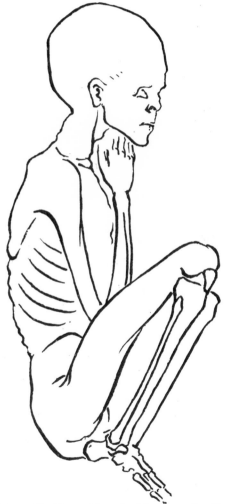

FIGURE 20. Mummy from burial cave at Site 26, island near Mummy Island

The cave nearest the water contained the scattered bones of several individuals, of which we took the only remaining mandible.[19] In the upper cave or shelter was an open cist or grave surrounded by stones. Grave robbers had already removed all of the bones, leaving only a blue glass bead and a few fragments of plank, presumably the cover for the cist. In a small cave or chamber below this shelter we found the partially mummified body of a woman in a wooden coffin (Fig. 20). The planks of the coffin were so well adzed that we could not tell whether a stone or a steel tool had been used. The coffin was of the same type as those in Palutat Cave, although it did not seem to have been covered with earth, and when found was disarranged. Since the mouth of the cave was completely blocked by stones and earth, the disturbance of the coffin could not have taken place in recent times. The body lay on the left side, the arms and legs tightly flexed, the head to the north or northwest and the feet toward the mouth of the tiny rock chamber. The body had been wrapped in depilated sealskins, on which were traces of purple-red paint. That the body had also been clothed, or that garments were included in the wrappings, is indicated by the remains of a sealskin boot upper or sleeve and by a fragment of a fringed garment made of several skins stitched together. Two pieces of a 4-strand braided sinew cord were found among the fragments and had probably been used to tie up the mummy bundle. The side of a birchbark basket lay on top of one of the coffin boards. Unless animals had managed to open the coffin, its disturbance was the work of ancient grave robbers, which suggests that the burial may have been that of a distinguished person, since the robbers must have thought there were valuable grave goods to be found.

Site 34, Port Gravina

According to Paul Elie Chimowitski's description, the mummy which he found on

[19] Oetteking, 1945, pp. 59 f.

this small island in Olsen Bay was that of a youth about 17 years old. It was lying on a board, the head to the west (?) resting on a wooden pillow. The legs were extended and were crossed at the ankles; the arms were folded across the breast with the hands at the shoulders. The body was covered by a board, but there were none at the sides. From the description this sounds like an incomplete (or partially destroyed) coffin. The grave was in the shelter of an overhanging rock and was not an interment. Although we visited the place with Paul as a guide, no trace of the burial remained.

7. GRAVE AT PORT WELLS

In 1794 one of Vancouver's survey parties discovered a grave in Port Wells, at what I have tentatively identified as the north point of Harrison Lagoon.

At one of the points where the party had occasion to land, a sepulchre was discovered; Mr. Whidbey, in the course of his excursion [along the mainland north from Cape Puget and along the southwest shore of Knight Island] had observed similar monuments before, but they were all so old, decayed, and mutilated, that it was not an easy matter to determine exactly for what specific purpose they had been originally intended; but it was now proved that their conjectures had been rightly formed. This tomb being of more recent date, Mr. Whidbey had it examined; a hole was found dug about a foot deep, five feet long, and four feet wide; at the bottom were some thin planks, and across them, nearly in the middle of the grave, two pieces of wood were placed about a foot asunder, and about nine inches thick, between which were deposited the remains of a dead body, rolled up in a seal skin, and carefully tied with thongs of the same material. These remains consisted of some ashes and calcined bones, which were concluded to be human; and as all the parts of the grave shewed evident signs of the action of fire, it is natural to infer, that consuming their dead by fire is the practice of the inhabitants. The relics thus deposited were covered over with another plank, over which were strewed stones, moss, and some old broken paddles. The direction of the grave was nearly north and south, with a small pole about eight feet long erected at its south end. The curiosity of the party having been thus satisfied, every thing was restored to its former state.[20]

[20] Vancouver, 1801, V, 311 f.

From the description of the tomb itself —its size, the flooring and covering with wood, the stone and paddles on the lid, the pole set up near one end—we should judge this to be a typical Eskimo grave. The coffin was, however, incomplete, since there is no mention of planks at the ends and sides of the hole, unless these had collapsed and were represented by the 2 pieces of wood near the center of the grave. The cremated remains are harder to explain. Vancouver's account would imply that the body was burned in the grave, since the interior of the hole showed the action of fire. Yet the fact that the ashes and calcined bones were wrapped in sealskin would suggest that the cremation had taken place outside, especially since it requires a large fire with a good draft to consume a human body. Something other than the corpse (food, grave offerings, or a purificatory fire) may have been burned in the grave before the ashes were deposited. Unfortunately Vancouver's men did not examine any of the other, presumably similar burials, so that we do not know what they contained.

Our Chugach informants denied cremation, and the only archaeological evidence suggestive of the practice was the burned human bones near a hearth in Palutat Cave. The only reference to cremation in Prince William Sound is in the very brief passage on the Chugach written by Merck, one of the members of Billings' expedition (1790). "They are supposed to burn their dead," he writes,[21] but gives us no authority for this extraordinary bit of information.

Since the Tanaina of Cook Inlet, who lived within easy access of Port Wells, consistently cremated their dead, we might well suppose this grave to be that of some Indian visitor. Most of the Tanaina groups erected a pole at the place where the ashes were buried, but we have no information as to whether they used a coffin.[22] Therefore, especially as the tomb itself seemed to be like others in the western part of the sound,

[21] Jacobi, 1937, p. 133: "Ihre Toten sollen sie verbrennen."
[22] Osgood, 1937, pp. 166.

we cannot be sure that these remains were those of an Indian. Since the Chugach lived between the Tlingit, Eyak, and Tanaina, all of whom practiced cremation, it should not be too surprising if the Chugach themselves sometimes copied this method of corpse disposal. In this connection we might note that Hrdlička makes the following report on finds from the large site at Uyak Bay, Kodiak Island, suggesting that cremation may have been not unknown here at one time: "Remains of a cremated intermediary-period adult male skeleton were found; and one adult female with one juvenile body had been burned partially during what appears to have been a wide conflagration in the settlement at one time."[23] He even found cremated remains in one or 2 caves on Kagamil Island in the Aleutians. One of these finds represented 2 bodies; the second consisted of the partially consumed bones of at least 10 young women, which were covered by a large stone slab at the bottom of the cave.[24]

In our excavations [in the Aleutians] we found the remains of one or two cremated bodies in every rock-shelter that had been used for burials; and in the warm Kagamil cave, at its lowest part and under a huge slab, there were the calcined remains of several females and children. All the cremated had doubtless been slaves, for the Aleuts did not cremate their free kind. A detail of interest—the cremation was achieved by fire, evidently very hot, of rich-in-fat whale bones.[25]

Hrdlička also quotes a passage from Veniaminof to the effect that the Atka Aleut used to torture captives, especially men, by burning them alive in fires or on heated rocks.[26] The implication is that the captives were tortured to death, but this is not clear, and there is no indication that their bodies were cremated and the ashes deposited in burial caves. It is more likely, I suspect, that the cremated remains found by Hrdlička represented a special method of corpse disposal.

[23] Hrdlička, 1944, p. 228.
[24] Hrdlička, 1945, pp. 267, 399.
[25] Ibid., p. 150.
[26] Ibid., p. 182.

Lantis cites a report from Nunivak Island in Bering Sea that the Eskimo there cremated the recovered bodies of those who had died by drowning.[27] Did this same custom obtain among the Aleut, Koniag, and Chugach? The bodies of most of those who drowned were probably never recovered, which would explain why the archaeological evidence for cremation is so scanty in these areas and why it has not been mentioned by informants. The motive for such a method of disposal might be fear of this type of dead. While Makari said that the Chugach were not, ordinarily, afraid of ghosts, his daughter told of a family that recently had had to move out of Simpson Bay because the ghost of a man who had been drowned at Orca cannery in Cordova Bay used to bother them. The Chugach evidently shared to a certain extent the Eyak and Tlingit belief that land otters were persons who had drowned and been transformed into evil monsters. The Aleut believed that the sea otter was a transformed human being.[28]

Such speculation, however fascinating, should be recognized for what it is. We really do not know how to interpret Vancouver's grave, and are not likely to be able to discover the answer, since the old natives who might have known are now dead.

8. OTHER MUMMY CAVES

A number of burials are known to us only through brief reports. Thus we were told that mummies had been found on an island at the mouth of Fish Bay, in Port Fidalgo; mummies without clothing or wrappings had been taken from an island in Boulder Bay, Port Fidalgo; and mummies were found on Bligh Island opposite Ellamar. These three localities are all within the territory of the Tatitlek People.

There are more numerous reports from the western part of the sound, from the territory of the Chenega People. A burial

[27] Lantis, 1947, pp. 15 f.
[28] Birket-Smith and de Laguna, 1938, pp. 236 f., 286-89, 508.

cave was reported on Bainbridge Island, and there were mummies in caves on Culross Island (Site 51). At Site 59 on Mummy Island (in Drier Bay, Knight Island) 7 mummies are said to have been found in the rock shelter, squatting with their backs to the wall. The adzed planks found here in 1930 suggest that some may have been enclosed in coffins. Several paintings were on the overhanging face of the cliff (Fig. 24; Pl. 7, *1*). The mummies found in a deep cave in Mummy Bay, Knight Island, are said to have been lashed to planks leaning against the rock; the cords passed through holes drilled along the edges of the planks. It is difficult to know how much credence should be given this report. Meany saw the mummies of 2 men and one woman which had been obtained from this site in 1905 and taken to Ellamar. The bodies had evidently been eviscerated, for he reports that they were stuffed with grass and bits of otter skin. The woman was supposed to have originally held a baby in her arms.[29]

Captain Jacobsen, who made collections in 1881-83 for the Könlige Museum in Berlin, describes 3 burial caves on Chenega Island and one on Knight Island, although he fails to give any exact location. The first cave was only a few miles from Chenega Village, but some one had preceded him, and on his first visit he obtained only 2 wooden masks. The next day he went again to the cave with an interpreter and Captain Andersen, the skipper of the *Three Brothers*.

This time after a long search we discovered the mummies of an adult and a child. They were, however, almost completely decayed, and by using the greatest caution we were able to get only one of them on board without its falling to pieces. As far as can be learned, the legs of the corpse were bent up so that the mummy was in a hunched position. Over it was a covering of skins that had been tied up with thongs. Outside this again was a second covering of depilated sealskin (*Seehundsleder*). The mummies were in a cave-like hollow in which they were protected from the rain. The remains of the child were so rotted that they could not be transported. In spite of the apparently great age of the bodies, I could not take for granted that they had lain here in the same spot perhaps for centuries, for I found beside the mummies a piece of wood that had been cut with a saw.

We went a bit farther with our boat along the high, steep, almost overhanging shores, with caves in various places, and thus discovered a second burial place where we found more mummies. These were completely decayed, so that we were able to rescue only a single small example. It was also wrapped in skins and lay in a round wooden hoop which resembled a Labrador snowshoe but was actually a child's cradle. Fortunately we found in this place a few well-preserved skulls. Because of a flood or high tide, the sea had entered the burial cave and had washed away most of the human remains. As grave goods I found a few pieces of wooden masks, but no hunting equipment or weapons, as formerly seemed to be the case in this area.

Jacobsen had to agree to send half of the collection to the Messrs. Fischer in St. Paul.

. . . We went on again some miles farther in the boat and again found a burial place. Here the roof of the cave had been destroyed and had fallen down on the human remains so that we first had to make room to work in before we could investigate the graves. After a great deal of effort we succeeded in securing a well-preserved skull. It would appear that this was the oldest burial place of all that I saw on these shores, not so much because of the condition of the cave, as especially because the bodies were covered with pieces of wood and planks, which had evidently not been worked with our modern tools, saw and ax, but had been split in the old way with wedges. A few bodies were also covered with spruce bark. I had the impression that these graves in this last place had a certain resemblance to the graves of the ancient inhabitants of Labrador; although to be sure the latter differ from these in that many objects are found in them, while on the other hand no wooden plank covers can be cited in treeless Labrador. In the vicinity of these old burial places of Chenega Island, there ought to be still some larger caves filled with mummies, yet we were unable to obtain more exact information from the natives.

Next day I went with Captain Andersen and an Eskimo over to Knight Island, where there was also an old burial place, as I had been informed. It was under an overhanging cliff. As in the last place visited yesterday, there were corpses buried in coffins made out of rough planks. Altogether, the remains were in a very decayed state, so that we had the greatest trouble to discover four partially preserved mummies from among the multitude of graves. In addition, we collected six skulls here. To-

[29] Meany, 1906, p. 468.

gether in one grave were the bodies of a woman and a child. Eager though I was to take the contents of this grave also, it was possible to secure intact only the cradle and the skull of the woman. It was very difficult to carry the mummies and parts of skeletons down the steep bank from the cave to the shore. All of the mummies were wrapped in animal skins. We were, moreover, not the first investigators of this place, but had been preceded by collectors for the Smithsonian Institution.[30]

Dall has described a mummy from Prince William Sound. This was collected by agents of the Alaska Commercial Company, who maintained a post at Port Etches, and was forwarded to the U.S. National Museum from the company's headquarters at San Francisco. With the mummy were sent 7 wooden masks, which Dall not unreasonably assumed were found in the same cave or rock shelter as the mummy, although there was no information as to the provenience of any of this material. We do not even know that it came from the vicinity of Nuchek, since the company apparently had dealings with the natives all over the sound, and the agents must have traveled about.

The mummy was stripped of its coverings, if it ever had any; and was that of an adult male. It had been eviscerated through the pelvis and bore marks of the incisions (made by most of the Innuit) for labrets. These were below the corners of the mouth, one on each side. The hair was long and black with no indications of the tonsure [characteristic of northern Alaskan Eskimo]. A string around the neck with a few old-fashioned Russian beads upon it, fixed the date as subsequent to the advent of traders. There were no other articles of use or ornament with the remains, which were well preserved.[31]

Meany reported that "Agent Smith, of the Alaska Commercial Company at Nuchek," had taken 2 mummies from Palutat Cave about 15 years or so before Meany's visit, i.e., about 1880, and had shipped them to the company's headquarters in San Francisco. These were later given to the University of California (see quotation from Meany in Chapter II, section 14). I therefore entered into correspondence with Dr. Robert F. Heizer and Dr. E. W. Gifford in order to trace these mummies, if possible. Dr. Gifford reported that the Museum of Anthropology at Berkeley had one such mummy (number 12-3487), which had come to it without data, and kindly furnished me with photographs and a description. The mummy is that of a man with a slight moustache. It is well preserved, except that the left leg and a good part of the lower left side of the body have been torn away. There is no trace of evisceration. In the center of the lower lip is a labret hole. The body is tightly flexed, the hands lying one above the other slightly below the chin; the head is bent forward a little, and the right leg is folded tightly against the chest. It is believed that this mummy was one which had been in the Bancroft Library.

The mummy in the library is mentioned by Bancroft in his *Literary Industries.* It was obtained by Ivan Petroff, when he visited Kodiak Island in July, 1878, while engaged in historical research for Bancroft's *History of Alaska.* The Mr. McIntyre to whom reference is made was an agent of the Alaska Commercial Company.

Mr McIntyre presented Mr Petroff with a mummy, which was sent to the Bancroft Library and placed in a glass case. It was obtained by Mr McIntyre from Nutchuk island, from a cave on the side of a steep mountain very difficult of access. In this cave were the dried bodies of a man and two boys. One was secretly shipped, but when the others were about to be placed in a box the natives interfered, and required their burial for a time. It was Mr Oliver Smith, a trader at Nutchuk, who undertook their removal, and who obtained for Petroff the legend connected with them. The body is well preserved, with finely formed head, bearing little resemblance either to Aleut or Kolosh. The hair is smooth and black; it has the scanty mustache and goatee, sometimes noticeable among Aleuts. The nose has lost its original shape. Brown and well dried, with chin resting on the raised knees, this strange relic has a curious appearance as it views its new surroundings.[32]

Oliver Smith is certainly the same as "Agent Smith," mentioned by Meany;

[30] Jacobsen, 1884, pp. 381-84, my translation.
[31] Dall, 1878, p. 32. See also Dall, 1884, pp. 124-28.

[32] Bancroft, 1890, pp. 555-56.

"Nutchuk" is evidently Nuchek on Hinchinbrook Island, although it is hard to understand why Bancroft, who is usually so careful in identification of localities, should refer to the island by this misspelled and uncommonly used name. From this account, we infer that the mummy in question did not come from Palutat Cave, for not only is that cave far to the north but it is very easy of access. In that case, what became of the mummies that Smith obtained from Palutat? Bancroft's mummy seems to have come from one of the caves which were reported to us as located in the hills above Nuchek Village. In any case, it is not altogether clear that Bancroft's mummy is the same as the one now in the Museum of Anthropology, although this is a reasonable assumption. From the photographs it is evident that the chin of the latter did not rest on the knees; the back appears to be too straight for the chin to have rested even on the now missing left leg. There is some hair on the head and a mustache, but apparently no goatee. However, the whole passage in Bancroft seems to be rather hastily and perhaps inaccurately written, so that too much value should not be placed on his description.

According to the legend connected with the mummies, long before the Russians appeared the Copper River People, called "Medonopky" (in Russian) or "Ssootchetnee," raided the Nuchek People, killing men and boys and carrying off women, among whom was the daughter of the chief. Years later the Nuchek People were able to kill a party of Ssootchetnee sea otter hunters and recaptured the chief's daughter. Her father had died, and the new chief of Nuchek refused to recognize her because she had married one of her former captors. She took refuge in a cave in the mountains where she found the naked bodies of her husband and 2 sons (evidently where the Nuchek People had put the corpses). A female spirit, "Wilghtnee," that lived in a lake above the cave and controlled the runs of salmon and other fish, took pity on the

woman. The spirit not only miraculously preserved the bodies with water from her lake, so that they became "shining like the flesh of the halibut," but punished the cruel chief and many of his followers with death from starvation by withholding the salmon. The woman then became chief and taught the people how to preserve their dead.

The "Ssootchetnee," a Copper River people who hunt sea otter in or near the home waters of the Nuchek People and who are enemies of the latter, would appear to be the Eyak, although the name is one with which I am totally unfamiliar. It is possibly a garbled version of the Chugach word for "men," cukit, which they usually apply to themselves; it also suggests Chitina, a place on the Copper River in the territory of the Atna. I am not familiar with "Wilghtnee," who is apparently the "owner" of the salmon, although the concept of a spirit at the headwaters of each stream who controls the salmon run is a common Tlingit idea. In general, this story which describes the mummies as non-Eskimo and the methods of preservation as supernatural or mysterious, and which stresses the refusal at first to take back the stolen woman who had married her alien captor, is consistent with themes in other Chugach legends and explanations of mummies in caves.

9. Conclusion: Summary

We have presented evidence concerning a number of different methods of corpse disposal practiced by the Chugach. Most of the recorded finds of human remains have been made in caves and rock shelters, since this is almost inevitable when rapid and relatively superficial surveys are made. Many of these caves are on rather small uninhabited islands. In addition, we have established the fact that the Chugach sometimes interred the dead in shallow graves dug in the village refuse heaps, a custom widely practiced by the Aleut and Eskimo of southwestern Alaska. The placing of the body of a prominent person on top of an almost inaccessible rocky islet or high cliff also has a wide distribution. The uncertain evidences of cremation in Prince William Sound have been discussed. Disarranged skeletons or scattered human bones have been compared with similar finds in other parts of southwestern Alaska. We should note in this connection, however, that we found no evidence of purposely dismembered skeletons or of cut and utilized human bones, features which were characteristic of Kachemak Bay III and a comparable period on Kodiak Island.[33] We did not find any trophy skulls, although Stepan told us that the head of a slain enemy was cut off, brought back to the village, and kept for a time in a wooden box outside the house. After all the neighbors had seen it, it was buried in a sequestered spot—a practice which probably explains why we found none. Trophy skulls are known from the Northwest Coast, Kachemak Bay (in the Second Period, at any rate), Kodiak Island, Alaska Peninsula, Bristol Bay, and the Aleutian Islands.[34]

It is interesting that in spite of all the many known examples Makari at first denied that caves were used as burial places. Later he admitted that chiefs and their families were sometimes put in caves. Fred Allen, Lee Pratt's informant, a Nuchek man like Makari, also specified that cave burial was only for chiefs or important people. Yet Black Stepan of Chenega said that all persons, regardless of status, used to be buried in caves. Is it possible that this difference of opinion reflects differences in practice between the eastern and western parts of the sound? In other words, was cave burial more common in the Chenega area (were there perhaps more available caves?) than in the region around Hinchinbrook and Hawkins islands? Or did an equally common practice and the memories of that practice survive better in the west? Certainly in 1933 the Chenega natives seemed

to have retained more of the old ways than had the other Eskimo in the sound. Cave burial is, of course, well known from Kodiak and the Aleutians.[35] On Kodiak it was for prominent persons, chiefly for shamans and whalers, while among the Aleut cave burial was more common. Ordinary people and slaves might be put into caves or under shallow rock shelters with no attempt to prevent decomposition, but deep caves were used by the Aleut for the carefully prepared mummies of important persons. I think it quite likely that the more desirable caves or the more sheltered portions of caves were reserved by the Chugach for their illustrious dead, and that the less important (not necessarily the more recently deceased, as suggested by Meany) were accommodated only in the more exposed positions or under small overhanging rocks. There have been reports of cave burial in Kachemak Bay, but neither Jacobsen nor I was able to confirm them, and I do not know whether the caves were supposed to have been used by the Tanaina for cremated remains or by the earlier Eskimo for corpses.[36]

✓ 10. Mummification

Our informants did not know anything about artificial attempts to preserve the bodies of the dead, such as the removal of the viscera. Fred Allen in fact told Lee Pratt that the bodies were just naturally dried by the "good air" in the caves. Yet evidence cited from Dall and Jacobsen indicates that removing the internal organs and stuffing the body cavity with dried grass, bits of fur, etc., was practiced even after contact with the Russians. The one complete mummy which we obtained from Palutat Cave showed no evidence of an abdominal incision, at least in that part of the body which we could examine without injuring the remains. The Aleut and Koniag also eviscerated the bodies of important persons when preparing them for

[33] De Laguna, 1934, pp. 44-47, 102; Hrdlička, 1944, pp. 323, 351.
[34] De Laguna, 1947, p. 79; add Hrdlička, 1944, p. 227; 1945, p. 149, Fig. 177.

[35] Dall, 1878; Jochelson, 1925, pp. 45 ff.; Hrdlička, 1944, pp. 89 f.; 1945, pp. 178-94, 412-20; Lantis, 1947, p. 11; and sources cited.
[36] Jacobsen, 1884, pp. 371, 373; de Laguna, 1934, pp. 21, 48 f.

deposition in caves or tombs. Laughlin believes that the Aleut practice of "mummification of the dead of certain outstanding families cannot have long preceded the advent of the Russians. . . . This custom, undoubtedly introduced by the Neo-Aleuts [from the east], never reached the people of Attu and Agattu islands at the western end of the chain."[37]

The Chugach seem to have wrapped the naked corpse (whether eviscerated or not) in skins and mats. Clothing may sometimes have been included as part of the wrappings, as is suggested by the finding of fragments of garments with the partially mummified body at Site 26, with the mummy from Palutat Cave, and on the surface of the cave, but we have no clear evidence that the corpse was actually dressed in these clothes. The beads with Skeleton III at Palugvik were in place as if she had been wearing an apron, but that is all we can say. On the other hand, if corpses were always dressed in their clothes we should not have received so many reports of naked mummies. In some cases (Glacier Island, especially), the corpse wore ornaments, but the labrets had been removed from the mummy described by Dall. The wrappings of the rich, according to our informants, included valuable furs (sea otter, ground hog, etc.), but the outer wrappings of these bodies, as well as the sole wrappings of the poor, were said to be seal or sea lion skins, often the cover taken from an old bidarka or umiak. That these wrappings were sometimes secured by lashings is supported by Jacobsen's description of a mummy bundle from Chenega Island and by our finds of cords associated with burials at Site 26 and Palutat Cave. On the other hand, the loosely flexed position of a number of skeletons would indicate that lashings might be omitted in some cases, or else that little attempt was made to achieve a compact bundle. We have no way of knowing whether as complex a mummy bundle as

those described for the Aleut was ever made, but the basic method of preparation was the same.

Although at least one of the infants found at Palugvik had been summarily stuffed under some stones and the others may have been given equally careless disposal, Chugach babies, according to Jacobsen's account, were sometimes put into their cradles before being deposited in caves. His description suggests that the cradle was a wooden hoop filled with some kind of netting or possibly matting. Our informants mentioned skin cradles which could be either hung or leaned against the wall of the house, and Dr. Otteking found evidence of slight cradleboard deformation in the woman's skeleton from Glacier Island. Aleut cradles containing babies have also been found in caves and in a wooden tomb.[38] These cradles were hoops of wood, sometimes reinforced across the back with extra slats, to which was fastened an asymmetric pouch of matting or skin. One was made entirely of twined basketry, like a bag with part of the side cut away, and another seems to have been of bark.

That the Chugach may sometimes have tied the bodies of adults into frames is suggested by the dubious report of mummies lashed to drilled planks leaning against the wall of a cave in Mummy Bay, Knight Island. The frames in which Aleut mummy bundles were fastened have been described as "a cradle or swing," "a sort of wooden cradle," "a small boat made of drift-wood," and a "frame of suitable size, in the shape of a prism, and covered with skins."[39] Dall illustrates and describes what is evidently a frame of this last type, obtained from a cave on Kagamil Island,[40] and it is very similar to the baby's cradle from the same cave. These frames were usually suspended

[37] Dall, 1878; Jochelson, 1925, pp. 42, 44; Hrdlička, 1944, pp. 89-90; Hrdlička, 1945, pp. 182 ff.; Lantis, 1947, p. 9; Laughlin and Marsh, 1951, p. 82.

[38] Dall, 1878, Pl. V, no. 17483; Weyer, 1929, Fig. 7; Hrdlička, 1945, Figs. 17, 61, 174 to 176. For cradles on Kodiak Island and the resulting slight deformation, see Hrdlička, 1944, pp. 37, 270 f., 366 f., 396.

[39] Hrdlička, 1945, pp. 178, 414; Sarytschew, 1807, Part II, p. 77; Lantis, 1947, p. 10.

[40] Dall, 1878, pp. 16-18, Pls. II and III.

from a rack erected in a cave; they might also be hung (temporarily?) in the house or in a wooden tomb, or laid in such a tomb. Those found in a wooden sarcophagus on top of "Split Rock" or "Fortress Rock" near Unalaska Island are described by Weyer as "an oval hoop to which was attached loosely an animal skin, like a loose drum head."[41] There was no difference, except in size, between those made for 2 of the 3 adults and the child's cradle also found in the same tomb. We are evidently dealing with 2 types of frame: one is a cradle-like hoop, often reinforced, and covered with skin, basketry, or bark; the other, to judge from its comparison with a wooden boat or wooden cradle (I assume a European model is implied), suggests something suspiciously like a dugout canoe, a point to which I shall refer again. It is perhaps significant that this latter type is reported only from the Fox Islands (Unalaska district), where driftwood was not as hard to obtain as it was farther west, although Jochelson mentions "troughs resembling cradles," which may or may not be the same thing, in which Atka whalers were suspended.[42]

From some reports it would appear that the Chugach sometimes deposited the wrapped corpse or mummy in a sitting position, leaning against the back of the cave, although we made no finds of this nature. This squatting position was commonly used by the Aleut, not only for mummy bundles deposited in caves but for interments in the village refuse heaps.[43] The skeleton of a child was found in this position in a Third Period site on Kachemak Bay, and there was a similar adult burial at Port Graham.[44]

Lantis has questioned the statements of Dall and Pinart that Kodiak and Aleut mummies were sometimes placed in lifelike positions in caves, as if engaged in their favorite occupations, the women sewing or nursing a child, the men hunting, fishing,

or beating a drum.[45] In such cases the mummies were not wrapped in bundles, but were dressed in ordinary clothes or armor, and might or might not wear a mask on the face. Dall also claims that they were customarily supplied with wooden models of weapons and tools, rather than with articles of real value, and that there were wooden effigies of the animals being hunted. Dall himself actually saw a mummy from a cave in Ugamuk Strait, Kodiak Island, that when found had been dressed in a gutskin frock. It still held in its hand a spear with a long double-edged slate blade on which was impaled a figure cut out of depilated sealskin. The latter was supposed to represent a demon, whose enmity the dead man averted in return for the offerings of food that the natives had been regularly bringing to the cave.

Although the descriptions of more elaborately arranged mummies, reported by Dall apparently from hearsay, do strain our credulity, we must remember that some of the disarticulated skeletons from Kachemak Bay III and Hrdlička's Kodiak site had holes drilled in the bones as if they had sometime been reassembled (perhaps even as marionettes?). And from Kachemak Bay sub-III and III and Kodiak we also have skeletons with artificial eyes in the orbits, in the first case embedded in clay masks.[46] Such finds indicate that there may have been elaborate and lifelike arrangements of corpses in ancient times.

There is also some evidence that the Chugach may have known some of the practices claimed by Dall. Thus, Makari told us that the dead chief might be dressed in his sea otter fur garments or in his armor and "chamois skin shirt and pants," his head and feet bare. Every day the people used to go to look at his body lying in the rock shelter and bring him a share of whatever they had to eat. Meany reported that the mummy of a woman from the cave in

[41] Weyer, 1929, p. 231.
[42] Jochelson, 1925, p. 44.
[43] *Ibid.*, p. 42 f., etc.
[44] De Laguna, 1934, pp. 16, 24.

[45] Dall, 1878, pp. 27 f.; 1884, p. 139; Lantis, 1947, p. 11.
[46] De Laguna, 1934, pp. 43 f., 46, 72, 113; Hrdlička, 1944, p. 351, Figs. 40 and 41.

Mummy Bay, Knight Island, is said to have held the body of an infant in her arms. Stepan's story about Palutat Cave would also indicate a lifelike posture for the bodies and that the women there held their children. The wooden model of a harpoon head from the same cave (Pl. 34, 3) also suggests that imitations were used as grave goods.

11. MASKS

Dall also claimed that some of the unwrapped lifelike Aleut and Kodiak mummies wore masks on their faces, and that masks were sometimes deposited as grave offerings in the caves.[47] As Lantis points out, it is not really clear whether the masks found in these caves were actually put on the face of the dead or were merely left beside the body,[48] and the same uncertainty attaches to Chugach masks. Jacobsen found masks in 2 burial caves on Chenega Island but does not tell us explicitly where they were placed. Makari said that some of the 6 seated mummies in Palutat Cave wore masks, and that masked mummies had been found in a cave on Knight Island. The Aleut seem to have had the custom of depositing in caves the masks and drums that had been used in ceremonies,[49] which might account for the finding of masks in caves which incidentally had also been used as burial places. Makari also said that the Chugach stored the rattles, drums, and masks used by shamans in caves to protect them from possible defilement by the touch of a menstruant (perhaps also to protect the laymen from their supernatural powers?). Masks worn at ceremonies, into which a shaman may or may not have put his spirits, were also kept in a cave, "to keep them from the young girls." Makari said that several masks had been found in a cave on Mummy Island, where they had presumably been cached. Among both the Chugach and Aleut, masks were supposed to represent the familiar spirits of shamans,

and might be in either anthropomorphic or animal form.

Dall would distinguish between Aleut dancing masks used in ceremonies and those placed on or with the dead.[50] The former, to judge by Sauer's illustrations, 2 of which Dall reproduces,[51] are naturalistic portrayals of the Aleut's own physical type, whereas the mortuary masks, as represented by 3 specimens from rock shelters on Unga Island in the Shumagins, depict a clumsy face, with very large nose (high bridge, flaring alae), prominent chin, rather fierce-looking teeth (inserted pegs), and ears set on too high up.[52] However, these Unga masks had also been worn, for the crossbar in back, which was to be held in the mouth like a bit, showed the marks of the wearer's teeth. The nostrils are pierced vertically, and since the eyes are solid (not holes), the wearer could only have looked downward through the nose of the mask, a circumstance which fits some descriptions of Aleut ceremonial masks.

Our best knowledge of Chugach masks, aside from the somewhat unclear descriptions given by Makari and Stepan, is derived from the 7 specimens described by Dall, which seem to have come from a burial cave, although he identifies them as dancing masks.[53] These were crudely carved and hollowed out of nearly flat slabs of spruce, and originally had feathers attached to holes around the edges. They were partially painted with red ochre; usually one eye only was so colored, and a few also had a crescent painted on the forehead, while 2 also had small silhouette figures of seals or fish, etc., on the face. The workmanship is certainly inferior to that of other Eskimo and Aleut specimens. These masks were held on the head by one or 2 crossbars and a wooden latticework across the back, and some also had a wooden bit to be held in the teeth. (Makari said that masks were

---

[47] Dall, 1878, pp. 5, 28; 1884, pp. 139-42.
[48] Lantis, 1947, p. 12.
[49] Hrdlička, 1945, p. 157.

[50] Dall, 1884, pp. 137-43.
[51] Dall, 1884, Pl. XXVIII, 71, 72.
[52] Ibid., Pls. XXVIII, 73, XXIX, 74, 75.
[53] Ibid., pp. 124-28, text fig. on p. 126, Pls. XXXIII, 51 to 53, 54 to 56, XXIV, 59, 60 to 62, XXV, 63 and 64, 65.

tied on around the head with a thong and lacked a mouthpiece.) Two had evidently been worn, for red paint from the wearer's face had rubbed off on the inside. Like the Shumagin Aleut masks, the eyes of these specimens were nonfunctional, and the nostril openings served as peepholes. One of the Chugach masks which has no visible means of suspension shows an eyeless face with round protruding mouth and high pointed head. Dall believes it represents a bowhead whale, but the high pointed head suggests much more closely certain descriptions of shaman's spirits. Dall compared this mask with an ivory image from the site at Port Möller on the Alaska Peninsula. The doll is obviously a shaman's puppet, like similar dolls with pointed heads from Kachemak Bay.[54] The other 6 masks in the collection are rectangular in outline, with long narrow slots for the mouth, in one case slanting. The wood is cut away below the brows and around the nose, leaving the eyes, or the single eye on one side, to project like pegs. Two masks also have a hole like a cyclopean eye in the middle of the forehead. On 2 masks one eyebrow is raised. The top of one mask is rounded; on the other 5 it is deeply indented so that the 2 upper corners project like high ears or horns. Makari had said that some "funny masks" might have only one eye, sometimes in the middle, or a crooked mouth, a description confirmed by these examples.

The most curious statement made by Makari was that the only persons who would be buried in masks were the 6 members of a secret society at Chenega, known as the aqlat, "winds," because they were so wild and used to frighten and even kill people. This is not the place for a lengthy discussion of this complex problem which has been dealt with by Dr. Birket-Smith in his ethnographic monograph, but I judge from Stepan's statement that similar groups existed in other villages besides Chenega. The whole thing sounds very much like the men's secret tribal society

which, according to Margaret Lantis' brilliant argument, existed among the Aleut, Kodiak, and other Eskimo groups as far north as Norton Sound, and which had as an important function the terrorizing of the uninitiated women and children.[55] The presence of masks in caves within this area may thus have some connection with these societies and perhaps with burial rites appropriate to their leaders.

12. COFFINS

Although Makari denied that coffins were used, and Stepan said that they were a recent innovation, "since Noah and the flood," we have cited ample evidence that coffins were common and date back to the earliest period of which we have any archaeological record in Prince William Sound. The most carefully made examples were composed of separate planks that lined shallow graves. At Site 22 on Mummy Island coffins are reported to have been pegged together and may have been above-ground, but we are unable to verify this statement. In any case, the coffins were never deeply buried; at most there could have been only a few inches of dirt over the lids, and in some instances I suspect that the upper part may have protruded above the surface. Less pretentious were the cists of planks and stones, or of stones alone, some (or all?) of which had plank lids like the wooden coffins. There were also incomplete coffin frames consisting of a few boards above, below, or beside the body. And lastly there was the shallow grave, covered simply with sheets of bark or some stones. Coffins were found not only in caves and rock shelters but in the Palugvik midden, and were reported by Vancouver on points of land or other places presumably visible from the water and removed from any village.

Wooden tombs comparable to the Chugach coffins were used by the Aleut. Most of these were apparently subterranean, but others are reported to have been above-

[54] De Laguna, 1934, pp. 114 f., 208.

[55] Lantis, 1947, pp. 27-33.

ground, despite Jochelson's denial that any were above the surface.[56] Thus Veniaminof describes an aboveground wooden tomb, shaped like a hut with gable roof, in which the mummy bundle of a chief was hung; and Sauer pictures a wooden tomb at Unalaska which was apparently slightly raised above ground by 4 posts and was decorated on the sides.[57] It seems to be identical in construction with the wooden sarcophagus on "Split Rock" or "Fortress Rock" near Unalaska, described by Weyer, except that it is uncertain whether the latter was originally buried or not.[58] In both cases, earth was piled on the lids. These boxes were made of small planks and split logs, evidently pegged or fastened by some means to the corner posts. The lids were double, with matting between. Weyer's tomb was large enough to hold the mummies of 3 adults and a child, as well as a considerable amount of grave offerings. Dall has described what appears to be an aboveground tomb with a door in the side at Chernoffsky Harbor, Unalaska. It is not clear whether he himself saw the sarcophagus. It was

a unique wooden tomb, constructed and carved with the ancient stone implements, in a very careful and elaborate manner, with the door so hung on wooden pins that it might be raised and the contents viewed, and by its own gravity would close itself on being released. In this tomb were the remains of a noted hunter, a toyon [chief] of eminence among the natives, surrounded by an enormous store of sea otter skins, garments, etc., all then in good preservation.[59]

The more common type of tomb, however, seems to have been underground. Thus, on Atka Island, important persons were put into a small hut, lined with mats and covered over with earth.[60] According to Jochelson, the Aleut might inter the dead in a walled-off sleeping room of the house, or they might make instead a burial pit desig-

nated by a special term meaning "a possible house."[61] These tombs might have wooden floors and roofs (Jochelson says nothing about walls), especially on Umnak where driftwood was relatively plentiful, but elsewhere whale bone would be used for the rafters. When the structure collapsed the tomb would appear as a circular depression from one to 2 meters in diameter, and therefore seems to have been larger than any known Chugach coffin. In some places these little "huts" were arranged in rows along one side of the house, an orientation which suggests that of the coffin at Palugvik and a box burial at Cottonwood Creek in Kachemak Bay. The skeletons which Jochelson found in these graves were squatting or flexed on the side. Sarychef is evidently describing an interment in such a tomb when he writes:

The entrails are taken out of the corpse; which is stuffed with hay. Persons in mean circumstances are put without any ceremony into the ground, or the cavities of the rocks, but the rich are laid in tombs, made of wood, expressly for the purpose. Into these earth is first shaken, and then covered with grass and skins, upon which the body is laid, and bound with thongs, in the position in which one usually sits in the baidar, with the feet approaching towards the breast, and the hands folded round the latter. Another mat is then laid over it, and covered with another layer of earth, upon which broken pieces of the baidar are placed.[62]

The custom of shaking earth into the coffin and making a grass bed may explain the dust and trash, such as spruce needles, etc., in the Palutat coffins, especially as Meany seems to have found evidence of a bough bed. Obviously the less important people would not have a carefully made "hut" or coffin, but merely a protecting cist or coffin frame of some kind, comparable to those of Prince William Sound. Thus, Hrdlička reports that burials in Aleut village middens "were occasionally laid upon, covered with or surrounded by pieces of whale ribs or a portion of whale scapula."[63] Appar-

---

[56] Jochelson, 1925, pp. 45 f.; Lantis, 1947, p. 10.
[57] Veniaminof in Hrdlička, 1945, p. 182; Sauer, 1802, Fig. 4, also in Hrdlička, 1945, as Fig. 39.
[58] Weyer, 1929, pp. 228-30. "The parts were expertly mortised together and bone nails added rigidity."
[59] Dall, 1787, p. 8.
[60] Veniaminof in Hrdlička, 1945, p. 179.

[61] Jochelson, 1925, pp. 49-52.
[62] Sarytschew, 1807, Part II, p. 77.
[63] Hrdlička, 1945, p. 485. Cf. skeleton on Amoknak Island surrounded by large whale bones (p. 219, Fig. 9), or a skeleton on Agattu lying on several whale bones and covered with rocks (p. 306).

ently the Aleut did not use wooden coffins for cave burials, although the dead might be laid on a wooden flooring or scaffolding composed of driftwood and planks, sometimes protected by a tentlike canopy of skins on poles.[64]

Coffins were evidently used on Kodiak Island. Hrdlička illustrates one from Uyak Bay which is exactly like the Chugach wooden coffins except that it is made of large slabs of slate and lacks a bottom.[65] He also encountered traces of wood in association with some of the burials in the midden on Uyak Bay, which might be interpreted as parts of coffins or of coffin-like frames or covers. Occasionally stone slabs seem to have been used also for such cists.[66] To judge from the photographs, all the interments were very shallow, as on Kachemak Bay and Prince William Sound. Equally suggestive of a knowledge of coffins or cists is the trace of a plank found above a Kachemak Bay II skeleton, or the stone slabs over the squatting burial at Port Graham, as well as the clearly defined box-like holes in which were found some of the dismembered burials of Kachemak Bay III.[67]

13. INHUMATION

In denying the use of coffins, Makari was evidently referring to the most common type of interment practiced by the Chugach, which was presumably the simple basic method used for common people all over southwestern Alaska and even farther north, the type from which were developed the more elaborate graves for the illustrious.[68] These graves, he said, were at some distance from the village, and if some one died away from home he was buried on the spot. The body was wrapped in skins, usually just sealskins for ordinary people,

although chiefs and wealthy persons would also have wrappings of fur and might wear labrets, beads, and other ornaments. The grave was "dug down to the gravel," a phrase which suggests deep inhumation, although I suspect that all interments were really shallow. The body was placed in an extended position on the back, the arms at the sides, and the head to the south. Later, he modified this last statement to indicate that the dead faced their homes. This information on orientation and position was not verified by our finds, however, as will be indicated below. Small objects might be placed in the grave on each side of the corpse, and larger possessions left aboveground, but the leaving of the goods of the deceased at the grave seems to have depended on the economic and social status of the family and also on what bequests the dead person might have made. In most cases there were no grave goods, as we discovered. Finally, stones were piled on top of the grave. Makari later specified that stones were piled only on the graves of persons who had been killed (murdered?), but the wide distribution of stone-covered graves or graves set about with stones in the whole area suggests that this was probably a common practice, though perhaps one more carefully followed in the case of murder. The grave was marked by setting up the digging stick or shovel which had been used or by lopping off all but the topmost branches of a near-by tree. Several of these "lob-sticks," to use the popular phrase, were observed in 1930, generally near the end of a point, but at that time their possible significance was not known. This type of burial, Makari said, was the same for men, women, children, whalers, and shamans. A similar practice seems to have been common on Kodiak Island, where the grave was covered with large stones or pieces of wood, and poles were erected.[69]

Lantis has suggested that this kind of shallow inhumation under a pile of stones,

[64] *Ibid.*, pp. 238, 243 f., 325 f. The photograph of the cave at Shiprock, Umnak Pass, shows what looks suspiciously like part of a wooden coffin, or a cist of planks and stones (Fig. 117).

[65] Hrdlička, 1944, pp. 95 f., Fig. 7.

[66] *Ibid.*, pp. 146, 148, 160, 166, 172, 250, 300, Figs. 144 and 145.

[67] De Laguna, 1934, pp. 16, 42, 45, 46.

[68] Lantis, 1947, pp. 13 f.

[69] De Laguna, 1947, p. 90; Lantis, 1947, p. 11.

wood, or sod was perhaps related to true cairn burial in the far north. Inhumation is certainly very ancient in northwestern North America,[70] and in the far north the shallow veneer of unfrozen soil above the permanent ground frost would prevent the digging of a grave and force the substitution of a cairn or pile over the body if the intention were to cover it. Thick turf, tree roots, and hard soil of any kind would likewise tend to discourage the digging of deep graves by a people who had only wooden shovels or digging sticks, and suggest instead the piling up of stones or wood on the grave. It would be natural to arrange these in a ring or frame around the corpse and to use them like a lid or cover. These natural tendencies to protect the body from disturbance or to prevent it from walking were reinforced, I believe, by the diffusion of more elaborate methods of burial from Asia via the Aleutian chain. This relatively recent circum-Pacific culture drift was responsible, I have argued,[71] for the introduction of the true wooden coffin, which appears typically in the form of an elevated box like a cache, or as a grave house sometimes holding a separate inner coffin, or more simply as a wooden coffin resting on the ground. The use of a boat, especially a dugout canoe, is another variant, and one which may be reflected in the wooden boat-like containers for Aleut mummies or in the Kodiak use of the bidarka. The underground tombs and coffins would represent a real fusion of the earlier forms of inhumation and the imported coffin.

14. ORIENTATION OF CORPSE

In view of Makari's statement with respect to the position and orientation of the body, it may be of interest to present in tabular form the data which we obtained on this topic. Since most of the skeletons were found in caves or rock shelters, usually lying close to the back wall, the orientation of these bodies was controlled by that of the rock, with a possible choice of only two directions. Such burials are marked with an asterisk. As will be seen, there is no uniformity in orientation or in position, except that in almost all cases the bodies were flexed to some extent. Nor is there any correlation of orientation or position with the sex or age of the deceased.

Skeleton	Sex	Direction of Head	Position of Body
Palugvik I	male	north	flexed, on right side
Palugvik II	female	north	flexed, on left side
Palugvik III	female	west	flexed, on right side
Palugvik IV	infant	northwest	flexed, on left side
Palugvik V	infant	west	extended, on back
Palugvik East Point I	male (?)	west*	flexed, on right side
Palugvik East Point II	female (?)	northeast	flexed, on left side
Palugvik East Point III	male	east*	flexed, on back
Palutat A	male	north*	legs flexed (?), on back
Palutat B1	female (?)	south*	flexed, on left side
Palutat B2	male	south*	(disturbed), on face

70 De Laguna, 1947, pp. 86 f., 271.   71 Ibid., pp. 87-90, 113, 278.

Palutat B3	female	south	legs under body, on face
Palutat C1	male	east	flexed, on left side
Palutat C2	male	?	partly disarticulated
Palutat D	female	south	legs flexed to right, on back
Palutat E1	female	south*	legs flexed to left, on back
Site 16, small shelter	male	west or southwest*	(disarranged), on back
Site 20, A	male	east or southeast*	flexed (disturbed)
Site 20, B	female	east or southeast*	flexed, on right side
Site 26	female	north or northwest*	flexed on left side
Site 34 (reported)	male	west (?)	extended, on back
Glacier Island I	male (?)	northeast*	legs flexed to left, on back
Glacier Island II	female	northeast*	legs flexed above body, on back

CHAPTER IV

skip

Rock Paintings

1. CHUGACH PICTOGRAPHS

THE ROCK PAINTINGS in Prince William Sound, like those of Cook Inlet, are painted in silhouette, with the exception of a few outlined symbols. The paint in both cases seems to be red hematite mixed with fat (?) and is insoluble in water. The paintings in the sound are much weathered, but where the rock was not too badly disintegrated to touch, it was possible to brighten the pictures temporarily by light applications of wood alcohol so that they could be traced. The drawings reproduced in Figures 21 to 24 were made from these tracings. Dotted lines indicate indistinct outlines; hatched lines represent cracks or breaks in the rock. The pictures are about as large as those in Tuxedni Bay, Cook Inlet.[1]

Paintings on rocks were found at 5 localities in Prince William Sound: (1) a cliff on the eastern side of a small bight on the north shore of Boswell Bay, near Site 9, Hinchinbrook Island; (2) a cave, Site 12, on the south shore of Hawkins Island, one mile west of Palugvik; (3) a cliff, Site 13, ¼ mile west of Palugvik; (4) the rock shelter (Site 43) on Glacier Island from which 2 skeletons were obtained; (5) a burial cave, Site 59, on Mummy Island in Drier Bay, Knight Island.

Paintings were reported by the natives at 3 additional localities: (6) on the mainland in Orca Bay opposite Channel Island

[1] De Laguna, 1934, Pls. 62 to 64.

(this area was explored in 1933, but we did not find the pictures, which are said to represent men); (7) Siwash Bay in Unakwik Inlet; (8) the east shore of Port Wells, between Esther Passage and Golden, now defaced by prospectors.

The 2 pictures at Site 9 in Boswell Bay, Hinchinbrook Island, represent an anthropomorphic figure or bear (Fig. 21B) and an inverted V, perhaps a highly conventionalized anthropomorphic figure also (Fig. 21A). The foot of the cliff on which they are painted is just reached by the tide, and the pictures are about 5 feet above the level of the beach. There is supposed to have been a camping place on the beach at the site now occupied by an abandoned cannery, and a few yards beyond the pic-

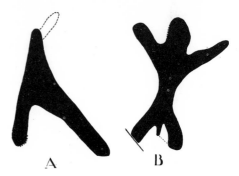

A   B

FIGURE 21. Paintings on cliff near Site 9, Hinchinbrook Island. Scale 1/3 natural size
A, Conventionalized figure; B, anthropomorphic figure

102

tures is a dry shelter under an overhang of the cliff. There was nothing in this shelter.

The pictures in the burial cave, Site 12, one mile west of Palugvik, are at the back and west end of the cave, all 5 or 6 feet above the floor. The elaborate anthropomorphic symbol, reminiscent of Northwest Coast style (Fig. 22C), is directly above the recess where the bones of an adult and 2 infants were found. At the western end of the cave is a group of paintings representing a human face (Fig. 22A), a jumping whale (Fig. 22B), a horizontal row of circles between 2 parallel lines, and 8 additional paintings which were so blurred that their outlines could not be determined. There is also a large smudge of paint near the eastern end of the rear wall.

Site 13, just west of Palugvik, was evidently a rock shelter at one time, but the land has sunk at least 4 feet and the original floor is now covered by the beach (Pl. 2, 3). The pictures are scattered along a distance of about 15 feet and are at 2 levels. The lower level is from 6 inches to 3 feet

above the sloping beach gravel. Proceeding in order from the landward end of this lower group, the pictures are: a headless human figure (Fig. 23E) 6 inches above the gravel; a sea mammal (?) (D) above E on a small overhang; a man with clenched fist (B); a human face (A) and a sticklike symbol (G), the last 2 above E, B, and D, and about 3 feet above the gravel; an unidentified symbol (K) 3 feet above the beach; a headless man (C) 2½ feet above the beach; an umiak with 5 paddlers (?) (F) 6 inches below C; and lastly several smudges near F. The pictures on the upper level are 4 feet above a natural ledge which is itself 8 feet above the beach. The ledge is not wide enough to stand on at the present time, but may have been wider when the paintings were made; otherwise, the painters must have had a scaffold. These upper pictures are in order: a cross or X (Fig. 23I), an oval (J), a boat with 3 men (H), and a smudge.

The single painting at Site 43 on Glacier Island is an indistinct blob on the fallen rock between the head of Skeleton I and the back wall of the shelter, perhaps made in mixing the pigment with which the face of the corpse was painted.

The pictures at Site 59 on Mummy Island in Drier Bay, Knight Island, are on the back wall of the rock shelter, some 5 feet above the floor. The wall has weathered so badly that several paintings could not be traced (Pl. 7, 1). These pictures represented a seal (?) (Fig. 24A), a cross (B), and 2 boats with paddlers, one of which was copied (C); the remaining pictures could not be deciphered.

These paintings seem to be very old. Their age is suggested not only by the sinking of the land at Site 13 on Hawkins Island but by the vagueness of the native traditions concerning them. Only the pictures in Orca Bay, in Unakwik Inlet, and in Port Wells were known to the Eskimo before our visit in 1933. Even Makari, who was well informed about localities in the eastern part of the sound, knew nothing

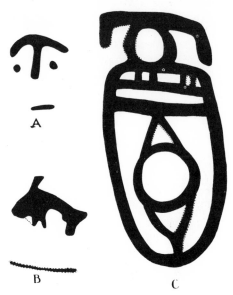

FIGURE 22. Paintings in burial cave, Site 12, Hawkins Island. Scale slightly over ¼ natural size

A, Face on western wall of cave; B, whale, below and to left of A; C, conventionalized figure, above grave at rear of cave

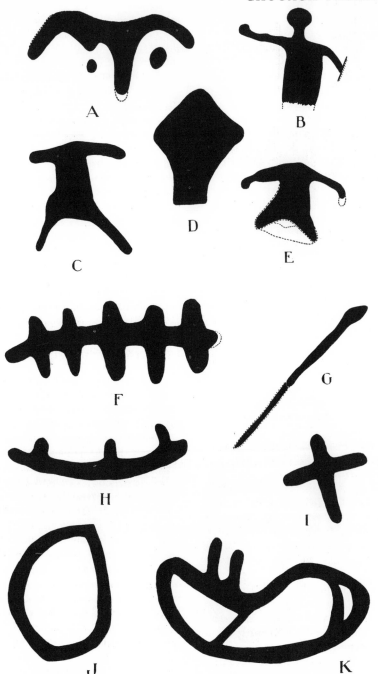

FIGURE 23. Paintings on cliff, Site 13, Hawkins Island. Scale 1/3. See Plate 2, 3
A, Face; B, man; C, headless man (?); D, sea mammal (?); E, headless man (?); F, boat with 5 paddlers (?); G, unidentified symbol; H, boat with 3 occupants (on cliff above high ledge); I, cross (on cliff above high ledge); J, oval (on cliff above high ledge); K, unidentified symbol

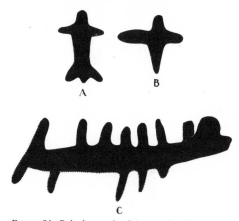

C

FIGURE 24. Paintings at burial cave, Site 59, Mummy Island, Drier Bay, Knight Island. Scale slightly under ¼ natural size. See Plate 7, *1*.
A, Seal (?); B, cross; C, boat with 7 or 8 occupants

about the pictures on Hinchinbrook and Hawkins islands before we discovered them. He suggested 2 conflicting explanations of the paintings. According to the account which he offered with the greater confidence, the pictures in Orca Bay near Channel Island were made by a man-eating spirit, Kapaxcuci, who used to live at the head of Cordova Bay, and about whom he told us several myths. When we discovered the other paintings, Makari and his daughter accepted them as evidence of Kapaxcuci's wanderings. Old Man Dude, an Eyak shaman who lived in Simpson Bay, also knew of the paintings in Orca Bay and said that they were supposed to have been made by Kapaxcuci to record his wicked exploits. In answer to direct questioning, Makari also told us that whale killers used to make paintings "of all kinds of animals" on the rocks in secret places. "This was their luck." Black Stepan of Chenega said that rock paintings were made by persons who wished to become shamans. The would-be shamans spoke to the pictures and gave them pieces of clothing and food. Soon afterward they acquired shamanistic powers. The rock paintings made by the ancient Cook Inlet Eskimo, to which the pictures in Prince William Sound bear a close resemblance, were also

made in secret places, probably in connection with whaling rituals or other hunting magic.[2]

2. PICTOGRAPHS AND PETROGLYPHS IN NEIGHBORING AREAS

Prince William Sound and Cook Inlet lie near the edge of a Northwest Coast and Plateau area in which pictographs and petroglyphs are found. Before analyzing the pictures in the sound, it may be helpful to review the localities where red paintings are known.

An Eskimo from Kodiak Island and another from Afognak Island in the Kodiak group reported many red pictographs on these islands, similar to those of Cook Inlet. According to the first informant, they were made to tell others of game which had been killed, and according to the other were to bring luck in hunting. It is curious that Hrdlička did not find any paintings on Kodiak. There are, however, 2 groups of petroglyphs, chiefly of faces, on Cape Alitak at the southwest end of the island.[3] No pictures have been found on the Aleutians, although Jochelson was told of a cave on Agattu Island in which a shaman was supposed to have made representations (carved?, painted?) of female genitals.[4]

Farther north, Jenness discovered pictures in red and black paint "of human beings in various attitudes" on the Tuksuk River, 17 miles above Teller, Alaska. These were believed by the Eskimo to represent a war between themselves and the Siberians.[5]

The Tena Indians reported red pictographs at 3 localities in the Yukon drainage area. Nothing is known about those at 2 of these places. Pictures at the third locality, in the Tanana Valley at the confluence of the Chena and Little Chena rivers about 10 miles from Fairbanks, are of a row of human beings in silhouette about 12 inches

[2] *Ibid.*, pp. 153 f.
[3] Photographs given the author by Stephen R. Capps, USGS; Hrdlička, 1944, Figs. 17 and 18. Heizer, 1947, has published the most complete account.
[4] Jochelson, 1925, p. 122.
[5] Jenness, 1928, pp. 78 f.

high. This is the spot where Raven made the first human beings out of transformed men.[6] Giddings has published rock paintings at the confluence of Moose Creek with a slough of the Tanana River, some 18 miles above Fairbanks, which may possibly be the same place as that mentioned by my informants. These are silhouettes, 4 to 25 inches high, of men and anthropomorphic figures, and of 2 boats with 5 and 6 occupants.[7]

I am indebted to the late Harlan I. Smith for detailed information about petroglyphs and red pictographs in southeastern Alaska and British Columbia,[8] which indicates that rock paintings are most numerous in Coast Salish, Kwakiutl, and Bella Coola territory, less common in Bella Bella, Tsimshian, and Tlingit country, rare among the Nootka, and as yet unreported from the Haida. The subjects are men or anthropomorphic beings, faces or masks, boats (including some modern sailing ships), coppers, dishes, whales, ravens, and other animals, and geometric symbols. The Coast Salish of Seechel Island told Smith that they made pictographs to mark the boundaries of family hunting territories.

Petroglyphs are more common than pictographs on the Northwest Coast, especially north of the Salish area. Emmons reported that the petroglyphs in Tlingit territory are so old that the present inhabitants are unable to interpret them and believe them to be the work of strangers who passed through the country before it was inhabited by the Tlingit.[9] Keithahn points out that Tlingit petroglyphs are usually on beach boulders near the mouths of sockeye salmon streams and are so placed that they not only face the sea but are submerged at high tide; he argues that they were made to insure or increase the salmon runs by supernatural means.[10] According to our in-

formants, some Tlingit petroglyphs seem to have been made as records of property sacrificed at potlatches or in settling disputes,[11] or as records of other important events. A number reflect sib crests and could be "read like totem poles," serving to record sib territorial claims. Pictographs were variously supposed to commemorate the killing of captives or the exploits of shamans, or were ascribed to Tsimshian war parties.[12]

Petroglyphs near the present village of Bella Coola, representing the faces of anthropomorphic beings, are said to be connected with ceremonies of the winter secret societies. The members pound on them while singing, according to Smith's informants.

The numerous red pictographs in the territory of the Interior Salish (Lillooet, Thompson, Shuswap, Okanagon) were made as records of the puberty observances of boys and girls, and also of objects seen in dreams. Making the pictures was supposed to help in the attainment of supernatural power. Teit also records the belief among the Thompson Indians that the pictures were the work of local water spirits.[13]

The Carrier also made red pictographs. I am indebted to Dr. Jenness for a photograph of paintings at Stuart Lake, representing anthropomorphic beings, animals, and symbols in outline and silhouette. Morice suggests that these are representations of guardian spirits. In addition, he reports that the Carrier made abbreviated signs, sketched in charcoal on rocks and trees, as a "means of communication between different hunting parties."[14]

Petroglyphs are relatively rare in the interior of British Columbia and are in the same scratchy outline style as the paintings in that area.

6 De Laguna, 1947, pp. 38, 43, 225.
7 Giddings, 1941, Pl. IX.
8 Cf. H. I. Smith, 1927a, and files of the National Museum of Canada.
9 Emmons, 1908, p. 221.
10 Keithahn, 1940.

11 Cf. Garfield, 1947, p. 441.
12 Field notes, 1949 and 1950.
13 Teit, 1900, pp. 239, 381; 1906, p. 282; 1909, p. 590.
14 Morice, 1894, Fig. 190, pp. 207, 209 f.

3. ANALYSIS AND COMPARISON

The figure of a man (Fig. 23B) at Site 13, Hawkins Island, is almost identical with a painting on Bear Island in Kachemak Bay,[15] except that the latter is much smaller and shows the left arm with exaggerated fingers and the legs widespread, whereas the left arm and legs of the former are obliterated. These figures are similar to a Thompson pictograph in outline and a petroglyph at Cape Alitak on Kodiak Island.[16]

The man or bear with penis or tail at Site 9 in Boswell Bay (Fig. 21B) closely resembles figures at Tuxedni Bay, Cook Inlet, which have already been compared to crude figures of men made by the Thompson, Shuswap and Lillooet and are also somewhat similar to pictures in the Tanana Valley and to some of the Cape Alitak petroglyphs.[17] The animal-like characteristics of the figures at Boswell Bay, Tuxedni Bay, and possibly Kodiak suggest that they may represent spirits. According to the Chugach, such spirits (kałaγat) included man-eating demons like Kapaχcuci, some of the familiars of shamans, and wicked persons who became cannibal monsters either during life or after death. They are described as covered with fur and having pointed heads, long teeth and claws, and other animal traits.

Two pictures at Site 13 (Fig. 23C and E) suggest the bodies of men without heads, as does an inverted V-shaped figure at Boswell Bay (Fig. 21A). They are not dissimilar to a Shuswap painting[18] and one in the Tanana Valley.

The schematized faces at Sites 12 and 13 on Hawkins Island (Figs. 22A, 23A) have no analogies in Cook Inlet, but there are many similar faces at Cape Alitak on Kodiak Island[19] and in British Columbia and

southeastern Alaska. The latter include Tsimshian pictographs on the Skeena River, on Douglas Channel, and on Venn Passage;[20] Tlingit petroglyphs near Wrangell;[21] Kwakiutl petroglyphs at Fort Rupert and on Meadow Island;[22] and Salish petroglyphs on Yellow Island near Comox.[23] The petroglyphs near Bella Coola, supposed to be connected with the winter secret societies, include 2 similar faces, and there is another Bella Coola example on South Bentnick Arm.[24] An anthropomorphic figure in red outline on Dean Channel on the Bella Bella and Bella Coola boundary has the features shown in similar style.[25] This type of face is thus very common on the Northwest Coast, although some of the examples cited include such details as ears or the outline of the face, not found in the Chugach paintings. Lastly there is a single example of a similar face in red paint on a boulder in Thompson Indian country.[26]

Four pictures in Prince William Sound seem to represent men in boats. At Site 59 on Mummy Island near Knight Island there are 2 umiaks, one with 7 or 8 occupants (Fig. 24C, Pl. 7, 1), the other with 3 or 4 (unillustrated). These are very similar to pictures at Tuxedni Bay on Cook Inlet, and in the Tanana Valley.[27] A picture at Site 13 on Hawkins Island (Fig. 23F) may also represent a boat with 5 paddlers, and this may be compared to a Carrier drawing in charcoal which is equally crude.[28] Another picture at Site 13 (Fig. 23H) suggests a boat with 3 occupants. It is more likely to be an umiak or dugout than a

15 De Laguna, 1934, Pl. 65B.
16 Teit, 1900, Pl. XX, 21c; Heizer, 1947, Fig. 4.
17 De Laguna, 1934, Pls. 62C, 2; 63A, 2, 3, B, 1, E, pp. 151 f. Add: Teit, 1906, Pl. IX, 1; Giddings, 1941, Pl. IX; Heizer, 1947, Fig. 4.
18 Teit, 1909, Fig. 252L (man with mask of fir boughs).

19 Hrdlička, 1944, Figs. 17, 18; Heizer, 1947, Figs. 4, 5C, E, pp. 282, 288.
20 H. I. Smith, 1927b, Fig. 1; Drucker, 1943, Pl. 9c, d, p. 110.
21 Niblack, 1890, Pl. XX, 76; Emmons, 1908, Figs. 62, 63; H. I. Smith, 1909, Pl. XXVIIIa, b.
22 Boas, 1897, Fig. 24; Drucker, 1943, Pl. 9f, p. 110.
23 H. I. Smith, 1907, Fig. 115.
24 H. I. Smith, 1925, Fig. 1.
25 Canadian National Museum photograph 61788 by H. I. Smith.
26 Teit, 1900, Pl. XX, 8.
27 De Laguna, 1934, Pls. 63B, 2; 64, 5; Giddings, 1941, Pl. IX.
28 Morice, 1894, Fig. 197L (significance unknown).

3-man bidarka, since the latter was a Russian innovation of the late eighteenth century and the picture would appear to be older than this. In style it may be compared to pictographs of the Heiltsuk at Namu, of the Coast Salish at Codrington Point,[29] and of the Lillooet.[30]

The oval at Site 13 (Fig. 23J), just to the left of the boat (H), suggests a similar combination of figures in a group of red paintings on the Stikine River, B. C., near the mouth of the Anook River, which are said to have been made in the middle of the nineteenth century to commemorate the massacre here of Stikine (Wrangell) Tlingit by the Nass River Tsimshian, and the capture of a canoe-load of slaves.[31] The "boat" (if it is one) is in this case much more conventionalized.

The more complicated oval figure at Site 13 (Fig. 23K) has no known analogies.

Other geometric paintings in Prince William Sound are the crosses at Site 13 (Fig. 23I) and Site 59 (Fig. 24B), the oblique line with a bulge at one end (Fig. 23G), and also at Site 13 a horizontal row of circles touching each other, above and below which is a horizontal line (unillustrated). Such geometric symbols as lines, ovals, circles, crosses, spirals, etc. are not uncommon among the pictographs and petroglyphs in the areas previously mentioned, and comparisons may be omitted.

The seal (?) at Site 59 (Fig. 24A) and the more amorphous sea mammal at Site 13 (Fig. 23D) are similar to seals or sea otters and a walrus (?) on Bear Island in Kachemak Bay.[32] The jumping whale at Site 12 (Fig. 22B) is almost identical with paintings in Tuxedni Bay and at Sadie Cove in Kachemak Bay, although the latter lack a line below suggesting the water.[33] The sperm whale, killer whale, porpoise,

or beluga are represented among the Cape Alitak petroglyphs,[34] and jumping whales in red are common in British Columbia, especially in southern Kwakiutl and Coast Salish territory.

The most elaborate painting is that above the small recess at Site 12, Hawkins Island, where human remains were found (Chapter III, section 6). It vaguely suggests a living form, perhaps with pendant ears or drooping hat brim (Fig. 22C). No parallels are known, but the general style, especially the suggestion of an eye in the middle of the body, is not unlike that of the Northwest Coast, although in the latter art the eye is horizontal.[35] It is possible that the Hawkins Island painting represents a spirit (kałaₐq) who has a single eye placed sideways in the middle of his body. It is characteristic of the Eskimo in general that they conceive of spirits as having misplaced body parts, as lacking certain parts, or as composed of parts of different species. We have already suggested that some of the anthropomorphic figures also represented spirits. Heizer interpreted some of the faces on Cape Alitak as masks, and this explanation might be correct for all the faces there, as well as for our Prince William Sound examples. In one Chugach story a helping spirit was described as "a little mask," and in the whole area shamans made masks to represent their familiars. Since spirits could also change their forms and often appeared in animal or bird guise, according to our informants, it is possible that all of the Pacific Eskimo pictographs and petroglyphs portray such spirit helpers. This interpretation would be consistent with Black Stepan's statement that would-be shamans used to make offerings to the paintings.

Whatever explanation we favor, it is clear that the paintings in Prince William

29 Information from H. I. Smith.
30 Teit, 1906, Pl. IX, 42.
31 Letter from Dr. Diamond Jenness, 22 February, 1935, quoting report by Forest A. Kerr, Geological Survey of Canada, 22 January, 1932.
32 De Laguna, 1934, Pls. 65E, 1; 66; 67D.
33 De Laguna, 1934, Pls. 63G; 64, 2; 68 (the last are blackfish whales).

34 Heizer, 1947, p. 288, Fig. 3.
35 Cf. eyes in petroglyphs of a human face and a killer whale near Wrangell (Niblack, 1890, Pl. XX, 76, face, and 77, whale); the same figures are illustrated by Emmons, 1908, Figs. 62 and 53; the face by H. I. Smith, 1909, Pl. XXVIIIa.

Sound find their closest analogy in the Eskimo pictographs of Cook Inlet. At the same time the Chugach pictographs stand closer than the Cook Inlet pictures to the Kodiak petroglyphs and to the pictographs of the southern Kwakiutl and Salish, and also to the petroglyphs of the Tlingit and other Northwest Coast tribes. The Cook Inlet and Chugach paintings are also very similar to the Tena pictures in the Tanana Valley. In style and technique, however, the Kodiak petroglyphs resemble Northwest Coast rock carving more closely than do the Chugach paintings. Heizer finds with justice that the Kodiak petroglyph complex was probably derived from the Northwest Coast before the full development of the characteristic Northwest Coast art style.[36] Chugach pictographs seem to have been only lightly touched by this specifically northern Northwest Coast–Kodiak movement, which is rather curious since one would suppose that the transfer of motifs and techniques must have taken place through their territory. It is also curious that, where Chugach pictographs seem to reflect influences from beyond the Pacific Eskimo area, these suggest the southern Northwest Coast and the Plateau. We are probably dealing here with several periods of development, the sequences of which we are not yet able to unravel.

[36] Heizer, 1947, pp. 292 f.

CHAPTER V

Archaeological Specimens from Prince William Sound

1. Introduction

THE BULK OF THE collections which are described in this chapter were excavated at the Palugvik midden, although important additions, especially of perishable materials and of grave offerings, were found in Palutat Cave and at Palugvik East Point. The Palugvik midden yielded the following number of artifacts (finished specimens, broken objects, worked fragments), excluding those found on the beach or in slumped portions of the shell heap which could not be assigned to any of the 4 layers composing the midden:

	Bone, Antler, Ivory	Stone	Other Materials
Layer 4	98	85	4 copper 4 paint 1 shell
Layer 3 or 4	30	15	1 copper 1 shell
Layer 3	74	69	1 shell
Layer 2 or 3	24	25	1 paint
Layer 2	142	101	1 paint 2 shell
Layer 1 or 2	37	26	1 shell
Layer 1 (exclusive of Grave III)	121	123	22 wood
Totals	526	444	39

It is thus evident that the lower half of the midden, Layers 1 and 2, was richer than the upper half. There were, however, many other sites (see Chapter II, section 16) which appear to have been of the same age as the upper half of the midden.

In the following pages, the archaeological specimens are described according to type. They consist of tools, weapons, utensils, ornaments, objects of ceremonial significance or unknown use, boats, clothing, etc. The materials of which they are made are bone, antler, ivory, shell, copper, greenstone, sandstone, slate, and other rocks, wood, bark, roots, skin, and grass. The treatment of these specimens is not completely logical, since they are not discussed in an order based entirely upon function or entirely upon material, but the text attempts to combine both considerations. In the plates, the objects to be illustrated are arranged primarily according to material, in order to exhibit techniques of manufacture. For explanation of the catalogue numbers, see the Preface.

2. Splitting Adzes

Our collections contain 98 complete or fragmentary blades for splitting adzes. These heavy blades, which are thicker than they are wide, were lashed directly to an elbow or T-shaped handle and were presumably used for rough work, such as chopping down trees, splitting logs, etc., while

110

the smaller planing adzes (see section 3) were used for finer tasks, such as shaping planks and dugout canoes.

The splitting adz is not only a numerically common type but one represented at almost every site in Prince William Sound, in part because the heavy blades stand a good chance of preservation when washed out by the sea, and the majority of our examples were recovered from beaches. Only 13 specimens were found in Palugvik midden, and, of these, 6 came from the uppermost layer, indicating that the splitting adz became much more common in the last period of occupation. This agrees with the evidence from Kachemak Bay, where the splitting adz seems to be confined to the latter half of the Third Period; it also appears to be late on Kodiak Island.[1] Splitting adzes were relatively more common in the sound than in Kachemak Bay, while the reverse is true of bone wedges, even though comparisons are limited to the latter half of Kachemak Bay III. This is consistent with the theory that the splitting adz partially displaced the bone wedge. We can, of course, say nothing about the role of the wooden wedge, since it is rarely preserved.

Almost all the splitting adzes from Prince William Sound are made of greenstone or altered rocks of the basalt-greenstone series, but there are a few of dolerite, basic schist, and unidentified volcanic materials.

A considerable number are poorly made. The shape is irregular, the usual groove for the lashing poorly defined, and the surface unfinished except at the cutting edge. A few are made of such asymmetric slabs that it is doubtful whether they could strike a true blow (Pl. 11, 5).

The sides and the bottom (next to the handle) of the more carefully made adzes have been evenly pecked all over. On some, these surfaces are flattened to produce a subrectangular cross section (Pls. 10, 3, 9; 11, 1). On others, the top, sides, and bottom are rounded and the cross section is oval

[1] De Laguna, 1934, p. 130; 1947, pp. 154-56; Hrdlička, 1944, p. 333; Heizer, 1946, p. 149; Birket-Smith, 1941, Fig. 30a, d, f, h.

(Pls. 10, 2, 11; 11, 5). The top is usually arched or humped longitudinally and the bottom curved up to meet it at the cutting edge.

The specimens average 20 cm. in length, 6.5 cm. in thickness, and 4 or 4.5 cm. in width, but there are many variations. The length ranges from 11 cm. (Pl. 48, 2) to 29 cm. (Pl. 11, 10), the thickness from 3.5 cm. (Pl. 48, 2) to 9 cm. (Pl. 11, 6), and the width from 2.7 to 6 cm. The widest is a broken specimen from Palugvik 1 which was reshaped as a planning adz.

Of the 98 specimens, 20 are fragments which fail to show how they were lashed to the handle. Sixty-seven out of the remaining 78 specimens were furnished with some arrangement of grooves or knobs to prevent the lashing from slipping. The grooves are 2.5 to 5 cm. wide and are cut across the top and sometimes partway down the sides. The arched top often gives the effect of a ridge or ridges on one or both sides of the groove; on some specimens the adz is carefully shaped to leave a knob or knobs, 1.4 to 2 cm. high.

On 40 blades there was only a single groove, set a little to the rear of the middle or sometimes quite near the butt. As can be seen from the table at the end of this section, these specimens come from both the upper and lower halves of the Palugvik midden and from sites all over the sound (Pls. 10, 4, 9, 11, 12; 11, 1, 3 to 5, 8, 9).

Two specimens have a ridge or knob just aft of the groove (Pl. 11, 2), and 3 have only a single knob (Pl. 11, 6). On 4 adzes the groove is set between 2 knobs or ridges (Pl. 10, 3, 6); on 4 additional specimens a pair of knobs or grooves produces the effect of a groove, although the space between them is not cut below the level of the top of the adz (Pl. 11, 10).

Seven specimens have 2 grooves, both placed toward the butt (Pl. 10, 7); on 5 others the 2 grooves are separated by a ridge or knob; one specimen has 3 ridges and 2 or 3 grooves.

There are, lastly, 11 specimens without

groove or ridge to hold the lashing. These include a very long, picklike blade with an exceedingly narrow cutting edge (Pl. 10, *1*) ; the smallest specimen of all (Pl. 48, *2*) ; 2 broken blades, one reworked as a planing adz, the other reshaped so the original groove can no longer be used (Pl. 11, *7*) ; and others (Pl. 10, *2*). A number of heavy, grooveless blades are reported by Hrdlička from Kodiak Island, from both the earlier "Pre-Koniag" and the later "Koniag" levels. Some may be splitting adzes; others, listed as "axes," are evidently only large planing adz blades.[2]

It is to be noted that the more elaborate arrangements for securing the lashing seem to be characteristic of the western part of the sound. The Chenega Church Collection, in particular, had a large proportion of adzes with various combinations of grooves and knobs. On the other hand, the plainer type with single groove, although represented in all areas, was more characteristic of the southeastern part.

These splitting adzes were subjected to violent use and were frequently broken.

A common situation in Chugach folklore deals with the plight of the slave who has broken his master's adz while chopping firewood and fears a beating. A number of the broken specimens have been reshaped or put to other uses. Thus, 2 damaged adzes (Pl. 11, *7*, *9*) show signs of reworking for further use, and 3 were reshaped as planing adzes. Another has had the butt end sharpened to serve either as a planing adz or as an ax (Pl. 11, *8*), and a specimen which may have originally been a large pick, not an adz, was reshaped as an ax (Pl. 11, *4*). Three broken blades were used as chisels or hammers (Pl. 11, *10*).

A private collection from the vicinity of Tatitlek (on loan to the Washington State Museum) contains a single example of a type of adz not represented in our collections. This blade is wide and flat like a planing adz (not thick and narrow), yet has a groove like a splitting adz. I have named this flat grooved form an "intermediate type adz." It is also known from Kodiak.[3]

The distribution of splitting adzes is:

Palugvik 4	with groove (33-37-102, 105)
	with groove, reworked (Pl. 11, *9*)
	with knob (33-37-104)
	fragments (33-37-103, P.733)
Palugvik 3 or 2	fragment (P.734)
Palugvik 2	with groove (33-37-350, 351)
	fragments (33-37-346, P. 991)
Palugvik 1	without groove, reshaped as planing adz (33-37-454)
	fragment, identification uncertain (P.999)
Palugvik, layer (?)	with groove (33-37-525)
	without groove (P.1046)

[2] Hrdlička, 1944, pp. 333, 343, Fig. 113.

[3] De Laguna, 1934, p. 56; 1947, p. 156; Birket-Smith, 1941, Fig. 30c.

PLATE 10. Splitting adzes. Scale slightly over ⅓ natural size

1, Ungrooved, greenstone, Chenega Church Collection (33-37-645) ; 2, ungrooved, greenstone, Ellamar (Site 40) (33-37-590) ; 3, with groove and 2 knobs, greenstone, Site 65B, Montague Island (33-37-612) ; 4, with groove, greenstone, Site 6, Hinchinbrook Island (30-25-47) ; 5, with groove and 2 ridges, altered volcanic rock, Site 45, Long Bay (30-25-114) ; 6, with 2 knobs and groove, altered volcanic rock, Site 2, Hinchinbrook Island (30-25-46) ; 7, with 2 grooves, greenstone, Site 45, Long Bay (D30-25-119) ; 8, with knob and 2 grooves, greenstone, Site 65A, Montague Island (33-37-599) ; 9, with groove, dolerite, from man's grave under rock, Site 16, Hawkins Island (33-37-579) ; 10, with one (or 2 ?) knobs, greenstone, Site 56, Chenega Island (33-37-626) ; 11, with groove, greenstone, Site 65A, Montague Island (33-37-598) ; 12, with groove, greenstone, Site 45, Long Bay (30-25-115)

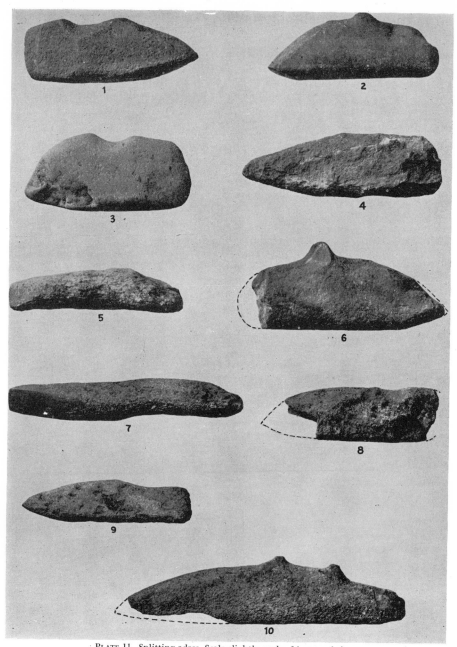

PLATE 11. Splitting adzes. Scale slightly under ⅓ natural size

1, With groove, basalt, Site 62, Evans Island (P.1162); 2, with groove and knob, greenstone, Chenega Church Collection (P.1122); 3, with groove, now waterworn, igneous rock, Site 56, Chenega Island (P.1135); 4, splitting adz or pick, broken butt partly reshaped as an ax, greenstone, Site 65A, Montague Island (P.1140); 5, splitting adz with groove, greenstone (seen from above), Site 65B, Montague Island (P.1149); 6, with knob, igneous rock, 18 to 24 inches below surface, Palutat Cave (P.1203); 7, ungrooved, greenstone (seen from above), Site 7, Hawkins Cut Off (P.1106); 8, with groove, broken butt reshaped as ax, Site 65B, Montague Island (P.1150); 9, with groove, greenstone, Palugvik, Layer 4 (P.732); 10, with 2 knobs, basalt, used as hammer after being broken, Site 65B, Montague Island (P.1147)

Palugvik East Point,
   Grave III   without groove (Pl. 48, 2)

Site 2, Hinchinbrook   with 2 knobs and groove (Pl. 10, 6)
   Island

Site 6, Hinchinbrook   with groove (Pl. 10, 4, 30-25-48)
   Island

Site 7, Hawkins Cut Off   with groove (30-25-69, P.1107)
                    reworked, now without groove (Pl. 11, 7)

Site 8, Hinchinbrook   with groove (30-25-55, 57, 60 to 63, D30-25-56, 58)
   Island   with 2 knobs (P.1118)
                    fragment (30-25-59)

Site 16, Hawkins Island,
   Small Burial Shelter   with groove (Pl. 10, 9)

Site 17, Hawkins Island   reported

Site 22, Mummy Island   without groove (30-25-87)

Site 23, Mummy Island   with groove (30-25-83)
                    fragment (30-25-89)

Site 27, Grass Island   with 2 grooves (30-25-40)

Site 31, Sheep Bay   without groove (33-37-587)

Site 32, Sheep Bay   with groove (30-25-100)
                    fragment (30-25-102)

Site 35, Gravina Bay   with 2 grooves (P.1167)
                    fragment (P.1168)

Near Tatitlek   loan collection in WSM includes splitting adzes and
                    intermediate type adz

Site 40, Ellamar   with groove (30-25-105, P. 1175)
                    without groove (Pl. 10, 2)
                    with 2 grooves (WSM X-158)
                    reshaped as planing adz (30-25-103)

Site 42, Galena Bay   with groove (30-25-112)

Site 44, Long Bay   with groove (Pl. 10, 12, 30-25-116 to 118, 120)
                    with groove and 2 ridges (Pl. 10, 5)
                    with 2 grooves (Pl. 10, 7)

Palutat Cave,
   depth 6″   fragment (P.1212)
   depth 1′6″-2′   with knob (Pl. 11, 6)

Chenega Village   with 2 (?) grooves (P.1177)

Chenega Church
   Collection   with groove (33-37-642)
                    without groove (Pl. 10, 1)
                    with groove and knob (Pl. 11, 2, P.1123)
                    with groove and 2 ridges (33-37-643)
                    with 2 grooves and knob, (33-37-644)
                    with 3 (?) grooves and 3 ridges (P.1127)
                    fragment (P.1124), used as chisel (P.1125)

Site 56, Chenega Island	with groove (Pl. 11, *3*)
	with groove and 2 ridges (33-37-624)
	with 2 grooves (33-37-622, 627)
	with 2 grooves and knob (33-37-623, 625, P.1134)
	with knob (P.1136)
	with 2 knobs or ridges (Pl. 10, *10*)
Knight Island	reported
Site 61, Bainbridge Island	without groove (30-25-122)
	fragment (30-25-123)
Site 62, Evans Island	with groove (Pl. 11, *1*)
	with 1 or 2 knobs (P. 1161)
Site 65A, Montague I.	with groove (Pl. 10, *11*, 33-37-601)
	without groove (P.1139, P.1141)
	with 2 grooves and knob (Pl. 10, *8*)
	reshaped as planing adz (33-37-597)
	adz (or pick?) with groove, reshaped as ax (Pl. 11, *4*)
	fragment (33-37-600)
Site 65B, Montague I.	with groove (Pl. 11, *5*, 33-37-610, P.1148, WSM X-121)
	with groove, reshaped as ax (Pl. 11, *8*)
	with groove and 2 knobs (Pl. 10, *3*)
	with knob (33-37-614)
	with 2 knobs, used as hammer (Pl. 11, *10*)
	fragment (33-37-615), used as hammer or chisel (P.1153)

3. PLANING ADZES

There are 63 planing adz blades, in addition to 3 specimens made from broken splitting adzes. Planing adz blades are grooveless celts, wider than they are thick, and smaller and lighter than blades for splitting adzes. The smaller planing adz blades may have been set into bone (or wood?) heads or hafts, which were in turn attached to wooden handles. Although such bone hafts were found on Kachemak Bay, the Alaska Peninsula, and Kodiak Island,[4] none was obtained in Prince William Sound. The larger blades were undoubtedly lashed directly to an elbow-shaped handle. These larger blades, especially those with fairly thick, oval sections, somewhat resemble the grooveless splitting adzes, and the 2 types tend to merge.

Most of the planing adzes are of green chert (altered greenstone) and greenstone, but there are a few of schist and slate. The average length is between 8 and 12 cm., although blades range in size from 4.5 (?) by 3 cm. (Pl. 14, *12*), perhaps a scraper blade, up to 17.8 by 7.3 cm. (Pl. 13, *8*). The greatest width is usually at the cutting edge. Some blades are flat, with both surfaces more or less polished (Pls. 12, *2*, *5*, *7*; 13, *4*, *6*, *8*; 14, *15*). Others with oval section are almost as thick as they are wide

[4] De Laguna, 1934. Pl. 19, *1*, *5*, *6*, pp. 59, 173; 1947, pp. 157-59; Hrdlička, 1944, Fig. 114. The collections from Kodiak Island contain several types of haft.

PLATE 12. Planing adzes, axes, and picks. Scale ½ natural size

1, Combination splitting adz and ax, greenstone, Site 65B, Montague Island (33-37-616); 2, planing adz, greenstone, Site 6, Hinchinbrook Island (30-25-51); 3, planing adz, green chert, Palugvik 2 (33-37-348); 4, planing adz, green chert, Dooly's Island, near Site 31, Sheep Bay (33-37-585); 5, planing adz, green chert, Site 65A, Montague Island (33-37-596); 6, double-pointed pick, greenstone, Site 31, Sheep Bay (33-37-586); 7, planing adz, greenstone, Site 8, Hinchinbrook Island (30-25-54); 8, chisel, greenstone, Site 32, Sheep Bay (30-25-101); 9, ax, greenstone, Site 28, Point Whitshed (30-25-93); 10, ax, greenstone, Site 58, Little Bay, Knight Island (Lutz Collection); 11, pick (?), schist, Site 7, Hawkins Cut Off (30-25-76)

(Pls. 12, *3, 4;* 13, *5, 7;* 48, *1*). The average thickness is between 1.2 and 3.5 cm. Methods of shaping were by chipping and grinding or by pecking and grinding. Fewer specimens show evidence of sawing than we should have anticipated from the number of stone saws found. The butt is sometimes left rough, sometimes rounded off, and the degree of finish varies greatly. The cutting edge is usually asymmetric because it is ground more from one face than from the other.

There are also 8 blades, shaped like adzes but so small that they may have been used for scrapers. Most of these are made from slate or schist, which breaks more easily than greenstone or chert. Six of these small blades are from Palugvik 4 (Pls. 13, *2;* 14, *12;* 33-37-84, 92, 94, P.747), one from Palugvik 3 or 4 (33-37-100), and the last from Palugvik 3 (33-37-190). Small adz-like slate blades, probably scrapers, are known from Kachemak Bay III, where some even have the paddle shape characteristic of Chugach specimens identified as scrapers (see section 13). In fact, slate scrapers date from Kachemak Bay I to the Tanaina Indian culture which succeeded the Eskimo in this area. Similar small slate blades for adz or scraper are also known from Kodiak.[5] Only in Prince William Sound do such small blades appear to be late.

The distribution of ordinary planing adzes (see below) contrasts with that of the splitting adzes. The planing adz was less well represented in collections obtained from beaches, probably because it is more fragile, although it was more common than the splitting adz at excavated sites. Thus, 23 planing adzes and 8 scraper-like blades were found in the Palugvik midden, in contrast to only 13 splitting adzes. The youngest layer here yielded only 2 planing adzes but 6 splitting adzes, while the oldest contained 9 planing and only 3 splitting adz blades (one reshaped as a planing adz). These figures, if large enough to be significant, may be explained in 2 ways, depending upon what function is ascribed to the small blades. If these were scrapers, then it would appear that the planing adz declined in importance as the splitting adz took over some of its functions. If, however, the small blades were actually for adzes, we cannot say that the planing adz declined, but rather that it developed a specialized form for delicate work, while the splitting adz, which was adapted for heavy work, became relatively common.

The provenience of the planing adzes, other than the 8 small blades, is:

Palugvik 4	2 (33-37-101, P.745)
Palugvik 3	2 (33-37-193, 194)
Palugvik 2 or 3	2 (Pl. 13, *4, 7*)
Palugvik 2	7 (Pl. 12, *3;* 33-37-343, 345, 347, 349, P.736, P.739)
Palugvik 1 or 2	(33-37-344)
Palugvik 1	9 (Pl. 13, *6;* 33-37-449 to 453, P.740, P.741, P.998)
Palugvik, layer (?)	9 (33-37-522 to 524, P.742, P.1040, P.1041, P.1185, 2 uncatalogued in DNM)
Palugvik East Point	
Grave III	(Pl. 48, *1*)
Burial Ledge	(P.1094)
Site 6, Hinchinbrook Island	(Pl. 12, *2*)
Site 7, Hawkins Cut Off	4 (Pl. 13, *8;* D30-25-77, 30-25-78, P.1109)

[5] De Laguna, 1934, Pl. 34, *4, 5, 7*, pp. 77, 182; 1947, p. 186; Birket-Smith, 1941, Fig. 30b, p. 154.

PLATE 13. Hunting pick and planing adzes. Scale slightly under ½ natural size

1, Double-pointed pick, greenstone, Palugvik 4, (P.731) ; 2, scraper-like planing adz, greenstone, Palugvik 4, (P.746) ; 3, planing adz, greenstone, waterworn, Chenega Church Collection (P.1126) ; 4, planing adz, greenstone, Palugvik 2 (or 3) (P.738) ; 5, planing adz, greenstone (seen from the edge), Site 31, Sheep Bay (P.1176) ; 6, planing adz, greenstone, Palugvik 1 (P.737) ; 7, planing adz, greenstone, Palugvik 3 (or 2) (P.735) ; 8, planing adz, slaty greenstone, Site 7, Hawkins Cut Off (P.1108)

Site 8, Hinchinbrook Island	2 (Pl. 12, 7; 33-37-580)
Beach below Site 21, Mummy Island	(30-25-90)
Site 23, Mummy Island	(30-25-84)
Site 28, Point Whitshed	(30-25-94)
Site 31, Sheep Bay	(Pl. 13, 5)
Dooly's Island, near Site 31	2 (Pl. 12, 4; 33-37-584)
Chenega Church Collection	5 (Pls. 13, 3; 14, 15; 33-37-640, 641, WSM X-91)
Site 65A, Montague Island	2 (Pl. 12, 5; P.1142)
Site 65B, Montague Island	(P.1151)

4. Axes

From Site 28 at Point Whitshed is an anomalous blade of cherty greenstone (Pl. 12, 9), 18 cm. long. The lashing groove is at right angles to the cutting edge, indicating that the specimen was hafted as an ax, even though the slight asymmetry of the blade would prevent it from being very serviceable.

Mr. Lutz found a well-made ax of greenstone (Pl. 12, 10), 19.5 cm. long, 6.5 cm. wide, and 3 cm. thick, at Site 58, near Little Bay, Knight Island. The blade is symmetrical, and there is a well-defined groove for lashing.

A broken greenstone celt from Site 23, Mummy Island, seems to have been an ax, although lack of a lashing groove prevents certain identification (30-25-85). It is, of course, possible that some of the specimens classed as grooveless splitting adzes were hafted as ax blades.

There are, in addition, 4 axlike implements. A specimen in the private collection from the vicinity of Tatitlek has a blade at each end, at right angles to each other; when it was hafted, one blade would have served as an adz, the other (now broken) as an ax or axlike pick. A greenstone specimen (point broken from a splitting adz?) from Site 65B, Montague Island, also has a cutting edge at each end, at right angles to each other, producing a combination ax-adz (Pl. 12, 1). A grooved splitting adz from the same site has a sharpened butt (Pl. 11, 8). If both blades, now broken, had been serviceable at the same time, it would also have been a combination adz-ax. The butt of a battered splitting adz (or pick?) from Site 65A has been sharpened as an ax. The specimen is now an ax-pick (Pl. 11, 4).

Axes as tools are very rare in northwestern North America. They seem to be confined to the Chugach and Eyak, and even here are far outnumbered by adzes.[6]

5. Stone Chisels

Another anomalous specimen is a blade of green chert (Pl. 12, 8) from Site 32, Sheep Bay. It is shaped like a rather thick planing adz, 14 cm. long; the battered butt indicates use as a chisel.

A broken splitting adz in the Chenega Church Collection, now 9.5 cm. long, was evidently reshaped as a chisel (P.1125).

There are, in addition, 17 or 18 delicate

[6] De Laguna, 1947, p. 164.

PLATE 14. Men's knives, chipped blades, slate chisels. Scale ¾ natural size
1, Man's knife like ulo, slate, Palugvik, layer (?) (33-37-509); 2, toy ulo, slate, Palugvik 2, (33-37-307); 3, man's knife like ulo, slate, Palugvik 2 (33-37-312); 4, chipped blade, green chert, Palugvik, layer (?) (33-37-510); 5, chipped blade, green chert, Palugvik 4 (33-37-96); 6, copper blade fragment, Palugvik 4 (33-37-63); 7, single-edged knife blade, slate, Palugvik East Point burial ledge (33-37-563); 8, chipped blade, black chert, Palugvik, layer (?) (33-37-511); 9, chipped blade, slightly metamorphosed slate, Palutat Cave, depth 18 to 24 inches (33-37-668); 10 and 11, adzlike chisels, slate, Site 16, Hawkins Island (30-25-34, 33); 12, scraper or small planing adz, schist, Palugvik 4 (33-37-93); 13, knifelike chisel, slate, Site 65B, Montague Island (33-37-609); 14, knifelike chisel, slate, Palugvik 4 (33-37-85); 15, planing adz, gray chert, Chenega Church Collection (33-37-639); 16, adzlike chisel, slate, Site 16, Hawkins Island (30-25-2); 17, adzlike chisel, slate, Palugvik 4 (33-37-87)

chisel-like implements, all of slate, except for one of greenstone, varying in length from 5 to 13.9 cm. The cutting edges have been formed in 2 ways. On 6 the blade has been sharpened from both sides to produce a knifelike implement (Pls. 14, *13, 14;* 15, *3, 6*), admirably adapted for fine wood carving, cutting grooves, setting arrow feathers into slits, etc. One specimen in this group has a blade at each end (Pl. 15, *9*). On 11 specimens the blade has been sharpened from both edges to make an implement like a tiny splitting adz (Pls. 14, *10, 11, 16, 17;* 15, *2*). One of these even has a faint groove near the butt (Pl. 15, *8*), and another found by Lee Pratt at Site 17, Hawkins Island, is grooved like a miniature splitting adz. These 2 specimens may have been toy adzes, or, like the other 9 grooveless implements in the group, have

served as woodworking tools. Another possibility is that the 11 adzlike blades were hafted as spikes for war clubs. I can cite no close parallels from southwestern Alaska to these small Chugach chisels. However, they suggest comparisons with the various slate and schist tools of the northern Tlingit (Angoon, 1950; Yakutat, 1952), which were presumably used for cutting and grinding bone and wood. The whole group, Chugach and Tlingit, may have been remotely related to the ground burin-like tools of the Greenland "Stone Age," Dorset, Old Bering Sea, and Ipiutak Eskimo, which in turn are obviously derived from the true burins of Cape Denbigh and the Brooks Range in Alaska, and from the Dorset culture.[7]

The distribution of the small Chugach chisels is:

	Adzlike	*Knifelike*
Palugvik 4	Pl. 14, *17*	Pl. 14, *14*
	33-37-86	Pl. 15, *3* (greenstone)
		Pl. 15, *6*
Palugvik 3		Pl. 15, *9* (double-bladed)
Palugvik 2		33-37-342 (frag., type?)
Palugvik, layer (?)	Pl. 15, *2*	
Site 2, Hinchinbrook Island	30-25-285	
Site 16, Hawkins Island	Pl. 14, *10*	
	Pl. 14, *11*	
	30-25-36	
Site 17, Hawkins Island	Pl. 14, *16*	
	Pratt's specimen (grooved)	
Palutat Cave,		
12" below surface	P.1209 (unfinished)	
Site 65B, Montague Island	Pl. 15, *8* (grooved)	Pl. 14, *13*
		33-37-608
		field no. X-141 (lost)

6. Bone and Wooden Wedges

Although bone wedges were common in all periods on Kachemak Bay and Kodiak Island, and are known from the Alaska Peninsula and the Aleutians,[8] the type is represented by only 7 specimens from

Prince William Sound. This was to be expected, however, in view of the extreme development here of the splitting adz. These wedges (possibly some are chisels) are of whale or other hard bone, from 9 to 12 cm. long and from 1.7 to 3.7 cm. wide, usually

[7] Collins, 1953, pp. 36-39 and sources cited there; also Irving, 1951, pp. 52-53. The specimens from Kodiak Island, called "chisels" by Hrdlička (1944, Fig. 69, pp. 333, 343; cf. de Laguna, 1947, p. 168), are larger, and may well have been small adzes.

[8] Jochelson, 1925, Pl. 26, *2* to *8;* de Laguna, 1934, pp. 100 f., 199; 1947, pp. 168 f.; Hrdlička, 1944, Fig. 85, pp. 329, 334, 346; 1945, p. 457; Heizer, 1946, p. 149.

PLATE 15. Chisels and wedges. Scale ⅗ natural size

1, Chisel, bear penis bone, from post hole at bottom of Palugvik 1 (P.787); 2, adzlike chisel, slate, Palugvik, layer (?) (P.1199); 3, knifelike chisel, greenstone, Palugvik 4 (P.717); 4, wedge or chisel, bone, Palugvik 2 (?) (P.1012); 5, chisel, bone, Grave D, Palutat Cave (P.1218); 6, knifelike chisel, slate, Palugvik 4 (P.718); 7, wedge, bone, Palugvik 1 (P.954); 8, adzlike chisel, slate, Site 65B, Montague Island (P.1159); 9, knifelike chisel with 2 blades, slate, Palugvik 3 (P.650); 10, wedge, wood, bottom of Palugvik 1 (P.1197)

with marks of blows at the butts and damaged fore ends. They come from Palugvik 4 (Pl. 41, 7; 33-37-44, P.957), Palugvik 2(?) (Pl. 15, 4), Palugvik 1 (Pl. 15, 7), and from 1 to 4 feet below the surface of Palutat Cave (P.1215). The last is a cut whale rib. A whale bone wedge fragment (33-37-406) from Palugvik 1 has a drilled pit on one side, showing that it had been used as a drill rest, like so many bone wedges from Kodiak and the Aleutians.

The only wooden wedge (Pl. 15, 10), a nicely finished specimen 30.5 cm. long and 3.5 cm. in diameter, was found at the very bottom of the Palugvik midden. Since wooden wedges were presumably more common than bone wedges, to judge from ethnographic reports, it is curious that no other specimens of wood were found. They might have been expected in Palutat Cave, where there were so many coffins made of split planks.

7. Bone Chisels

Six chisels, all apparently of bear penis bone, from 5.5 to 10 cm. long, come from Palugvik 4 (Pl. 41, 8), Palugvik 3 (Pl. 41, 2), Palugvik 1 or 2 (P.942, fragment), a post hole at the bottom of the midden (Pl. 15, 1), the beach (P.1054, point only), and Grave D, Palutat Cave (Pl. 15, 5, point only).

A small chisel from Kachemak Bay III, made of moose(?) bone, and a presumably later specimen from Port Graham are somewhat similar to the Chugach specimens. Hrdlička's collections from Kodiak Island also contain a few small implements which may have been chisels, although most of the illustrated specimens are probably bone wedges.[9] With these exceptions, the bone chisel, especially of bear penis bone, seems to be restricted to Prince William Sound.

8. Whetstones

There are 49 whetstones, comprising not only small specimens which could be held in the hand, and which were presumably used for shaping and sharpening small stone and bone objects, but also heavy grinding blocks or slabs on which large adz blades seem to have been sharpened. All of the larger and many of the smaller specimens are of sandstone, but among the latter there are also specimens of slate, shale, altered tuff, felsite, diorite, and other rocks. There are no apparent chronological differences among the various sizes and shapes of these artifacts. We were also told that the Chugach used to sharpen adzes by fastening them under a heavy log which they dragged over the frozen beach.

There were 8 of the large blocks. One from Palugvik East Point midden was an oval boulder shaped like a lamp in outline, but with one surface polished from use.[10] Other blocks were deeply grooved (Pl. 22, 4, 5). There were no large thin grinding slabs, like those of Kachemak Bay II and III which were used in conjunction with a small handstone like a mano.[11]

The smaller whetstones are flat slabs, 5.5 to 15 cm. long, ground on one or both surfaces (Pl. 16, 15), or small bars or blocks, ground along the sides and edges (Pl. 16, 8, 12). Some have grooves in which small objects, such as shafts, awls, needles, etc., were shaped or sharpened (Pl. 16, 10, 11, 15). One slab was evidently used in mixing red paint. There are only a small broken felsite bar from Palugvik 3 (Pl. 17, 13) and a little sandstone block from Palugvik East Point midden (Pl. 16, 12) which suggest in any way the hexagonally or octagonally faceted bars of tuff and felsite characteristic of Kachemak Bay III.[12]

Four whetstones were found in graves: 2 slate bars from the large burial cave at Site 16, Hawkins Island (Pl. 16, 8); a shale slab with Skeleton III, Palugvik East Point (Pl. 48, 6); and a dolerite slab from Grave B1, Palutat Cave.

A broken slate whetstone from Palugvik

9 De Laguna, 1934, Pl. 46, 6, 8, p. 100; Hrdlička, 1944, Fig. 85, pp. 334, 346, and unpublished specimens.

10 Cf. de Laguna, 1934, Pl. 18, 6.
11 Ibid., Pl. 13D, p. 60.
12 Ibid., Pl. 22, 14, 15. Some Kodiak specimens approach this type (Hrdlička, 1944, Fig. 141).

2 is so well made as to suggest a mirror, were not the polished surface concave. A whetstone from the same layer was made from a broken slate scraper, and another was used as a scraper.

The distribution of these specimens is:

Palugvik 4	grinding block (P.726)
	2 slabs (33-37-111, P.774)
	bar or broken slate object (Pl. 17, *12*)
Palugvik 3	grinding block (33-37-200)
	2 slabs (33-37-197, 199)
	bar (Pl. 17, *13*)
	grooved whetstone (Pl. 16, *10*)
Palugvik 2 or 3	grinding block (P.760, fits Pl. 22, *4?*)
	grooved whetstone (Pl. 17, *10*)
Palugvik 2	5 slabs (33-37-359, 360 P.766, P.771, P.776)
	3 grooved whetstones (Pl. 16, *11;* P.761, P:763)
	mirror-like whetstone (33-37-362)
	whetstone used as scraper (P.765)
	whetstone made from scraper (P.772)
Palugvik 1 or 2	grinding block (Pl. 22, *5*)
	grooved whetstone (P.761)
Palugvik 1	8 slabs (33-37-468 to 470, P.767, P.768, P.777, WSM 958, 971)
	grooved whetstone (Pl. 17, *11*)
Palugvik, layer (?)	3 grinding blocks (Pl. 22, *4,* fits P.760?; P.1179, P.1180)
	5 slabs (Pl. 16, *15;* P.1069 with red paint, 33-37-528, 529, WSM 1125)
Palugvik East Point Midden	grinding block (not saved)
	bar (Pl. 16, *12*)
Grave III	slab (Pl. 48, *6*)
Site 7, Hawkins Cut Off	slab (30-25-73b)
Site 16, Hawkins Island Large Burial Cave	2 bars (Pl. 16, *8;* P.1112)
Near Tatitlek	bar in loan collection at WSM
Palutat Cave, Grave B1	slab (33-37-669)

In addition to the above, there are 8 stone plaques which may have been whetstones (Pls. 16, *7, 9;* 19, *5, 7* to *10;* P.775) but which, because of their unusual or decorative features, are described in sections 65 and 66.

A small ball of yellow-gray pumice, worn from use as an abrasive, was found in Palugvik 1 (33-37-471). It resembles the soft, light Katmai ejecta of 1911, although it is, of course, much older. The distance from active volcanoes explains why pumice is so rare in Prince William Sound, in contrast to its frequent occurrence in sites on Kachemak Bay, Kodiak, and the Aleutian Islands.[13]

[13] Jochelson, 1925, Pl. 16, *22, 23, 25;* de Laguna, 1934, pp. 62 f., 176; Hrdlička, 1944, pp. 328, 341.

9. STONE SAWS

There are 62 saws made of thin slabs of abrasive stone (mostly coarse granular basic schist, some sandstone, granite gneiss, etc.), which were used for cutting rock and probably bone. The edge is not notched but shows wear from use as a file, and may be straight or slightly curved. The specimens may be classified according to type: (1) those with one cutting edge, (2) rectangular saws with 3 (or 4) cutting edges, and (3) paddle-shaped saws. In addition, there are (4) fragments with one cutting edge, (5) with 2 parallel edges, and (6) with 2 edges meeting at right angles.

There are 14 complete or almost complete saws with a single cutting edge (Pl. 17, 8). These are roughly shaped like an ulo, and range in size from only 6 by 2.5 cm. (combination saw and whetstone, Palugvik 4) to a saw probably 20 by 8.5 cm. when complete (Pl. 16, 5). One specimen (Pl. 17, 9) has a notch at one end, like those found on ulo blades for attaching a winding about the grip in place of a handle.

In addition to the 14 complete or nearly complete saws of this type, there are 17 fragments with one cutting edge, but these may have been broken from specimens with 2 or more edges.

There are 8 fragmentary saws with 2 parallel cutting edges (Pl. 17, 5, 6). They vary in width from 2.6 to 10 cm. but are broken at the ends and may therefore be parts of rectangular or paddle-shaped saws. There is no evidence that the long double-edged saw of Kachemak Bay was used in Prince William Sound.[14]

Twelve saws have 2 cutting edges meeting at right angles (Pl. 17, 2), all but 2 probably broken from rectangular blades. One of the apparently unbroken specimens was perhaps intended to have a third edge. Another, made of a fire-cracked boulder chip, seems originally to have had a single edge, but after accidental breakage a second was formed which shows slight signs of use.

There are 7 rectangular saws, 5.5 by 3.7 cm., to 12 (?) by 7.4 cm. Five of these have 3 cutting edges (Pls. 16, 2, 3; 17, 4) and appear to be complete, although the fourth edge is left rough and may indicate that they were broken from paddle-shaped specimens. The remaining 2 rectangular saws, however, have 4 edges each (Pl. 17, 1, 7).

There are, lastly, 4 paddle-shaped specimens, roughly rectangular but narrowed somewhat at one end for a grip (Pl. 16, 4). There is a short cutting edge across the other end, and 2 lateral cutting edges meet this at a rather obtuse angle. One specimen (Pl. 17, 3) differs from the others in having only a single cutting edge across the end, but may be unfinished. The largest (Pl. 16, 1) is 11.5 by 6.3 cm., and the others are only slightly smaller. These paddle-shaped saws were the only type not found in the upper half of the Palugvik midden.

Chugach saws differ from those of Kachemak Bay by being often made of very thin, small slabs, the surfaces of which are usually ground smooth, while the Kachemak Bay specimens are on the whole rougher and

14 De Laguna, 1934, Pl. 22, 2, 4.

PLATE 16. Stone saws, whetstones, scrapers. Scale ½ natural size

1, Paddle-shaped saw, basic schist, Palugvik 2 (33-37-357); 2, rectangular saw, schist, Site 41 near Ellamar (30-25-111); 3, rectangular saw (?), basic schist, Palugvik 1 (33-37-462); 4, paddle-shaped saw, basic schist, Palugvik 1 (33-37-464); 5, single-edged saw, basic schist, Palugvik 1 (33-37-465); 6, paddle-shaped scraper, slaty greenstone, Palugvik 3 (33-37-189); 7, plaque or whetstone with notched edge, soft altered tuff, Palugvik 2 (33-37-361); 8, bar whetstone, slate, large burial cave, Site 16, Hawkins Island (33-37-578); 9, plaque or whetstone with notched edges, Palugvik 1 (33-37-467); 10, whetstone grooved for sharpening points, sandstone, Palugvik 3 (33-37-198); 11, whetstone grooved for sharpening points, sandstone, Palugvik 2 (33-37-364); 12, whetstone, sandstone, Palugvik East Point midden (33-37-572); 13, ulo-shaped scraper, basic schist, Palugvik 1 or 2 (33-37-341); 14, scraper, greenstone, Site 61, Bainbridge Island (30-25-126); 15, whetstone, sandstone, Palugvik, layer (?) (30-25-8)

PLATE 17. Stone saws and whetstones. Scale slightly under ½ natural size

1, Rectangular saw, sandstone, Palugvik 3 (P.715); 2, broken rectangular saw, sandstone, Palugvik 1 (P.709); 3, paddle-shaped saw, sandstone, Palugvik 1 (P.699); 4, rectangular saw, sandstone, Palugvik 3 (P.698); 5, broken rectangular saw, sandstone, Palugvik 4 (P.710); 6, broken rectangular saw, Palugvik East Point burial ledge (P.1093); 7, rectangular saw, Palugvik 1 (P.714); 8, single-edged saw, sandstone, Palugvik 2 (P.697); 9, single-edged saw with notches, sandstone, Palugvik 1 or 2 (P.695); 10, grooved whetstone, sandstone, Palugvik 2 or 3 (P.770); 11, grooved whetstone, sandstone, Palugvik 1 (P.764); 12, whetstone, slate, Palugvik 4 (P.769); 13, bar whetstone, felsite, Palugvik 3 (P.773)

cruder. Only one saw with 3 edges was found in Kachemak Bay, and 3 specimens with 2 parallel edges; all the rest had only one cutting edge. None was older than Period sub-III.[15]

Only 11 saws and fragments were found in the upper part of the Palugvik midden (Layers 3 and 4), and 40 in Layers 1 and 2. None came from the northern and western parts of the sound. This distribution is hard to understand.

The following table does not include a combination saw and ulo (Pl. 27, 6) from Palugvik 2 described in Section 22.

	Saws with 1 Edge	Rectangular Saws	Paddle-shaped Saws
Palugvik 4	33-37-110 P.713	33-37-526	
Palugvik 3	33-37-195	Pl. 17, 1 (4 edges) Pl. 17, 4 P.704	
Palugvik 2	Pl. 17, 8 33-37-356 P.696		Pl. 16, 1
Palugvik 1 or 2	Pl. 17, 9 (notched)		
Palugvik 1	Pl. 16, 5 33-37-458 459 P.693 P.694 P.712	Pl. 16, 3 Pl. 17, 7 (4 edges)	Pl. 16, 4 Pl. 17, 3
Palugvik, layer (?)			33-37-527
Palugvik East Point Grave III	Pl. 48, 3		
Site 41, near Ellamar		Pl. 16, 2	

	Fragments with 1 Edge	Fragments with 2 Parallel Edges	Fragments with 2 Right-angled Edges
Palugvik 4		Pl. 17, 5 33-37-108 109	
Palugvik 3	33-37-196		
Palugvik 2 or 3	P.982a, b		P.707
Palugvik 2	33-37-352 354 358 P.700 P.702	33-37-353	33-37-355
Palugvik 1 or 2	33-37-460	30-25-16	D30-25-17

[15] *Ibid.*, p. 61.

Palugvik 1	33-37-453	P.703 (un-	Pl. 17, 2
	456	finished	33-37-455 (whole?)
	457	rectangular?)	461
	P.701		466
	P.708		P.705
	P.711		P.706
			P.1312
			WSM 1061
Palugvik, layer (?)			WSM 1121 (boulder
			chip)
Palugvik East Point			
Midden		P.1098	
Burial Ledge	33-37-566	Pl. 17, 6	
Site 35, Gravina Bay	P.1172		

10. DOUBLE-POINTED WAR PICKS

A pick of greenstone with conical points at both ends (one of which is now broken) and a groove between 2 ridges for hafting was found in Palugvik 4 (Pl. 13, 1). It was probably 23 cm. long when complete and is 4.2 cm. thick and 2.6 cm. wide. It was identified by Makari, our Eskimo informant, as an unhafted dagger, used in warfare. We can be confident, however, that it was hafted to a T-shaped handle like that of a splitting adz. It closely resembles 2 Tena Indian specimens from the Yukon, identified by a local Indian as weapons for hunting bears as well as for cutting wood.[16] I believe that the Chugach specimen was the head of a picklike war club.

A broken specimen of the same type was found at Site 31 in Sheep Bay (Pl. 12, 6). It is oval in section, with 2 encircling ridges at the middle setting off a groove for lashing. Although both points are now broken off, they seem to have been more sloped from the upper than from the lower side.

11. CHIPPED STONE PICKS (?)

One complete specimen and 5 (or 7?) fragments represent a type which we have called "stone picks." The name is descriptive only of the shape. The specimens, if

hafted, could have been used for digging or, like the double-pointed picks, have been the heads of picklike weapons.

The complete specimen (Pl. 12, 11) is from Site 7 in Hawkins Cut Off. It is made of actinolite schist and is shaped something like a very narrow splitting adz, 26 cm. long and 7 cm. thick. It has been worked entirely by chipping and pecking, and shows no polishing or grinding even at the point. The butt ends of 2 similar implements were also found at the same site (D30-25-70, 30-25-71). An almost complete specimen of greenstone, now (24) cm. long, 7.7 cm. thick, and 4.6 cm. wide, is from Site 35 in Gravina Bay (P.1169). Other fragments were found at Site 2, in Port Etches, Hinchinbrook Island (30-25-284), and Site 32 in Sheep Bay (30-25-99).

In addition, there is a specimen of coarse micaceous schist from Palugvik 4 (33-37-106), 17 by 5.8 cm., and shaped entirely by chipping. It may have been either a pick or an unfinished planing adz blade. Another chipped specimen of schist, with a faint groove for a lashing, comes from Site 65B, Montague Island (33-37-613). It may be the butt end of a splitting adz rather than a fragment of a pick.

What may be a specimen similar to the Chugach chipped stone picks is mentioned by Hrdlička[17] as coming from the latest oc-

---

[16] De Laguna, 1947, Pls. X, 9, XI, 2. The Chugach seem to be the only Eskimo group to have adopted this typically Northwest Coast weapon (pp. 162 f.).

[17] Hrdlička, 1944, p. 333.

cupation levels at Uyak Bay, Kodiak. Aside from this, I know of no other examples from southwestern Alaska.

12. Chipped Blades

Very few chipped stone blades were found in Prince William Sound, in contrast to the many specimens from Kachemak Bay, where they were especially common in the lower layers. In this respect, the Chugach stone industry not only seems to represent an advanced stage of the tendency observable in Kachemak Bay to rely more and more upon ground slate and less upon chipped siliceous stone, but it also resembles more closely that of the Northwest Coast, where chipped stone is virtually unknown.

In addition to the chipped scrapers (section 13) and the chipped slate ulo blades (section 23), there are only 10 examples of chipped stone blades in the collections.

From Palugvik 4 there is a broken and unfinished lance blade of green chert (altered greenstone). It is leaf-shaped with a broad tang, is 3 cm. wide, and was probably 6 cm. long when complete (Pl. 14, 5).[18]

A broken chert knife or lance blade (Pl. 14, 4), 2.6 cm. wide, finely retouched along both edges and on both surfaces, comes from Palugvik, layer unknown. One end is broken off.

Also from Palugvik, layer unknown, is half of an oval flake of black chert, retouched on one surface (Pl. 14, 8). It is 8.5 cm. long and was probably the blade for a knife or scraper.[19]

Another knife or scraper blade was found about 2 feet below the surface of Palutat Cave (Pl. 14, 9). It is a triangular flake of slightly altered slate, 7 by 4.8 cm., retouched along 2 edges which meet at right angles; the third edge is blunt.[20]

A triangular blade of chipped micaceous slate, 4.5 by 2 cm., probably for an arrow or dart, was found one foot below the surface of Palutat Cave (Pl. 28, 10). A similar

blade of phyllitic slate, 6.5 by 1.2 cm., comes from Palugvik 2 (Pl. 29, 10). These resemble some of the phyllite blades from Kachemak Bay, which are especially characteristic of the Second Period.[21]

There are also 4 unfinished rectangular blades, chipped along the 2 longer edges. These were possibly blanks being worked into blades for scrapers, lances, or knives. Two are of slate, measuring about 3.5 cm. in width and now 7 cm. long, and come from Palugvik 4 (33-37-95) and Grave B2, Palutat Cave (33-37-667). The third, from Site 62, Evans Island (33-37-620) is of slaty greenstone and is possibly a broken planing adz blade which was being reshaped into a scraper like that illustrated in Plate 16, 14. A similar fragment of chipped greenstone is from Palugvik, layer unknown (P.1047).

In addition, only 4 boulder chips, that is, sharp oval fragments split from beach cobbles, were found in Prince William Sound, in striking contrast to the hundreds discovered in Kachemak Bay from every site and every culture stage. One of these is a large specimen of sandstone, 16 by 11 cm., which was among the few grave goods recovered from the large burial cave at Site 16, Hawkins Island (33-37-577). There was also a specimen from Palugvik 1 or 2 (P.726) which may have been used as a scraper, and another from Palugvik, layer unknown, which has already been mentioned in section 9 as a saw. It is not clear whether this chip was intentionally formed or whether it was accidentally split from a fire-cracked boulder. The fourth boulder chip, a scraper from Palugvik 1 (Pl. 18, 8), is described in section 13.

13. Stone Scrapers

In addition to the specimens already mentioned in section 12, which may have been used as scrapers, or intended for such use, the collections contain 32 large chipped blades which were probably scrapers for working skins.

[18] Cf. de Laguna, 1934, Pl. 30, 26, from Kachemak Bay III or later.
[19] Cf., ibid., Pl. 30, 24, from Kachemak Bay III.
[20] Cf. ibid., Pl. 30, 37, from Kachemak Bay III.

[21] Ibid., p. 69, Pl. 30, 8.

Seven blades with straight dull back and curved working edge have the semilunar shape traditionally associated with ulo blades (Pl. 16, *13*). They are of slate, schist, and dolerite, ranging in size from 7 by 5 cm. (Pl. 18, *10*) to 12 by 14.6 cm. (Pl. 18, *14*). One made from a slate chip with polished surfaces (Pl. 18, *9*) should perhaps be included among the chipped ulo blades (section 23). One is narrowed at one end as if for a lateral grip (33-37-340), and another (Pl. 18, *11*) is almost paddle-shaped. These ulo-shaped scrapers are all from Palugvik 1 and 2.[22]

Closely related to these is a scraper from Palugvik 1 (Pl. 18, *8*) made of a greenstone boulder chip, 6.2 by 7.2 cm. A boulder chip from Palugvik 1 or 2 (P.726) may also have been used as a scraper. Both of these have been mentioned in the preceding section.

We may think of the ulo-like shape as being modified in 2 ways: first, by a lateral elongation to produce a rectangular scraper with one or 2 long edges (i.e., like some of the straight-edged blades for ulos or for men's knives); and, second, by a dorsal prolongation to produce a paddle-shaped scraper with handle and short transverse edge (i.e., like the paddle-shaped saws).

There are 10 (or 12?) paddle-shaped scrapers of slate, slaty greenstone, schist, etc. (Pls. 16, *6;* 18, *1, 2, 4* to *6*). The surface may be partially smoothed, and occasionally one of the long edges of the handle may also show wear. These scrapers range in size from 7.5 by 3.3 cm. (Pl. 18, *1*) to

over 17.5 cm. in length (Pl. 18, *6*) or 6 cm. in width. Only one specimen (Pl. 18, 2) has a sharp edge. It is now (5) by 2.1 cm. and may have been hafted, perhaps in an adzlike handle. A second doubtful specimen, showing no signs of use, was found in Grave A, Palutat Cave. Paddle-shaped scrapers seem to be fairly evenly distributed through the layers of the Palugvik midden, and similar specimens with polished edge are known from Kachemak Bay III.[23]

There are 6 rectangular scrapers with fairly well-defined shape. One of these, a slate slab with rough surface and 3 chipped edges, measuring 22.1 by 13.1 cm. (Pl. 18, *12*), may possibly be an unfinished ulo. The largest is a split slab of slate, 30.4 by 7.7 cm., evidently used without further shaping (P.778). The smallest is of dolerite, only 9.5 by 4 cm., with one slightly curved working edge (Pl. 18, *3*). These rectangular specimens are all from Palugvik 1 and 2 and Sites 61 and 62 (Pl. 16, *14*). We have already mentioned (section 12) similar specimens from Palugvik, layer unknown, and Site 62.

There are also 6 or 7 scrapers of irregular shape, some of which appear to be variants of the rectangular form. One (Pl. 18, *13*) is simply a slab of sawed slate; another was broken and reused as a whetstone (P.772); a third has been used as both scraper and whetstone (Pl. 18, *7*).

It is curious that, of 24 specimens from the Palugvik midden, only 3 are definitely known to come from the upper half, and all of these are paddle-shaped. One irregular specimen is from Layer 2 (or 3).

[22] Cf. chipped quartz scraper from Kachemak Bay III (*ibid.*, Pl. 35, *3*).

[23] *Ibid.*, Pl. 34, *5, 9*.

PLATE 18. Stone scrapers. Scale ⅓ natural size

1, Chipped, unfinished, paddle-shaped scraper, Palugvik 1 or 2 (P.1007); 2, paddle-shaped scraper (?) with sharp edge, Palugvik, layer (?) (P.1200); 3, rectangular scraper, dolerite (working edge to left), Palugvik 2 (P.689); 4, paddle-shaped scraper, slaty schist, Palugvik 2 (P.690); 5, paddle-shaped scraper, chipped slate, Site 35, Port Gravina (P.1170); 6, paddle-shaped scraper, Palugvik 3 (P.1330); 7, stone slab used as scraper and whetstone, Palugvik 2 (P.691); 8, boulder chip used as scraper, greenstone, Palugvik 1 (P.990); 9, ulo-shaped scraper, chipped slate, Palugvik 1 (P.719); 10, ulo-shaped scraper, dolerite, Palugvik 1 (P.688); 11, ulo-shaped scraper, slate, Palugvik 1 (P.687); 12, scraper or unfinished ulo, slate, Site 62, Evans Island (P.1165); 13, sawed slate used as scraper, Palugvik 2 (or 3) (P.989); 14, ulo-shaped scraper, Palugvik 2 (P.725)

PLATE 19. Stone plaques. Scale ⅔ natural size

1, Decorated slate plaque, Palugvik, layer (?) (P.1066) (see Fig. 31) ; 2, decorated slate plaque, Palugvik 1 (P.780) (see Fig. 27) ; 3, decorated slate plaque, Palugvik 1 (P.782) (see Fig. 26) ; 4, decorated slate plaque (inverted), Palugvik 2 (P.781) (see Fig. 25) ; 5, slate plaque with hole (fits No. 8?), Palugvik East Point burial ledge (P.1096) ; 6, notched greenstone plaque, Palugvik 2 (P.730) ; 7, polished slate plaque, Palugvik 2 (P.728) ; 8, notched slate plaque (fits No. 5?), Palugvik 1 (P.984) ; 9, notched plaque, mica schist, Palugvik 1 (P.729) ; 10, notched plaque, sandstone, Palugvik 2 (P.983)

	Ulo-shaped	Paddle-shaped	Rectangular	Irregular
Palugvik 4		33-37-519		
Palugvik 3		Pl. 16, 6		
		Pl. 18, 6		
Palugvik 2 (or 3)				Pl. 18, 13
Palugvik 2	Pl. 18, 14	Pl. 18, 4	Pl. 18, 3	Pl. 18, 7
	33-37-340	33-37-338	P.778	P.772 (whetstone)
Palugvik 1 or 2	Pl. 16, 13	Pl. 18, 1		P.1183
		33-37-339		
Palugvik 1	Pl. 18, 9	33-37-447	33-37-446	Pl. 18, 8
	Pl. 18, 10		P.692	
	Pl. 18, 11			
	33-37-448			
Palugvik, layer (?)		Pl. 18, 2	(cf. P.1047)	33-37-521
		33-37-520		
Site 35, Port Gravina		Pl. 18, 5		
Site 61, Bainbridge Island			Pl. 16, 14	
Site 62, Evans Island			Pl. 18, 12	
			(cf. 33-37-620)	
Palutat Cave		P.1211		P.1210
		(Grave A)		

14. GROOVED STONES AND BOLA (?)

Nine grooved stones, all but one of simple types, were found in Prince William Sound. These are ovoid or egg-shaped boulders of sandstone, diorite, greenstone schist, or other compact, fine-grained rocks, ranging in length from 8 to 13 cm., and grooved for the attachment of a cord. Fred Allen, Lee Pratt's Chugach informant who died before 1930, told him that a common weapon was made of a round or oblong boulder, about the size of a doubled fist, with a groove around the middle to which was fastened a long line of sealskin. The natives were supposed to be able to kill bear, black or Kodiak brown, by throwing this weapon. Paul Elie Chimowitski said that the throwing stone was fastened to the user's wrist by a line 3 or 4 fathoms long (the length is surely exaggerated). It was a weapon used for braining personal enemies. The murderer traditionally waited on the roof of his victim's house to attack him

when he came out at night to urinate. Makari reported at first that the grooved stone was tied by a thong 6 feet long to a man's wrist, and that it was thrown like a ball. Later, he claimed that the strap was much shorter and that the weapon was used only to brain a person coming out of a house. The stone was called an·uaq. Black Stepan of Chenega gave the name aη·uaq to the grooved stone, but reported that one was tied to each end of a thong about 3 or 4 feet long. The thong was grasped in the middle and whirled around the head to strike a direct blow, not thrown. This weapon was used in war. Although these accounts are not completely consistent, there is no doubt that our grooved stones were used as weapons, and several are, in fact, battered from hard and violent usage.

Two specimens, from Palugvik 1 (Pl. 21, 4) and from the beach at Palugvik East Point (Pl. 20, 7), are grooved around the longer circumference. A third stone, from

Palugvik, layer unknown (Pl. 21, 6), which has been partially shaped by pecking, should also be classed with these, since there are partial grooves over both ends.

Five specimens are grooved about the shorter circumference. These are from Palugvik 2 (Pl. 20, 8), Palugvik 1 or 2 (33-37-367), Palugvik 1 (P.749), Site 6 on Hinchinbrook Island (D30-25-50), and Site 56 on Chenega Island (33-37-628).

The most elaborately grooved specimen is from Palugvik 4 (Pl. 21, 7). It is grooved around the middle and over both ends. The groove at one end is very short and may be simply the result of battering; the other is prolonged down one side to meet the encircling groove.

In addition to these grooved specimens, a ball of greenstone (Pl. 20, 6), 6 cm. in diameter, and a partially shaped ball of quartzite (Pl. 20, 5), 6 by 7 cm., were found together in Palugvik 3. The second specimen would have been considered only as a battered hammerstone, were not the greenstone ball so carefully shaped. Although neither specimen is grooved, their associa-

tion suggests that they were weights for a double bola, like the weapon described by Black Stepan, in which case they may have been tied up in skin bags for attachment to the cord.

15. HAMMERSTONES

There are 46 hammerstones in the collections from Prince William Sound. These fall into 2 types: rounded or ovoid beach stones, from 5 to 11.7 cm. in diameter, pounded on the ends and sometimes on the edges and sides (Pls. 20, 9, 11; 21, 1, 3); and elongated beach stones, naturally shaped like pestles, which were pounded on one or both ends (Pls. 20, 4; 21, 2). The latter vary in length from 7 to 23.5 cm. The rocks selected were greenstone, sandstone, slate, granite, dolerite, serpentine, etc. A pestle-shaped specimen from Site 65B, Montague Island, was originally a splitting adz or a stone chisel (P.1153). Another specimen from the same site is of slate and has also served as a whetstone (P.1156).

The distribution of these hammerstones is:

	Ovoid	Pestle-shaped
Palugvik 4	33-37-112	33-37-113
	P.750	114
		115
Palugvik 3	Pl. 20, 11	P.754
	33-37-201	P.755
	P.752	
	P.753	
	P.757	
Palugvik 2	33-37-368	
Palugvik 1 or 2	P.756	

PLATE 20. Grooved stones, hammerstones, mauls. Scale ⅓ natural size

1, Large double-edged lance or knife blade, slate, Site 65B, Montague Island (33-37-606); 2, ulo blade, unpolished slate chip, Palugvik 4 (33-37-76); 3, knife blade, green chert, Palugvik East Point burial ledge (33-37-565); 4, pestle-shaped hammerstone, slate (?), Site 65B, Montague Island (33-37-617); 5 and 6, bola (?) balls of quartzite and greenstone, found together, Palugvik 3 (33-37-204, 203); 7, grooved stone, sandstone, Palugvik East Point beach (30-25-29); 8, grooved stone, sandstone, Palugvik 2 (33-37-366); 9, hammerstone, sandstone, Site 6, Hinchinbrook Island (30-25-49); 10, pestle, sandstone, Site 54, Jackpot Bay (33-37-646); 11, hammerstone, dolerite, Palugvik 3 (33-37-202); 12, unfinished hunter's lamp (?), Site 6, Hinchinbrook Island (30-25-53); 13, maul head, sandstone, Site 65A, Montague Island (33-37-602); 14, maul head, altered porphyry, Site 2, Hinchinbrook Island (30-25-44); 15, maul head (?), sandstone, Site 65B, Montague Island (33-37-611); 16, maul head, granite, near Site 21, Mummy Island (30-25-91)

PLATE 21. Grooved stones, hammerstones, pestles. Scale ⅓ natural size

1, Hammerstone, Palutat Cave, depth 18 to 24 inches (P.1204) ; 2, hammerstone, Site 65B, Montague Island (P.1152) ; 3, hammerstone, Palùgvik 1 (P.751) ; 4, grooved stone, Palugvik 1 (P.1182) ;
5, maul head, Site 65A, Montague Island (P.1144) ; 6, grooved stone, Palugvik, layer (?) (P.1050) ;
7, grooved stone, Palugvik 4 (P.748) ; 8, pestle, meta-greenstone, Chenega Church Collection
(P.1128) ; 9, pestle fragment, Palùgvik 1 (P.1184) ; 10, maul head, Site 65A, Montague Island
(P.1143)

Palugvik 1	Pl. 21, *3*	
	33-37-472	
Palugvik, layer (?)	33-37-531	33-37-532
	P.1045	533
		P.1044
Site 2, Hinchinbrook Island	D30-25-45	
Site 6, Hinchinbrook Island	Pl. 20, *9*	
Site 7, Hawkins Cut Off		D30-25-73a
		30-25-74
		75
Site 16, Hawkins Island	30-25-32	
Site 17, Hawkins Island	30-25-4	
Beach at Site 20, Mummy Island		30-25-88
Site 40, Ellamar		30-25-104
Palutat Cave, surface	33-37-670	
18″-2′	Pl. 21, *1*	
Chenega Church Collection		33-37-647
Site 56, Chenega Island	P.1137	
Site 61, Bainbridge Island	30-25-124	30-25-125
Site 62, Evans Island	33-37-621	
	P.1164	
Site 65A, Montague Island	33-37-603	
	P.1145	
	WSM X-114	
Site 65B, Montague Island		Pl. 20, *4*
		Pl. 21, *2*
		P.1153
		P.1156
		WSM X-130

In addition to the specimens listed above, there is a sandstone boulder from Palugvik, layer unknown, measuring 15 by 9.5 cm. (33-37-534), which is deeply pitted by blows on one side. It may have been used either as a hammerstone or as an anvil. A similar specimen from Palugvik 1 (?) (P.779), 12.8 by 9.9 cm. in diameter and 4.1 cm. thick, is battered on the edges and ground hollow on one face. It was probably used as an anvil, possibly as a mortar.

16. Maul Heads

Five maul heads, grooved for hafting, and one doubtful specimen were obtained. Mauls may have been used for driving wedges or stakes or for working native copper. These heads are made of granite, sandstone, and altered porphyry; they range in length from 11 to 16.5 cm. and in their maximum diameter at the striking end from 5.5 to 10.5 cm. Three specimens are oval or round in section; 2 of these have a wide groove which runs only part way around, like the groove on a splitting adz. These are from Site 65A, Montague Island (Pl. 21, *10*), and from Site 2, Hinchinbrook Island (Pl. 20, *14*). A smaller cylindrical specimen, from Site 65A, is almost encircled by a narrow groove (Pl. 20, *13*).

The last 2 specimens are roughly triangular in section with an interrupted groove across the 3 angles. They come

PLATE 22. Mortars, pestles, grinding blocks. Scale ½ natural size

1, Pestle, hard crystalline rock, near Site 16, Hawkins Island (35-26-1) ; 2, mortar, sandstone, Ellamar, Site 40 (33-37-591) ; 3, mortar, whale vertebra, Site 7, Hawkins Cut Off (33-37-582) ; 4, grinding block, arkosic sandstone, Palugvik layer (?) (33-37-530) ; 5, grinding block, arkosic sandstone, Palugvik 1 or 2 (33-37-363)

from Site 65A (Pl. 21, *5*) and from the beach below the small burial cave, Site 21, on Mummy Island (Pl. 20, *16*).

A broken specimen from Site 65B (Pl. 20, *15*) is shaped like the butt end of a large splitting adz but is made of sandstone, an unsuitable material for an adz blade. Since one end is broken, the identification of this specimen is uncertain.

A completely grooved hammer head comes from Kachemak Bay, as does a maul head like that in Plate 20, *14*. A specimen similar to the latter was found in the Port Graham area, but none of these can be dated.[24] Hrdlička found grooved heads for mauls and for hammers at Uyak Bay, Kodiak Island. On the basis of a preliminary survey, Heizer finds that mauls were relatively more important in the earlier than in the later layers.[25]

17. PESTLES

In addition to the hammerstones which may have been used as pestles, we obtained 3 carefully shaped stone pestles, and 2 more have also been found in Prince William Sound.

A fine specimen of meta-greenstone is from the Chenega Church Collection (Pl. 21, *8*). It has a flaring circular base or striking end, 10 cm. in diameter, and a conical shaft or hand grip which tapers to a diameter of 5.5 cm. just below the enlarged head. The head has 8 facets, making a flattened octagonal cross section 7 cm. wide, the 2 wider facets on each side being slightly concave. The total height of the specimen is 18.8 cm.

A pestle of hard crystalline rock from the vicinity of Site 16 on Hawkins Island (Pl. 22, *1*) is almost identical with the first, except that it stands 21 cm. high. The third pestle is of sandstone and is said to have been found on the little island, Site 54, at the mouth of Jackpot Bay (Pl. 20, *10*). It

is not only smaller than the others, measuring 6 cm. in diameter at the base and 16.5 cm. in height, but the faceted "head" is so much longer in proportion—11 cm. long— that the head, and not the tapering shaft below, must have served as the handle. Lee Pratt found a pestle with faceted head on Knight Island.

Will Chase of Cordova has a sandstone pestle shaped like a telephone receiver, which is said to have come from one of the Egg Islands between Prince William Sound and the mouth of the Copper River. These islands were uninhabited but were visited by both Eyak and Chugach sea otter hunters.

Two broken specimens of sandstone, carefully shaped by fine pecking, come from Palugvik 1 (Pl. 21, *9*) and Site 65A, Montague Island (33-37-595). They are rounded at the end and have a flattened oval cross section, 8.5 by 6.4 and 7 by 4.5 cm., respectively. They are now (11.5) and (17) cm. long, and appear to have been the tops of pestles.

A battered implement of greenstone from Site 42, "Indian Village" in Galena Bay, may be a broken pestle (30-25-111). It is now (9) cm. long, and is circular in section with a diameter of 5.5 cm. at the broken end. This end has been shaped into a rough wedge by violent blows, suggesting an attempt to rework the broken implement into a chisel or adz blade.

Although these specimens have been described as pestles because of their shape, they may have served as hammers or pile drivers rather than as implements to crush materials placed in a mortar. Two modern Chugach pestles in the Washington State Museum, used to crush berries, are made of wood and have a slender handle attached to an almost disklike base.

18. MORTARS

There are 3 stone mortars and one of bone in the collections, in addition to a number of doubtful stone specimens which have been tentatively identified as lamps.

[24] *Ibid.*, Pls. 17, *1*; 21, *6*, pp. 58 f.
[25] Hrdlička, 1944, Figs. 75, 76 (mauls), 118 (hammer; although this is described as having pits for the fingers, it looks rather as if it had been hafted), p. 344; Heizer, 1946, p. 149.

PLATE 23. Lamps. Scale slightly under ½ natural size

1, Lamp, arkosic sandstone, Chenega Church Collection (33-37-648)-; 2, naturally hollow sandstone boulder used as a lamp, Palugvik 2 (33-37-369) ; 3, bowl, sandstone, Palugvik East Point
burial ledge (33-37-567) ; 4, lamp, altered gabbro, Palugvik 3 or 4 (33-37-107) ; 5, lamp, Palutat
Cave, depth 3 feet to 3 feet 6 inches (33-37-671) ; 6, unfinished hunter's lamp, Site 42, Galena
Bay (30-25-113)

One mortar is an irregular sandstone boulder from Site 40 at Ellamar (Pl. 22, 2), in which a circular depression, 7.5 cm. in diameter and 4 cm. deep, has been made by grinding and pounding. A similar but smaller boulder from Site 62, Evans Island (P.1163), has a pecked hollow 5.5 cm. in diameter and only 1 cm. deep. From Palugvik, layer unknown (Pl. 24, 7), is a roughly circular sandstone dish, 23.6 by 24.5 cm. in diameter, evidently a naturally hollow stone, in which the depression has been enlarged by pecking. The rim is damaged, and there are no signs of use, either as a mortar or as a lamp, so that identification is uncertain.

There are also 2 other doubtful stone specimens. One is a round beach pebble from the Chenega Church Collection (Pl. 24, 6) with a slight depression on one side, which may have been a small mortar, an unfinished toy lamp, or even a pitted hammerstone. The second, a battered ovoid pebble with a shallow depression ground on one surface, comes from Palugvik 1 (?) (P.779), and has already been mentioned as a possible hammerstone or anvil. It may, however, have been a small mortar.

A mortar made from a whale vertebra (Pl. 22, 3) was found by Makari at Site 7, Hawkins Cut Off, and was identified by him as a mortar for snuff, an article which was, of course, introduced by the Russians. The shape, that of a goblet, also seems to be modern. The specimen is 11 cm. high and 16 cm. in diameter at the rim. Hrdlička has published the picture of a similarly shaped but cruder Aleut specimen, without, however, any information as to age or provenience.[26]

In Joe Bourke's collection at Valdez there are one or 2 whale vertebra mortars, also supposed to have been used in the preparation of snuff. These are, however, simple bowls, without narrowed stems and distinct bases, like a modern Aleut bone mortar for tobacco published by Jochelson.[27] Similar

bone vessels from Kodiak and the Aleutians have been variously described or identified as dishes, pots, lamps, and lamp stands, but their functions remain rather uncertain since few of them exhibit signs of charring, of organic incrustations, or of pounding, which might determine their uses.[28] Some may, of course, have been mortars. In any case, we have evidence that bone vessels were used in late prehistoric times in southwestern Alaska, and that such utensils were adapted as snuff mortars when tobacco was introduced.

A well-made stone mortar was found in Kachemak Bay, although it cannot be assigned to any particular cultural stage. A fragment, probably of a worn-out mortar, comes from the Third Period. Here, as in Prince William Sound, there are other crude stone vessels which might be either makeshift lamps or mortars.[29]

19. LAMPS

Twenty-six stone lamps were obtained in Prince William Sound. They are oval or roughly oval in outline, but are usually broader at the back than at the front end where the lip was placed. These lamps were used for light alone, not for cooking, which was carried on at the fire in the center of the main room of the house. If lit in the small "sweat bath" and sleeping room of the house, the lamp must have afforded a little heat as well as light. Although lamps were found in all areas of the sound, they are not as common as might have been expected, perhaps because they were not needed very much when the fire in the main room was burning brightly.

These lamps vary in size from 26.6 by 23.4 cm. (Pl. 24, 4) to 12 by 10 cm. (Pl. 23, 2). The longer diameter of most specimens is between 15 and 20 cm. The height or thickness ranges from 5 to 10 cm. (Pl. 25, 2), with an average of about 7 cm. The

26 Hrdlička, 1945, Fig. 195.
27 Jochelson, 1925, Pl. 20, 10.

28 Ibid., Pl. 20, 1, 2, 5, 7 (lamps), 6 (bowl), pp. 73 ff.; Hrdlička, 1944, Fig. 154 (lamp), pp. 223, 245, and unpublished specimens; 1945, Fig. 196 (pots), pp. 57, 441, 451.
29 De Laguna, 1934, Pls. 18, 4; 21, 4, pp. 60, 63, 174.

PLATE 24. Lamps and stone vessels. Scale $\frac{3}{10}$ natural size

1, Lamp, sandstone, near middle burial cave, Site 26, near Mummy Island (P.1178); 2, lamp, Palugvik 1 (P.759); 3, lamp, Palugvik, layer (?) (P.1049); 4, lamp, iqałʋq island in Port Gravina (P.1173); 5, hunter's lamp, Chenega Village (P.1119); 6, pitted pebble used as mortar or toy (?), Chenega Church Collection (P.1120); 7, dish, sandstone, Palugvik, layer (?) (P.1181)

bowl may be from 1 to 4 cm. deep. A number of specimens have a lip for the wick at the narrower end of the bowl. Materials are arkosic sandstone, greenstone, gabbro, granite, syenite, volcanic tuff, diorite, and unidentified hard rocks.

Some of the specimens are made of naturally hollow beach boulders, the shape of which has been very little altered, and the identification of these as lamps is therefore somewhat uncertain. Such specimens are from Palugvik 2 (Pl. 23, 2) ; Site 7, Hawkins Cut Off (30-25-72) ; and Site 35, Gravina Bay (33-37-589).

Other lamps made from boulders have had the bowl hollowed out by pecking and grinding. Two such specimens are from Site 56 on Chenega Island (33-37-629, 630), and one of these has a well-defined wick lip, like a spout cut through the rim. A lamp from Palugvik 1 (Pl. 24, 2) also has a clearly marked lip for the wick and a polished area on 'the thick bottom below the lip.

Two rather crude lamps, from Ellamar (Pl. 25, 3) and the Chenega Church Collection (P.1121), are so shaped that they tilt to one side, as if the wick had been laid against the side, not at one end. This feature was also noted on a crude lamp from Kachemak Bay.[30]

The collections contain 5 rather narrow oval lamps. A specimen from the Chenega Church Collection (Pl. 23, 1), another from Ellamar (P.1174), and a third from Site 65A, Montague Island (33-37-604), are all of sandstone and lack a lip. A broken sandstone lamp from Site 56, Chenega Island (P.1138), seems to have been irregular in shape but has a wick lip. A rather nicely made lamp from Site 7 in Hawkins Cut Off has an unusually broad lip, 3 cm. wide (P.546). This lamp was found by Makari and was actually used by him for a time.

A lamp from Ellamar (Pl. 25, 1) is unusual in having a little shelf, 3 cm. wide, on the inside of the bowl instead of the ordinary wick lip customarily cut into the rim.

Other lamps are more nearly circular in outline. A typical specimen, from the Chenega Church Collection (Pl. 25, 4), is so shaped that the flat bottom of the bowl tips forward toward the wick lip. The small pit in the bowl is probably due to an accident. A smaller lamp of the same kind is from Palugvik, layer unknown (Pl. 24, 3). Other lamps, not quite so broad, are from Ellamar (WSM X-170) and Site 65A on Montague Island (Pl. 25, 2). On all of these the rim and side are evenly rounded.

Two lamps, one from iqaɬʋq Island in Port Gravina (Pl. 24, 4) and a broken specimen from Site 65B on Montague Island (33-37-618), are broad and flat with a wide, horizontal, and slightly concave rim, halfway through which has been cut a crescentic lip about 6 cm. wide. A lamp of this kind was found in Kachemak Bay, and the style is reported to be characteristic of southwestern Kodiak Island and of the latest period at Uyak Bay.[31]

There are 2 lamps with almost straight rear ends and rather pointed fore ends, rather similar to certain Aleut lamps that Jochelson called "sadiron shaped."[32] One of these is the decorated specimen from Palugvik described below (Pl. 23, 4), and the other is a rather crude vessel from a depth of about 3 feet below the surface in Palutat Cave. The latter (Pl. 23, 5) has a wick lip like the spout of a pitcher.

The remaining 5 lamps from Prince William Sound have very slight ornamental features suggesting the more elaborately decorated lamps of Kachemak Bay III and Kodiak Island. The first of these is a broken greenstone specimen (33-37-583) from Site 7 in Hawkins Cut Off, with a bulge on the outside at the front. A specimen of altered gabbro from Site 23 on Mummy Island (Pl. 25, 5) has a more pronounced bulge in the same place. An egg-shaped sandstone lamp, found near a burial cave at Site 26, near

---

[30] Ibid., p. 63, Pl. 23, 1.

[31] Ibid., Pl. 24, 1; Hrdlička, 1944, Fig. 147, p. 457; Heizer, 1946, p. 159.

[32] Jochelson, 1925 pp. 74, 77. Cf. Hrdlička, 1945, Fig. 123, "Kashega-type"; Quimby, 1946a.

Mummy Island (Pl. 24, *1*), has a slightly concave side interrupted by a ridge 4 cm. wide below the lip. The most carefully finished specimen of all is from Palugvik 3 or 4 (Pl. 23, *4*). It is of gabbro, sadiron-shaped, with a very evenly rounded rim and bottom and almost vertical side. The bowl is polished, and the grinding has resulted in a groove along each side of the bowl which undercuts the rim on the inside. On the exterior, just below the lip, is a vertical ridge 4 cm. long and 2 cm. wide. A groove around the outside of the lamp is interrupted at this ridge and also at the straight back of the lamp.

An encircling groove on the outside was reported on a stone "dish" or lamp, said to have been found in Sheep Bay. The specimen was described as about 25 cm. in diameter and only 4 or 5 cm. thick. Lamps and stone "dishes" decorated with "flowers" are said to have been found in a sub-beach midden in Port Gravina. While this report should be treated with caution, it suggests that some Chugach lamps may have had festoon-like decorations, similar to those on the outside of the large lamps with human figure found on Cook Inlet and Kenai Peninsula, and ascribable to Kachemak Bay III.[33]

The collection also contains a fragment of worked stone from Palugvik 3 (P.988), which may represent the rim of a lamp decorated by a ridge between 2 grooves.

The provenience of these lamps is: Palugvik 3 or 4, Pl. 23, *4;* Palugvik 3, P.988 (lamp? fragment); Palugvik 2, Pl. 23, *2;* Palugvik 1, Pl. 24, *2;* Palugvik, layer unknown, Pl. 24, *3;* Site 7, Hawkins Cut Off, 30-25-72, 33-37-583, P.546; Site 23, Mummy Island, Pl. 25, *5;* Burial Cave, Site 26, Mummy Island, Pl. 24, *1;* iqaɫuq Island, Gravina Bay, Pl. 24, *4;* Site 35, Gravina Bay, 33-37-589; Site 40, Ellamar, Pl. 25, *1, 3,* P.1174, WSM X-170; Palutat Cave, depth 3 feet, Pl. 23, *5;* Chenega Church Collection, Pls. 23, *1,* 25, *4,* P.1121; Site 56, Chenega Island, 33-37-629, 630, P.1138; Site

65A, Montague Island, Pl. 25, *2,* 33-37-604; Site 65B, Montague Island, 33-37-618.

20. HUNTERS' (?) LAMPS

Seven specimens are unusually small, and may have been intended not for ordinary use as lamps in a house but for emergency service on hunting trips. Small lamps were carried by sea otter hunters, who not only used them for light when camping but also warmed themselves by squatting over them. Hunters' lamps were found in Kachemak Bay, Kodiak, and the Aleutians.[34]

Two naturally hollow stones have already been mentioned in the previous section. One from Palugvik 2 (Pl. 23, *2*) measures only 12 by 10 cm.; the second from Site 35, Port Gravina (33-37-589), is 11 by (?) cm. In addition, there is a broken sandstone lamp, 12 by 9 (?) cm., with a slight lip, from Site 65B, Montague Island (P.1155). A flat pebble, 9.3 by 7.2 cm., with a shallow oval bowl, comes from the beach at Chenega Village and was identified by the natives as a lamp (Pl. 24, *5*). Three partially worked beach pebbles, about 10 cm. in diameter, may also have been intended for hunters' lamps. One, from Site 42 in Galena Bay (Pl. 23, *6*), has a pecked groove outlining the unfinished bowl. The other 2, from Site 40 at Ellamar (D30-25-106) and Site 6, Hinchinbrook Island (Pl. 20, *12*), may possibly be pitted hammerstones.

21. STONE DISH

In addition to the stone vessels tentatively identified as mortars or lamps, there is a broken bowl of fine-grained sandstone from the burial ledge at Palugvik East Point (Pl. 23, *3*). It was originally hemispherical, 11 or 12 cm. in diameter. The specimen is badly weathered, and it is now impossible to ascertain its function. It should be remembered that the Chugach Eskimo did not use stone vessels as cooking pots. Food was boiled in baskets by means

---

[33] De Laguna, 1934, Pls. 69; 70, *2.*

[34] Jochelson, 1925, p. 74; de Laguna, 1934, p. 67; Hrdlička, 1944, pp. 442 ff., refers to them as "baby lamps."

PLATE 25. Lamps. Scale approximately ⅕ natural size

1, Lamp, grano-diorite, Ellamar, Site 40 (30-25-108) ; 2, lamp, arkosic sandstone, Site 65A, Montague Island (33-37-605) ; 3, lamp, volcanic tuff, Ellamar, Site 40 (30-35-107) ; 4, lamp, arkosic sandstone, Chenega Church Collection (33-37-649) ; 5, lamp, altered gabbro, Site 23, Mummy Island (30-25-86)

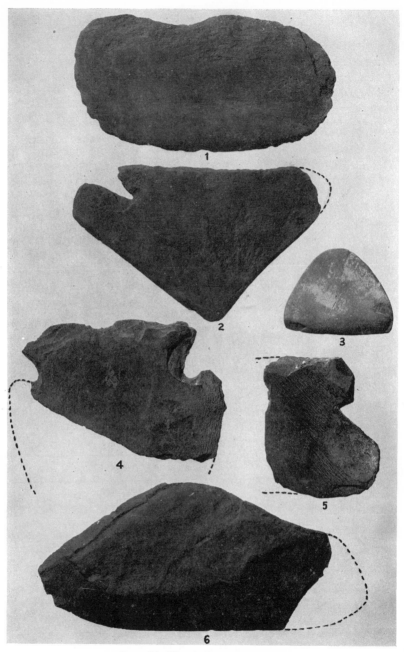

PLATE 26. Ulos. Scale ⅗ natural size

1, Ulo with curved edge, slate, Palugvik 3 (33-37-164) ; 2, ulo with 2 straight edges and notch, slate, Palugvik East Point burial ledge (33-37-560) ; 3, ulo with straight edge, slate, Palugvik 4 (33-37-74) ; 4, ulo with notches, slate, Palugvik, layer (?) (33-37-506) ; 5, ulo with notch, slate, Palugvik 2 (33-37-306) ; 6, ulo with straight edge, slate, Palugvik, layer (?) (33-37-507)

of hot rocks, baked in pits lined with hot rocks, or roasted on hot stone slabs or spits.

This specimen might be compared to the stone and "pottery" vessels described by Quimby from Amaknak Island—elliptical or oval bowls which were apparently used for cooking. Although some seem to show evidence of a certain amount of modeling while the material was relatively soft, I suspect that they were made primarily by carving and gouging out partly indurated clay, already naturally "tempered" with sand and/or grit, and that this material turned to stone and "pottery" when dried and heated.[35] The Aleut vessels would then, if I am correct, represent stoneworking techniques more closely than those associated with true pottery.

22. ULO BLADES

There are 26 slate ulo blades in the collections, and 9 fragments which are probably parts of such blades. The complete specimens range in size from 5.5 by 4.2 cm. (Pl. 26, 3) to 13.4 by 7 cm. (Pl. 26, 1). A broken specimen from Site 65A, Montague Island (33-37-594), was probably 16 or 17 cm. long when complete, and a blade from the Palugvik East Point burial ledge is 11.1 cm. long and almost 10 cm. wide (Pl. 27, 7).

Although it is impossible to divide the specimens into sharply defined groups, 16 have rather straight cutting edges (Pls. 26, 3, 6; 27, 1), and 11 have convexly curved edges (Pls. 26, 1; 27, 7, 8).

Some of the straight-edged specimens are unusual in having 2 cutting edges. For example, a broken blade from Palugvik 3 (33-37-165) and another from Palugvik 2 (33-37-310) are sharpened on the unbroken end as well as on the long edge. A fragment from Palugvik 3 (33-37-167) has 2 sharp edges meeting at an obtuse angle. A very unusual specimen from the burial ledge at Palugvik East Point (Pl. 26, 2) has 2 sharp edges meeting at right angles.[36]

Eight blades, including both straight and curved edge forms, are notched near the back for a lashing or for hafting (Pls. 26, 4, 5; 27, 2, 7). Thirteen blades, however, seem to have been unnotched. The unusual blade from Palugvik East Point (Pl. 26, 2) has only one notch, unless there was once a very small second notch in the corner now broken off.

A few of the blades show signs of breakage and resharpening (P.666). A broken blade of slaty schist from Palugvik (Pl. 27, 6) seems to have been a combination ulo and saw. The cutting ulo edge is curved, and the dull saw edge is at the end of the blade.

In addition to the full-sized blades, a toy ulo of micaceous schist was found in Palugvik 2 (Pl. 14, 2). It is shaped to represent a straight-edged blade hafted in a plain straight handle. Since no ulo handles of bone were found, we must suppose that in Prince William Sound, as in Kachemak Bay, the ulo handles were of wood.[37] There were no blades with holes for attachment to the handle, unless the notches on a specimen from Palugvik 1 or 2 (Pl. 27, 2) were made after the holes had broken out. The smoothing at the base of the notches could have been caused as easily by the rubbing of a winding as by the action of a drill. Although 2 fragments of slate blades with drilled holes were found (see section 29), it is impossible to identify the type of blade. Drilled holes were not uncommon in Kodiak ulo blades, however.[38]

In the following table the symbol "(u)" indicates that the blade was unnotched, while "(n)" indicates notching. Two fragments from Palugvik 1 (33-37-432, 433), here classed as ulo blades, may have been pieces of mirrors or some other kind of object. One has a dull curved edge; the other has 2 dull edges meeting at right angles.

[35] Quimby, 1945a. I have had the opportunity of examining some of this material.
[36] Cf. de Laguna, 1934, Pl. 33, 7, from Kachemak Bay III.

[37] Ibid., Pl. 56, 17.
[38] Birket-Smith, 1941, Fig. 31a, b, j, k; Hrdlička, 1944, Fig. 112. Heizer (1946, p. 149) finds them relatively more common in the earlier layers at Uyak Bay.

	Straight Edge	Curved Edge	Fragment
Palugvik 4	Pl. 26, 3 (u)	P.673	33-37-78 (n)
	Pl. 27, 1 (u)		
	P.674		
Palugvik 3	33-37-165 (u)	Pl. 26, 1 (u)	33-37-166
	167		
Palugvik 2	Pl. 14, 2 (toy)	Pl. 26, 5 (n)	33-37-308
	P.667 (n)	Pl. 27, 6 (with saw)	309
	P.671 (u)	P.666 (n)	P.670
		P.668 (u?)	
Palugvik 1 or 2	Pl. 27, 2 (n)		
Palugvik 1	33-37-434		33-37-432
	WSM 941		433
Palugvik, layer (?)	Pl. 26, 6 (u)	30-25-6	Pl. 26, 4 (n)
	30-25-27 (u)		
Palugvik East Point			
Burial Ledge	Pl. 26, 2 (n)	Pl. 27, 7 (n)	
	33-37-561 (u)	33-37-562 (n)	
Palutat Cave	Pl. 27, 5 (u)		33-37-664
Site 64A, Montague Island		33-37-594 (u)	
		WSM X-99	
Site 65B, Montague Island		Pl. 27, 8 (u)	

23. CHIPPED ULO BLADES

Besides the polished slate ulo blades, there are 5 of chipped slate with unground edges. A rough slate chip, 18.5 by 9 cm., with a sharp, unretouched, straight edge was found in Palugvik 4 (33-37-75). A second specimen from the same level is rectangular in shape, 18.5 by 10 cm. (Pl. 20, 2). The cutting edge and back are straight, and both show retouching. A heavy specimen from Palugvik 3, also rectangular, 19 by 13.5 cm. and 1.5 cm. thick (33-37-205), has a retouched and battered edge. The surface has been partly smoothed. A chipped triangular blade from Palugvik 2 (33-37-314), 11 by 6 cm., may have been used for cutting or scraping. There is lastly an irregular and possibly unfinished chipped slate blade from Palugvik 1 (Pl. 27, 10), measuring (16) by 9.7 cm., with a notch at one corner, like the notches on some polished ulo blades; the other end is broken.

It is difficult to determine whether these 5 specimens should be considered as a distinct type of ulo, or simply as unfinished ulo blades, or scrapers. Similar chipped slate blades were characteristic of Kachemak Bay II and III and were relatively more common in the earlier layers at Uyak Bay, Kodiak Island.[39]

[39] De Laguna, 1934, pp. 77 f.; Hrdlička, 1944, Fig. 111; Heizer, 1946, p. 149.

PLATE 27. Ulos and men's knives. Scale ½ natural size

1, Ulo with straight edge, slate, Palugvik 4 (P.665); 2, ulo with straight edge and holes or notches, slate, Palugvik 1 or 2 (P.663); 3, copper knife blade, Palugvik 4 (P.979); 4, unfinished (?) man's knife like ulo, chipped slate, Palugvik 1 (P.994); 5, ulo with straight edge (to right), slate, Palutat Cave, depth 1 foot (P.1206); 6, combination ulo and saw, slaty schist (cutting edge down, saw edge to right), Palugvik 2 (P.672); 7, ulo with curved edge and notches, slate, Palugvik East Point burial ledge (P.1095); 8, ulo with curved edge, slate, Site 65B, Montague Island (P.1158); 9, man's knife like ulo, slate, Site 7, Hawkins Cut Off (P.1110); 10, unfinished (?) ulo with notch, chipped slate, Palugvik 1 (P.664)

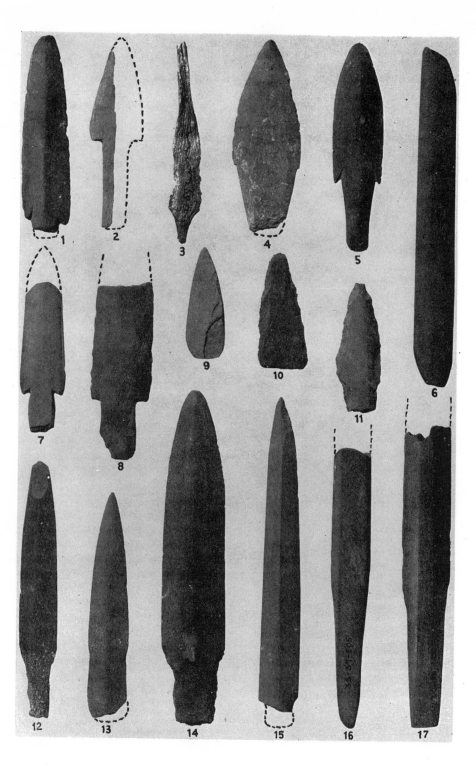

24. Men's Knives Like Ulos

There are 9 slate blades which appear to have been for men's knives like ulos; they cannot, however, be clearly differentiated from women's knives. Three of these blades are complete. The smallest is an unfinished (?) chipped slate specimen, 6.6 cm. long and 1.7 cm. wide, and comes from Palugvik 1 (Pl. 27, 4). A complete blade from Palugvik, layer unknown, measures 7 by 2.4 cm. and has a straight cutting edge, chipped dull back, and rounded ends (Pl. 14, 1). The third and largest specimen is from Site 7, Hawkins Cut Off (Pl. 27, 9). It is 14.1 by 6.4 cm. and also has a straight cutting edge and dull back for a grip.

There are in addition 4 broken specimens from Palugvik 2. Two of these have a straight cutting edge and dull back (P.675, 33-37-313), a third has a concave cutting edge (33-37-311), and the fourth a convexly curved edge (Pl. 14, 3). A doubtful specimen was found in the midden on Palugvik East Point (33-37-570). A waterworn blade of greenstone, 8 by 3.5 cm., from Site 28 at Point Whitshed (30-25-95), is probably also for a man's knife.

In addition to the 9 specimens just mentioned, there are 3 broken double-edged slate blades which have apparently been made to serve as blades for men's small knives, like the baleen shaves of the more northern Eskimo. These are from Palugvik 4 (P.683), Palugvik 2 (P.679), and layer unknown (33-37-508). Similar small slate knife blades are known from all periods represented at Kachemak Bay and from the Aleutians.[40]

[40] Jochelson, 1925, Pl. 16, 2, 3, 9, 15; de Laguna, 1934, pp. 76, 185.

25. Copper Knife Blade

From Palugvik 4 there is a copper blade, 5 cm. long and 1.5 cm. wide (Pl. 27, 3). It is notched at both ends, like a small ulo, and was probably the blade for a man's knife like an ulo or baleen shave.

We found no specimens like the very large sickle-shaped copper blades (for ulos?) found in the uppermost layer at Yukon Island in Kachemak Bay.[41]

26. Miscellaneous Knife Blades

From Palugvik East Point burial ledge is a triangular slate chip, 7.3 cm. long, sharpened along one edge. It is evidently the blade for a knife (Pl. 14, 7).

A beautifully finished blade of green chert, 13 by 8 cm., was found at the same place (Pl. 20, 3). The back of the blade is narrowed to a tang or handle 6 cm. long and 6.5 cm. wide. The blade is too thin to have served as an adz, and the edge too curved to have been serviceable as a scraper.

A 2-edged triangular knife of polished greenstone from Palugvik 1 (P.676), 10.6 by 7.6 cm., has been shaped to fit, unhafted, in the hand.

Double-edged slate blades, some of which may have been used for knives, are described in the next section. Bone blades for knives or weapons, a wooden knife handle, bone knives or scrapers, and bone daggers, picks, and stilettos are described in sections 52 to 55.

27. Double-edged Slate Blades

The collections contain 53 double-edged slate blades for arrows, lances, harpoons, knives, etc., although in most cases it is im-

[41] De Laguna, 1934, Pl. 49, 14, 15, p. 118.

PLATE 28. Double-edged slate blades and copper arrowhead. Scale ⅘ natural size

1, Blade with barbs, Chenega Village (33-37-637); 2, blade with pronounced shoulders, Palugvik 2 or 3 (33-37-161); 3, copper arrowhead, Site 65A, Montague Island (33-37-593); 4, blade with shoulders like barbs, Palutat Cave, depth 2 feet (33-37-665); 5, blade with barbs, Palutat Cave, depth 6 to 9 inches (33-37-662); 6, blade with straight edges, "Halibut Cove type," Site 7, Hawkins Cut Off (30-25-79); 7, blade with barbs, Palugvik 4 (33-37-68); 8, blade with barbs, Palugvik 3 (33-37-160); 9, leaf-shaped blade with sharp point and dull edges, Palugvik 4 (33-37-73); 10, chipped, triangular, micaceous slate blade, Palutat Cave, depth 1 foot (33-37-666); 11, unfinished (?) blade with tang, Palugvik 1 (33-37-425); 12 and 13, blades with tang, Palugvik 4 (33-37-70, 69); 14 and 15, blades with tang, Palugvik 1 (33-37-428, 431); 16, blade with tang, Palugvik, layer (?) (33-37-505); 17, blade with tang, Palugvik East Point burial ledge (33-37-559)

possible to determine for what kind of implement or weapon they were intended. On typological grounds they may be divided into 17 blades with barbs, 16 blades with tang but without barbs or distinct shoulders, and 16 almost straight-edged blades, shaped like a slender leaf without a tang ("Halibut Cove type"). There are also 14 miscellaneous, fragmentary, and unfinished blades which cannot be classified.

There are 17 barbed blades which were certainly intended for weapons, presumably for lances. They average between 8 and 12 cm. in length and from 1.5 to 2 cm. in width, the longest measuring 16.7 by 2.6 cm. (Pl. 29, *14*), and the shortest and widest, 7.5 by 3.4 cm. (Pl. 29, *9*). Typical specimens tend to be rather slender and straight-edged, with the greatest width just above the barbs, and may be slightly or strongly faceted, with lozenge- or diamond-shaped cross sections; the tangs are apt to be flattened or wedge-shaped (Pls. 28, *1, 7;* 29, *2, 3, 4, 14*). There are 2 fragments, probably of the same barbed blade, with flattened hexagonal section, from Palugvik East Point midden. Also rather unusual are 3 specimens from Palutat Cave. Two are rather short, leaf-shaped blades with lenticular cross sections and diminutive barbs (Pls. 28, *4;* 29, *9*). Either could have fitted the wooden lance head found in the cave (Pl. 34, *7*). The third specimen from the cave is only slightly faceted, with the greatest width at the middle, not at the barbs (Pl. 28, *5*). Another interesting specimen comes from Palugvik 4 (Pl. 29, *1*). It is waterworn and was evidently once on the beach, where perhaps it had washed from an older part of the midden.

In addition to the 17 barbed specimens, a blade from Palugvik 2 or 3 (Pl. 28, *2*) has the long tang set off by shoulders that are so pronounced they may have functioned as barbs.

There are 16 blades that are narrowed to a tang but lack barbs or distinct shoulders. Two are lenticular in section; the rest are more or less faceted with lozenge or hex-

agonal cross sections. The average dimensions are 8.8 by 1.7 cm. (Pl. 28, *13*), to 13.3 by 2.7 cm. (Pl. 28, *14*), or even to about 16 cm. (Pl. 29, *15*). Other typical examples are shown in Plates 28, *12, 15* to *17*, and 29, *5*. On one specimen from Palugvik (WSM 1135) the tang is so slightly detached that the blade is almost leaf-shaped. An unusual specimen from Palugvik 1, only 5 by 1.8 cm., perhaps intended for an arrow, has ground surfaces but chipped edges and may be unfinished (Pl. 28, *11*). Another unusual specimen, also unfinished, was found with a number of unworked slate splinters in the same layer. It is lancet-shaped and, though broken at both ends, is still (22) by 3.5 cm. (Pl. 29, *17*).

Related to the 16 tanged specimens is the largest blade in the collection (Pl. 20, *1*), found at Site 65B, Montague Island. Though perhaps half has been broken off, the fragment is (23.5) cm. long and 6 cm. wide. It is very slightly faceted and has a wide tang or handle. It was probably a large flensing knife and could have been used without a separate handle or haft.

There are 16 slender leaf-shaped blades with lenticular section, probably for knives, which resemble the long, narrow, straight-edged specimens found at Halibut Cove in Kachemak Bay.[42] Since most of the Chugach examples are fragmentary, identification is uncertain. Complete specimens vary in length from 5.1 (?) by 1.2 cm. (Pl. 29, *7*) to an unfinished blade, 13.5 by 1.5 cm. (Pl. 28, *6*). The latter, from Site 7, Hawkins Cut Off, and a waterworn specimen from Site 41 near Ellamar (30-25-109) were identified by the natives as blades for a man's knife, naγu·ṭeq. A much weathered specimen was found with the incomplete and disarticulatd skeleton C2 in Palutat Cave (Pl. 29, *11*). Other specimens are broken (Pl. 29, *6, 12*). Three of these were apparently reworked for use as blades for men's knives like small ulos, and have already been mentioned in section 24.

Among the miscellaneous specimens, im-

[42] *Ibid.,* Pl. 32, *8, 14, 19.*

possible to classify, are a heavy, leaf-shaped blade, 12.7 by 3.5 cm., probably unfinished, from Palutat Cave (Pl. 29, *16*) ; 2 small leaf-shaped or trianguloid specimens from Palugvik 4 (Pls. 28, *9;* 29, *8*) that resemble a blade from Kachemak Bay in having a sharp point but dull edges;[43] and a slender blade with oval section, (9.2) by 1.2, from Site 65B, Montague Island, that seems to be related to the type of weapon point described as a slate "awl" in the next section. Chipped blades of micaceous and phyllitic slate from Palutat Cave (Pl. 28, *10*) and Palugvik 2 (Pl. 29, *10*) have already been mentioned in section 12.

There are, lastly, 3 broken blades with lozenge-shaped sections, one with hexagonal section, and 4 fragments of unfinished blades, chipped but not polished.

As can be seen from the table given below, knife (?) blades of the Halibut Cove type seem to be represented in almost equal proportions in the various layers at Palugvik and are about equal in number to either the barbed blades or the barbless blades with tang. However, the 2 oldest layers at Palugvik contained only one barbed blade, as against 10 barbless blades with tang (although 2 of the latter were unfinished, and so difficult to classify). The upper half of the midden yielded 7 barbed blades and only 3 with tangs alone, and here the proportion is similar to that found in Yukon Island III, although on the whole barbed blades were even more numerous than tanged blades in Kachemak Bay III.[44] No large leaf-shaped blades like those of Kachemak Bay were found in the sound.[45] Most of the Chugach specimens are faceted, producing definite lozenge-shaped or hexagonal cross sections, while only a few blades from Kachemak Bay had facets, and these were seldom pronounced. Neither Prince William Sound nor Kachemak Bay yielded blades as long as those of the Kodiak Island whaling lances.[46]

The proveniences of the slate blades are as follows:

	Barbed	Tanged	Halibut Cove Type	Other
Palugvik 4	Pl. 28, 7	Pl. 28, 12	P.683 (reused)	Pl. 28, 9
	Pl. 29, 1	Pl. 28, 13	33-37-72 (waterworn)	(leaf-shaped)
	(waterworn)	Pl. 29, 5		Pl. 29, 8
	Pl. 29, 2			(leaf-shaped)
	Pl. 29, 4			33-37-71 (frag.)
	33-37-67			
Palugvik 3 or 4	P.655			P.680 (frag.)
Palugvik 3	33-37-160		33-37-162	
			163 (unfinished)	
			P.685 (unfinished)	
Palugvik 2 or 3			Pl. 29, 7	Pl. 28, 2 (with
			P.681	shoulders)
Palugvik 2		Pl. 29, 15	33-37-304	33-37-305
		WSM 1135	P.679 (reused)	(chipped tang)

[43] *Ibid.,* Pl. 32, *12.*
[44] *Ibid.,* pp. 71 f.

[45] *Ibid.,* Pl. 32, *20 to 23.*
[46] Birket-Smith, 1941, p. 139, Figs. 15a, b, 16; Heizer, 1952b, p. 15, Pl. 2j, k, 1.

Palugvik 1	Pl. 29, *3*	Pl. 28, *11* (unfinished?) Pl. 28, *14* Pl. 28, *15* Pl. 29, *17* (unfinished) 33-37-426 429 P.661 P.662	P.682	33-37-427 (frag.) 430 (frag.) 30-25-15 (unfinished) P.644 (unfinished)
Palugvik, layer (?)	P.1048	Pl. 28, *16*	33-37-508 (reused)	
Palugvik East Point Midden			Pl. 29, *12*	
Burial ledge	P.1100-1101	Pl. 28, *17*		
Site 7, Hawkins Cut Off			Pl. 28, *6*	
Site 12, Hawkins Island	Pl. 29, *14*			
Site 41, near Ellamar			30-25-109	
Palutat Cave Surface	Pl. 29, *9* 33-37-663			Pl. 29, *16* (unfinished)
6″ to 9″	Pl. 28, *5*			
24″	Pl. 28, *4*			
Grave C2			Pl. 29, *11*	
Chenega Village	Pl. 28, *1*			
Site 65A Montague Island	WSM X-102		Pl. 29, *6*	
Site 65B Montague Island		P.1154		Pl. 20, *1* (flens- ing knife) 33-37-607 (awl- like) P.1157 (unfinished)

PLATE 29. Double-edged slate blades. Scale ½ natural size

1, Blade with barbs, waterworn, Palugvik 4 (P.656) ; 2, blade with barbs, Palugvik 4 (P.653) ; 3, blade with barbs, Palugvik 1 (P.652) ; 4, blade with barbs, Palugvik 4 (P.654) ; 5, blade with tang, Palugvik 4 (P.657) ; 6, blade with straight edges, "Halibut Cove type," Site 65A, Montague Island (P.1146) ; 7, blade with straight edges, "Halibut Cove type," Palugvik 2 (or 3) (P.677) ; 8, leaf-shaped blade with sharp point and dull edges, Palugvik 4 (P.686) ; 9, blade with barbs, Palutat Cave, surface (P.1207) ; 10, chipped blade, phyllitic slate, Palugvik 2 (P.678) ; 11, blade with straight edges, "Halibut Cove type," Grave C2, Palutat Cave (P.1263) ; 12, blade with straight edges, "Halibut Cove type," with saw cut, Palugvik East Point midden (P.1099) ; 13, fragment of triangular blade, greenstone, Palugvik 4 (P.997) ; 14, blade with barbs, burial cave, Site 12, Hawkins Island (P.1117) ; 15, blade with tang, Palugvik 2 (P.1010) ; 16, unfinished leaf-shaped (?) blade, Palugvik Cave, surface (P.1205) ; 17, unfinished blade, Palugvik 1 (P.651)

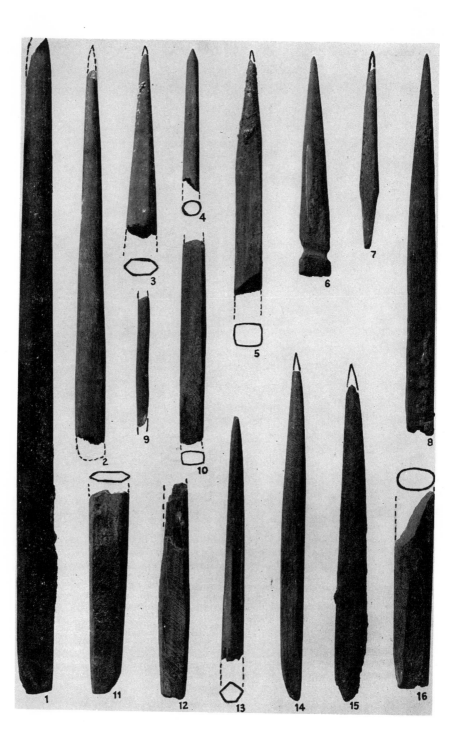

In addition to the slate specimens listed above, there are 3 blades of ground greenstone. One from Palugvik 4 is the point of a double-edged blade, possibly a triangular blade for harpoon or lance (Pl. 29, 13). No triangular blades of slate were found, although they should have been expected, since the type is represented by ethnological Chugach specimens.[47] A fragment of polished greenstone blade is from Palugvik 3 (33-37-191). The third greenstone specimen is the triangular knife from Palugvik 1 (P.676), described in section 26.

Blades of native copper, similar to the double-edged slate blades, are described in section 37.

28. SLATE "AWLS"

In Prince William Sound we found 128 specimens of a type which we have called slate "awls" for lack of a better name. We do not believe, however, that they were used to make holes. The points, when preserved, show no signs of wear, and moreover slate would be a poor material for awls since it is very brittle. These "awls" must have been objects in common use, since so many were found, yet were not placed in graves to give us a clue to the sex of the users. The butt ends show that these slate implements were always (generally?) hafted. Some with hexagonal cross section are so flat, and the facets so sharp, that the specimens look like exceedingly slender lance blades. It is believed, therefore, that the slate "awls" are a specialized type of lance point, probably intended to break off in

the wound, and presumably used for hunting whales and large sea mammals. Similar awl-like lance points were found in Kachemak Bay III and on Kodiak Island. The latter are said to have been over 12 inches long.[48]

Almost all the specimens from Prince William Sound are broken. The 18 or so complete or almost complete specimens show that the lengths ranged from 7 and 7.5 cm. (Pls. 30, 7; 31, 7) to something over 27 cm. (Pl. 30, 1), with the majority falling between 9 and 15 cm. The diameters vary from 0.5 (Pl. 30, 9) up to 2.1 cm. (Pl. 30, 11), but the average is about 1 to 1.3 cm.

On 33 specimens the butts have been preserved. These are rounded or finished off bluntly on 8 examples (Pls. 30, 8; 31, 5, 11). On 3 the butts taper (Pl. 30, 14, 15). One of the unbroken specimens has a broad flat butt, grooved for attachment to a shaft or haft (Pl. 30, 6). Another is scarfed on one surface (Pl. 31, 9). All of the remaining 20 specimens are more or less flattened at the butt, which, on the more carefully finished, resembles a wedge-shaped tang (Pl. 30, 7). It seems clear, therefore, that these slate points were hafted in a handle or shaft, presumably of wood, since no bone shaft has been found to fit them.

The slate "awls" vary in the shape of their cross sections. In general, they tend to be round or oval at the point, hexagonal in the middle, and rectangular near the butt, although there are specimens which seem to have been oval, hexagonal, or rec-

[47] Museum für Völkerkunde, Berlin, IV-A-6238, barbed wooden lance head; 6240 and 6363, toggle harpoon heads.

[48] De Laguna, 1934, p. 79 (18 specimens from III and sub-III, but identified as drills); Hrdlička, 1944, Fig. 119; Birket-Smith, 1941, pp. 138 f.

PLATE 30. Slate "awls." Scale ¾ natural size

1, With oval section and wedge-shaped butt, Palugvik 1 (33-37-441); 2, with oval section and flattened butt, Palugvik 1 or 2 (33-37-445); 3, with hexagonal section, Palugvik 2 (33-37-320); 4, with round section, Palugvik East Point burial ledge (33-37-564); 5, with rectangular section, Palugvik 3 (33-37-180); 6, with flat wide butt, grooved for attachment, Palugvik 2 (33-37-316); 7, with round section and wedge-shaped butt, Palugvik 2 (?) (33-37-337); 8, with hexagonal to rectangular section, Palugvik 2 (33-37-334); 9, with round section, Palugvik 1 (33-37-437); 10, with rectangular section, Palugvik 1 (33-37-444); 11, with flat hexagonal section, Palugvik 3 (33-37-178); 12, with flat hexagonal section, Palugvik 2 (33-37-321); 13, with pentagonal section, Palugvik 1 (33-37-443); 14, with oval to subrectangular section, Palugvik 3 (33-37-171); 15, with subrectangular section, Palugvik 4 (33-37-80); 16, with oval section, Palugvik 2 (33-37-325)

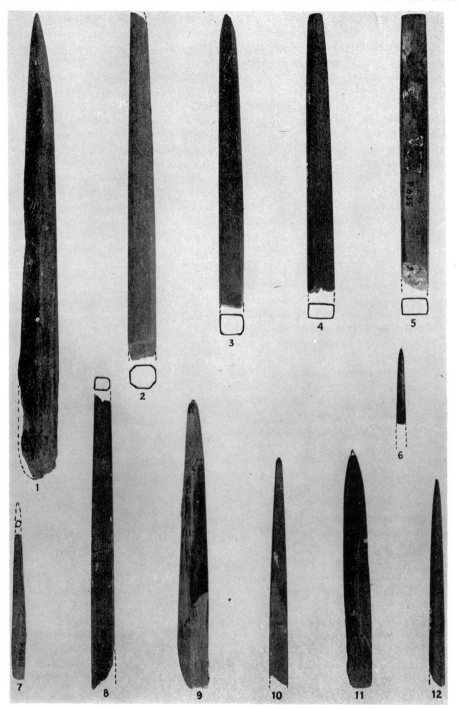

tangular throughout the greater part of their length. A few are pentagonal, octagonal, or diamond-shaped in section.

There seems to be no chronological or regional significance in the variations of shape. It is interesting, however, that the upper half of the midden at Palugvik yielded 37 specimens, while the lower half produced 72; there were in addition 8 "awls" which could not be assigned to either half. It is also noteworthy that no specimens were found in Palutat Cave, and that only one awl-like, double-edged slate blade was found at Sites 65A and B on Montague Island, although this double village yielded 6 double-edged slate blades. If our identification of the slate "awls" as lance blades is correct, this distribution suggests that the type of hunting for which

they were adapted became less common in the later period of occupation of the sound. This may have been either because of a shift to other hunting techniques (with barbed blades?) or perhaps because of a change in the types of sea mammals that were hunted. The absence of slate "awls" at Palutat Cave and at Montague Island also suggests that the game for which these points were intended did not frequent the waters near these sites. Furthermore, the relative scarcity of slate "awls" in Kachemak Bay, contrasted with their abundance in Prince William Sound and Kodiak Island, might also be explained by a difference in the type of game available to the hunters.

The distribution of the Chugach specimens is:

Palugvik 4	9	(Pls. 30, *15;* 31, *6, 8;* 33-37-79, 83; P.608, P.614, P.620, P.622)
Palugvik 3 or 4	5	(33-37-81, 82; P.598, P.609, P.642)
Palugvik 3	22	(Pls. 30, *5, 11, 14;* 31, *4* [unfinished], 31, *9;* 33-37-172 to 177, 179, 181 to 187; P.602, P.610, P.638)
Palugvik 2 or 3	3	(P.611, P.628, P.629)
Palugvik 2	38	(Pls. 30, *3, 6, 7, 8, 12, 13, 16;* 31, *2, 7;* 30-25-10, D30-25-18, 33-37-317 to 319, 322 to 324, 326, 328 to 330, 332, 333, 335; P.594, P.606, P.612, P.613, P.616, P.619, P.621, P.623, P.625 to 627, P.631 [unfinished], P.634, P.636, P.1011)
Palugvik 1 or 2	5	(Pls. 30, *2;* 31, *1, 11, 12;* 33-37-338)
Palugvik 1	31	(Pls. 30, *1, 9, 10, 13;* 31, *3, 5, 9, 10;* 30-25-19, 33-37-435, 436, 438 to 440, 442; P.597, P.599, P.604, P.615, P.617, P.618, P.624, P.632, P.637 chisel?, P639a to c, P.660, P.1008, P.1324, WSM 937, 1029)

PLATE 31. Slate "awls." Scale slightly over ⅔ natural size

1, With oval section, Palugvik 1 or 2 (P.595); 2, with round to octagonal section, Palugvik 2 (P.607); 3, with hexagonal to rectangular section, Palugvik 1 (P.641); 4, with rectangular section and wedged-shaped butt (butt end up), Palugvik 3 (P.630); 5, with rectangular section (butt end up), Palugvik 1 (P.635); 6, with very fine point, Palugvik 4, (P.643); 7, with round section and flattened butt, Palugvik 2 (P.600); 8, with oval to rectangular section, Palugvik 4 (P.633); 9, with oval section and scarfed butt, Palugvik 3 (P.605); 10, with rectangular section, Palugvik 1 (P.603); 11, with rectangular section and rounded butt, Palugvik (1 or) 2 (P.601); 12, with pentagonal section, Palugvik (1 or) 2 (P.596)

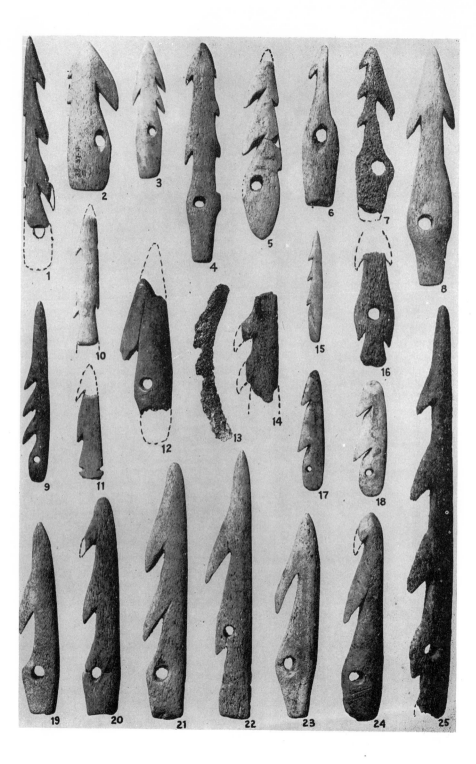

Palugvik, layer (?)	5	(33-37-513, 515, 516; P.1042, P.1070)
Palugvik East Point		
Midden	2	(33-37-571, P.1102)
Burial ledge	2	(Pl. 30, *4;* P.1097)
Site 26, Point Whitshed	1	(30-25-97)
Site 35, Port Gravina	1	(P.1171 chisel?)
Chenega Church Collection	3	(33-37-638, P.1130, P.1131)
Site 62, Evans Island	1	(33-37-619)

29. WORKED SLATE AND GREENSTONE

In addition to the slate specimens described in separate sections, there are 25 fragments of worked slate which cannot be identified. Other broken pieces were found in the course of excavation but were not saved. Some of these worked pieces are narrow sawed strips, possibly unfinished "awls"; others may be fragments of ulo blades, lance blades, etc. These fragments show that in Prince William Sound, as in Kachemak Bay III, slate was shaped by sawing and chipping and finished by grinding and polishing. One of the narrow strips from Palugvik 4 (33-37-89) shows how the hexagonal section of many of the "awls" would result naturally from the process of sawing out the piece from both sides of a flat slab of slate. From Palugvik 3 and from the big burial cave at Site 16, Hawkins Island, are fragments of blades with drilled holes. These are the only specimens suggesting that blades were hafted by pegging or lashing through holes. Holes for hafting were apparently rather common on Kodiak slate blades and not unknown on Kachemak Bay.[49]

Eighteen fragments of greenstone and green chert are probably pieces broken from adz blades in the course of manufacture.

The distribution of these worked stone fragments is:

Palugvik 4	slate (33-37-88, 89, 90, 91; P.721, P.724, P.987)
	greenstone (33-37-99, P.727a, b, P.746)
Palugvik 3 or 4	greenstone (33-37-97, 98; P.996)
Palugvik 3	slate (33-37-118, P.720, P.723, P.986, P.995, P.1000)
	greenstone (33-37-192, P.744, P.1001, field nos. 220, 272)

[49] Birket-Smith, 1941. Fig. 31a, b, j, k; Hrdlička, 1944. Fig. 112, last 6 specimens; de Laguna, 1934, p. 75; Pl. 32, *1*.

PLATE 32. Detachable barbed heads. Scale ⅔ natural size

1, With 3 large and 3 ornamental barbs, Palugvik, layer (?) (33-37-487); 2, with one large and 2 ornamental barbs, Palugvik 4 (33-37-4); 3, asymmetrically barbed, Palugvik 1 (33-37-371); 4, with 2 large and 3 ornamental barbs, Palugvik 2 (33-37-214); 5, with 2 large and 2 ornamental barbs, Palugvik 3 (33-37-119); 6, asymmetrically barbed, Palugvik 1 or 2 (33-37-221); 7, asymmetrically barbed, Palugvik 2 (33-37-215); 8, symmetrically barbed, Palugvik 2 (33-37-218); 9, barbed on one edge, Palugvik 4 (33-37-5); 10, with 2 large and one ornamental barb, Palugvik, layer (?) (33-37-490); 11, barbed on one edge, notched for attachment of harpoon line, Palugvik 1 (33-37-370); 12, decorated fragment, barbed on one edge, Palugvik 1 (33-37-372); 13, copper fragment, barbed on one edge, Palugvik 3 (33-37-124); 14, fragment barbed on one edge with groove for blade, Palugvik 3 (33-37-123); 15, barbed on one edge, lacking line hole (unfinished?), Palugvik 2 (33-37-222); 16, symmetrically barbed, Palugvik, layer (?) (33-37-489); 17, barbed on one edge, Palugvik 3 or 4 (33-37-6); 18, barbed on one edge, Palugvik, layer (?) (33-37-486); 19, originally with 2 barbs (?) on one edge, reshaped with one barb, Palugvik 4 (33-37-2); 20 and 21, barbed on one edge, Palugvik 2 (30-25-11, 33-37-217); 22, barbed on one edge, butt broken and line hole redrilled, Palugvik 2 (33-37-219); 23, barbed on one edge, Palugvik 2 (33-37-216); 24, barbed on one edge, Palugvik 1 (33-37-373); 25, barbed on one edge, butt broken and line hole redrilled, Palutat Cave, surface (33-37-650)

Palugvik 2 or 3   greenstone (30-25-24, field no. 259)

Palugvik 2   slate (33-37-360, P.669, P.702)
                                   greenstone (field nos. 445, 643)

Palugvik 1   slate (P.722)
                                   greenstone (P.743, P.999)

Palugvik, layer unknown   slate (33-37-517, 518; P.1201)
Palugvik East Point
    Burial Ledge   slate (P.1092)

Large Cave, Site 16,
    Hawkins Island   slate (33-37-575, P.1113, P.1114)

Palutat Cave   slate (P.1208)

30. DETACHABLE BARBED HEADS

Whereas the toggle harpoon head with socket was rather uncommon in Prince William Sound, the detachable barbed head with tang was in general use for the hand-thrust harpoon, the throwing-board dart, and the harpoon arrow. The 87 specimens in the collections can be divided into 4 types: 56 heads barbed only on one edge, 9 heads with large barbs on one edge and small ornamental barbs on the other, 7 heads barbed asymmetrically on both edges, and 7 heads with more or less symmetrically paired barbs. These distinctions are not rigid, however, and the last 3 types grade into one another.

The specimens range in size from 3.2 cm. (a very small specimen recut as a fishhook barb, Pl. 36, 9) or 3.5 cm. (Pl. 33, 16) to 18.8 cm. (Pl. 32, 25), represented by a broken and reshaped specimen which was originally longer. The majority are about 8 or 10 cm. long. The heads in general have an oval section, but those made of pieces of animal leg bone may be flattened or even slightly concave on the side formed by the original inner surface of the bone. The barbs vary in size and shape, some being more detached than others, but the majority are curved convexly above and concavely below. The butt end of the head is usually flattened on both sides to produce a wedge-shaped tang to fit the oval cavity of the socket pieces (see section 33). With a few exceptions which will be noted, the harpoon line which attached the head to

the shaft or to a bladder was run through a hole in the upper part of the tang. This hole was made either by a hand drill or by a bow (or cord) drill and is almost never in the center of the tang, even on heads which were otherwise symmetrical, but is placed toward one edge, invariably the barbed edge on unilaterally barbed specimens, or the edge with the larger barbs on bilaterally, asymmetrically barbed heads. The tang itself usually expands asymmetrically to accommodate the hole. Some of the bilaterally barbed heads, however, have symmetrically placed holes.

These barbed heads were used for harpooning seals, sea otter, and fish, according to our Chugach informants. The smallest heads, ranging up to about 5 cm. in length, were presumably used for sea otter arrows. There are 7 of these in the collections—6 of them barbed on one edge, and one barbed asymmetrically on both edges. These small heads are from Palugvik 4 (Pls. 33, 8, 16; 36, 9), Palugvik 3 (Pl. 33, 7), Palugvik 2 or 3 (Pl. 33, 22), and Palugvik 2 (Pl. 32, 15).

A few specimens are decorated, perhaps to render them magically more effective, or perhaps the design served as an owner's mark for purposes of reclaiming the head and the game caught with it. These simple designs are described below.

Heads Barbed on One Edge

These form by far the most numerous group, and number 56. They include both the smallest and the largest specimens in the collections. The tang of the smallest has been split through the line hole, and the head has been reshaped as a barb for a fish-hook (Pl. 36, 9). Another small specimen (Pl. 32, 15) is evidently unfinished and lacks the line hole. The hole is also missing on a broken and recut specimen (P.587), and the method of attachment of the line is un-certain. Another small head (Pl. 32, 11) has a pair of notches on the tang to hold the line. The original tang has been broken on one specimen with 2 barbs (Pl. 32, 22), but the head has been reshaped for further use with a hole through the lower barb. This barb has been whittled down until it is smaller than the upper one. The present butt end has been cut off squarely, and there are several small notches on its dorsal edge. A similar accident has been repaired in the same way in the case of the largest head of all, which comes from Palutat Cave (Pl. 32, 25). Two other heads, both orig-inally with 2 barbs (?), have 2 holes in the tang, the upper one of which was drilled after the first had broken, and on one of these heads the second hole has also broken out (P.1328). The butt of a fifth head has split through the original hole, and has subsequently been grooved about for the line (Pl. 33, 5). One of the sea otter heads has a drilled pit just below the line hole as if a second hole or a different position for the hole had been intended at one time (Pl. 33, 8). All other heads on which the tang has been preserved had a single line hole.

A number of heads have lost the upper-most barb and have been resharpened at the point (Pls. 32, 19; 33, 19, 20). Other heads were originally made with a rather long point above the barbs (Pls. 32, 9, 25; 33, 14), like heads from Port Graham, Cook Inlet.[50]

Three heads are grooved up one side of the point to hold a blade. A complete head of this type, 6.8 cm. long, was found in Grave A, Palutat Cave (Pl. 33, 1). The groove is only 1 cm. long and 0.3 cm. wide.

[50] De Laguna, 1934, Pl. 39, 6, 23, 24.

The second is a broken specimen from which the tip of the point is missing; the remaining portion of the groove is still (1.5) cm. long and 0.7 cm. wide (Pl. 32, 14). The third specimen is too fragmentary to measure. The blades to fit these grooves must have been shaped like awls, but no bone or stone specimens could be identified with certainty as intended for such use. Heads with similar grooves come from Kachemak Bay III, and heads with grooves or scarfing for the attachment of blades are also represented in Hrdlička's collections from Kodiak.[51]

Three specimens, all from Palugvik 4 (Pl. 33, 9, 16; 33-37-7), have unusually shaped barbs. The tip of the barb is cut off rather abruptly and is hollowed out below. Under-cut barbs are also found on heads from Kodiak and probably also from the Aleu-tians, although here there is a tendency to make the profile of the barbs very elaborate. I suspect that undercutting or hollowing the barbs is a relatively late style.[52]

One small head with 4 barbs (Pl. 33, 7) has the 2 lower barbs set so close to-gether that they appear like one barb which has been cut in two.

A few specimens are decorated. Two, from Palugvik 1 (Pl. 33, 17) and from the beach (Pl. 33, 3), have a longitudinal groove or line down one side; the other side is the naturally hollow or cancellous inner surface of the bone. Another head from Palugvik 1 (Pl. 32, 12) has a line trailing up from the notch of the barb and 2 fine transverse lines (metal cut?) above the line hole. A specimen from the house pit in Palugvik 4 (P.577) has a transverse band of crosshatching below the barb on one surface. The point of the head has been cut off. A groove leads down into the line hole, a feature commonly seen on Eskimo toggle harpoon heads with sockets.

[51] Ibid., Pl. 39, 8, 16, p. 84, unpublished speci-mens from Kodiak.
[52] Birket-Smith, 1941, Fig. 14f, p. 135; Quimby, 1948, Fig. 17C. (I am not convinced that Quimby's dating of this material as belonging to the "Middle Period" is satisfactory.) Laughlin (1952, Pl. 2H) finds such "castellated barbs" late on Umnak Island.

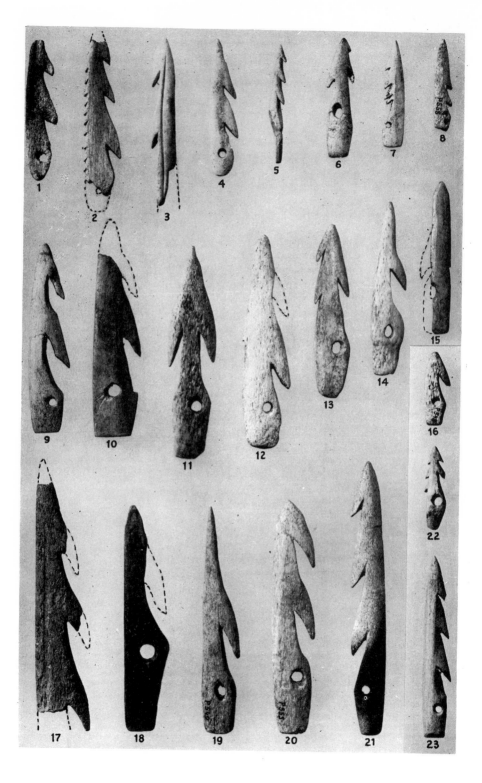

A specimen from the Chenega Church Collection (Pl. 33, *18*) which appears to be of rather recent manufacture has traces of a red stain.

In addition to the small head which was recut as a fishhook barb, we should mention 2 other reworked specimens. One of these, from Palugvik 4 (Pl. 35, *10*), is now a harpoon foreshaft. A very slender specimen from Palugvik 1 (P.1013), originally with 3 or 4 barbs, has had the barbs trimmed off and the butt sharpened to a blunt point.

The distribution of heads with barbs on one edge is given below. Broken specimens, the classification of which is uncertain, are indicated by parentheses.

A head of copper with at least 2 barbs, but with point and tang missing, was found in Palugvik 3 (Pl. 32, *13*) but has not been included in the above count.

	1 Barb	*2 Barbs*	*3 Barbs*	*Fragments*
Palugvik 4	Pl. 32, *19*	Pl. 33, *4*	Pl. 32, *9*	Pl. 35, *10*
	Pl. 33, *16*	Pl. 33, *8*	(P.556)	33-37-1
	Pl. 36, *9*	Pl. 33, *9*		7
	(P.577)	(33-37-8)		10
		(P.566)		P.567
Palugvik 3 or 4		Pl. 32, *17*		
		P.1328		P.576
Palugvik 3		Pl. 33, *23*	Pl. 33, *7,*	Pl. 32, *14*
		(33-37-122)	4 barbs	P.564
		(P.571)		P.568
Palugvik 2	Pl. 32, *23*	Pl. 32, *20*	Pl. 32, *15*	33-37-213
	Pl. 33, *14*	Pl. 32, *21*	Pl. 33, *21*	
	Pl. 33, *19*	Pl. 32, *22*		
	D30-25-12	Pl. 33, *5*		
		Pl. 33, *20*		
		(P.587)		

PLATE 33. Detachable barbed heads. Scale ⅔ natural size

1, Barbed on one edge with groove for blade, Grave A, Palutat Cave (P.1261); 2, with 3 large and 10 ornamental barbs, Palugvik 4 (P.569); 3, barbed on one edge with decorative line on one side, Palugvik, layer (?) (P.1051); 4, barbed on one edge, Palugvik 4 (P.553); 5, barbed on one edge, reshaped at butt, Palugvik 2 (P.586); 6, asymmetrically barbed, Palugvik 4 (P.948); 7, barbed on one edge, Palugvik 3 (P.559); 8, barbed on one edge, with second, incompletely drilled hole in butt, Palugvik 4 (P.558); 9, with 2 barbs on one edge, hollowed out below, Palugvik 4 (P.554); 10, barbed on one edge, Palugvik 1 (P.551); 11, symmetrically barbed, Palugvik 2 (P.561); 12, with 2 large and one ornamental barb, Palugvik 3 (P.552); 13, asymmetrically barbed, Palugvik 2 or 3 (P.562); 14, barbed on one edge, Palugvik 2 (P.550); 15, with ornamental barb, recut as knife, Palugvik 2 (P.588); 16, with one barb hollowed out below, Palugvik 4 (P.548); 17, barbed on one edge with decorative line on one side, Palugvik 1 (P.565); 18, relatively modern, barbed on one edge, stained red, Chenega Church Collection (P.1132); 19, originally with 2 barbs (?) on one edge, reshaped with one, Palugvik 2 (P.549); 20, originally with 3 barbs (?) on one edge, reshaped with 2, Palugvik 2 (P.555); 21, barbed on one edge, Palugvik 2 (P.560); 22, asymmetrically barbed, Palugvik 2 or 3 (P.563); 23, barbed on one edge, Palugvik 3 (P.557)

Palugvik 1 or 2					P.575
Palugvik 1	(Pl. 32, *12*)	(Pl. 32, *11*) Pl. 32, *24* (Pl. 33, *10*) WSM 1024	Pl. 33, *17* (P.1013, 3 or 4 barbs?)		
Palugvik, layer (?)		Pl. 32, *18* (Pl. 33, *3*) (DNM uncat.)		33-37-587	30-25-28
Palugvik East Point Midden				33-37-568	
Chenega Church Collection	Pl. 33, *18*				

Palutat Cave
  Surface
  Grave A
		Pl. 33, *1*	Pl. 32, *25*,
			4 barbs		

Heads with Ornamental Dorsal Barbs

There are 9 heads with large barbs on one edge and one or more small barbs on the other. The latter could not have been effective and were presumably for ornament. There are, in addition, 2 heads on which the dorsal barbs are possibly large enough to have been useful, and these specimens have therefore been described among the asymmetrically barbed heads, even though exact classification is impossible.

One head, originally with a single large barb opposite the ornamental one, has been recut, perhaps to serve as a knife (Pl. 33, *15*). Two heads had one ornamental barb and 2 large barbs. On the first, the dorsal barb lies opposite the space between the large ones (Pl. 33, *12*); on the second, the lower end of which is unfortunately missing, the dorsal barb is paired with the lower of the 2 large ones, but there may, of course, have once been additional barbs (Pl. 32, *10*). There are 2 heads with 2 ornamental barbs. On one of these, evidently recut after the fore end had been broken off, the 2 small barbs are combined with one large barb (Pl. 32, *2*). On the other specimen the 2 small barbs are combined with 2 large ones (Pl. 32, *5*). A third specimen (P.572) is represented by a fragment on which 2 large and 2 small barbs are paired.

One very flat, slender head has a combination of 3 small barbs and 3 larger ones. The lowest pair of barbs are notched, perhaps for decoration, perhaps for attachment cf the line, since the specimen is now broken at the line hole (Pl. 32, *1*). Another head combines 3 ornamental barbs and 2 large ones (Pl. 32, *4*). At the level of the line hole there is a rectangular projection or shoulder on the dorsal edge.

A fragmentary head from which both ends are missing has 3 large barbs and 10 very small ones (Pl. 33, *2*).

Asymmetrically Barbed Heads

The 7 heads of this type could be considered as ones on which the dorsal barbs had become large enough to be effective, and they are also similar to heads which are symmetrically barbed on both edges. In fact, no clear lines can be drawn among these 3 groups.

Thus, on one specimen a single large barb is combined with 3 smaller ones (Pl. 32, *7*), and, on 2 other heads, with 2 smaller barbs (Pl. 33, *6, 13*). On a third very small head, measuring only 4 by 1 cm. (Pl. 33,

22), 2 larger barbs balance 3 smaller ones. There is a gouged-out triangular area above the line hole on this specimen. A. fourth head, now broken, evidently had at least one large barb and one small, almost ornamental one (Pl. 32, 6). The line hole is symmetrically placed. All of these heads are, therefore, very similar to the specimens with purely decorative barbs.

Only one specimen in the group has 3 barbs of the same size, 2 on one edge and one on the other (Pl. 32, 3). A tang similar to that on this specimen was found in Palugvik 1 (P.581), but the type of head cannot be identified.

Symmetrically Barbed Heads

The remaining 7 heads are so nearly symmetrical that they may all be classed together, even though none is perfect.

There are 3 complete specimens with a single pair of barbs, as well as 2 broken heads which had at least one pair and may have had more. One of the complete heads may have been recut from a larger specimen with more than one pair of barbs (Pl. 33, 11). The line holes of 4 of these specimens are somewhat asymmetrically placed (Pls. 32, 8; 33, 11; 33-37-374, 120; P.574).

Two fragmentary specimens evidently had at least 2 pairs of barbs. On both, the lower barbs are not quite symmetrically placed, while the upper pair (now missing) seem to have been more carefully paired. The line holes of both were in the center. One head was subsequently equipped with a new line hole between the lower set of barbs (Pl. 32, 16; P.573).

There are in addition 6 symmetrical tangs which may have been broken from heads of this type, and one tang which is too small to classify at all.

The distribution of the bilaterally barbed heads is:

	Ornamental Barbs	Asymmetric	Symmetric	Fragments
Palugvik 4	Pl. 32, 2 Pl. 33, 2	Pl. 33, 6	(33-37-3, tang only)	P.581
Palugvik 3	Pl. 32, 5 Pl. 33, 12 P.572		33-37-120	P.582
Palugvik 2 or 3		Pl. 33, 22 Pl. 33, 13		
Palugvik 2	Pl. 32, 4 Pl. 33, 15	Pl. 32, 7	Pl. 32, 8 Pl. 33, 11 P.574 (33-37-212 and 227, tangs only) (P.578 and P.579, tangs only)	
Palugvik 1 or 2		Pl. 32, 6 (33-37-220)	P.573	

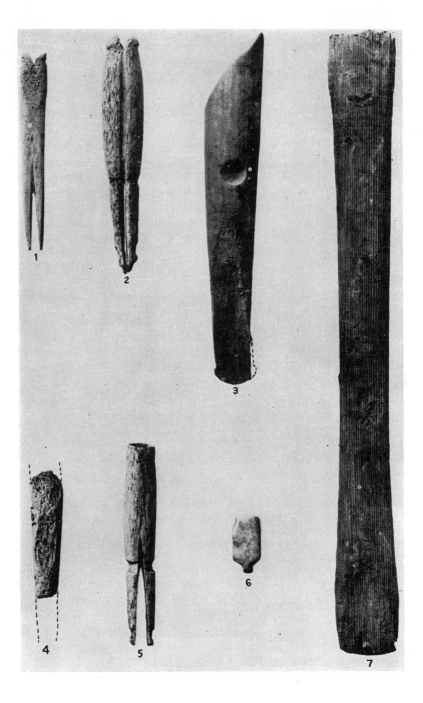

Palugvik 1		Pl. 32, *3*	33-37-374 (P.580, tang only)	
Palugvik, layer (?)	Pl. 32, *1* Pl. 32, *10*	(33-37-488)	Pl. 32, *16*	
	9	7	7 heads 6 tangs	2

Although the upper part of Palugvik midden yielded 34 heads and 3 unclassifiable fragments, and the lower half 29 heads and 5 unclassifiable fragments, the distribution of the different types throughout the midden fails to reveal any temporal distinctions between them.

All over southwestern Alaska tanged barbed heads predominate over toggle heads with socket (see the following section). On Kachemak Bay, during all periods, unilaterally barbed heads are even more numerous in proportion to bilaterally barbed forms than they are on Prince William Sound. In contrast, bilaterally barbed heads, especially asymmetric forms, predominate in archaeological collections from Kodiak and the Aleutians.[53] Heads that exhibit a combination of large barbs on one edge and small, often ineffective barbs on the other are characteristic of the Alaska Peninsula and the Aleutians and are not uncommon in Hrdlička's material from Kodiak Island. Small ornamental dorsal barbs seem to be more common on Prince

[53] De Laguna, 1934, pp. 82-85; 1947, pp. 199-201; Hrdlička's unpublished collections. Laughlin and Marsh (1951, p. 81) found that asymmetrically barbed weapon points were characteristic of the lowest layers at the Chaluka site on Umnak Island, while symmetrically barbed heads were more common in the latest layers. Their statement, however, makes no distinction among the various types of detachable and fixed heads.

William Sound than on Kachemak Bay, where only 4 specimens were found, on 2 of which the dorsal barb is really more like a shoulder than a barb.[54]

31. HARPOON HEADS

Only 3 toggle harpoon heads with socket were found in Prince William Sound. According to Makari, such heads were used for seals, sea lions, and small whales. The head was made of the wrist bone of a sea lion and was equipped with a blade of stone. A model of a bladder dart which he made has a harpoon head with closed socket, a barbed blade at right angles to the line hole, and a symmetrically placed spur.

A large harpoon head of whale bone was found in Palugvik 4 (Pl. 35, *9*). The socket is closed, and the blade slit at right angles to the line hole. There is no hole for pegging in the blade. The spur is somewhat asymmetrically placed; its tip is now broken off, but was probably always blunt. The line hole has been drilled from both sides, and on both sides a small groove leads down from it to accommodate the harpoon line. The head measures 8.7 (plus) by 2 cm.

A defective wooden head of the same general type was found on the surface of Palutat Cave and may perhaps have been

[54] De Laguna, 1934, Pls. 39, *1, 9, 10;* 40, *16,* p. 190.

PLATE 34. Harpoon head, lance foreshaft, socket pieces. Scale slightly under natural size
1, Socket piece or arrowhead with blade slit (?), Palugvik 1 (P.796); 2, socket piece or arrowhead with blade slit (?), Palugvik 1 (P.949); 3, unfinished or defective wooden model of toggle harpoon head with bed for blade (inverted), Palutat Cave, surface (P.1232); 4, fragment of bone pin or shaft, Palugvik 4 (P.951); 5, socket piece for harpoon or dart, Palugvik 3 (P.797); 6, bone stopper for harpoon bladder (?), Palugvik, layer (?) (P.1060); 7, wooden foreshaft for lance, with blade slit and wedge-shaped butt, Palutat Cave, surface (P.1230)

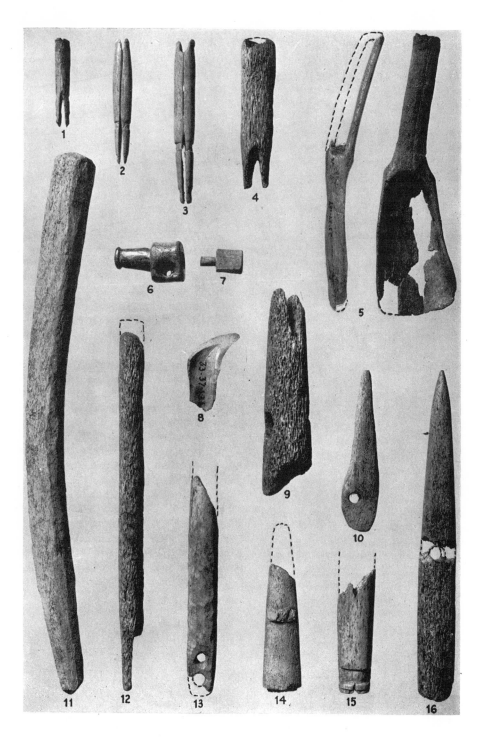

intended only as a model for funerary use (Pl. 34, 3). It measures 10.9 by 1.7 by 1.5 cm. No socket has been made, although the head is obviously intended to have a closed one, and the line hole is indicated only by a drilled pit on one side. There is a bed, not a slit, for the blade, cut on the same side as the incomplete line hole; on the other side is a shoulder to hold the lashing which secured the blade. This blade must have had a long, flat, pointed tang, and the plane of the blade would have been at right angles to the line hole.

The third archaeological specimen is a small fragment from Palugvik, layer unknown (P.952). It originally had a closed socket, now broken out, and was ridged on each side of the line hole. Both the spur and the fore end are missing.

According to Quimby,[55] the older heads from Amaknak Island have beds for attachment of the blade and exhibit a rather elegant silhouette. The younger heads, including a specimen very similar to our Plate 35, 9, have a slit for the blade and for the most part have rather clumsy silhouettes. The blade on both groups was at right angles to the line hole. These late Aleut and Chugach heads stand thus in rather marked contrast to the more elegant closed-socket harpoon heads from Kachemak Bay III.[56]

32. HARPOON FORESHAFTS

Three specimens were probably foreshafts for toggle harpoon heads. The most perfect of these is a heavy bone shaft from Palug-

[55] Quimby, 1946b.
[56] De Laguna, 1934, Pl. 38, 1 to 5.

vik 4 (Pl. 35, 16). It is broken in the middle at the line hole and, when complete, must have been over 13 cm. in length. It is oval in section, with a diameter of 1.5 cm. The point is rather sharp, and the shaft swells toward the butt, which is rounded off abruptly. Another specimen from Palugvik 4 (33-37-9) is much smaller. The point is missing, and the specimen is now only (5) cm. long. The tang is wedge-shaped, with a symmetrically placed line hole. Another specimen from the same level (Pl. 35, 10) was originally a unilaterally barbed head from which the barb or barbs have been cut. It is 6.7 cm. long.

In addition, a doubtful specimen was found in Palugvik 2 (33-37-227). It is a fragment of a bone shaft with a centrally placed line hole and a roughly pointed butt. The rest of the specimen beyond the hole is missing. It has already been listed among the symmetrical tangs. Other tangs, described in section 30 on Detachable Barbed Heads, may, of course, have been broken from foreshafts. Foreshafts and barbed heads seem to have had similarly shaped butt ends, probably so they could be used interchangeably on the same dart or harpoon.

If the Chugach foreshafts were like those of the Koniag, they were not attached directly to the shaft but had, fastened to the hole, a small loop (of quill) through which was run the harpoon line connecting the detachable head and the shaft (or bladder). When the animal was harpooned, the foreshaft would also come loose from the socket piece or shaft. Specimens comparable to the

---

PLATE 35. Harpoon head, foreshafts, socket pieces. Scale ¾ natural size
1, Socket piece for harpoon arrow, Palugvik 2 (33-37-228); 2, socket piece or arrowhead with blade slit (?), Palugvik 1 or 2 (33-37-230); 3, socket piece or arrowhead with blade slit (?), Palugvik 1 (30-25-14); 4, socket piece for harpoon or dart, Palugvik 4 (33-37-21); 5, antler spoon, Palugvik 3 (33-37-137); 6, ivory mouthpiece for harpoon bladder, Palugvik 4 (33-37-24); 7, bone stopper for mouthpiece, Palugvik 4 (?) (33-37-25); 8, blade for crooked knife, bear canine, Palugvik 3 (33-37-136); 9, toggle harpoon head, whale bone, Palugvik 4 (33-37-17); 10, harpoon foreshaft, made of reshaped barbed head, Palugvik 4 (33-37-19); 11, unfinished socket piece, Palugvik 4 (33-37-42); 12, socket piece for harpoon or dart, Site 7, Hawkins Island (30-25-80); 13, bone shaft (fragment of socket piece?), Palugvik 2 or 3 (33-37-125); 14, bone pin with transverse knob, Palugvik 1 (33-37-377); 15, fragment of socket piece, Palugvik 1 (33-37-376); 16, harpoon foreshaft, Palugvik 4 (33-37-20a, b)

Chugach foreshafts were found in Kachemak Bay I to III.[57]

33. Socket Pieces

There are 19 socket pieces in the collection, not including doubtful specimens described as shaft fragments (see section 35). The dominant type in Prince William Sound was like that used in recent times; it was made in one piece with bifurcated tang, although none of the archaeological specimens is as long and slender as the modern specimens purchased by Mr. Lutz at Makaka Point, Hawkin Island.[58] The proportions of the archaeological Chugach specimens resemble those of socket pieces from Kachemak Bay III, although the socket piece with bifurcated tang was not as important on Cook Inlet as on Prince William Sound.

These socket pieces were attached to the fore ends of darts and arrow shafts and received the butt ends of either detachable barbed heads or foreshafts for socketed harpoon heads. No complete specimens were found large enough to have been used with the hand-thrust harpoon, so presumably the barbed heads for these were set directly into the end of the wooden shaft. The bone socket piece made possible a more secure hafting of the detachable head than would have been possible with a slender dart or arrow shaft alone, which would have been likely to split, and the socket piece also gave balance to the light dart or arrow in flight. When the seal or sea otter had been struck and the head detached, the socket piece served to weight down the forepart of the shaft so that it floated vertically in the water, not only impeding the escape of the harpooned animal but signaling its movements to the hunter by the feathered rear end of the shaft, which stuck up out of the water. The harpoon line was always divided

into 2 parts, and each end of this martingale was fastened to an end of the shaft, so that the entire shaft acted as a brake.

The largest specimen, tentatively identified as an unfinished socket piece, comes from Palugvik 4 and measures 21.5 by 1.8 cm. (Pl. 35, 11). It is now warped; there is no socket at the fore end; and the butt has been slightly wedged. It is, therefore, impossible to say how the butt would have been finished. Another bone object, from Site 7 in Hawkins Cut Off (33-37-581), measuring (10) by 2 cm., also appears to have been an unfinished socket piece. At the latter site a much worn and defective specimen was also found (Pl. 35, 12). It is now 15 cm. long and about 1.2 cm. in diameter. The fore end has been broken and rounded off bluntly, perhaps to serve as a blunt head for a practice dart. The butt end is scarfed with one short, laterally placed tang, but it may once have been bifurcated. Two diagonal cuts on the middle of the specimen, slanting down from left to right, may be a decoration or an owner's mark.

There are 13 specimens with bifurcated butts. Five of these have circular or oval sockets, sometimes rather shallow, but are clearly socket pieces. This group includes both the longest (33-37-22), a broken specimen probably 13 cm. long when complete, and the shortest (Pl. 35, 1), only 3.6 cm. long, evidently the socket piece for a sea otter harpoon arrow. There are also 5 additional specimens, shaped exactly like the first, except that they have an expanded slit in the fore end, shaped like an oval socket with open ends. These were at first believed to be arrowheads with blades.[59] However, the slits are not cut down as far as those on arrowheads from Kachemak Bay III, in which the remains of stone blades were actually found,[60] and the Chugach specimens are more likely to have been socket pieces. The slitting of the socket, about which there was a lashing, may have been intended to give a little spring to the

[57] Birket-Smith, 1941, Fig 14a to c; de Laguna, 1934, Pl. 41, 1, 2, 3.
[58] Cf. de Laguna, 1934, Pl. 56, 1, made by a Kodiak Eskimo living in Kachemak Bay; and presumably late Aleut specimens in Jochelson, 1925, Pls. 26, 16; 23, 20 to 24; late Aleut specimens in Laughlin and Marsh, 1951, p. 83; and in Laughlin, 1952, Pl. 2A.

[59] De Laguna, 1934, pp. 89, 155, 215: "Bone arrowhead for inserted blade."
[60] Ibid., Pl. 41, 16, 17.

grip which held the tang of the detachable barbed head. There are, lastly, 3 specimens with bifurcated butts which have lost the fore ends, so that classification is impossible. Both types with bifurcated butt are likely to be grooved around the base of the tangs for a lashing to secure the shaft, and to have grooves for lashings about the fore end and about the base of the bifurcation to prevent splitting (Pls. 34, *1, 5;* 35, *1, 2*). They may be decorated by a pair of longitudinal lines rising from the cleft of the bifurcation (Pls. 34, *2, 5;* 35, *3*) or by 4 longitudinal lines (Pl. 35, *2;* P.591). There is one specimen with oval, closed socket in the expanded fore end which lacks both lashing grooves and decoration (Pl. 35, *4*).

There are, lastly, 3 tangs (Pls. 35, *15;* 47, *7*) which appear to be fragments of larger socket pieces with bifurcated butts.[61] These are from 1.3 to 1.7 cm. wide, and because of their size may be fragments of socket pieces made in 2 parts.

Socket pieces in 2 parts predominate over other forms in Kachemak Bay I to III and are also well represented on Kodiak, the Alaska Peninsula, and the Aleutian Islands.

Forms with central tang are known from Kachemak Bay III and the Aleutian Islands. The common prehistoric Chugach type with bifurcated butt and closed socket is known from Kachemak Bay III, Kodiak, and the Aleutian Islands, but I do not know of any specimens with slit socket outside of Prince William Sound. The general trend in southwestern socket pieces seems to have been from 2-piece to one-piece forms and from short to long slender shapes, with a few notable exceptions from the Aleutians.[62]

Although not enough specimens were found in Prince William Sound to permit of definite conclusions, it is suggestive that the type with slit socket was found only in the lower half of the Palugvik midden, while the corresponding type with plain socket was characteristic of the upper half, with Layer 2 apparently representing a transitional period. This apparent shift from one type to the other strengthens our suspicion that the specimens with slit fore end were socket pieces, not arrowheads.

The distribution of these specimens is:

Palugvik 4	1 unfinished, central tang (?) (Pl. 35, *11*)
	3 bifurcated base, closed socket (Pl. 35, *4;* 33-37-22, P.591)
Palugvik 3	1 bifurcated base, closed socket (Pl. 34, *5*)
	1 bifurcated fragment (P.950)
Palugvik 2	1 bifurcated base, closed socket (Pl. 35, *1*)
	2 bifurcated base, slit socket (Pl. 34, *2;* D30-25-13)
	1 bifurcated fragment (33-37-229)
Palugvik 1 or 2	1 bifurcated base, slit socket (Pl. 35, *2*)
Palugvik 1	2 bifurcated base, slit socket (Pls. 34, *1;* 35, *3*)
	1 bifurcated fragment (P.592)
	1 tang (Pl. 35, *15*)
Palugvik, layer (?)	1 tang (33-37-491)
Palugvik East Point Grave III	1 tang (Pl. 47, *7*)
Site 7, Hawkins Cut Off	1 with scarfed tang (?) (Pl. 35, *12*)
	1 unfinished (33-37-581)

[61] Cf. *ibid.*, Pl. 41, *13*.

[62] *Ibid.*, pp. 86 f., 194 f.; de Laguna, 1947, p. 201; add Hrdlička, 1945, Fig. 202, and unpublished specimens from Kodiak. The socket piece in 2 parts was the only type found throughout all layers of the Chaluka site on Umnak Island, although the long, slender, one-piece form with bifurcated butt belongs only to the late prehistoric or modern layers (Laughlin and Marsh, 1951, pp. 81 f.).

34. Mouthpiece for Bladder

Some of the Chugach harpoons were furnished with inflated bladders attached to the shaft. From Palugvik 4 (Pl. 35, 6) is the mouthpiece by means of which such a bladder was inflated and was also attached to the shaft. The specimen measures 2.8 by 1.8 cm. and consists of a rectangular block with a cylindrical projection at one end which fitted into the bladder. The hole for inflating is oval in section and is enlarged at the outer end to hold the plug or stopper. The piece appears to have been made from a large bear canine, and the oval hole is simply the nerve canal of the tooth. The hole for fastening the mouthpiece to the harpoon shaft was made with a fine bow drill and was reamed out at each end by a hand drill.[63]

A bone stopper for such a mouthpiece was also found in Palugvik 4 (Pl. 35, 7). It is too small, however, to fit this particular specimen. It has a rectangular grip at one end and a short cylindrical plug. The specimen measures 1.8 cm. long and 0.8 cm. wide. A very similar specimen, measuring 1.9 by 0.9 cm., was found on Palugvik beach (Pl. 34, 6). It may also have been a stopper, although the projection is sharpened like a drill point.

35. Bone Shafts

In the collections there are 9 fragments of bone shafts which may be parts of harpoons or lances. From Palugvik 3 or 4 is a fragment (7.3) cm. long and 1.5 cm. in diameter (33-37-23). The section is oval, and the specimen tapers toward one end as if toward a point. Both ends are, however, missing. A similar but smaller fragment, only 1.2 cm. in diameter, comes from Palugvik 4 (Pl. 34, 4). Another bone shaft fragment, 1.5 cm. in diameter (P.953), is also from Palugvik 4, and a piece 2 cm. in diameter is from Palugvik 3 (P.956). From

Palugvik 2 or 3 there is a fragment with oval section, 2 cm. in diameter (Pl. 35, 13). At one end—the other is broken—it narrows to a wedge-shaped butt, which is pierced by 2 holes. The lower hole is now broken out. The fragment is (9) cm. long and was possibly the lower end of a socket piece with central tang, like one from Kachemak Bay III.[64] Two specimens, from Palugvik 2 (P.798) and Palugvik 1 (P.958), 1.7 and 1.5 cm. in diameter, respectively, are tapered and shouldered at one end. They may also be parts of socket pieces, or possibly parts of lance heads. A fragment of bone shaft (9.5) cm. long, with flattened oval section 1.7 cm. in diameter, was found on the surface of Palutat Cave (33-37-656). The unbroken end is shaped to a blunt point. A second specimen, (9) cm. long and 1.9 cm. in diameter, was found 4 feet below the surface of the cave (33-37-655).

Identification of these specimens is impossible. Some may have been parts of heavy socket pieces or lance heads. It is unlikely that the others were parts of the shaft of a harpoon or spear, since plenty of wood was available and would probably have been more serviceable for such a use. The only large objects made of bone which these fragments suggest are the whale bone "bayonets" or picks described in section 55.

36. Wooden Lance

A wooden foreshaft or head for a lance was found on the surface of Palutat Cave (Pl. 34, 7). It is not unlike an ethnological specimen from Kodiak Island which holds a slender barbed slate blade.[65] The Palutat specimen is 19.4 cm. long and has an oval cross section 1 cm. in diameter at the middle and expanding to 2.4 cm. at the flattened fore end, with the blade slit. Stains made by a lashing about the slit extend for a distance of 4 cm. The butt has been faceted to a wedge-shaped tang. This specimen probably had a slate blade and, like the Kodiak specimen, was probably used in whaling,

[63] The Koniag used bladders on sealing darts (Birket-Smith, 1941, Fig. 13; Heizer, 1952b, Pl. 1f) with rather similar mouthpiece (Heizer, 1952b, Fig. 1. 7). Mouthpieces of somewhat different shape were found on Umnak (Jochelson, 1925, Fig. 75A, B).

[64] De Laguna, 1934, Pl. 41, 8.
[65] Birket-Smith, 1941, Fig. 16, especially k.

since our informants stated that the slate blade of the whaling lance was set into a foreshaft of hard wood. The foreshaft was intended to pull loose from the shaft and to remain, with the blade, in the wounded animal. The hunter could then refit his lance with a new foreshaft and blade (i.e., with a new head) and continue the hunt.

Also in Palutat Cave was found a wooden lance shaft (Pl. 57, 1), one fragment of which had been left in Grave A by recent looters. The total length of the shaft was over 108.5 cm. The section is subrectangular, and the shaft has been tapered toward the fore end, which has been hollowed on one side to make a deep bed for the blade. This bed is 8 cm. long and 2 cm. wide. Stains made by the lashing which secured the blade can be seen, but there are no grooves to hold the lashing. The blade was evidently rather thick and was probably, therefore, of chipped stone.

37. PLAIN BONE AND COPPER ARROWHEADS

From Prince William Sound there are 6 bone arrowheads without barbs or inserted blades. Two specimens and one fragment are simply flat strips of bone with a slightly enlarged leaf-shaped point. One of these, from Site 17, Hawkins Island (Pl. 36, 20), is like a flat bone.pin, 11.3 cm. long. The second complete specimen is from Palutat Cave and measures 9.2 by 1 cm. (Pl. 36, 21). A fragment from Palugvik 4 is part of a thin bone blade (33-37-28). Two other specimens, from Palugvik 4 (Pl. 36, 22) and Palugvik 3 (Pl. 36, 18), have faceted points and measure, respectively, 8.2 and 15.9 cm. in length. An unfinished head (14.7) cm. long, with flat elliptical section, comes from Palugvik 3 or 4 (Pl. 37, 7). There is also a slender bone pin, 10.9 cm. long, with sharp point, oval section, and somewhat flattened sharp butt. It may also have been an arrowhead, though identification is doubtful (Pl. 37, 12). It comes from Palugvik, probably from the upper part of the midden. A fragment of a rather blunt bone pin from Palugvik 2 (P.947) appears

to have been part of a similar specimen.

Copper arrowheads of the same type as the bone specimens have also been found. A rather defective specimen, 8 by 1.5 cm., comes from Site 65A, Montague Island (Pl. 28, 3). The tang is broken off, and the edges of the blade near the point are crushed. H. J. Lutz has a very fine specimen from a site on the northern end of Elrington Island (Pl. 36, 19). It is leaf-shaped, with a flat hexagonal section and a distinct tang, and it is 13 cm. long and 1.8 cm. wide. A third copper arrowhead, 6.1 by 1.3 cm., was found in Palugvik 4 (or 3?). It, too, is leaf-shaped, with 2 pairs of shoulders setting off the flat, pointed tang (Pl. 37, 10). These copper specimens should also be compared with some of the smaller double-edged slate blades which may have been arrowheads.

38. BONE ARROWHEADS WITH BARBS

The collections contain a number of barbed points, some of which are described in the next section on Slender Barbed Points. The exact function of these is uncertain, but there are, in addition, a number of specimens which were evidently arrowheads, presumably for hunting land animals, since the heads were not detachable.

The most perfect specimen is from Palugvik 3 (Pl. 36, 4). It is 9 cm. long and 0.9 cm. wide, with a pointed conical tang 1.6 cm. long, separated from the body of the head by a distinct shoulder. There are 3 small barbs, set close together on one edge. Another complete specimen with 3 barbs was found in Palugvik 4 (Pl. 37, 3). The head is thin, measuring 16.7 by 1.5 cm., and has a plain wedge-shaped butt. A third specimen with 3 barbs was found in Palutat Cave (Pl. 37, 6). It is of whale bone, and has a broken point now bluntly reshaped. The barbs are only slightly detached and are near the middle of the head. The butt end has been left rough, and the specimen measures 9.9 by 1 cm.

A defective specimen made of a splinter

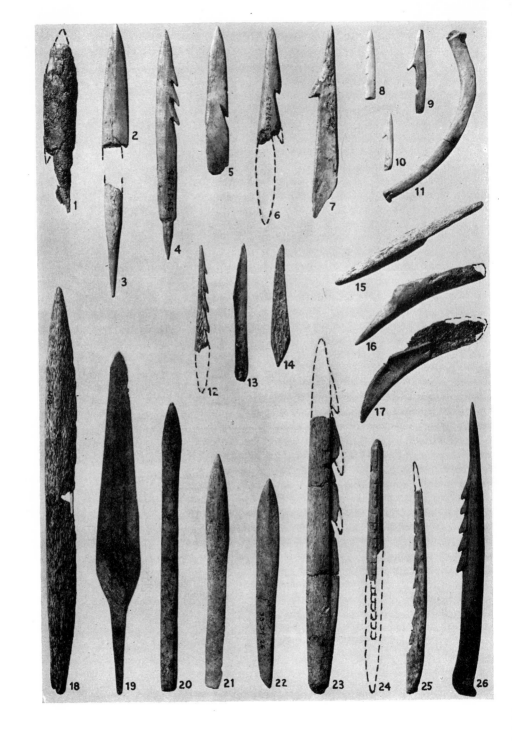

of a large animal bone was found in the modern site in Boswell Bay (Site 11, Hinchinbrook Island). It is 6.5 cm. long and 1.4 cm. wide (Pl. 36, *1*). The conical tang is set off on one side by a barb, now broken, and on the other side by a slight shoulder. A fragment of a faceted head with one barb was found in Palugvik 4 (Pl. 36, *2*), a similar fragment in Palugvik 3 (33-37-128), and a doubtful one in Palutat Cave (33-37-654).

A slender bone pin with a sharp conical point at one end and the remains of a faceted blade at the other end, which is broken, appears to be the tang broken from an arrowhead, perhaps one like that in Plate 36, *4*. The fragment is from Palugvik 1 (Pl. 36, *3*).

There are 2 flat arrowheads with one barb, both neatly made. The first from Palugvik 1 or 2 has a notch above the barb (Pl. 36, *5*). There is now no tang; the specimen seems to have been reshaped without one, and now measures (5.8) by 1 cm. The second head is a flat leaf-shaped or bladelike specimen, 7.3 by 1 cm., and comes from Palugvik 3 or 4 (Pl. 37, *8*). It appears to have been recut from a head with a single barb on one edge. The edges have been ground dull, and both ends are pointed. Identification as an arrowhead is uncertain.

A number of barbed fragments may be parts of arrowheads, detachable barbed heads, or slender barbed points. Specimens with 2 barbs are from Palugvik 3 (P.1327), Palugvik 2 (Pl. 36, *6*), and from layer unknown (P.1052). Another fragment with 4 poorly cut barbs is from Palugvik 4 (P.589), as is also a fragment of a slender point, asymmetrically barbed on both edges (P.570).

Arrowheads with flattened bladelike ends, barbed or unbarbed, seem to be characteristic of Prince William Sound as opposed to other areas in southwestern Álaska. On the other hand, the characteristic type on Kachemak Bay was a slender pinlike form with fore end slit to hold a tiny blade, a type represented on Kodiak and the Aleutians but not on Prince William Sound.[66] Plain bone pins were common on Kachemak Bay and represented the most popular type of arrowhead on Kodiak, but were rare on Prince William Sound.[67]

39. SLENDER BARBED POINTS

The slender barbed points so characteristic of Kachemak Bay and Kodiak Island[68] are represented on Prince William Sound by only a few specimens. They may have been arrowheads, dart heads, or the central prong for multipronged barbed leisters, although Makari denied that multipronged darts or arrows were used.

[66] De Laguna, 1934, Pl. 41, *16* to *18*; unpublished specimens from Kodiak; Jochelson, 1925, Fig. 57.
[67] De Laguna, 1934, Pl. 43, *25* to *30*, pp. 94 f. Identification of these specimens is much less certain than that of Hrdlička's specimens from Kodiak.
[68] Hrdlička, 1944, Fig. 124; de Laguna, 1934, Pl. 42.

PLATE 36. Arrowheads, fishhooks, fish spears. Scale ⅖ natural size

1, Barbed bone arrowhead, Site 11, Hinchinbrook Island (30-25-65); 2, barbed bone arrowhead, Palugvik 4 (33-37-27); 3, tang of arrowhead, Palugvik 1 (33-37-380); 4, barbed bone arrowhead, Palugvik 3 (33-37-126); 5, barbed bone arrowhead, Palugvik 1 or 2 (33-37-225); 6, fragment of slender barbed point, Palugvik 2 (33-37-223); 7, barb for large fishhook or fish spear, Palugvik 4 (33-37-14); 8, fishhook barb, Palugvik, layer (?) (33-37-492); 9, fishhook barb made from small detachable barbed head, Palugvik 4 (33-37-12); 10, fishhook barb, Palugvik 2 (or 3) (33-37-231); 11, shank for fishhook, small animal rib, Palugvik 4 (33-37-15); 12, slender barbed point, Palugvik 2 (33-37-224); 13, bird bone point, Palugvik 3 or 4 (33-37-31); 14, barb for fish spear or fishhook, Palugvik 2 (33-37-232); 15, barb for fish spear, Palugvik 4 (33-37-16); 16, barb for fish spear, Palugvik 3 or 4 (33-37-18); 17, barb for fish spear, Palugvik 2 (33-37-233); 18, bone arrowhead, Palugvik 3 (33-37-127); 19, copper arrowhead, Elrington Island (Lutz Collection); 20, bone arrowhead (?), Site 17, Hawkins Island (30-25-3); 21, bone arrowhead, Palutat Cave, depth unknown (33-37-653); 22, bone arrowhead, Palugvik 4 (33-37-11); 23, slender barbed point, "Yukon Island I" type, Palugvik 4 (33-37-11); 24, slender barbed point, variant of "Yukon Island III" type, Palugvik 1 (33-37-375); 25, barbed point for leister (?), Palutat Cave, depth 4 feet (33-37-651); 26, side prong for bird dart, Palutat Cave, depth 12 to 18 inches (33-37-652)

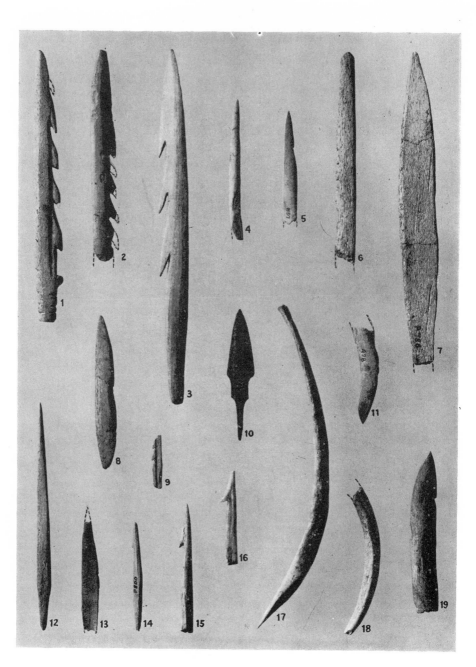

From Palugvik 4 is a broken example of the large "Yukon Island I" type of barbed point, slender but rather flat in section (Pl. 36, *23*). It has 2 barbs (originally 3?), and is now (11.2) cm. long. Another specimen from the same layer, the butt end of which is missing, had at least 5 barbs and is (10) cm. long (Pl. 37, *2*). A complete specimen, from which only the uppermost of 5 barbs has been broken, measures 12.9 cm. in length (Pl. 37, *1*). There are a number of notches at the butt and a rectangular projection below the barbs and opposite a larger notch, presumably to facilitate hafting. The specimen comes from Palugvik 1.

Also from Palugvik 1 is a variant of the smaller "Yukon Island III" type (Pl. 36, *24*). There seem to have been 3 barbs (perhaps more), spaced about 1 cm. apart. Above each barb the ridge between the 2 longitudinal lines which outline the row of barbs is cut by fine transverse notches. A fragment from Palugvik 4 (P.1009) is possibly part of a slender barbed point of the same type.

A fragment of a very small, flat specimen from Palugvik 2 (Pl. 36, *12*) has 4 very fine barbs, but the tang is missing.

A specimen of whale bone with a broken and reshaped blunt point and 3 barbs was found in Palutat Cave (Pl. 37, *6*). It has already been described as an arrowhead, although it may also be mentioned here.

We should note that none of the Chugach specimens had slits for end blades, although these are present on slender barbed points from Kachemak Bay, Kodiak, and the Aleutians. Specimens in these other areas range in size from small points suitable for arrows to large heads for war or whaling lances.[69]

A very slender barbed point from 4 feet below the surface at Palutat Cave is made of the rib (?) of a small animal (Pl. 36, *25*). It is 8 cm. long and only 0.7 cm. in diameter. There are 8 barbs cut in the natural ridge of the bone. These barbs are very little detached; the upper 2, in fact, are hardly more than notches. The curved shape of the specimen suggests that it was one prong of a multipronged barbed leister. Leister prongs seem to be known from Kachemak Bay III, Kodiak, and the Aleutians.[70]

40. SIDE PRONG FOR BIRD DART

A typical Eskimo side prong for a bird dart was found in Palutat Cave at a depth of 12 to 18 inches (Pl. 36, *26*). It is 11.5 cm. long, with 5 barbs, outlined by a pair of longitudinal lines, on the inner (concavely curved) edge. The point is long and sharp; but the butt is flat and curved in on the side with the barbs, with a small shoulder opposite to hold the lashing which fastened it to the shaft. Although rare in southwestern Alaska, similar specimens are known from Kachemak Bay sub-III, Kodiak, the Alaska Peninsula, and the Aleutians. Identification of some of these is admittedly uncertain.[71]

[69] De Laguna, 1934, pp. 90-92, 192-94; 1947, pp. 203-7. Add: Hrdlička, 1945, Fig. 200 (some have beds for blades); unpublished specimens from Kodiak; Laughlin and Marsh, 1951, p. 83; Laughlin, 1952, Pl. 2.
[70] Jochelson, 1925, Pl. 24, *1* to *6*; de Laguna, 1934, p. 91; Hrdlička, unpublished specimens from Kodiak.
[71] De Laguna, 1934, Pl. 43, *20*, p. 196; Hrdlička's unpublished material from Uyak Bay.

PLATE 37. Arrowheads, fishhooks, fish spears. Scale slightly over ⅔ natural size

1, Slender barbed point, "Yukon Island I" type, Palugvik 1 (P.584); 2, slender barbed point, "Yukon Island I" type, Palugvik 4 (P.585); 3, barbed bone arrowhead, Palugvik 4, (P.583); 4, bird bone point, Palugvik 4 (P.812); 5, bird bone point, Palugvik, layer (?) (P.1055); 6, barbed bone arrowhead, Palutat Cave, surface (P.1213); 7, unfinished bone arrowhead, Palugvik 3 or 4 (P.786);.8, barbed bone arrowhead, Palugvik 3 or 4 (P.964); 9, fishhook barb, Palugvik 3 or 4 (P.590); 10, copper arrowhead, Palugvik 4 (or 3) (P.593); 11, barb for fish spear, Palugvik 2 (P.940); 12, bone pin or arrowhead, Palugvik 3 or 4 (P.820); 13, bird bone point, Palugvik 1 (P.917); 14, fishhook barb, Palugvik 1 (P.800); 15, fishhook barb, Palugvik 2 (or 1) (P.801); 16, fishhook barb, Palugvik 4 (P.802); 17, pointed animal rib, Palugvik 2 (P.937); 18, pointed animal rib, Palugvik 1 (P.939); 19, barb for fish spear, Palugvik, layer (?) (P.1053)

41. Bow and Arrows

A carefully smoothed fragment of wood, about (29.5) cm. long and 3 cm. in diameter, was found at the bottom of the Palugvik midden (P.1196). It is probably a fragment of a bow, although identification is uncertain.

A toy arrow made of wood was found on the surface of Palutat Cave (Pl. 49, 9). The shaft is 27 cm. long and 0.4 cm. in diameter. It is slightly thicker in the middle than near the ends and widens out at the butt to a knob in which is cut the notch. At the point there seem to be the remains of a small barb, the plane of which is parallel to that of the notch. A broken wooden shaft (12.5) cm. long, with a sharp, fire-hardened point, was possibly also a toy arrow (P.1247). It was found near the surface in Palutat Cave.

Several pieces of wood which appear to have been arrow shafts were found in the cave. None of them is complete, however, and the ends were not found. One fragment (33-37-676a, b) is (88) cm. long and 1.3 cm. in diameter. It tapers to a flat point, now badly rotted, the shape of which suggests that something was lashed to it. A shaft with a similarly flattened point (P.1253a, b) had a diameter of 1.4 cm. and was at least 86 cm. long. Another shaft with a diameter of 1.4 cm. was over 72 cm. in length (P.1250a, b, and 33-37-677). A fragment with the same diameter is flattened on one side and bears faint traces of red paint (P.1222).

42. Fish Spear Barbs (?)

Makari described a fish gaff, and, although he at first denied that the Chugach used 3-prong fish spears, he later admitted that they were used for herring. Ten specimens were found which may have been the barbs for the side prongs of such spears, or the prongs for gaffs. Identification is, however, very uncertain.

One specimen is a bone pin from Palugvik 4 (Pl. 36, 15), 6.5 cm. long, scarfed at the butt as if for lashing to the side prong.

Another, from Palugvik 3, of animal rib, is 8 cm. long and has several ill-defined notches at the butt (33-37-129). A bone pin (33-37-235) from Palugvik 2, about 4.5 cm. long when complete, has a wedge-shaped butt, evidently for insertion into a hole (in the side prong?).

The remaining 6 specimens are of animal rib, sharply pointed at one end; the butts are missing, but the specimens are all over 5 or 6 cm. in length. They are from Palugvik 3 or 4 (Pl. 36, 16), Palugvik 2 (Pls. 36, 17; 37, 11; 33-37-234), Palugvik 1 (P.910), and the beach (Pl. 37, 19). The last has a very small, ineffective barb near the point. If correctly identified, it is the only example from Prince William Sound of a barbed barb for the side prong of a fish spear.

The unbarbed specimens may be compared with examples from Kachemak Bay I to III, the Alaska Peninsula, Kodiak, and the Aleutians. Barbed barbs are also known from the same areas, but are restricted in Kachemak Bay to Periods II and III.[72]

43. Fishhooks

Our Chugach informants told us that some fishhooks were made from the wishbone of the large loon, although we did not find any of this type. A V-shaped one-piece hook was used for codfish, and a 2-piece hook for halibut. The line was of kelp, of which pieces 9 feet long could be obtained. Codfish, ducks, and gulls were also taken with a wooden hook made like a gorge with a crosspiece. A number of wooden pins were found (see section 58) but could not be identified as parts of hooks. However, 11 bone barbs for compound fishhooks and one bone fishhook shank were obtained from archaeological sites. These were parts of V-shaped hooks of the common type in Kachemak Bay, Kodiak Island, and the Aleutians.[73]

The shank (Pl. 36, 11) is made from the rib of a small animal and has a shoulder

[72] De Laguna, 1934, Pls. 40, 8 to 11 (barbed); 43, 14, 15 (unbarbed), pp. 92 f., 195 f.; unpublished specimens in Hrdlička's collections.
[73] De Laguna, 1934, Pl. 43, 5 to 13; Birket-Smith, 1941, Fig. 23; Jochelson, 1925, Pl. 25, 40 to 51.

at each end. The shoulder at the larger end is simply the dorsal epiphysis which has been trimmed; the shoulder at the smaller end has been artificially shaped. (The specimen is shown upside down in the illustration, since the fishline should be attached to the smaller end of the shank, and the barb to the larger end.) The specimen is 7.5 cm. long and comes from Palugvik 4. On all of the more carefully made fishhook shanks found by Hrdlička on Kodiak and on the Aleutians, the larger end has an oblique groove in which the barb rested. This groove is, however, lacking on our specimen. On the inner (concavely curved) edge at the smaller end of the shank there is almost invariably a groove in which the fishline was placed, presumably to prevent it from being bitten through by the fish. On our specimen, however, this groove is placed at one side. Bone fishhook shanks were common on Kodiak and the Aleutians but were not found in Kachemak Bay, even though the barbs were numerous there.[74] The shanks must have been made of wood, as were, presumably, the majority in Prince William Sound.

The barbs were lashed to the shank with their own small barbs turned inward. The 11 complete barbs in our collections are all straight, like those of Kachemak Bay and Kodiak, not curved like the Aleutian specimens. They range in length from 2.8 (Pl. 36, 8) to 7.5 cm. (Pl. 36, 7) and are usually unnotched at the butt, which may be blunt or pointed.

The smallest specimen was found on the beach at Palugvik (Pl. 36, 8) and has 3 barbs on one edge and 3 notches on each edge of the butt for attachment to the shank. A broken specimen from Palugvik 3 or 4 (Pl. 37, 9) has 2 barbs (possibly 3, originally) and is grooved up one side.

All of the other specimens have only one barb. One of these, from Palugvik 4 (Pl. 36, 9), was originally a small detachable barbed head and has already been described

(see section 30). It is 3.2 cm. long. The line hole has broken out, and in the reshaping of the specimen the remains of the hole have been utilized as a notch for the lashing. A specimen from Palugvik 2 (Pl. 36, 10) is 5 cm. long and has a pair of notches at the butt. Five other specimens have plain butts and come from Palugvik 4 (Pls. 36, 7; 37, 16; 33-37-13), Palugvik 2 or (1?) (Pl. 37, 15) and Palugvik 1 (Pl. 37, 14). A broken specimen is from Palugvik, layer unknown (P.967).

44. BIRD BONE POINTS

There are 13 bird bone points, exclusive of specimens classed as unfinished needles or broken awls, which may be compared with bird bone points from Kachemak Bay.[75] They were probably hafted, perhaps as barbs for compound fishhooks.

These specimens are simply pointed slivers of bird bone, the butts rounded off or left rough. The only complete specimens (Pls. 36, 13; 37, 5) are about 5.5 cm. long, but others may have been over 7 cm. in length (Pl. 37, 4). Three specimens have a notch or series of notches near the butt, presumably to facilitate hafting (Pls. 36, 13, on side not illustrated; 37, 13; P.936). Two have a small barb (Pl. 37, 5; 33-37-493).

These bird bone points are from Palugvik 4 (Pl. 37, 4), 3 or 4 (Pl. 36, 13), 3 (33-37-133, P.809), 3 or 2 (P.936), 2 (P.944, field nos. 616, 624), 1 (Pl. 37, 13), and the beach (Pl. 37, 5; 33-37-493).

In addition, there are from Palugvik 1 (33-37-379) and 2 (Pl. 36, 14) 2 similar points made of splinters of animal bone. The second of these is pointed at both ends and might have been a gorge, a device used to catch both fish and birds.

45. BONE PINS

Curiously enough, no specimens resembling the bone pins so common in Kachemak Bay were found in Prince William

---

[74] De Laguna, 1934, p. 93.

[75] Ibid., Pl. 43, 16 to 19, p. 94.

Sound.[76] Two nondescript specimens were found at Palugvik in 1930. One of these, from Palugvik 3 (?) (30-25-21), may be the tang of an arrow; the other, from the beach (30-25-7), is too waterworn to be identified. Three broken specimens from Palugvik 3 (33-37-130, 131, 132) and another from Palugvik 2 (33-37-226) appear to be points broken from weapons (barbed heads?) or from awls. A bone object from Palugvik 4 (33-37-116), described in the field catalogue as a bone rod or pin, (9.5) cm. long, sharpened at one end and broken at the other, was unfortunately lost. A second specimen from the same layer (P.804) is 5.2 cm. long and may have been an awl.

From Palugvik 3 or 4 there is a decorated bone pin, broken at both ends (33-37-51). It is (3.5) cm. long and 0.5 cm. in diameter. At the wider end there is an obliquely drilled pit or groove, possibly some kind of socket (?). From this end 4 longitudinal lines run about halfway down the specimen. At the other, smaller end there are a pair of spiral lines which make a complete turn about the pin and end on a level with the ends of the 4 longitudinal lines. All of these lines appear to have been cut with a metal tool. The smaller end is slightly flattened on the side of the groove. We can offer no suggestion as to the use of this specimen.

[76] *Ibid.*, Pl. 43, *25* to *30*, pp. 94 f., 197. Some of these pins may have been arrowheads, and others barbs for halibut hooks, teeth for fish rakes, or gaffs, bodkins, awls, etc. Many of the bone pins from Kodiak have detached conical tangs and thus are clearly arrowheads; others have ornamented butts and are awls or bodkins. In general, it is much easier to determine the functions of this Kodiak material.

46. BONE AWLS

Fifteen awls of bird bone, 10 of animal bone, and 2 specimens tentatively identified as handles for awls were found in Prince William Sound.

All but 3 of the bird bone awls were broken. One complete specimen, of cormorant ulna (?) with the proximal articulation left as a handle, is 11 cm. long and comes from Palugvik 4 (Pl. 38, *16*). On the 2 other complete awls, both from the burial ledge at Palugvik East Point, the butt end has been trimmed. One is 6.5 cm. long (33-37-557); the other, 6.8 cm. long, was found near the hand of Skeleton III (Pl. 47, *6*). Broken bird bone awls were found in Palugvik 4 (Pl. 39, *3, 9;* 33-37-38, P.805, P.813), Palugvik 3 (P.814), Palugvik 2 (33-37-243), Palugvik 1 or 2 (33-37-249), and Palugvik 1 (Pl. 38, *17;* 33-37-393, 394; WSM 1026).

In addition, there is an awl from Palugvik 2 or 3 (Pl. 38, *15*) made of a bird bone point set into a larger bird bone for a handle. Since both ends are broken, identification as a compound awl is uncertain.[77] A roughly shaped fragment of animal bone 7.2 cm. long, from a depth of 4 feet or more in Palutat Cave, may also be the handle for an awl (Pl. 39, *26*), since it has a groove on one edge to hold the point, and notches for a lashing.

There are 10 awls of animal bone, varying in length from 7 cm. (Pl. 39, *16*) to over 11.3 cm. (Pl. 38, *14*). The most carefully made specimen is a rod (16) cm. long,

[77] A similar specimen, broken in the same way, comes from Kachemak Bay III (*ibid.*, Pl. 44, *10*, p. 96).

PLATE 38. Needles, awls, drills. Scale natural size

1, Needle, broken and reshaped with new eye, Palugvik 2 (33-37-242); 2, needle, broken at eye, Palugvik 1 or 2 (33-37-239); 3, needle, Palugvik 2 or 3 (30-25-9); 4, needle, Palugvik 1 (33-37-386); 5, needle, Palugvik 3 or 4 (33-37-37); 6, needle, Palugvik 1 (33-37-384); 7, needle, without eye, Palugvik (1 or) 2 (33-37-240); 8, needle, Palugvik 3 (33-37-140); 9, tube, goose bone, Palugvik 4 (33-37-50); 10, drill point, greenstone, Palugvik 2 (30-25-20); 11, drill point, greenstone, Palugvik, layer (?) (33-37-512); 12, drill point, greenstone, Palugvik 3 (33-37-168); 13, drill point, greenstone, Palugvik 2 or 3 (33-37-169); 14, awl, bear fibula, Palugvik 1 (33-37-392); 15, awl (?), one bird bone thrust inside another, Palugvik 2 or 3 (33-37-142); 16, awl, cormorant (?) ulna, Palugvik 4 (33-37-39); 17, awl, bird bone, Palugvik 1 (33-37-395); 18, hand drill, bone, Palugvik 3 (33-37-134); 19, hand drill, slate, Palugvik 3 (33-37-170)

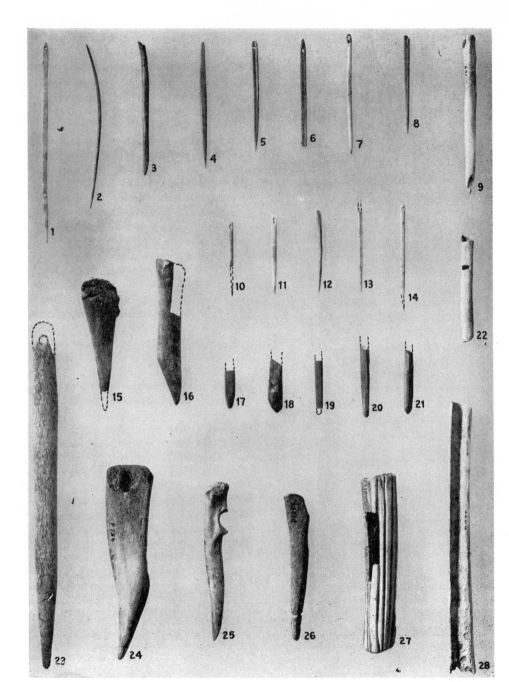

with suboval cross section (Pl. 39, 23). The point is charred and the butt broken at the suspension hole. In shape the specimen resembles the pick found with Skeleton III at Palugvik East Point (Pl. 48, 7). The remaining 9 specimens are made of bear fibula, porcupine (?) ulna, seal tibia (?), etc., or of sections cut out of animal bones. On 2, the articulation has been left as a handle (Pls. 38, 14; 39, 25). Another has a hole drilled through the butt, apparently for suspension (Pl. 39, 24). These specimens are from Palugvik 4 (P.796), Palugvik 3 (Pl. 39, 25), Palugvik 2 (Pl. 39, 16, 24; P.791, P.852) and Palugvik 1 (Pls. 38, 14; 39, 15; P.806).

In addition, some of the sharp bone points, identified as barbs for the side prongs of fish spears, and some of the sharpened sections of animal rib described in the next section may also have been awls.

47. Cut Ribs

In addition to the pointed animal ribs which were tentatively identified as barbs for fish spears (section 42), there are also 4 ribs with sharp points. The complete specimens are 15.5 (Pl. 37, 17) and 27 (Pl. 41, 9) cm. long, and both are from Palugvik 2. The 2 fragments are from Palugvik 3 or 4 (33-37-33) and Palugvik 1 (Pl. 37, 18). These may have been awls.

Three animal ribs have blunt points. A specimen from Palugvik 1 (33-37-396) made of a large rib (porpoise or beluga?), (16) cm. long, has a worn blunt point. Another from the same layer (P.959) and one

from Palugvik 4 (P.966) are of smaller ribs. The latter has been split in two and partly smoothed. The point is flat and blunt, and there are notches along the edge. These specimens may have been used as flaking tools, even though Makari denied that the Chugach possessed such tools.

There are, lastly, 2 fragmentary pieces of cut animal rib from Palugvik 4 (P.941, P.1325).

Similar cut ribs are known from Kachemak Bay and Kodiak.[78]

48. Needles

Thirty-five (or 36?) needles with eyes were found in Prince William Sound. Makari's daughter told us that ordinary sewing used to be done with a needle of native copper, but no copper needles were seen. When heavy skins were to be sewed, the holes were first made with a bone awl, and the thread was then carried by a bone needle. With one or 2 exceptions, all the needles in our collections are made of splinters of bird bone. Whereas the needles from Kachemak Bay had been ground down to a circular cross section,[79] most of those from the sound are simply flat strips of bone. There is even one from Palugvik 1, made from a very small, unsplit bird bone (Pl. 39, 5). The needles with oval cross section are flattened at the eye. The eyes are usually made with a hand drill or are fine slits cut with a knife. On only 7

[78] *Ibid.*, Pls. 45, *1* to *4*; 56, *10*; Hrdlička's unpublished collections.
[79] De Laguna, 1934, Pl. 44, *1* to *8*, pp. 96 f.

PLATE 39. Needles, awls, drills. Scale ¾ natural size

1, Needle, Palugvik 1 (P.823); 2, needle, Palutat Cave, depth 12 to 18 inches (P.1262); 3, awl, bird bone, Palugvik 4 (P.811); 4, needle without eye, Palugvik 2 (P.821); 5, needle of unsplit bird bone, Palugvik 1 (P.822); 6 and 8, fragments of same needle, Palugvik 1 (P.1014a, b); 7, needle, Palugvik 2 (P.825); 9, awl, bird bone, Palugvik 4 (P.792); 10, needle, Palugvik, layer (?) (P.1056); 11, needle, Palugvik 1 (P.824); 12, needle without eye, Palugvik 2 (P.833); 13, needle, Palugvik 2 (P.830); 14, needle, Palugvik 3 (P.826); 15, awl, animal bone, Palugvik 1 (P.789); 16, awl, animal bone, Palugvik 2 (P.788); 17, drill point, greenstone, Palugvik 2 (P.646); 18, drill point, greenstone, Palugvik 1 (P.648); 19, drill point, greenstone, Palugvik 3 (P.649); 20, drill point, greenstone, Palugvik 2 (P.647); 21, drill point, greenstone, Palugvik 1 (P.645); 22, whistle, bird bone, Palugvik 4 (P.814); 23, awl or miniature pick (?), Palugvik 3 (P.794); 24, awl with suspension hole, animal bone, Palugvik 2 (P.784); 25, awl, animal bone, Palugvik 3 (P.785); 26, awl handle, bone, Palutat Cave, depth 4 feet (P.1214); 27, bird bone tube, cut for needles, Palugvik 3 (P.970); 28, bird bone tube, split in two, Palugvik 3 (P.935)

specimens does the eye seem to have been made with a bow drill. These are from Palugvik 3 (Pls. 38, *8;* 39, *14*), Palugvik 2 or 3 (Pl. 38, *3*), Palugvik 1 (Pl. 39, *1, 5*), layer unknown (Pl. 39, *10*), and Grave III, Palugvik East Point (Pl. 46, *14*).

The length of the complete specimens ranges from 3.2 (broken and reshaped) or 3.7 cm. (Pl. 38, *6*) up to 10.8 cm. (Pl. 38, *8*). Two needles 10 cm. long (Pl. 46, *16, 17*) were found, together with some very long unfinished (?) specimens and fragments, lying across the chest of Skeleton III at Palugvik East Point. This range of sizes is greater than that of the needles from Kachemak Bay, and the Chugach specimens are on the whole much coarser.

Two needles, from Palugvik 2 (Pl. 38, *1*) and Palugvik 1 or 2 (WSM 1126), were broken at the eye and reshaped with a new eye. Another broken needle from Palugvik 2 was reshaped without an eye (P.835).

There are also 24 (or 25?) unfinished (?) needles, completely shaped except that they lack eye, notch, groove, or any other obvious means of attaching a thread. With Skeleton III, Palugvik East Point, were 7 specimens, 12.2 to 14.8 cm. long (Pl. 46, *1* to *4, 6* to *8*), found with 6 needles with

eyes (Pl. 46, *11, 12, 14* to *17*), and 4 fragments (Pl. 46, *5, 9, 10, 13*) which may or may not have had eyes. Eyeless specimens from the Palugvik midden vary in length from 4 (Pl. 39, *12*) to 8.5 cm. (33-37-657). One from Palugvik 2 is pointed at both ends (Pl. 39, *4*). It is possible that these eyeless specimens were never intended as needles, but were perhaps used as awls; or the thread may have been fastened to them in some way, though they lack the groove characteristic of Aleut eyeless needles. They may, of course, be simply unfinished needles, although it seems unlikely that so many specimens, all of which are well made, should have been left incomplete.[80]

There are in addition 20 fragments which were probably broken from needles, even though the butt ends are missing. Sixteen pieces of bird bone, split but otherwise unshaped, exhibit the technique of manufacture.[81] The ends were evidently cut off a bird bone of convenient size, and this tube was then sawed longitudinally into narrow strips (Pl. 39, *27*). Whetstones with grooves in which these strips could be smoothed down and sharpened are illustrated in Plate 16, *10, 11*.

The provenience of these specimens is:

	Eyed Needles	Eyeless Needles	Fragments	Bone Cut for Needles
Palugvik 4		33-37-35 P.834		P.969
Palugvik 3 or 4	Pl. 38, *5*	P.837	33-37-36 P.1361a to c	P.840
Palugvik 3	Pl. 38, *8* Pl. 39, *14* 33-37-139	33-37-138 141 P.838	P.829	Pl. 39, *27* P.1318
Palugvik 2 or 3	Pl. 38, *3* P.1319			P.836

[80] Similar specimens from Kachemak Bay were evidently not as common and were interpreted as

unfinished needles *(ibid.,* Pl. 44, *9,* p. 97).
[81] Cf. *ibid.,* Pl. 44, *26.*

Palugvik 2	Pl. 38, *1*	Pl. 38, *7*	33-37-237	33-37-244
	Pl. 39, *7*	Pl. 39, *4*	P.881	245
	Pl. 39, *13*	Pl. 39, *12*	P.1329a to c	246
	33-37-241	33-37-236		248
	P.827	238		
	P.835.................reshaped			
	P.975	P.971		
	field no. 293			
Palugvik 1 or 2	Pl. 38, *2*		P.832	33-37-247
	WSM 1126			
Palugvik 1	Pl. 38, *4*	33-37-390	33-37-382	33-37-387
	Pl. 38, *6*	P.839	P.974	391
	Pl. 39, *1*	P.973	P.976	P.968
	Pl. 39, *5*		P.977	P.972
	Pl. 39, *6 & 8*		P.1317	WSM 1048
	Pl. 39, *11*			
	33-37-381			
	383			
	385 & 389			
	388			
	P.828			
Palugvik, layer (?)	Pl. 39, *10*	33-37-494	P.1057	P.1068
		495		
Palugvik East Point Grave III	Pl. 46, *11,* *12, 14* to *17*	Pl. 46, *1* to *4* *6* to *8*	Pl. 46, *5,* *9, 10, 13*	
Palutat Cave Depth 12″ to 18″	Pl. 39, *2*			
Depth 4′			33-37-657	

One fragmentary needle from Palugvik 1 (P.922) is made of a flat strip of bone 1.1 cm. wide, split from an animal rib. The hole is a cut slit. This specimen is not included in the list given above because it was probably not used for sewing but rather perhaps for stringing fish.

49. DRILLS

The holes in bone, ivory, shell, and slate objects show that both the hand drill and a mechanical drill (bow or cord) were used in Prince William Sound throughout the period represented by the sites explored.

The hand drill seems to have been used less often than the bow or cord drill, but all 3 types were mentioned by our informants.

From Palugvik 3 is a hand drill made of a piece of animal leg bone, 7 cm. long, unshaped except at the point (Pl. 38, *18*). A hand drill of slate was found in the same layer (Pl. 38, *19*). It is 5.5 cm. long; one surface is polished, the edges are chipped, and the butt is enlarged for a grip.

There are also 12 drill bits of greenstone and one of slate, for hafting in a shaft of wood or bone and presumably used

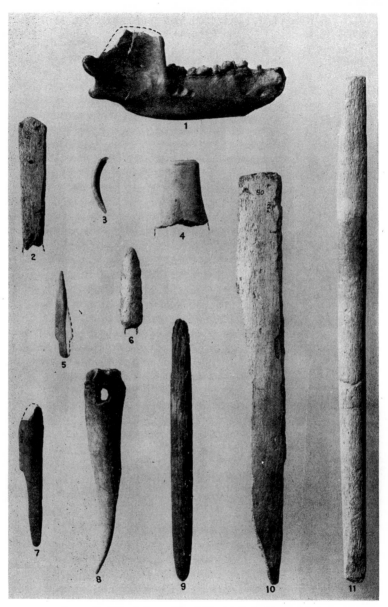

PLATE 40. Bone knives, picks, drill rest. Scale ⅔ natural size

1, Drill rest, bear mandible, Palugvik 1 (P.896) ; 2, handle for spoon (?) , whale bone, Palugvik 4
(P.908) ; 3, knife blade or engraving tool, porcupine incisor, Palugvik 2 (P.946) ; 4, handle,
section of animal leg bone, Palugvik 1 (P.929) ; 5, broken leaf-shaped blade, bone, Palugvik 3
(P.808) ; 6, point of ice pick (?) , bone, Palugvik 4 (P.810) ; 7, bone knife or scraper, Palutat
Cave, depth 12 to 18 inches (P.1217) ; 8, stiletto, animal bone, Palugvik 2 (P.783) ; 9, fire drill,
Palutat Cave, surface (P.1224) ; 10, pick, whale bone, Palugvik 3 (P.931) ; 11, pick or bone shaft,
Palugvik 1 (P.793)

with a bow or a cord drill. The holes which could be made with these bits range in diameter from 0.3 or 0.4 cm. (Pl. 38, *11, 12*) to 0.8 cm. (Pl. 38, *13*). The only complete specimen, unfortunately lost, came from Palugvik 1 and was described in the field catalogue as 2 cm. long and pointed at both ends (33-37-483). The other specimens are either broken or roughly shaped at the butts, and range in length from 1.9 (Pl. 39, *17*) to 5 cm. The sections may be flat (Pl. 38, *13*), triangular, rectangular (Pls. 38, *10;* 39, *17*), pentagonal (Pl. 38, *11*), or hexagonal (Pl. 39, *20, 21*). The distribution of these drill bits is: Palugvik 3 (Pls. 38, *12;* 39, *19*), Palugvik 2 or 3 (Pl. 38, *13*), Palugvik 2 (Pls. 38, *10;* 39, *17, 20;* 33-37-315, WSM 1134), Palugvik 1 (Pl. 39, *18, 21;* 33-37-483), Palugvik, layer (?) (Pl. 38, *11*), and large burial cave at Site 16, Hawkins Island (P.1111).

Hand drills and drill bits of stone and bone were also found in Kachemak Bay. Whereas bits of greenstone were peculiar to Prince William Sound, our Chugach collections did not include any of bone, although bone drill points were common in Kachemak Bay I to III. Drills or drill points seem to be very rare in other parts of southwestern Alaska or else have not been reported.[82]

A fragment of cut rib from Palugvik 3 or 4 with a natural groove near the cut end may be part of a bow for a drill (P.1326), similar to a specimen found by Hrdlička on Kodiak Island. The two ivory bear figures from the grave on Palugvik East Point (Pl. 46, *18, 19*) may perhaps have been handles for a cord drill (see section 64).

Although one of our informants said that a mouthpiece was used with the bow drill, no specimen of this type was found. It is probable that the upper end of the drill shaft used with a bow or cord drill rotated in a rest which was held in the hand or braced against the chest. Paul Elie

Chimowitski in fact specified that the rest for the fire drill was a round piece of wood which was held against the chest. Nine bone drill rests which could have been used in this manner were found in the lower half of the Palugvik midden.

One of these is a broken bone wedge from Palugvik 1 (33-37-406), already mentioned in section 6. From the same layer is a flat slab of bone, (7.9) by 2.3 cm., with a drilled pit near one end, showing its use as a rest for a mechanical drill.

There are 7 drill rests made from one half of a brown bear mandible, with from one to 7 drilled pits. One specimen of this type from Palugvik 1 (field no. 773), now unfortunately lost, served both as a drill rest and as a fat scraper, for the upper part of the ramus had been cut to form a sharp scraping edge, although it could have been used effectively only by a left-handed person. Other specimens are from Palugvik 2 (P.921), Palugvik 1 or 2 (33-37-258), and Palugvik 1 (Pls. 40, *1;* 41, *10;* P.895, P.930).

Bone wedges and scraps of bone or ivory were used as drill rests on Kachemak Bay, Kodiak, and the Aleutian Islands. These were all held in the hand or braced against the chest, and there is no clear evidence that the drill rest was ever held in the teeth, as it is among the more northern Eskimo.[83] The use of animal mandibles as drill rests can be duplicated on the Aleutians.

50. FIRE DRILLS

The fire drill was described as a cord drill. The board or hearth was of red cedar, found as driftwood, and the drill itself of yellow cedar. As already mentioned, the rest or brace was supposed to have been a circular piece of wood.

Four specimens from Palutat Cave seem to have been the shafts of fire drills. These

---

[82] *Ibid.*, Pl. 36, *1* to *11, 15, 18* to *20*, p. 78.

[83] Jochelson, 1925, Pl. 27, Fig. 1, *2, 5, 9;* de Laguna, 1934, Pls. 48, *12;* 52, *1c* (but not identified as a rest), pp. 103, 115, 185 (references to "mouthpieces" should be corrected to "rests"); 1947, p. 170; Hrdlička, 1944, p. 329 (bone wedges mentioned as "bases for the firemaking drill" should be corrected to "drill rests").

are wooden rods, circular in section, charred at the lower end which rotated in the fire board, and worn at the upper end which revolved in the pit of the drill rest. The 2 complete specimens (Pls. 40, *9;* 49, *5*) are 19 and 19.7 cm. long. The third is broken at the lower end, and may of course have been the shank for a drill with bit, not a fire drill (Pl. 50, *8*). The fourth, while broken at both ends, still shows charring at one (33-37-795). It has been gnawed by dogs.

The oblong wooden pillow found under the skull in Grave C1, Palutat Cave, is 35 by 10 cm. and has 2 charred, drilled pits. It was evidently used as a fire board or hearth (P.1298). The foot board of the coffin in Grave E, Palutat Cave (33-37-724), has 5 drilled pits on the surface which was turned outside. It may have been used as a hearth, although there is no charring visible now at the pits.

51. STRIKE-A-LIGHT

The collection contains a battered quartz pebble, 5.6 by 2.8 cm., which was identified by Matrona Tiedmann, Makari's daughter, as a stone used for striking fire (P.758). This stone comes from Palugvik 3 (or 2); similar lumps of quartz were found throughout the site but were not saved. Matrona also mentioned the use of pyrites in making fire but believed that this was learned from the Russians. It is more likely that the fire-making properties were known in prehistoric times, for a lump of pyrites, now disintegrated (P.1085a), lay near the hands of Skeleton I in the triple burial at Palugvik East Point.

Hrdlička also found a few pieces of pyrites in some of the Aleutian middens and quotes ethnological sources which indicate that the Aleut kindled fires by means of flint and quartz strike-a-lights and by means of fire drills.[84]

52. BONE BLADES FOR KNIVES OR WEAPONS

In addition to the knife blades described in sections 22 to 27, there are a few speci-

[84] Hrdlička, 1945, pp. 32, 99, 111 f.

mens of bone which may have been blades for knives.

A bear canine, split in two and sharpened along one edge, was found in Palugvik 3 (Pl. 35, *8*). It was apparently the blade for a crooked knife. One of our informants told us that crooked knives had double-edged blades of native copper, although we found no specimen of this type. A fragment of a cut and ground tooth from the beach (P.1058) may also have been a knife blade.

A porcupine incisor from Palugvik 2 has been ground at the tip to produce a sharp point (Pl. 40, *3*) and could have been used as a knife for cutting grooves or holes.[85]

Beaver teeth were said to have been used for sharpening knife blades. Copper blades were probably meant, since single-edged copper knives were said to have been used for cutting up meat.

A chip of naturally hollow animal leg bone from Palugvik 4 has been ground to a pointed, leaf-shaped blade with straight base, measuring 3.8 by 1 cm. (P.804). A broken bone blade from Palugvik 3, 6.6 cm. long and 1.6 (?) cm. wide, was ground to a leaf shape with hexagonal cross section and wedged butt (Pl. 40, *5*). These 2 specimens may have been blades for knives, lances, etc., and may be compared with similar slate blades.

A broken detachable barbed head from Palugvik 2 has been recut as a knife (Pl. 33, *15*).

53. KNIFE HANDLES

A wooden knife handle (Pl. 50, *5*) was found 6 inches below the surface of Palutat Cave. It is 12 cm. long, 1.8 cm. wide, and 1.2 cm. thick, with a rectangular section. The blade was originally lashed in a bed roughly cut out on one side of the handle. On the opposite side is a shoulder to hold the lashing. The lower end of the handle is slightly concave in outline. On the side with the shoulder, the handle is decorated with

[85] Birket-Smith (1941, Fig. 32a, p. 156) publishes a beaver tooth knife with wooden handle from Kodiak, of the type described by Lisiansky.

a medial longitudinal line which branches near the butt end to outline a cut triangular area. This decoration is very similar to that on the wooden bars from Grave B2 in the cave (see Fig. 34).

Another specimen, also from Palutat Cave, may be a knife handle (Pl. 50, 6). It is a flat wooden slat, 8 cm. long and 1.7 cm. wide, with a bed for the blade at one end. It lacks a shoulder or groove for the lashing. The specimen has clearly been shaped by a stone knife. Although smaller, it is no cruder than the wooden knife handle found in the Aleut burial cave on Kagamil Island.[86]

54. Bone Knives or Scrapers

From Palugvik 4 is a bone knife with a spatulate blade (Pl. 41, 5). The edges of the blade are dull; the handle is irregular in shape. The blade measures 8 by 1.8 cm., the handle 9 by 1.4 cm. It is likely that this specimen is unfinished.

A bone knife or scraper made of a split animal leg bone was found in Palugvik 1 (Pl. 41, 3). One end is broken off; the other is pointed and sharpened at the edges. The specimen was probably 12 cm. long when complete. A similar implement, now much rotted, is from Site 35 in Port Gravina, and is (33) cm. long (33-37-598). A piece of animal leg bone, 10.4 cm. long, with blunt point and the edges roughened by notching, may have been a knife or possibly a flaking tool. It comes from Palugvik 3 (P.955).

From 1 to 2 feet below the surface of Palutat Cave and at the bottom of the test pit in the cave were found 2 small tools made of split and trimmed animal leg bone, with rather dull edges and blunt flat points. The first (Pl. 40, 7) is 10.7 cm. long and 2 cm. wide; the second (Pl. 41, 6) is (15) cm. long and 1.4 cm. wide. These specimens may have been used as combination boot-sole creasers and scrapers or for other purposes connected with the preparation and sewing of skins. They may, however, have been used as marrow

extractors, since these were described as narrow, pointed bone tools.

A piece of caribou leg bone from Palugvik 3 which had been sawed in two lengthwise may have been intended as a 2-handed scraper (P.932). Neither of the 2 longitudinal edges, however, shows signs of wear.

A thin triangular blade with blunt edges, measuring (5.5) by 1.6 cm., has been cut from a large scapula (P.962). On one side are a few incised lines, which do not, however, form any clear pattern. This specimen comes from Palugvik 4 and may be a scraper or part of a scraper, perhaps for removing the inner bark of the hemlock, which was eaten by the Chugach because of its sweet taste. The scraper commonly used for scraping bark was said to have been a clam shell. Clam shell scrapers were also used for dehairing skins, as were paddle-shaped scrapers of wood.

The Chugach evidently had few bone scrapers, as compared with their relatives on Kachemak Bay. The latter possessed scapula scrapers with transverse or with longitudinal edge, scraper blades cut from scapulae, and scrapers of split leg bone with longitudinal edges, as well as smaller knife-like forms. Hrdlička also obtained a good collection of bone and ivory scrapers of various types from Kodiak Island.[87]

55. Daggers, Picks, and Stilettos

Our Chugach informants told us that a double-edged copper dagger was used in war. Sometimes this had a second, smaller blade set at the butt end of the handle. Daggers with stone blades were also mentioned. While no copper dagger was obtained, a bone dagger was found beside Skeleton III at Palugvik East Point (Pl. 48, 4). It is now curved, probably as a result of warping in the ground. The blade is lenticular in cross section, with sharp edges and point. The handle is roughly finished. The specimen is 37.5 cm. long and 4 cm. wide at the blade; the handle alone meas-

---

[86] Dall, 1878, Pl. 7, no. 17254.

[87] De Laguna, 1934, Pl. 45, pp. 98 f.; Hrdlička, unpublished collections.

PLATE 41. Bone knives, chisels, drill rest. Scale slightly over ⅔ natural size

1, Fragment of ice pick (?), Palugvik 4 (33-37-45) ; 2, chisel, bear penis bone, Palugvik 3 (33-37-135) ; 3, bone knife or scraper, Palugvik 1 (33-37-378) ; 4, stiletto, bear ulna, Palugvik 3 (33-37-143) ; 5, bone knife, Palugvik 4 (33-37-41) ; 6, bone knife or scraper, Palutat Cave, depth 5 feet (33-37-658) ; 7, wedge, whale bone, Palugvik 4 (33-37-43) ; 8, chisel, penis bone (?), Palugvik 4 (33-37-34) ; 9, sharpened bear rib, Palugvik 2 (33-37-250) ; 10, drill rest, brown bear mandible, Palugvik 1 (33-37-397)

ures 9 by 2.5 cm. The dagger is very similar to one from Port Graham and to a specimen from Umnak Island.[88] The point of a similar dagger, (9.7) by 2.4 cm. (Pl. 48, 5), was also found near Skeleton III but was possibly not associated with the burial.

The same skeleton had a "bayonet" or pick made of whale bone (Pl. 48, 7). This is a nicely finished shaft, 60.5 cm. long and about 2 cm. in diameter. It is circular in section at the point, oval in the middle, and squared at the butt, which is pierced by a drilled hole. Similar large whale bone picks are known from Kachemak Bay, Kodiak Island, and the Aleutians. The butts may be plain, pierced, knobbed, grooved around, or may possess a knob at the side. They were apparently used unhafted, and Jochelson reports that they were used for digging roots.[89] The fact that Skeleton III was also provided with a dagger suggests that the "bayonet" with him was a pick, not a weapon.

What appears to have been the butt end of a similar pick of whale bone was found in Palugvik 4 (P.795). It is oval in section, with a diameter of about 2.5 cm. In one end is a hole, now broken out. The other end has been cut off, and the object is now only 6.3 cm. long.

Two bone shafts may also have been picks. One from Palugvik 1 (Pl. 40, 11) is about 38 cm. long. It has a suboval cross section and a flattened blunt end on which are traces of red paint. The other end is broken or battered by hard usage. The second specimen is a whale bone slab from Palugvik 3, measuring 30.5 by 3.5 cm. and pointed at one end (Pl. 40, 10). Some of the whale bone specimens described as bone shafts (section 35) may have been fragments of similar picks.

A fragment of a bone shaft with transverse knob was found in Palugvik 1 (Pl. 35, 14). It resembles the bone pins with trans-

verse knob from Kachemak Bay III, except that it is much larger.[90] It may, however, be the butt end of a pick or "bayonet" like some of those from Kodiak Island. One end has been cut off roughly; the other end, toward which the fragment tapers, is unfortunately missing, and if our identification is correct this was the butt of the original pick. The specimen is (5) cm. long; the cross section is oval, with a maximum diameter of 1.7 cm.

Three animal leg bones, sharpened at one end and with the articulation left as a handle at the other, are typologically like large awls, but their size suggests that they were stilettos, probably for dispatching wounded game or fish. A rather short, heavy specimen from Palugvik 3 or 4 is made of a bear (?) bone and has a hole drilled for suspension through the butt end. The epiphysis has broken off, and the specimen is (8) cm. long (33-37-40). A stiletto of bear ulna from Palugvik 3 is 16 cm. long (Pl. 41, 4). The articulation has been trimmed and the shaft of the bone worked to a circular section. A similar stiletto from Palugvik 2 (Pl. 40, 8) has a suspension hole and is 15.8 cm. long. The end of a deer ulna (?), with a hole in it, was found in Palugvik 2 (P.960) and may possibly be the handle of a similar stiletto.

There are 2 broken bone objects from Palugvik 4 which may be parts of ice picks. The first is a wedge-shaped piece of bone, (3) by 2.8 cm., cut from a larger object with a hole (Pl. 41, 1). If it was part of an ice pick, it was presumably from the butt end and the hole served for attachment to a handle or shaft. The second object is a heavy bone point, (6.1) by 1 cm., decorated on one side by a medial line with alternating spurs on both sides, and on the other side by a line crossed by an oblique spur. The edges are blunt and have been roughly hacked (Pl. 40, 6). Two equally doubtful ice picks come from Kachemak Bay I and III.[91]

[88] De Laguna, 1934, Pl. 46, 14; Hrdlička, 1945, Fig. 199, left.
[89] Jochelson, 1925, Pl. 26, 37, 44; Hrdlička, 1944, Fig. 82, pp. 331, 346, and unpublished specimens; 1945, Fig. 199 (?), pp. 113, 446; de Laguna, 1934, Pl. 46, 13.

[90] De Laguna, 1934, Pl. 43, 1 to 4.
[91] Ibid., Pl. 46, 7, 9, p. 101.

56. Bone Handles (?)

A roughly shaped whale bone slab with a rectangular section, (9.9) cm. long and 2 cm. wide, may have been a handle, possibly of a spoon (Pl. 40, 2). It comes from Palugvik 4.

Another broken specimen, possibly a handle, is made of a section of animal leg bone (5) cm. long (Pl. 40, 4). There is a hole for suspension (?), not visible in the illustration, and the surface has been trimmed and polished. This fragment is from Palugvik 1.

Bone handles were also scarce on Kachemak Bay, although at Uyak Bay on Kodiak Hrdlička obtained a number which were clearly handles for knives.[92]

57. Spoons

An antler spoon was found in Palugvik 3 (Pl. 35, 5). It has a long, deep, shovel-shaped bowl, 5.7 by 3.3 cm., and a slender straight handle, 5.5 cm. long and 1.3 cm. wide. The handle is double, that is, it is split by a longitudinal slot which divides the handle into a dorsal and a ventral strip. The dorsal half has been broken off and the end of the remaining handle trimmed short.

A somewhat weathered wooden specimen from Palutat Cave may be the handle of a wooden spoon (Pl. 49, 8). It is flat on one side and convex on the other, and measures (16) by 1.4 cm.

A variety of bone and ivory spoons have been found in southwestern Alaska.[93]

58. Pins, Pegs, Stakes, and Miscellaneous Wooden Objects

A number of wooden pins and stakes and miscellaneously shaped pieces of wood were found in Palutat Cave.

Five pointed and curved (alder?) twigs from the cave may have been used as forks for serving meat. They are from 12 to 24 cm. long (Pls. 49, 1, 10; 51, 12, 17; 33-37-683).

Seven pointed pins, also from Palutat Cave, may have been the teeth for a composite comb, like the Aleut specimens from Kagamil Cave and Amlia Island which were made by lashing a number of wooden pins to a crossbar.[94] Five of the Palutat specimens are slender splinters, 8.5 to 15 cm. long and about 0.5 cm. in diameter (Pl. 51, 7; 33-37-685 to 688). The sixth is a flattened peg, 11.8 by 1 cm. (Pl. 51, 6), while the seventh is a twig 9 by 1 cm., roughly pointed at both ends (Pl. 50, 4).

A crude wooden plug or stopper, 6.8 cm. long and 2.5 cm. in diameter, has a groove around one end and was found at a depth of 1 to 4 feet below the surface of the cave (Pl. 51, 10).

A carefully made wooden object (9.2) by 1.3 cm., shaped like a thin rectangular bar, has a groove along one edge as if it had been lashed to a slender rounded shaft (Pl. 51, 8). One end is missing, but the other has a small, beaklike shoulder on the ungrooved edge.

A very carefully made cylindrical wooden rod, cut squarely at both ends, is 6.4 cm. long and 0.5 cm. in diameter (Pl. 49, 3). It may have been a treenail or a tally for a game. Similar well-shaped and sometimes decorated specimens of bone were found by Hrdlička on Kodiak Island, apparently in sets. A similar wooden rod, 6.7 by 0.8 cm., not quite as carefully finished, was also found in Palutat Cave (Pl. 51, 11). A larger rod, (13.9) cm. long, may have been a nail (Pl. 51, 16).

A number of wooden stakes and pegs from Palutat Cave may have been used for stretching skins. The largest of these (P. 1252), evidently cut down from some still bigger object, is 42.8 cm. long and 2.7 by 2 cm. in diameter. It has a roughly tapering point at one end and a shouldered enlargement at the other, like that on a modern tent peg. Two other stakes are 27.5 and 13 cm. long and about 1.5 cm. in diameter (33-37-691, 689). A pin, originally

---

[92] Ibid., p. 100; Hrdlička, unpublished specimens.
[93] Jochelson, 1925, Pl. 26, 10, 18, 19, 41; de Laguna, 1934, Pl. 49, 1, 2, 4, p. 201; Hrdlička, 1944, pp. 35, 332; 1945, Figs. 197, 198.

[94] Dall, 1878, Pl. 10, no. 17251; Hrdlička, 1945, Fig. 184, p. 433.

over 19 cm. in length and 1.2 cm. in diameter, has a blunt point at one end and tapers toward the other, the tip of which has been broken off (Pl. 51, *18*).

There are 3 flattened shafts or rods with a point at one end. Two measure 13.5 by 1.2 cm. (P.1244, P.1246); the third, (13.5) by 1.4 cm. (Pl. 51, *15*). There are also 2 fragments of similar specimens from which both ends are missing (P.1240, P. 1242).

An irregular wooden peg with a flat blunt point is decorated near the point with 3 diagonal lines (Pl. 50, *7*). The specimen measures 14 by 1.8 cm. and was found 1 to 4 feet below the surface of the cave.

A pointed wooden peg, 11.2 cm. long, was found in the large burial cave at Site 16 on Hawkins Island (P.1331). Two smaller pegs, 7.5 by 2.5 cm. and 8.5 by 1.8 cm., respectively, came from the midden at the same site (30-25-35a, b).

A number of pegs and stakes found at or near the bottom of Palugvik 1 are described in section 92.

Lastly, 2 chopped splinters of wood and 2 chips (P.1249a to c, 33-37-697) from Palutat Cave show marks made by a small gouging blade, presumably a stone adz. A fragment of a stick or shaft (P.1265), from a depth of 1 to 4 feet, has been whittled, the concave cuts suggesting a knife with a crooked blade (compare Pl. 35, *8*). A third chip (33-37-396), found on the surface of the cave, seems to be of rather recent origin, to judge by the fresher color of the wood, and was struck off by a steel ax. This is the only evidence from the cave of modern metal tools, and it was probably left by recent grave robbers.

59. CUT ARTICULATIONS

There are 24 articulations cut from the ends of animal and bird bones. They do not seem to have been used, but are rather the rejected parts of bones from which the shafts were utilized. As far as they can be identified they are: brown bear humerus; seal tibia, metatarsal, etc.; sea otter femur; dog tibia, humerus, etc.; caribou metatarsal; loon wing bone. Their distribution is:

Palugvik 4	P.903
Palugvik 3 or 4	33-37-48, 49, P.902, P.906, P.907
Palugvik 2 or 3	P.901
Palugvik 2	33-37-251 to 256, P.900, P.904
Palugvik 1·	33-37-398, 402, P.898, P.899, P.905
Palugvik, layer (?)	33-37-496, WSM 1095
Palutat Cave	P.1216
Site 6, Hinchinbrook Island	30-25 288

60. WORKED BONE

A good many pieces of cut animal bone were found, showing that the methods of working bone were by hacking, chopping, sawing, and grinding.

One large piece of worked whale rib from Palugvik 1 or 2 may possibly have been a club (P.943a, b). Similar clublike pieces of whale rib were common on Kodiak Island. Makari said that a curved wooden club was used by the Chugach for killing seals, and Black Stepan reported that his great-grandfather, who lived on Wooded Island off Montague Island and was a great whaler, used to kill bears with a club.

Two fragments of bone, one from Palugvik 3 (33-37-145) and the other from Palugvik 1 (33-37-408), appear to be waterworn. The only explanation we can offer is that they formed part of an earlier midden, were washed out on the beach, and were later carried back into the midden, perhaps with a basketful of gravel. It will be remembered that 2 waterworn slate blades were found in Palugvik 4 (Pl. 29, *1;* 33-37-

72). The piece of bone from Palugvik 1 is of particular interest in suggesting that the portion of the midden which we excavated may not have been the remains of the earliest habitation at the site.

The distribution of cut animal bones is:

Palugvik 4	33-37-46, 47, 117; P.913, P.926, P.927
Palugvik 3	33-37-144, 145, 208, 209; P.914, P.916, P.925, P.928
Palugvik 2 or 3	33-37-259
Palugvik 2	33-37-257, 260 to 264; P.912, P.915, P.933, P.934, P.938
Palugvik 1 or 2	P.943a, b (whale bone club?)
Palugvik 1	33-37-399 to 401, 403 to 405, 407 to 409; P.909, P.918, P.919, P.924, P.945, P.1015
Palugvik, layer (?)	33-37-497, P.1064
Grave III, Palugvik East Point	Pl. 47, *4, 5, 10* to *12*
Site 7, Hawkins Cut Off	30-25-289
Site 11, Hinchinbrook Island	30-25-66a to d
Large burial cave at Site 16, Hawkins Island	33-37-573
Site 17, Hawkins Island	30-25-5a, b
Site 27, Grass Island, Cordova Bay	30-25-39
Site 28, Point Whitshed	30-25-96a, b
Site 35, Port Gravina	P.1166
Palutat Cave, depth 1' to 4'	33-37-659
Site 64, Montague Island	33-37-592

The association of fragments of cut bone with the skeleton on Palugvik East Point may be accidental. However, such apparently meaningless fragments were found among the grave goods in burials in Kachemak Bay and probably represent raw material from which the ghost could make implements in the afterlife.[95]

61. Bird Bone Whistle

From Palugvik 4 is a bird bone tube with a small rectangular hole cut near one end (Pl. 39, *22*). This specimen was apparently a whistle. It is (5.2) cm. long, and both ends are missing.

62. Bird Bone Tubes

Besides the 3 decorated bird bone tubes from Grave III, Palugvik East Point, only 4 bird bone tubes were found. These are a specimen of goose bone 11 cm. long from Palugvik 4 (Pl. 38, *9*), half of a tube 13.2 cm. long from Palugvik 3 (Pl. 39, *28*), a specimen 4.5 cm. long from Palugvik 1, possibly a bead (WSM 954), and a broken specimen from the beach (WSM 1096). All the other fragments of bird bone tubes are either beads or pieces cut for needles.

A number of bird bone tubes, some with simple geometric decoration, come from Kachemak Bay and Kodiak Island, where they seem to have been more common than on Prince William Sound. Some seem to have been used as needlecases; others perhaps were beads.[96]

63. Decorated Bone Tubes

Three bird bone tubes, decorated with

[95] De Laguna, 1934, p. 43.

[96] *Ibid.*, p. 97, Pls. 44, *27;* 55, *17;* Hrdlička's unpublished collections.

spurred lines, were found with Skeleton III at Palugvik East Point. Two were found on the right side, near the hand; the third lay beside the feet near the long bone "bayonet."

The shorter of the 2 tubes (Pl. 47, *3*) found near the hands is 6.7 cm. long and 1.3 cm. in diameter. It is bifurcated at both ends, and the edges of the 4 projections thus formed have been rounded off. On the more convex side of the bone, the 2 ends are decorated by a pair of short oblique lines, crossed by deeply cut spurs. Though very simple, the tube resembles a decorated shaman's tube from the Northwest Coast. A similar small, but undecorated, specimen is in Hrdlička's collection from Kodiak.

A larger tube (Pl. 47, *1*) was found beside the first. It is 8.8 cm. long and 2 cm. in diameter. At one end are 2 holes, opposite each other; near the other end are also 2 holes, one larger than the other. All have been made with a hand drill. On one side of the tube is a design, made by lines crossed by short spurs, which represents a human being wearing a hat (?). The bottom of the tube is now broken, but there seem to have been 3 grooves on each side, below the 2 holes.

A smaller bone tube (Pl. 47, *2*), 4.6 cm. long and 1.9 by 1.2 cm. in diameter, was found near the feet of the skeleton. There are no holes in it, and both sides are decorated. The pattern on one side clearly represents a face, in this case an animal's with pointed ears (?) and rather pointed muzzle. All of the lines outlining the head and body are spurred on the outside. On the opposite side of the tube, the design also suggests an animal's head, but more conventionalized than the first. It is outlined by lines spurred on the outside or crossed by spurs, and the area of the pointed ears is filled with crosshatching. Near the lower end of the tube on each side of the muzzle are 2 longitudinal oval figures, spurred on the outside. Although they lie outside the area of the head, these figures suggest the

eyes and are similar to the eyes on one of the carved bears from the same grave (Pl. 46, *19*).

Although the purpose of these tubes is unknown, they suggest the paraphernalia of a shaman. We have already noted (Chapter III, section 3) that the combination of men's and women's implements with this skeleton may indicate that he was a transvestite.

64. IVORY BEAR FIGURES

Two ivory bear figures, perhaps used as buckles or as handles of a cord drill, were found together near the right hand of Skeleton III at Palugvik East Point. They are almost identical in size; one measures 6.5 by 2.8 by 2.5 cm. (Pl. 46, *18*), the other 6 by 2.5 by 2.1 cm. (Pl. 46, *19*). Both figures have a large hole drilled through the middle from side to side. The legs are represented by slightly raised semicircular ridges. The mouth is a deep notch or slit; the ears are low triangular knobs with a pit in the middle. On the larger bear the nostrils are 2 small gouges, and the edges of the mouth are notched to represent the teeth. The mouth of the smaller bear is unnotched, except for 2 small cuts on the upper jaw. The eyes of both are indicated by incised lines, but the patterns differ. The eyes of the larger bear are simply a pair of lines crossed by 3 deeply cut spurs. Those of the smaller are pointed oval figures, spurred on the outside, with a small gouge in the center for the pupil. A similar eye motif has already been noted for the highly conventionalized animal's head on the smallest bone tube found in the same grave (Pl. 47, *2*).

Both bears are decorated on the back by incised patterns of spurred lines. These patterns seem to have no realistic significance, that is, they do not represent the pattern of the animal's coat. Although they differ from each other, both are in the same style as the decorations on the bird bone tubes found in the grave. The lines, spurred on one side or with alternating spurs on both sides, like all the designs on objects from this grave, have been cut with a stone tool, and the spurs are more deeply gouged than the lines. The design on the back of the larger bear (Pl. 46, *18*) appears to be a simple geometric pattern; that on the smaller (Pl. 46, *19*), however, rather suggests an animal's head with pointed ears, similar to that on the smallest tube from the grave (Pl. 47, *2*), especially since the "eyes" are represented by the same motifs as are used for the eyes of the bear itself. This suggests, in turn, that the design on the back of the other bear may also be a highly conventionalized figure (a man with high, pointed head? i.e., a shaman's spirit?). If both bears actually have designs representing living beings, it is possible that these are intended to be the "souls" or "spirit owners" of the bears.

65. TRIANGULAR STONE PLAQUES

The collections contain 7 triangular or roughly triangular stone plaques which are described in this section, although it is by no means certain that they all had the same function or represent the same type.

The largest is of friable mica schist, measuring 10.8 by 5.8 cm., and comes from Palugvik 1 (Pl. 19, *9*). The surfaces are smoothed, and the edges are rounded and decorated with notches. A hole has been partially drilled from both sides at the rounded apex of the triangle. The shape and decoration of this specimen are strikingly reminiscent of a triangular slate mirror from Kachemak Bay III,[97] even though the Palugvik specimen does not have a surface smooth enough to give a reflection even when wet, and mica schist would seem to be a poor choice of material for a mirror when slate was obtainable. However, our specimen may have become badly weathered in the ground, so that we must not overlook the possibility that the surface was once smoother than it is now.

Two smaller greenstone plaques were

[97] De Laguna, 1934, p. 79, Pl. 37, *6*. Heizer (1946, p. 149) reports slate mirrors from the older levels at Uyak Bay, but gives no further details.

found in Palugvik 2. One, measuring 5.4 by 2.7 cm. (Pl. 42, *50*), is polished on both sides and deeply notched on the edges. The notches at the apex set off a projection by means of which the plaque could have been suspended as an ornament. The second plaque, measuring 5.4 by 3 cm. (Pl. 19, *6*), is notched only across the longest edge and partway up one of the others. The edges of both of these specimens are rather sharp, so that they could have served as saws. They are too small to have been useful as mirrors. The second plaque lacks means of suspension, so it could not have been a pendant, unless we are to suppose that it was never finished.

A semicircular, rather than triangular, slate plaque, finely polished on both surfaces, was also found in Palugvik 2 (Pl. 19, *7*). It measures only 4.4 by 2.1 cm. and is not notched on the edges. It is impossible to say whether or not it served the same function or functions as the greenstone plaques from the same layer.

From Palugvik 2 there is a fragment of roughly shaped sandstone which may have been broken from a large triangular plaque (Pl. 19, *10*). The fragment now measures (9.7 by 3.4) cm. and was evidently at least 2.5 cm. thick. At least one of the 2 surfaces was smooth, and one edge was ground slightly concave and deeply notched. It is possible that this specimen was only a whetstone.

Another sandstone fragment, found in Palugvik 3, also seems to have been part of a triangular plaque (P.775). It is now (8 by 4.1) cm. and is 1.8 cm. thick. Both surfaces are nicely smoothed, as are the edges. The edge forming the base of the triangle is grooved, and one of the sides is notched. This specimen may also have been a whetstone.

An irregularly shaped slab of altered tuff from Palugvik 2, 11 by 5 cm., is ground on one surface and notched along the curving edge (Pl. 16, *7*). Although it was probably a whetstone, it should be compared with the other notched triangular plaques.

66. SLATE PLAQUES WITH HOLES

A broken slate plaque, either a whetstone or an unusually heavy pendant, was found beside the hearth on the burial ledge at Palugvik East Point (Pl. 19, 5). It was apparently a flat oval beach stone, rubbed smooth on one surface and drilled for suspension at one end. The lower end of the specimen is missing, and it is (7) cm. long and 4.6 cm. wide.

A piece of worked slate from Palugvik 1 looks as if it might have been a piece of the same plaque (Pl. 19, 8). This is a fragment 4.5 cm. wide and (3.5) cm. long, which apparently once had a rounded end. The other end is broken off. There are a few notches along both edges. A similar slate fragment from the same layer, (5.5) by 4.5 cm., is polished smooth on one surface and is notched along both edges (Pl. 16, 9). The unbroken end is roughly ground. Both of these specimens from Palugvik 1 may have been parts of whetstones or of mirrors.

On the beach of Simpson Bay, in front of the cabin belonging to Old Man Dude, an Eyak Indian,[98] we picked up a rectangular slate plaque, 12.5 by 6.5 cm. (33-37-636). It had been sawed out and had a drilled hole near one end. The hole had been drilled by a bow or cord drill from both sides, and was reamed out by a mechanical drill on one side. The specimen is problematical, and it is possibly not of native manufacture, since there were no indications of an old site at this place.

67. DECORATED SLATE PLAQUES

Eight slate plaques (Figs. 25 to 32) and one 4-sided bar whetstone bear incised decorations. These plaques are irregular beach pebbles, unworked except for the polishing and decoration which is, with one exception, confined to one surface. These objects were not implements or tools of any kind. One is from Palugvik 2 (Pl. 19, 4); 4 are from Palugvik 1 (Figs. 28, 29; Pl. 19, 2, 3); 2 plaques (Fig. 30; Pl. 19, 1)

[98] This site is illustrated in Birket-Smith and de Laguna, 1938, Pl. 7, 1.

and the whetstone (P.1043) are from the beach; and the last plaque is from the midden at Palugvik East Point (Fig. 32). They thus appear to be limited to the earliest period of habitation thus far discovered in Prince William Sound.

The size of the plaques varies from 11 by 4.4 cm. (Pl. 19, 4) to fragments only half as large (Pl. 19, 1).

The plaque from Palugvik 2 (Fig. 25 and Pl. 19, 4; the specimen is shown upside down in the plate) is roughly rectangular. The decoration consists of 3 transverse bands, the upper 2 being "ladders" with the "crossbars" sloping up from left to right. The bottom band is composed of interlocking X's or crosshatching between bordering lines; below this projects a small rectangular element, also filled with crosshatching.

Another specimen with a fairly simple pattern is a broken slab from Palugvik 1 (Fig. 26 and Pl. 19, 3). Groups of longitudinal lines, one group bordering each (?) edge (one edge is missing) are connected by 3 transverse groups, each composed of slightly curved lines. The pattern is, in effect, a type of "ladder" motif, applied longitudinally to the slab. A similar design is very faintly incised on the surface of the whetstone found on the beach (P.1043).

An irregular slate slab from Palugvik 1 (Fig. 27 and Pl. 19, 2) has a decoration consisting of several transverse bands of crosshatching between bordering lines. These bands curve slightly upward in the middle. The lower band of crosshatching is actually composed of 11 bands.

From the beach is a triangular fragment, representing at the most only half of the original plaque (Fig. 30). It differs from the other specimens in that both sides are polished and decorated and one edge is notched. Unfortunately the decoration lies along the fractured edge, so that little of it is preserved. It was apparently the same on both sides, and consisted of at least 3 transverse and slightly curving bands of crosshatching set between bordering lines.

The remaining specimens have more

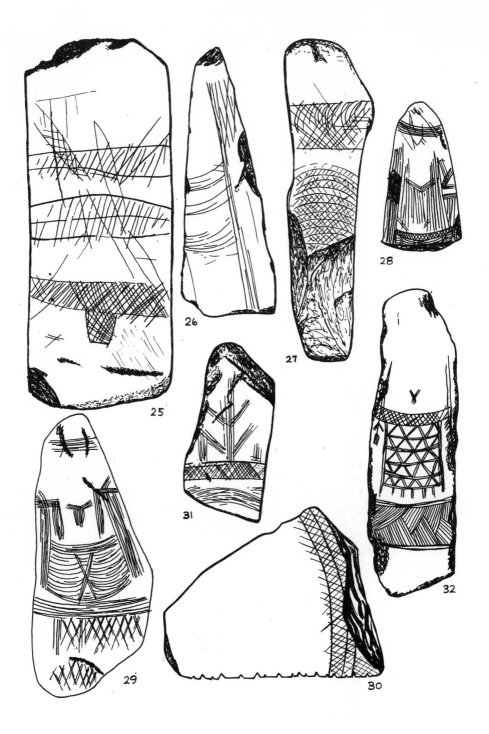

25

26

27

28

29

31

30

32

elaborate decorations. Two from Palugvik 1 have rather similar design layouts.

The first of these (Fig. 28) is half of a roughly oval plaque, (4.5) by 3 cm. If the specimen is held with the broken edge down, the decoration is seen as composed of several parts. First, there is a slightly curving or sagging band of transverse lines across the upper end. There are 2 long side panels, composed of longitudinal lines which are interrupted in the middle by short transverse and angled lines (the panel on the left is marred here by a fracture); the middle area between these panels is filled with longitudinal scratches across the top of which is superimposed a wide V-shaped figure. At the bottom is a slightly curved transverse band of crosshatching between bordering lines. Below this band, and interrupted by the break, are 4 pairs of vertical lines between which run transverse lines which sag in the middle of each space.

The second plaque (Fig. 29) measures 8.5 by 3.5 cm. and has a similarly arranged pattern. Across the upper end is a transverse band of straight lines. The middle area is bordered on the edges of the plaque by panels of longitudinal lines, the upper ends of which are crossed by angled figures. Between the upper ends of these panels is a detached Y-shaped or T-shaped element. The lower part of the middle area is filled with a wide band of sagging transverse lines on which is superimposed a large X. Across the top of the lower area is a transverse band of lines. The lower part of the plaque seems to have been filled with crosshatching, divided into longitudinal panels by groups of vertical lines, but this part of the design is now partially obliterated.

A fragment from the beach (Fig. 31 and Pl. 19, *1*) has a well-developed but somewhat different design. Across the wider end of the stone is a band of curving transverse lines. Above this is a band of crosshatching between bordering lines. Rising from this band and filling the upper portion of the plaque is a design composed of straight lines which suggests a squatting anthropomorphic figure with upraised arms. The "head" is missing.

The most elaborately decorated specimen is from the midden on Palugvik East Point (Fig. 32). It measures 9 by 2.5 cm. The design covers $2/3$ of the surface. Across the bottom is a band set off by borders of grouped lines and filled with oblique lines in groups which slant alternately down from right to left and then down from left to right, producing a braidlike pattern. Above this braided band is another composed of 5 transverse elements of zigzag lines, each set off by bordering lines. The zigzags are so arranged that they form lozenge or diamond-shaped patterns. These zigzag bands do not reach the edges of the stone, which is bordered by panels of longitudinal lines on each side. Between the zigzag band and the braided band are 5 short groups of longitudinal lines. Above the zigzag band, and running all the way across to the edges of the stone, is a transverse band of crosshatching between bordering lines. Pendant from this, in the spaces on each side of the zigzag bands, are 2 crude inverted Y-figures with central prong ("tree-figures"). Above the crosshatched band is a single detached Y.

These designs may be analyzed into the

FIGURE 25. Decorated slate plaque, Palugvik 2 (P.781). Scale natural size. See Plate 19, *4*

FIGURE 26. Decorated slate plaque, Palugvik 1 (P.782). Scale natural size. See Plate 19, *3*

FIGURE 27. Decorated slate plaque, Palugvik 1 (P.780). Scale natural size. See Plate 19, *2*

FIGURE 28. Decorated slate plaque, Palugvik 1 (33-37-423). Scale natural size

FIGURE 29. Decorated slate plaque, Palugvik 1 (33-37-424). Scale natural size

FIGURE 30. Decorated slate plaque, Palugvik, layer (?) (33-37-504). Scale natural size

FIGURE 31. Decorated slate plaque, Palugvik, layer (?) (P.1066). Scale natural size. See Plate 19, *1*

FIGURE 32. Decorated slate plaque, Palugvik East Point midden (33-37-569). Scale natural size

following elements: longitudinal bordering lines; transverse bands, straight or slightly curved, composed of lines, of crosshatching or X's (usually between borders), of zigzag lines arranged to form diamond-shaped figures, of oblique hatching (variation of "ladder" motif), and of "braiding" between borders; vertical bands of curved hatching between borders (variation of "ladder" motif); short vertical and horizontal groups of lines; angled elements like L's or V's; X figures; Y figures; Y figures with central prong ("tree-figures"); and lastly the figure suggesting a squatting person.

The decorations on these slate plaques are very different both in technique and in choice of motif from those incised on the bone and ivory objects from Grave III on Palugvik East Point (Pls. 46 and 47). The latter consist of single lines and short deep spurs and are therefore similar to Canadian Thule and northern Alaskan Eskimo designs. On the slate plaques, however, the lines are much finer, and a group of scratches is usually employed to render the motif. Spurred lines are absent. With the exception of 2 specimens from Palugvik 1, one from the beach, and one from Palugvik East Point, the composition is extremely simple. There is no real sense of the space to be filled, as is evident in the designs on the bone and ivory objects from the grave. The motifs on the stones are practically all simple bands, run transversely across the stone, one above the other, until the available space is more or less filled. The lack of spatial appreciation is also illustrated by the fact that the stones themselves are not shaped or the edges worked, except on the fragment with notched edge from the beach (Fig. 30). It is as if the artist had utilized the pebbles simply as convenient surfaces on which to experiment with various designs which he intended to apply elsewhere. That this impression is erroneous, however, is indicated by the 4 specimens with a more unified composition. These show that the deco-

ration of the stone was an end in itself. The designs are not representative in any ordinary sense, but one has the feeling that perhaps they do symbolize something, and this suspicion is in part confirmed by 2 specimens from the uppermost levels of the midden in Uyak Bay and by 25 from the vicinity of Kodiak City, Kodiak Island.[99] As is true of many Kodiak types, these are somewhat larger than any of our plaques, measuring up to 12.5 cm. in length. They are decorated on one or both surfaces with designs in the same general style as those on the Chugach plaques, except that spurred lines are prominent. What is more significant, however, is that the patterns on both sides represent highly conventionalized human figures. At the top, Y-shaped elements suggest the brows and the nose, and short transverse lines the mouth, or mouth and medial labret (cf. Figs. 28, 32). Occasionally the eyes are indicated by dots or small circles. Vertical lines on the cheeks or below the mouth (cf. Figs. 28, 29, 32) suggest flowing hair and beard or tattooing. The arms and legs are not represented, but simple patterns of horizontal and vertical lines and bands ("ladders," spurred lines) hint rather at clothing, possibly a long gutskin shirt with tufted seams or even a garment patched together from small skins. On one figure, pendant rectangular areas which suggest bibs or tails to the jacket might be compared with the crosshatched area on our Figure 25. Heizer has compared the treatment of the face, which is indicated on these pebbles simply by suggestions of the brows, nose, and mouth, with the faces of the petroglyphs at Cape Alitak on the southwestern part of Kodiak Island. These, as we have seen (Chapter IV, section 3), are again similar to some of the Chugach pictographs (Figs. 22A, 23A). Is it possible that the slate plaques are amulets?[100]

[99] Heizer, 1947, Fig. 6A, B, pp. 288 f.; Heizer, 1952a, Fig. 90, p. 266.
[100] Since the above was written, this hypothesis has been strengthened by finding in an historic Tlingit site on Admiralty Island 5 similar incised plaques, 3 of which bear designs suggestive of faces. These stones were hesitantly identified by one in-

68. LABRETS

There are 6 labrets from Prince William Sound. All are long and slender and could be classified either as novices' or as lateral labrets, although doubtless many were worn in the middle of the lower lip. Curiously enough, however, we did not find a single specimen with broad base and flat stud like the medial labrets of Kachemak Bay, Kodiak Island, and the Aleutians. Matrona Tiedmann said that women wore a labret in the middle of the lower lip and several smaller ones around the corners of the mouth, but did not describe the labret styles of the men. Meares reports, however:

The men have universally a slit in their under lip, between the projecting part of the lip and the chin, which is cut parallel with their mouths and has the appearance of another mouth. The boys have two, three, or four holes, where the slit is in the men, which is perhaps the distinctive mark of manhood. The women have the same apertures as the boys, with pieces of shell fixed in them resembling teeth.[101]

Portlock also writes that the Chugach slit the under lip in which "they have a bone or ivory instrument fitted with holes in it from which they hang beads as low as the chin."[102] Riobo, who was chaplain to Arteaga and Bodega y Quadra, says that the women "wore a string of big beads hanging down their chest from the corners of their mouth where they were attached," i.e., to labrets. "The men carried a bone artistically carved and ornamented on the upper lip."[103] The latter may refer to a nose pin, or to a labret in the *under* lip. Sarychef reports of the Chugach: "Some have their underlip cut through an inch and a half deep, and parallel with the mouth, wearing in the cavity little plates of green jasper, three quarters of an inch broad, and two inches three fourths long."[104] Captain Colnett, whose unpublished journal has been preserved in the British Public Record

Office, observed in 1788 that only the Chugach men wore medial labrets and sketched one from which hung 9 pendants, each composed of one long oval bead and several smaller beads of apparently 2 different colors. Such labrets seem to have been worn only on dress occasions; at other times a smaller plug of wood or bone was inserted, or the men amused themselves by playing with their tongues in the labret hole. Apparently Captain Colnett saw no Chugach women wearing labrets, for upon reaching Yakutat he commented upon the contrast between the large labret of the Tlingit women and the men's labret in Prince William Sound. He also reported that the Chugach and Yakutat expressed contempt of each other because of the difference in the sex wearing this ornament.

Captain Cook, however, has given us the fullest description:

But the most uncommon and unsightly ornamental fashion, adopted by some of both sexes, is their having the under-lip slit, or cut, quite through, in the direction of the mouth, a little below the swelling part. This incision, which is made even in the suckling children, is often above two inches long; and either by its natural retraction, when the wound is fresh, or by the repetition of some artificial management, assumes the shape of lips, and becomes so large as to admit the tongue through. This happened to be the case, when the first person having this incision was seen by one of the seamen, who called out, that the man had two mouths; and, indeed, it does not look unlike it. In this artificial mouth they stick a flat, narrow ornament, made entirely out of solid shell or bone, cut into little narrow pieces, like small teeth, almost down to the base or thickest part, which has a small projecting bit at each end that supports it when put into the divided lip; the cut part then appearing outward. Others have the lower lip only perforated into separate holes; and then the ornament consists of as many distinct shelly studs, whose points are pushed through these holes, and their heads appear within the lip, as another row of teeth immediately under their own.[105]

Plate 46 in the accompanying *Album* shows a man of Prince William Sound wearing 4 small labrets of this type. Cook also noted that some wore glass beads which they

formant as scratchers or amulets used by adolescent girls.

[101] Meares, 1791, I, xlix f.
[102] Portlock, 1789, pp. 248 f.
[103] Riobo, 1918, p. 86.
[104] Sarytschew, 1807, II, 22.

[105] Cook, 1785, II, 369 f.

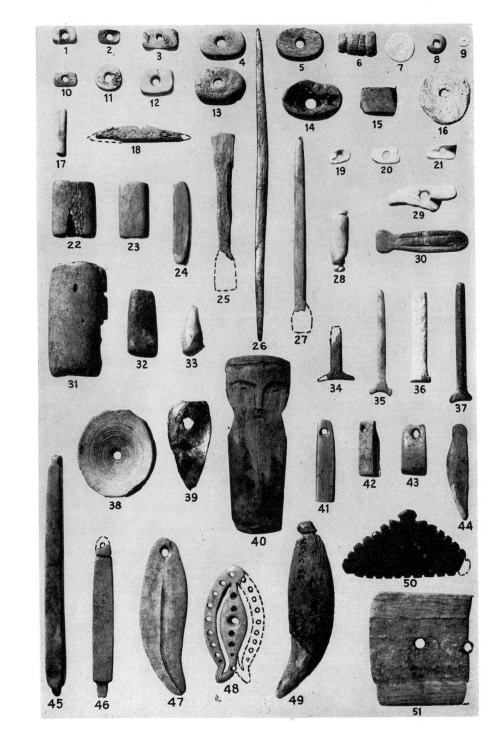

join to their lip-ornaments, which have a small hole drilled in each point to which they are fastened, and others to them, till they hang sometimes as low as the point of the chin. But in this last case, they cannot remove them [the labrets] so easily; for, as to their own lip-ornaments [without pendants], they can take them out with their tongue, or suck them in, at pleasure.

Plate 47 in the *Album* shows a woman wearing 5 small labrets from each of which hang 2 beads and a pendant (of dentalium?). Cook continues: "So fond are they, in general, of ornament, that they stick any thing in their perforated lip; one man appearing with two of our iron nails projecting from it like prongs; and another endeavoring to put a large brass button into it." One wonders whether in some cases such holes may not have served as "pockets" for carrying trifles, just as we put pencils behind the ears.

From Palugvik 3 or 4 there is a long slender labret of ivory with a crutch-shaped base. The base is 0.8 cm. wide, and the stud 4.8 cm. long (Pl. 42, *37*). A similar ivory specimen, measuring 4.3 by 1 cm., is from Palugvik 1 or 2 (Pl. 42, *35*). From Palugvik 1 there is a bone labret with a very

slender stud, now broken off to a height of (2) cm. The base is also broken, but was originally about 1.5 cm. long (Pl. 42, *34*). A labret of shell, 3.2 by 0.9 cm., is from Palugvik, layer unknown (Pl. 42, *36*). Another shell labret, 3.8 by 1.5 cm., was found in Palugvik 4 (Pl. 43, *31*). It has a small projection at the end of the stud. A very tiny labret, only 2.1 cm. long, comes from Palugvik 3 or 4 (Pl. 43, *33*).

A fragment of worked bone from Palugvik 4 may have been a broken labret, although identification is not certain (33-37-61).

In addition, a small ivory peg, carved from a tooth (?), was found in Palugvik 1 (Pl. 43, *34*). The specimen has a conical head, and thus could not have been worn comfortably as a labret, although it might have been used as an ear stud.[106] It measures 2.2 by 1 cm.

69. NOSE PINS

Matrona Tiedmann reported that both men and women wore nose ornaments. The description was not clear, but we gathered

[106] Cf. de Laguna, 1934, Pl. 51, *9*, from Kachemak Bay III.

PLATE 42. Ornaments. Scale ¾ natural size

1, 2, and 10, Rectangular beads, one ivory and 2 bone, found with 2 bone and 2 shell beads, Palugvik 2 (33-37-285); 3 and 4, rectangular and oval beads, (seal? tympanic bone), Palugvik 1 (33-37-414, 417); 5, oval bead, whale bone, Palugvik 2 (33-37-296); 6, carved bone object, Palugvik, layer (?) (33-37-498); 7 and 9, disk shell beads, Palugvik, layer (?) (33-37-501); 8, disk shell bead, Palugvik 3 (33-37-157); 11, disk bone bead, Palugvik 1 (33-37-415); 12, rectangular bone bead, Palugvik, layer (?) (33-37-501); 13, oval bead, seal tympanic bone, Palugvik 3 (33-37-153); 14, oval bead, seal tympanic bone, Palugvik 2 (33-37-284); 15, unfinished rectangular bone bead, Palugvik 2 (33-37-276); 16, disk shell bead, Palugvik 3 or 4 (33-37-57); 17, bead, section of bird bone, Palugvik, layer (?) (33-37-500); 18, bone toggle, Palugvik 1 or 2 (33-37-299); 19 to 21, rectangular shell beads, Palugvik, layer (?) (33-37-501); 22, bead, section of animal bone, Palugvik, layer (?) (33-37-501); 23, bead, section of animal bone, Palugvik 2 (33-37-278); 24, ivory bead, section of bear canine, Palugvik, layer (?) (33-37-501); 25, bone nose pin, Palugvik 3 (33-37-159); 26, copper nose pin, Palugvik 4 (33-37-62); 27, bone nose pin, Palugvik 1 (33-37-422); 28, shell nose pin, Palugvik, layer (?) (33-37-502); 29, rectangular shell bead, Palugvik, layer (?) (33-37-501); 30, whale figure (?), bone, Palugvik 2 (33-37-265); 31, bead, section of seal mandible, Palugvik 3 (33-37-150); 32, ivory bead, section of bear canine, Palugvik 2 (33-37-279); 33, tip cut from bear canine in making bead, Palugvik 2 (33-37-273); 34, bone labret, Palugvik 1 (33-37-421); 35, ivory labret, Palugvik 1 or 2 (33-37-300); 36, shell labret, Palugvik, layer (?) (33-37-503); 37, ivory labret, Palugvik 3 or 4 (33-37-60); 38, fish vertebra disk, Palugvik 3 (33-37-149); 39, operculum pendant, Palugvik 3 (33-37-148); 40, ivory doll, Palugvik 3 (?) (30-25-23); 41, ivory pendant, Palugvik 3 (33-37-147); 42, ivory pendant, Palugvik 1 or 2 (33-37-411); 43, ivory pendant, Palugvik 2 (33-37-266); 44, seal canine pendant, Palugvik 4 (?) (33-37-59); 45, ivory pendant, Palugvik 2 (33-37-267); 46, bone pendant, Palugvik 2 (33-37-268); 47, bear canine pendant, Palugvik 2 (33-37-269); 48, bone pendant, Palugvik 4 (33-37-52); 49, bear canine pendant, Palugvik 4 (33-37-58); 50, notched green chert plaque (pendant?), Palugvik 2 (33-37-302); 51, buckle, walrus ivory, Palugvik 2 or 3 (33-37-158)

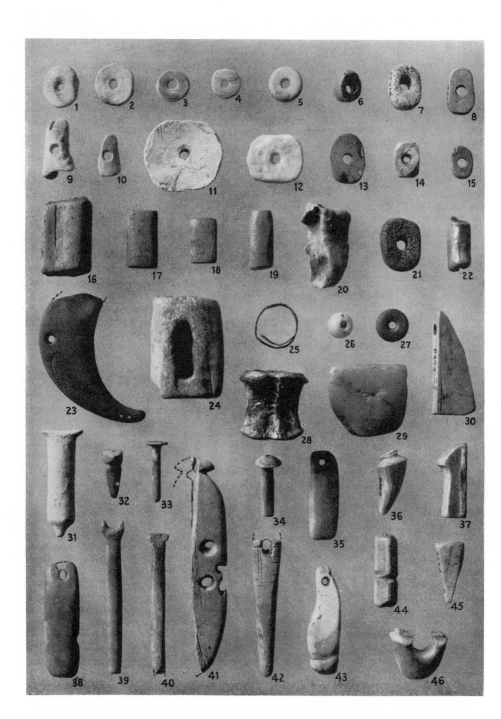

that these were usually straight pins and may sometimes have had pendants fastened to them (?). Seven pins or ornaments were found which could have been worn in the nose.

One of these, from Palugvik 4, is a pin of native copper, 12.5 by 0.4 cm., pointed at both ends (Pl. 42, 26). It has a rectangular section, and the laminated structure produced by pounding together thin layers of copper can be clearly seen, now that the specimen has been cleaned. It is thicker in the middle than at the ends and looks a little like the copper bracelet from Kachemak Bay III, if the latter were flattened out.[107]

A bone specimen from Palugvik 3 is broken at one end, but both ends seem to have had enlarged rectangular knobs (Pl. 42, 25). There is an angular swelling in the middle of the pin. When complete, the specimen would have measured 6.8 by 1 cm. A bone pin from Palugvik 1, (7) cm. long, formerly had an enlarged head at one end (Pl. 42, 27). The other end is pointed. In shape it resembles the nose pins from the Aleutian Islands.[108] A broken slender

bone pin from Palugvik 4, (4.9) cm. long, has a flat head at one end (Pl. 43, 40). We have tentatively identified it as a nose ornament, although it may have been a labret, and Makari even identified it as the handle of a toy paddle! An ivory nose pin from Palugvik 2 or 3 is blunt at one end and has a crutch-shaped head at the other (Pl. 43, 39). It is 5.3 cm. long. On the beach at Palugvik we found a very short pin made of the central column of a whelk shell. It is 2.5 cm. long and 0.6 cm. in diameter (Pl. 42, 28). About each end is a groove from which small pendants could have been hung, as from Aleut nose pins. Nose pins, labrets, and ear ornaments, varying slightly in local style, are common in southwestern Alaska.[109]

Cook has described the Chugach nose pin: "The *septum* of the nose is also perforated; through which they frequently thrust the quill feathers of small birds, or little bending ornaments, made of the above shelly substance [dentalia], strung on a stiff string or cord, three or four inches long, which gives them a truly grotesque appearance."[110] The man figured in Plate

---

[107] *Ibid.*, Pl. 49, 10.
[108] Jochelson, 1925, Fig. 95.

[109] De Laguna, 1934, pp. 204-7; Birket-Smith, 1941, pp. 132-33.
[110] Cook, 1785, II, 369.

PLATE 43. Ornaments. Scale slightly under 9/10 natural size

1 to 5, Disk shell beads, Palugvik, layer (?) (P.1059, P.1019 to P.1022); 6, disk bone bead, Palugvik 1 (P.869); 7, oval whale bone bead, Palugvik, layer (?) (P.1033); 8, oval bead, seal tympanic bone, Palugvik 1 or 2 (P.860); 9 and 10, rectangular shell beads, Palugvik, layer (?) (P.1024, P. 1025); 11, disk shell bead, Palugvik 4 (P.880); 12, oval shell bead, Palugvik, layer (?) (P.1017); 13 and 14, oval and rectangular beads, seal tympanic bone, Palugvik 1 (P.858, P. 864); 15, oval bead, seal tympanic bone, Palugvik 1 or 2 (P.862); 16, bead, section of animal bone, Palugvik 3, (P.868); 17 and 18, beads, sections of animal bone, Palugvik 2 (P.866, P.872); 19, ivory bead, section of bear canine, Palugvik, layer (?) (P.1038); 20, seal (?) tympanic bone, partly worked for bead, Palugvik 2 (P.911); 21, rectangular bead, whale bone, Palugvik 2 (P.861); 22, ivory bead, section of bear canine, Palugvik 2 (P.888); 23, slate pendant, Jackpot Bay (P.1129); 24, bead, walrus ivory, Palugvik East Point beach (P.1105); 25, copper finger ring, Palugvik 4 (P.978); 26, pale blue glass bead, "Cook type," Palutat Cave, surface (P.1220); 27, disk slate bead, Site 56, Chenega Island (P.1133); 28, spool-shaped ornament, halibut (?) vertebra, Palugvik 4 (P.893); 29, soapstone (?) pendant, Palugvik 2 (P.843); 30, ivory pendant, Palugvik 1 (P.873); 31, shell labret, Palugvik 4 (P.1004); 32, bone peg or nail, Palugvik 3 or 4 (P.817); 33, ivory labret, Palugvik 3 or 4 (P.816); 34, ivory pin or ear stud, Palugvik 1 (P.815); 35, ivory pendant, Palugvik 1 (P.876); 36, tip cut from bear canine in making bead, Palugvik 1 (P.883); 37, fragment of marble ornament, Palugvik 1 (P.965); 38, ivory pendant, Palugvik 1 or 2 (P.1005); 39, ivory nose pin, Palugvik 2 or 3 (P.818); 40, bone nose pin (?), Palugvik 4 (P.819); 41, bone pendant, Palugvik 3 or 4 (P.961); 42, bone pendant or bodkin, Palugvik 1 (P.799); 43, tooth pendant, Palugvik 2 (or 3) (P.875); 44, ivory toggle, Palutat Cave, bottom of deposit (P.1219); 45, bone pendant (inverted), Palugvik 1 (P.874); 46, broken ivory buckle, Palugvik 2 (P.892)

46 in the *Album* wears a nose pin which seems to be made of a straight stick with a large bead at each end; the woman in Plate 47 wears a double nose ornament, made of four dentalia strung on 2 semi-flexible rods. Meares writes: "Both sexes have the septum of the nose perforated, in which they generally wear a large quill, or a piece of the bark of a tree."[111] Portlock states: "In the hole in the nose they hang an ornament, as they deem it, made of bone or ivory two or three inches long."[112]

70. COPPER RING

A ring of native copper was found in Palugvik 4, just under the turf (Pl. 43, *25*). It is made from a strip 0.2 to 0.3 cm. wide, coiled in a spiral. The ring is 1.5 cm. in diameter and would just fit the little finger of a rather small hand. It is not unlike the copper bracelet from Yukon Island IV in Kachemak Bay.[113]

71. BUCKLES AND TOGGLES

No faceted rectangular buckles with a single hole, so typical of Kachemak Bay III, were found in Prince William Sound.[114] There are, however, 3 specimens of less distinctive style which could have been buckles.

A plaque of walrus ivory from Palugvik 2 or 3 was originally rectangular with somewhat rounded ends and measured 6 (?) by 4.5 cm. when complete (Pl. 42, *51*). It is pierced by 2 holes, 2 cm. apart, both made by a mechanical drill. The specimen is well finished except for the surface not illustrated, which was probably not intended to show. A fragment of ivory from the same level with one (or 2?) holes was perhaps a similar buckle (33-37-146). A third specimen, from Palugvik 2, appears to be half of an oval button or buckle of walrus ivory with a single hole (Pl. 43, *46*). It has been sawed in two, but was presumably about 4 by 1.7 cm. when complete.

There are also 3 small toggles which may have been used as buttons or buckles. A bone specimen from Palugvik 4 (P.1320) is 3.7 cm. long, and has a groove around the middle and blunt, conical ends. A bone toggle from Palugvik 1 or 2 measures 3.8 cm. in length (Pl. 42, *18*). It is straight along one edge; the other is convex with a notch in the middle; and the ends are pointed. The third specimen is a roughly cut ivory toggle from the bottom of the deposit in Palutat Cave (Pl. 43, *44*). The ends are blunt, and the groove about it is not quite in the middle. When working, the Chugach are said to have belted up their frocks with a belt of braided sinew fastened with a wooden toggle. It is impossible to identify any of the archaeological specimens as belt buckles, however. Belts seem to have been unknown, or at least very rare, on Kodiak, for example.[115]

72. FISH VERTEBRA RINGS AND DISKS

From Palugvik 4 is a flat ring made from the epiphysis of the vertebra of a large fish, probably a halibut (33-37-53). The diameter of the ring is 3.4 cm.; that of the central hole is 0.8 cm. The specimen resembles similar rings from Kachemak Bay III and specimens from the Aleutian Islands, said to be buckles for the shoulder straps of the kayak half-jacket.[116] Our Chugach informants mentioned the same garment, but failed to describe how it was buckled.

There are also 4 complete halibut (?) vertebrae with carefully trimmed edges and drilled hole in the center. These are from Palugvik 4 (33-37-54), Palugvik 3 or 4 (33-37-55), Palugvik 3 (Pl. 42, *38*), and Site 7, Hawkins Cut Off (DNM uncat.). A broken specimen was found in Palugvik 2 (?) (P.1016), as was a trimmed vertebra which lacked the central hole (P.894). From Palugvik 4 there is another halibut (?) vertebra which has been cut to a spool shape. A hole has been started from each end but is not finished (Pl. 43, *28*). These pierced

---

[111] Meares, 1791, I, lx.
[112] Portlock, 1789, pp. 248 f.
[113] De Laguna, 1934, Pl. 49, *10*.
[114] *Ibid.*, Pl. 50, *32* to *38*.

[115] Birket-Smith, 1941, p. 132.
[116] Jochelson, 1925, p. 100, Fig. 104; de Laguna, 1934, Pl. 51, *4*.

vertebrae were probably used as beads. The disks are identical with Aleut specimens from Dutch Harbor, Unalaska.[117] Hrdlička found a number of fish vertebra rings and disks of the same type on Kodiak Island. Eleven rings, 2 disks, and 11 more rings were found together in a set, as if they had been strung for a necklace.

73. BEADS

Two types of glass beads were found, the significance of which for dating has been discussed in Chapter II, section 16, and there were also many aboriginal beads. The latter consist of 11 tubular beads of ivory and 24 of bone; 170 flat oval or rectangular beads of bone, 18 of ivory, and 320 (plus 64 fragments) of shell; 13 disk-shaped beads of bone, 222 (plus 105 fragments) of shell, and 4 of stone; not including a few other specimens found but subsequently lost. Almost all the beads of native manufacture came from the lower half of the midden at Palugvik, the majority from the grave of the old woman (Skeleton III) in Layer 1. Matrona Tiedmann reported that the Chugach used to model toy animals of clay and shiny beads of clay mixed with seal oil, but we found nothing of this kind.

Glass Beads

The smaller blue, white, and black glass beads we have called the "Glacier Island type" because they were found about the neck and under the skull of Skeleton II (Pl. 45, *11* to *13;* 33-37-633) and Skeleton I (33-37-631, P.1305, blue beads only). Strings of presumably the same type of blue, white, and black beads, ascribed by Meany to the Hudson's Bay Company, were attached to a headband on the skeleton which he found on Glacier Island. Similar blue and white beads (33-37-574, P.1115) were among the bones in the larger burial cave at Site 16, Hawkins Island; and white beads of the same type, together with other beads and fragments of china (30-25-98) were found in front of the ruins of a large house at

Alaganik, the Eyak village on the Copper River, which was abandoned in 1892 or 1893.[118] Similar beads were found at historic Indian sites on the lower Yukon and in the Yakutat area.[119] It is probable that "Glacier Island type" beads were obtained from the Russians after 1778 or 1783, or even later.

The larger and rarer beads of pale blue glass, which we have called the "Cook type," evidently reached the Chugach during the protohistoric period before 1778 when Captain Cook saw them, but it has been impossible to date their first appearance. Two specimens of this kind (30-25-92) were found in the grave at Site 20 on Mummy Island; another (not saved) was in the upper burial shelter at Site 26 near Mummy Island; 2 (Pl. 43, *26;* 33-37-661) were probably derived from a disturbed grave in Section F, Palutat Cave; and one was found with other manufactured objects (30-25-42) at Nuchek on Hinchinbrook Island.

Tubular Ivory Beads

Ten ivory beads in the collections (Pls. 42, *24, 32;* 43, *19, 22;* 44, *33, 72*) are made of the central part of a bear canine, from which the tip and the root have been sawed off. The nerve canal, usually enlarged at one or both ends, has been utilized for stringing, and the outer surface or enamel ground off to expose the inner ivory. The beads are from 1.5 to 2.8 cm. in length and are oval to rectangular in section, with one end usually smaller than the other. In addition to the finished beads, 13 tips cut from bear teeth and partially shaped central sections were also found (Pls. 42, *33;* 43, *36*). There is also a tubular bead of walrus ivory, 3.5 cm. long and 2.6 by 1.5 cm. in diameter (Pl. 43, *24*).

Two tubular ivory beads come from the grave in Palugvik 1.

Tubular Bone Beads

Twenty-four beads made of sections of animal or bird bone were found, 5 in the

---

[117] Capps collection, University of Pennsylvania Museum.

[118] Birket-Smith and de Laguna, 1938, pp. 20 f.
[119] De Laguna, 1947, pp. 224 f; excavations near Yakutat, 1949 and 1952.

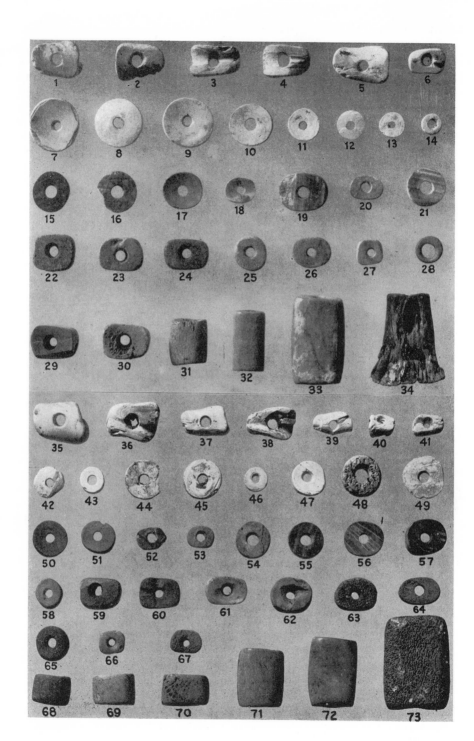

grave in Palugvik 1. Two specimens are simply pieces 1.7 and 1.9 cm. long, cut from naturally hollow bird bone (Pl. 42, *17*). Another, 4.5 by 2.5 cm., is made from a piece of seal mandible containing 2 teeth; the points of the teeth have been ground down and the natural canal used as the hole (Pl. 42, *31*).

More common are the beads made of sections or shaped pieces of animal bone, including whale bone (Pls. 42, *22, 23;* 43, *16* to *18;* 44, *31, 32, 71, 73*). Most of these are oval in section with a hole drilled or punched through the soft, spongy interior of the bone. They vary in length from 1.2 to 3.7 cm., and in diameter from just under 1 to 2 cm. A few approach in type the flat oval or disk-shaped bone beads.

Oval and Rectangular Bone and Ivory Beads

The collections contain 170 bone (6 additional specimens were lost) and 18 beads of ivory, of which 107 bone and 15 ivory specimens were in the grave in Palugvik 1. These beads are flat, and oval or rectangular in shape, rather similar to specimens of shell (see below). A few are almost disk-shaped; 2 others, 0.9 cm. thick, are almost tubular (Pl. 44, *69, 70*). The larger bone and ivory specimens are usually oval in outline; the smaller ones are apt to be rectangular; a few are almost square. The central hole is almost invariably made with a mechanical drill. There is a continuous range in size from only 0.7 by 0.5 cm. (P.1037) to 2.8 by 1.4 cm. (33-37-282), and it is impossible to separate the Chugach beads

into distinct types based on size or shape, or to find any correlation between variations in size or shape and depth in the Palugvik midden. The smaller specimens, well illustrated by a string of rectangular beads, 4 of bone, 2 of shell, and one of ivory (Pl. 42, *1, 2, 10*), found together in Palugvik 2, are identical with specimens from Kachemak Bay III,[120] where the larger bone and ivory specimens are lacking. The Chugach beads seem to be simply an exuberant development of the same pattern as that found on Cook Inlet.

About half of the flat oval or rectangular bone beads are made from the tympanic bones of seal, sea otter, or porpoise. They are ground flat on one side and on the other still show the natural irregularities of the inner surface of the bone (Pls. 42, *3, 4, 13, 14;* 43, *8, 13* to *15;* 44, *23, 61, 62*). A partially shaped piece of tympanic bone illustrates the process of manufacture (Pl. 43, *20*).

Less striking, but equally numerous, are beads made simply of pieces of whale or other animal bone (Pls. 42, *2, 10, 12;* 43, *7, 21;* 44, *22, 30, 63, 64, 67, 69, 70*). One bead seems to have been made from a piece of a small animal's skull (P.879); one from the old woman's grave in Palugvik 1 is made of a piece of animal jaw containing a tooth (P.1310). A plain bone specimen from Palugvik 2 (Pl. 42, *15*) may be either an unfinished bead or an inset (for a wooden vessel?).

In addition to the bone beads, there are

[120] De Laguna, 1934, Pl. 50, *4, 13*.

PLATE 44. Beads from apron and wooden box, with Skeleton III, Palugvik I. Scale natural size. (1 to 34, P.1307 to P.1315; 35 to 73, 33-37-420)

1 to 6, Rectangular shell beads; 7 to 14, disk shell beads; 15, 16, and 21, disk blue shell beads; 17, disk bone bead; 18 to 20, oval blue shell beads; 22 and 23, rectangular bone beads; 24 and 27, rectangular ivory beads; 25 and 26, oval bone beads; 28, disk blue shell bead; 29, oval ivory bead; 30, oval whale bone bead; 31 and 32, beads, sections of animal bone; 33, ivory bead, section of bear canine; 34, wooden box, at feet of skeleton; 35 to 41, rectangular shell beads; 42 to 49, disk shell beads; 50, 51, and 58, disk bone beads; 52, 53, 56, and 57, oval blue shell beads; 54 and 55, disk blue shell beads; 59 and 60, rectangular ivory beads; 61 and 62, rectangular and oval beads, seal tympanic bone; 63, 64, and 67, oval whale bone beads; 65 and 68, disk slate beads; 66, rectangular ivory bead; 69 and 70, unusually thick oval bone beads; 71 and 73, beads, sections of animal bone; 72, ivory bead, section of bear canine

18 similar specimens of ivory (Pls. 42, *1;* 44, *24, 27, 29, 59, 60, 66*).

Palugvik 2 contained a lump of seal tympanic bone (?) partially shaped into a ball 1.5 cm. in diameter (33-37-275). It may have been intended for a bead, but is not included in the count.

Oval and Rectangular Shell Beads

There are 320 rectangular and oval shell beads, of which 300 plus 64 fragments were found in the grave in Palugvik 1. They vary in size from 0.7 by 0.5 cm. to 2.8 by 1 cm., although there is a fragment broken from what was probably a much larger specimen. The range of size is thus similar to that of the bone and ivory beads of the same shape.

Most of the larger specimens are made of the hinge portion of clam shells; the majority of the smaller appear to be of cardium shell. The bead is so made that the hole may be drilled through the thinnest part of the shell. The smaller specimens are usually much more carefully made than the larger, which for the most part are simply irregular pieces (Pls. 42, *19* to *21, 29;* 43, *9, 10, 12;* 44, *1* to *6, 35* to *41*). The 2 small shell beads (P.881c, and one lost) found with the string in Palugvik 2 are identical with rectangular shell beads from Kachemak Bay III.[121] Among the shell beads in the old woman's grave are a few carefully shaped oval specimens of blue shell (Pl. 44, *18* to *20, 52, 53, 56, 57*). No blue shell beads were found elsewhere.

Disk-shaped Beads

The disk-shaped bone beads (Pls. 42, *11;* 43, *6;* 44, *17, 50, 51, 58*) are not very distinct from some of the shorter and broader oval bone specimens, and it has been almost impossible to draw a clear line between the 2 types. Some of the circular beads are made of tympanic bone, with diameters from 0.8 to 1.5 cm. Nine disk-shaped bone beads are from the grave in Palugvik 1.

There are 222 circular shell beads, of which 206 (plus 105 fragments) were found in the grave in Palugvik 1. These are made of flat thin pieces, much more carefully shaped than the oval or rectangular shell beads. They vary in size from one only 0.4 cm. in diameter (Pl. 42, *9*) to an irregular specimen, 2.8 by 2.5 cm. in diameter (Pl. 43, *11*). The holes are made with a mechanical drill, and some of the smaller beads are so perfect that they look as if they had been cut out with a pair of compasses (Pl. 42, *7* to *9, 16;* 43, *1* to *5, 11;* 44, 7 to *14, 42* to *49*). Among the beads in the grave were 5 of blue shell (Pl. 44, *15, 16, 21, 54, 55*). A large disk-shaped bead of white shell, found with Skeleton III on Palugvik East Point, disintegrated when touched.

There are 4 disk-shaped beads, all (?) of slate, from 0.8 to 1.1 cm. in diameter, and 0.4 to 0.8 cm. thick. Three were in the grave in Palugvik 1 (Pl. 44, *28, 65, 68*), and one came from Site 65 on Chenega Island (Pl. 43, *27*).

The distribution of all beads of native manufacture is:

Palugvik 4: 3 oval or rectangular bone beads (P.851, P.853, and DNM. uncat.), 1 disk shell bead (Pl. 43, *11*).

Palugvik 3 or 4: 1 bird bone tubular bead (33-37-56), 1 disk shell bead (Pl. 42, *16*).

Palugvik 3: 1 tooth cut for bead (P.885), 4 tubular bone beads (Pl. 43, *16;* 33-37-151, 152; P.878), 1 tubular bead of seal mandible (Pl. 42, *31*), 6 oval and rectangular bone beads (Pl. 42, *13;* 33-37-154 to 156; P.844; field no. 329, lost), 1 disk shell bead (Pl. 42, *8*).

Palugvik 2 or 3: 1 tooth cut for bead (30-25-22), 2 oval or rectangular bone beads (field nos. 231, 420, lost), 1 oval ivory bead (P.865).

Palugvik 2: string of rectangular beads: 4 bone, 1 ivory, 2 shell (1 lost) (Pl. 42,

---

[121] *Ibid.,* Pl. 50, *19.*

1, 2, 10; P.881a to c), 4 teeth cut for beads (Pl. 42, *33;* 33-37-270 to 272), 2 tubular ivory beads (Pl. 43, *22;* 33-37-279), 5 tubular bone beads (Pls. 42, *23; 43, 17, 18;* 33-37-277, P.870), 28 oval and rectangular bone beads in addition to those on the string (Pls. 42, *5, 14, 15;* 43, *20, 21;* 33-37-281 to 283, 286, 290 to 294, 297; P.845 to P.848, P.850, P.854, P.855, P.857, P.879, P.891, field nos. 644, 676, 677 [of these, 3 were unfinished]), 1 disk bone bead (field no. 286, lost).

Palugvik 1 or 2: 1 tubular ivory bead (P.1006), 1 tubular bone bead (P.871), 5 oval and rectangular bone beads (Pl. 43, *8, 15;* 33-37-287 to 289), 1 rectangular shell bead (33-37-298).

Palugvik 1 (not including Grave III): 6 teeth cut for beads (Pl. 43, *36;* 33-37-412, 413; P.884, P.887, WSM 1045), 3 tubular bone beads (P.876, P.889, P.890), 10 oval and rectangular bone beads (Pls. 42, *3, 4;* 43, *13, 14;* 33-37-416, 418; P.849, P.852, P.856, P.863), 3 disk bone beads (Pls. 42, *11;* 43, *6;* 33-37-419).

Grave III, Palugvik 1 (33-37-420, P.1307 to P.1315) (numbers refer to figures on Plate 44): 2 tubular ivory beads (*33, 72*), 5 tubular bone beads (*31, 32, 71, 73*), 107 oval and rectangular bone beads (*22, 23, 25, 26, 30, 61* to *64, 67, 69, 70*), 15 oval and rectangular ivory beads (*24, 27, 29, 59, 60, 66*), 300 oval and rectangular shell beads and 64 fragments (*1* to *6, 18* to *20, 35* to *41, 52, 53, 56, 57*), 9 disk bone beads (*17, 50, 51, 58*), 206 disk shell beads and 105 fragments (*7* to *16, 21, 42* to *49, 54, 55*), 3 disk stone beads (*28, 65, 68*).

Palugvik, layer (?): 4 tubular ivory beads (Pls. 42, *24;* 43, *19;* 33-37-501b, P.1065), 4 tubular bone beads (Pl. 42, *17, 22;* 33-37-499, P.1039), 20 oval and rectangular bone heads (Pl. 43, *7;* 33-37-501d to l, P.845, P.1029, P.1030, P.1032, P.1034 to P.1037, P.1062, P.1063), 1 oval ivory bead (P.1031), 16 oval and rectangular shell beads (Pl. 43, *9, 10, 12;* 33-37-501m to u, P.1018, P.1027, P.1028, P.1061), 14 disk shell beads (Pls. 42, *7, 9;* 43, *1* to *5, 11;* 33-37-50lv to bb, P.1023).

Palugvik East Point, beach: 1 tubular ivory bead (Pl. 43, *24*); burial ledge: 1 oval bone bead (P.1104), 1 rectangular shell bead (P.1103); Grave III: 1 disk shell bead (lost).

Site 56, Chenega Island: 1 disk stone bead (Pl. 43, *27*).

Palutat Cave, depth 4 feet: 1 tooth cut for bead (33-37-660).

It would be natural to assume that these beads were worn as necklaces, especially since the skeleton of a Kachemak Bay Eskimo woman is reported to have been found with a necklace of small rectangular shell beads.[122] The glass beads found with Skeletons I and II on Glacier Island would have been interpreted as necklaces without question, had not Meany found similar beads as pendants on the headband of a skeleton in a near-by grave. Our ethnological notes fail to mention necklaces specifically, nor are they described in the reports of the early explorers in Prince William Sound. None of the older skeletons had beads at the neck, so we cannot be sure whether or not the Chugach wore necklaces. The string of 7 small rectangular beads from Palugvik 2 is not long enough to have served such a purpose. On the other hand, Portlock describes beads hanging from the medial labret and strings of beads hanging from the ears to the shoulders.[123] Riobo also describes the women as wearing a string of beads hanging from the corners of the mouth down to the chest, evidently a string which connected two lateral labrets.[124] Dixon reports: "The ears of these Indians [i.e., the Chugach] were ornamented with plenty of small blue beads . . . [presumably]

[122] *Ibid.,* p. 47, Pl. 50, *19.*

[123] Portlock, 1789, p. 249. Colnett in 1788 sketched such a medial labret with beads, as described in section 68.

[124] Riobo, 1918, p. 86.

procured from the Russians."[125] Meares writes: "Their ears are full of holes, from which hang pendants of bone or shell."[126]

In Chapter II, section 16, we cited a passage from Cook and referred to the accompanying illustrations which indicate that the Chugach wore beads attached to their medial labrets and to their nose ornaments. Cook also writes: "Both sexes have the ears perforated with several holes, about the outer and lower part of the edge, in which they hang little bunches of beads, made of the same tubulous shelly substance used for this purpose by those of Nootka."[127] The men and women illustrated in Plates 46 and 47 of the *Album* wear a veritable fringe of dentalia hanging from the ears. The woman has at least six holes in the lobe and helix. Cook also noted that glass beads were worn in the ears and that "They also wear bracelets of the shelly beads [dentalia?], or others of a cylindrical shape, made of a substance like amber; with such also as are used in their ears and noses." Glass beads were also fastened to men's basketry hats; Plate 46 shows a row of such beads stitched around the brim and another about the top of the crown. Colnett found that the Chugach preferred transparent, smooth, round beads, no bigger than a large pea, though they would accept any color. He also remarks that they had quantities of beads of a different kind, not specified, with which they ornamented their dogs.

Beads were also fastened to various articles of dress. Thus the old woman buried in Palugvik 1 evidently wore an apron of some kind which hung from her waist to her knees and which was composed of or decorated with beads. These 800-odd beads were found in a mass extending over and between the femurs. No pattern could be determined, but it was evident that beads of the same material, size, and shape had been strung together in lines. Our Chugach informants told us that both sexes wore an apron or genital covering. The woman's apron was described as covering the breasts (i.e., it had a bib in front?). There were fringes along the edge, and some aprons were decorated with beads; others were ornamented with different colored skins. It is evident that the beads in this grave belonged to an apron of this type, although there is no archaeological evidence to show that it covered the body above the waist.

We were also informed that women wore beaded headbands, and that the chief's daughter (at puberty?) wore a hoodlike veil made of beads and dentalium shells which hung down her back, sometimes to the heels. Beads were said to belong only to chiefs and to members of their families; poor people never had any unless they had been given a few by a member of the chief's family. The beads belonging to a person were buried with the dead owner.

Dentalium shells, mentioned in connection with the veil of beads, were also used as nose ornaments. Spruce root hats were said to have been decorated with sea lion whiskers and dentalium shells.[128] These dentalium shells were obtained in trade from the Tlingit, but such trade was small because the Tlingit were so rich. We found no dentalium shells in Prince William Sound, and only one has been found in Kachemak Bay.[129]

74. PENDANTS

The pendants from Prince William Sound are of 5 types: those made of (1) bear or seal canines, (2) bone or ivory, (3) shell, (4) marine gastropod opercula, and (5) stone. It was reported that amber, found on the beaches of Kayak Island in Controller Bay, was used for ear ornaments, presumably in the form of pendants, but we found no amber.

[125] Dixon, 1789, p. 147.
[126] Meares, 1791, I, lxi.
[127] Cook, 1785, II, 369, 370.

[128] Cf. Birket-Smith, 1941, Fig. 7, a painted basketry hat, decorated with dentalium shells and small red, black, and white glass beads, tentatively identified as coming from Kodiak Island; and Fig. 8, various Kodiak hat ornaments, etc., made of sea lion whiskers, small glass beads, etc.
[129] De Laguna, 1934, Pl. 51, *8*, from Kachemak Bay III.

Tooth Pendants

There are 4 pendants made of bear canines, 3 of seal (?) canines, and one of an unidentified tooth. A bear canine from Palugvik 4 (Pl. 42, *49*) is simply grooved about the root for suspension. From Palugvik 4 (?) there is a seal canine which has been ground flat on both sides (Pl. 42, *44*). The natural constriction at the root apparently served for suspension. Two seal tooth pendants, from Palugvik 1 or 2 (P.886) and Palugvik 1 (P.882), are simply pierced at the root for suspension. A tooth pendant from Palugvik 2 (or 3?) has been somewhat shaped and has a hole (Pl. 43, *43*). A pendant from Palugvik 2 is made of a bear canine split in two to expose the nerve canal (Pl. 42, *47*). It is ground smooth and has a hole. With Skeleton III at Palugvik East Point were found 2 bear canines (Pl. 47, *8, 9*). These lay near the hands at the right shoulder and were presumably pendants, although they may have been buckles, etc. They are pierced near the root by 2 holes at right angles to each other, and the roots are encircled by 2 grooves.

Cut Bone and Ivory Pendants

There are 12 specimens of bone and ivory which are identified as pendants. The most elaborate of these is a broken ornament of bone from Palugvik 4, identified by Makari as an ear pendant (Pl. 42, *48*), and rather similar in style to 2 of Hrdlička's specimens from Kodiak. It is flat on one side (illustrated), slightly convex on the other, and oval in outline, with 2 pointed spurs at the base when complete. Two slots have been cut paralleling the edges, setting off a narrow border on each side which is joined to the central oval portion at the top and bottom. One of these bordering strips is broken off. At the upper end is the main suspension hole, and there is also a very small hole at the bottom. Along both (?) side strips are 7 small holes, and there is a large hole in the middle of the central section. On the flat side of the specimen there are also 5 drilled pits or unfinished holes in the central part, and one at the lower end of the bordering strip. When complete, the specimen might have suggested a highly conventionalized eye (or perhaps a fish). The central hole may have held an inset or itself have represented the pupil of the eye. Small pendants were probably suspended from the holes along the edges. The specimen is 4.8 cm. long and was about 3 cm. wide when complete.

A fragmentary bone pendant from Palugvik 3 or 4 is also rather elaborate (Pl. 43, *41*). The piece measures (7.5 by 1.3) cm. but was evidently cut from a leaf-shaped plaque about 8 cm. long and 2.5 cm. wide, of which our specimen represents most of the left half. The shape of the bottom cannot be determined, but it was probably rounded or pointed. The upper end was pierced for suspension and was also notched at the edges, setting off 2 earlike projections above the hole. Near the middle of the fragment are 2 holes, and there are also 2 holes at the edge, now broken out. There were presumably similar holes in the missing portion. The fragment is decorated on one surface by 2 longitudinal lines with downward slanting spurs on the outside. These curve apart near the lower end of the specimen, where there are 2 horizontal lines. If the other half had similar lines these would have produced a design consisting of a spurred oval in the center, flanked on each side by a spurred longitudinal line, with 2 connecting crossbars at the bottom. A somewhat similar bone pendant with incised decoration was found in Kachemak Bay III.[130]

Three pendants are simply rectangular ivory bars, 3.1, 3.4, and 3.9 cm. long, with a hole at one end. They are from Palugvik 1 (Pl. 43, *35*), Palugvik 3 (Pl. 42, *41*), and Palugvik 1 or 2 (Pl. 43, *38*). Two shorter rectangular ivory pendants are from Palugvik 2 (Pl. 42, *43*) and Palugvik 1 or 2 (Pl. 42, *42*). A bone pendant (Pl. 43, *45*) and a crude ivory specimen (Pl. 43, *30*), both

[130] *Ibid.,* Pl. 50, *24*.

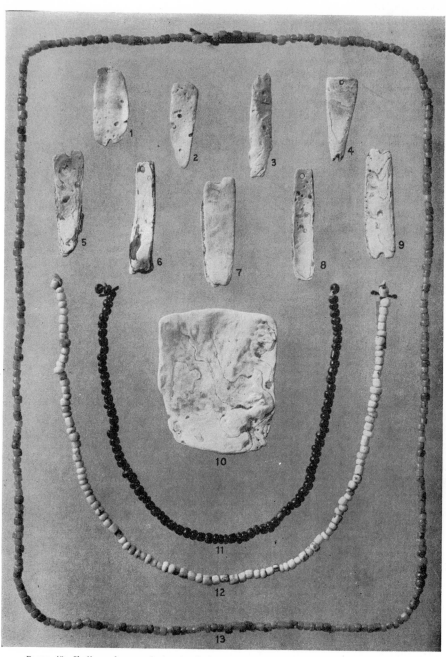

PLATE 45. Shell pendants and glass beads found with Skeleton II, Glacier Island, Site 43.
Scale slightly over ⅖ natural size

1 to 10, Shell pendants, representing one ear ornament (P.1304) ; 11, black glass beads (P.1303a) ;
12, white glass beads (P.1303b) ; 13, blue glass beads (P.1303c)

from Palugvik 1, are roughly triangular in outline and have the suspension hole drilled from edge to edge through the apex of the triangle.

From Palugvik 2 there are two 4-sided pendants, one of ivory, 9.8 cm. long (Pl. 42, *45*), the other of bone, 6.3 cm. long (Pl. 42, *46*). Both have small projections at the base. The hole in the ivory specimen is drilled from edge to edge, not from side to side as on most of the other specimens. The bone pendant appears to have had a suspension hole, now broken out, and has been refinished with a groove.

A bone specimen from Palugvik 1 is either a pendant or an ornamental bodkin of some kind (Pl. 43, *42*). It is a pin, circular in section at the smaller end and rectangular at the other, where it is pierced for suspension. This end has been sawed off through the hole, and the specimen is now 4.7 cm. long. There is a shallow groove across the lower end, and the 4 edges near the upper end have decorative notches.

Shell Pendants

Under the skull of the woman (Skeleton II) on Glacier Island were 2 groups of shell pendants which were probably ear ornaments.[131] Each group consisted of a large plaque and 9 smaller pendants, lying in a pile near each ear (Pl. 45, *1* to *10; 33-37-634*).

The larger plaques measure 5.2 by 4.5 cm. (Pl. 45, *10*) and 4.2 by 4.2 cm., and have a hole near one edge. There may have been holes along the lower edge from which the smaller pendants were hung, but the plaques are now too badly weathered to show any signs of such holes, and the larger plaques and smaller pendants may, therefore, have been hung from separate holes in the lobe and helix of the ear.

The smaller pendants are from 2.6 to 4.5 cm. long and about 1 cm. wide (Pl. 45, *1* to *9*). The majority are oval or rectangular in outline; 4 are triangular or narrower at one end than at the other. Ten specimens,

including 2 of the triangular pieces, have holes at both ends; 8 have holes at one end only. A nineteenth fragment of shell was apparently split from one of the other specimens. The arrangement of holes suggests that the pendants were hung in strings.

Pendants of Turbo Opercula

Two pendants, from Palugvik 3 (Pl. 42, *39*) and Palugvik 3 or 4 (P.877), are made of the triangular horny plate (operculum) from the foot of a turbo, or marine gastropod, by means of which the animal closes its shell. These measure about 3.5 by 1.7 cm. [132]

Stone Pendants

A pendant from Palugvik 2 is made of white, translucent soapstone (?), shaped like an oval plaque with one straight edge, measuring 2.5 by 2.3 cm., and 0.7 cm. in thickness (Pl. 43, *29*). Two holes for suspension are drilled obliquely through the corners at the straight edge.

The second pendant, said to have been found in Jackpot Bay in the northwestern part of the sound, is a broken crescent-shaped ornament of slate, originally 6 (?) by 4.5 cm. (Pl. 43, *23*). There is a drilled hole near the middle of the outer, convex edge, so that when the pendant was suspended the horns of the crescent would have hung down.

75. Chinese Coin

A Chinese coin was found just under the turf at Site 7 in Hawkins Cut Off (Fig. 33). The natives at Chenega said that they formerly wore coins of this type hung from holes in the ears or nose. As many as 5 were worn in each ear, suspended from the lobe and helix. The coin was identified by Miss Helen E. Fernald, formerly of the University of Pennsylvania Museum, as belonging to the K'ang Hsi period, A.D. 1662-1723. How and when it reached Alaska, it is impossible to say. Its position just under the turf indicates that this can-

---

[131] Strange (1928, p. 56) lists in his Chugach vocabulary the word for "An ear-ring of pearl shell."

[132] Strange (1928, p. 56) also gives the native word for "A rattle of dried barnacle shells," suggesting one use for these pendants.

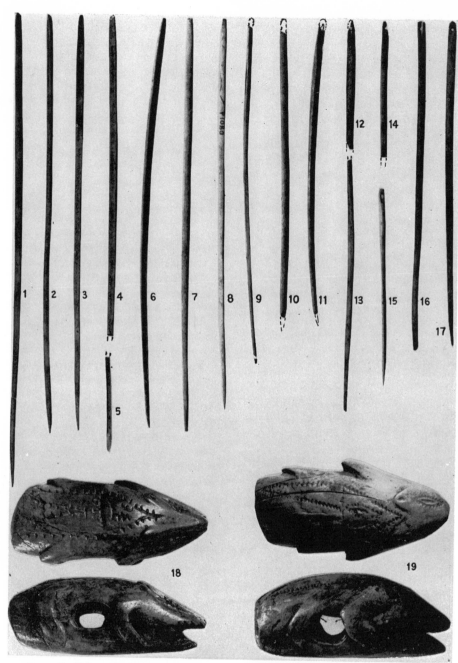

PLATE 46. Objects with Skeleton III, Palugvik East Point. Scale $\frac{9}{10}$ natural size (see Fig. 12)

1 to 4, 6 to 8, Eyeless needles or pins, on chest of skeleton (33-37-546 to 549, P.1078 to P.1080) ; 5, 9, 10, and 13, needle fragments, on chest of skeleton (33-37-550, P.1081 to P.1083) ; 11, 12, 14 to 17, needles with eyes, on chest of skeleton (33-37-543, 544, 545, P.1084, P.1085, P.1091) ; 18 and 19, bear figures, walrus ivory, used as handles for cord drill (?) , near hands of skeleton (33-37-539, P.1072)

FIGURE 33. Chinese coin (K'ang Hsi period, 1662-1723), Site 7, Hawkins Cut Off (30-25-81). Scale 1 1/3 natural size (*Sketch by Helen Fernald*)

not have been long ago, and the finding of the bone snuff mortar at the same site would indicate that, although the lower layers are prehistoric, the village was not abandoned until after contact with Europeans. It is interesting that near Yakutat in 1788 Colnett met an Indian whose dress was trimmed with Chinese money.

76. MISCELLANEOUS ORNAMENTS

A small flat piece of bone, 1.5 by 1 cm., decorated by 3 encircling grooves, was found on Palugvik beach (Pl. 42, *6*). It is possibly an unfinished bead, or a piece cut from a pendant or similar ornament.

A thin bone plate, (2.3) cm. long and 1.4 cm. wide, notched on the edges and cut off squarely at the undamaged end, may have been broken from a pendant. It comes from Palugvik 1 (P.923). A similar bone specimen, identified as a pendant, belongs to Kachemak Bay II.[133]

A fragment of ivory with incised lines comes from Palugvik 2 and may have been broken from a pendant or labret (33-37-410).

Half of a carnivore mandible, (6.5) cm. long, from which the ramus and anterior portion have been broken, comes from the upper half (or two-thirds?) of the Palugvik midden (P.897). The teeth are missing, and the edges of the 8 sockets are worn;

[133] De Laguna, 1934, Pl. 50, *18*.

in fact, the whole specimen has been polished smooth by much handling. It may possibly have been an amulet.

A small 4-sided bar of marble, 2.5 by 1 cm., has been thinned by grinding on both sides to leave a flange along one edge (Pl. 43, *37*). A beak-shaped projection or shoulder is carved at one end. This specimen was found in Palugvik 1.

In addition to the small ivory peg from Palugvik 1, described as a possible ear stud (Pl. 43, *34;* section 68), there is also an ornamental bone peg or nail from Palugvik 3 or 4 (Pl. 43, *32*). It is 1.7 cm. long, with a sharp point at one end and a flat triangular head, 0.9 cm. wide, set off by a groove at the other end. This peg is clearly intended to be pinned into something and may have been an article of personal adornment, such as an ear plug, or may have been an ornamental stud for some implement.

From Palugvik 2 is a thin bone object, 3.7 cm. long, the outline of which suggests a conventionalized whale (Pl. 42, *30*). On one side is a decoration consisting of 2 parallel longitudinal lines. It is possible that this object was a whaling amulet.

77. IVORY DOLL

Only one doll or human figurine was found in Prince William Sound. Makari reported that every shaman had several dolls which represented his familiar spirits, some strong and others weak. Makari had heard of only one childless woman who attempted to solace herself with a doll. This was a woman from Nuka Bay on the southern shore of Kenai Peninsula who was married to Apuluq, the chief of Montague Island in prehistoric times. He was a powerful shaman and made his wife a wooden doll, which she used to fondle and pretend to suckle. He could make the doll walk by putting his power into it. His wife dressed the doll in pearls, beads, and sea otter skins. Finally her breast rotted and she died and was buried with the doll.

A crude representation of a human being was found in Palugvik 3 (?) (Pl. 42, *40*).

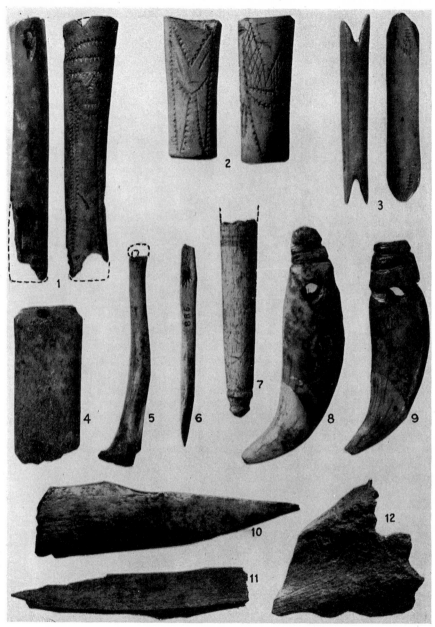

PLATE 47. Objects with Skeleton III, Palugvik East Point.
Scale slightly over ⅘ natural size (see Fig. 12)

1, Decorated bird bone tube, near hands (33-37-541) ; 2, decorated bird bone tube, near right
ankle (P.1075) ; 3, "shaman's" tube, near hands (33-37-542) ; 4, handle or shaft fragment, whale
bone, beyond skull, association with grave not certain (33-37-554) ; 5, marmot tibia with suspension hole, beyond skull, association with grave not certain (33-37-552) ; 6, awl, bird bone, near
hands (P.1077) ; 7, fragment of socket piece, beyond skull, association with grave not certain
(P.1088) ; 8 and 9, brown bear canines, near hands (P.1073 and 33-37-540) ; 10 to 12, fragments
of worked bone, beyond skull, association with grave not certain (P.1089, 33-37-553, P.1090)

It is made from a rectangular slab of walrus (?) ivory, concave on one surface and convex on the other. It measures 7.2 by 2.5 cm., the widest part being at the top of the head, the narrowest at the bottom of the body. The slab is notched on each edge to mark the neck, but there is no indication of limbs. The face is represented on the convex surface. An incised line, parallel to the top of the head, represents the hair or a cap and may be compared with an analogous line across the top of the human head incised on one of the decorated bone tubes from Palugvik East Point (Pl. 47, 1). The ivory is cut out below the brows and around the nose, which is long and narrow. The eyes are indicated by small gouges, the mouth by a very short transverse line. Although this specimen is very small it is similar in style to the faces carved on sections of split whale rib which Hrdlička found on Kodiak.[134]

According to Cook, the Prince William Sound natives had

a good many little images, four or five inches long, either of wood, or stuffed; which were covered with a bit of fur, and ornamented with pieces of small quill feathers, in imitation of their shelly beads [dentalia], with hair fixed on their heads. Whether these might be mere toys for children, or held in some veneration, as representing their deceased friends, and applied to some superstitious purpose, we could not determine.[135]

It is not clear from the passage whether these dolls or images were ever offered in trade or were merely carried in the natives' bidarkas.

In southwestern Alaska dolls or images representing human beings seem not to have been used as children's toys, but rather as magical paraphernalia. They were often shaman's puppets, as the specimens from Kachemak Bay II and III probably

were.[136] Lisiansky reports that childless women on Kodiak played with dolls,[137] probably in order to induce conception by magic, as perhaps poor Apuluq's wife tried to do. The Aleut, in apparently both ancient and modern times, prayed to an ivory image of the deity Kaadaraadar, which was suspended in the house. Carved bone images, sometimes representing seated men, were worn by the modern Aleut hunters on their hats, evidently as amulets; and 2 ivory ornaments with human faces were attached to a modern fur cap from Kodiak Island.[138] Faces, some suggestive of animals, others of men, were carved on hunting weapons of the prehistoric inhabitants of Umnak and Amaknak islands[139] and, perhaps like the decorations on the bone tubes from the shaman's grave at Palugvik East Point, were intended to represent guardian spirits.

78. Stone Ball for Game

A small egg-shaped pebble 3.8 cm. in diameter (33-37-365), found in Palugvik 2, was identified by Makari as a ball for a juggling game. This was not a competitive game but a solitary amusement, indulged in sometimes, if we are to believe the legends, by those unfortunates who are turning into evil spirits and who shun companionship, to wander up and down the beach, tossing their balls and catching them as they undergo this uncanny metamorphosis.

Similar specimens have been found in Kachemak Bay III, Kodiak, and the Aleutians. Hrdlička reports finding them in sets, and Jochelson specifies that the Aleut used to toss and catch 3 or 4 stone balls in the same hand.[140]

---

[134] Hrdlička, 1944, Fig. 51, is an unusually well-carved example of this type, broken off at the neck. It is the cruder, unpublished specimens which resemble the Palugvik doll. An unfinished doll (?) of the same kind was found in Yukon Island III (de Laguna, 1934, p. 114).

[135] Cook, 1785, II, 372 f. Strange (1928, p. 56) gives the native word for a "small Image."

[136] De Laguna, 1934, Pl. 52, pp. 114 f. Cf. Hrdlička, 1944, Fig. 161, pp. 347 f.

[137] Lisiansky, 1814, p. 178.

[138] Aleut image of deity (Laughlin and Marsh, 1951, pp. 72, 82 f.); Aleut hat ornaments (Steller in Golder, 1925, II, 95; Ivanov, 1930; and other sources cited in Hrdlička, 1945, pp. 78 f.); Kodiak cap ornaments (Heizer, 1952b, Fig. 2).

[139] Jochelson, 1925, Figs. 81 to 83; Hrdlička, 1945, p. 158; Quimby, 1948, Figs. 16 to 18.

[140] Jochelson, 1925, Pl. 17, 27, 29; de Laguna, 1934, p. 104; Hrdlička, 1944, Fig. 161, p. 287.

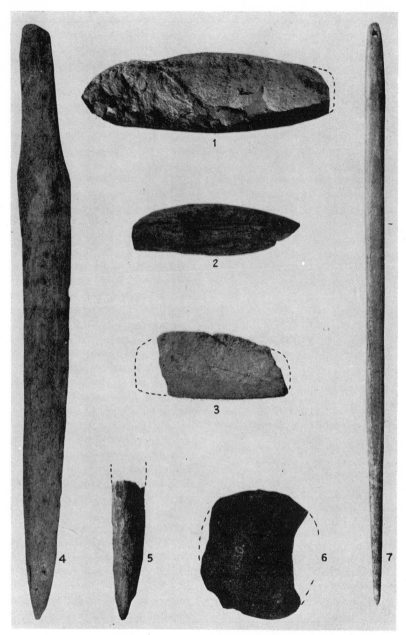

PLATE 48. Objects with Skeleton III, Palugvik East Point (see Fig. 12).
Scale slightly under ½ natural size except for No. 7

1, Planing adz, near left shoulder (P.1076) ; 2, splitting adz, without groove, near left shoulder
(33-37-556) ; 3, saw, sandstone, beyond skull, association with grave not certain (P.1086) ; 4,
dagger, whale bone, at right side (33-37-551) ; 5, point of similar dagger, beyond skull, association
with grave not certain (P.1087) ; 6, whetstone, shale, beyond skull, association with grave not
certain (33-37-555) ; 7, pick or "bayonet," whale bone, at right leg (P.1074) , scale ³⁄₁₀ natural size

79. ARMOR

Several pieces of wooden armor were found in Palutat Cave. According to our informants, such armor, made of round wooden slabs tied together with thongs, reached to the armpits and was worn in warfare. The natives denied the use of helmets or shields. These fragments of armor which we found may have been on one of the mummies in the cave, since the body of a chief was said to have been dressed in his armor.

One fragment consists of 2 wooden slats fastened together with thongs (Pl. 50, 1). These slats are 24.5 cm. long, 1.6 cm. wide, and 1 cm. thick. They are only 1.4 cm. wide on the side worn next to the body, so that when lashed together they would form a curved garment fitting the shape of the body. At the ends of each piece there are holes drilled from side to side. Two pairs of narrow thongs pass through these holes and lash the 2 slats together at the top and bottom, leaving a space 0.2 cm. wide between them. In the middle of the slats there are also a pair of holes, 7 cm. apart, drilled from edge to edge. Originally another pair of thongs through these holes must have strung the slats together. On the outer surface the slats are decorated by a longitudinal line up the middle. It will be noted that the right-hand slat in the illustration (the specimen is turned upside down) is cut obliquely across one end (the lower end, as pictured), so that the edge away from the left-hand slat is slightly longer than the nearer edge. This fragment of armor must be part of a suit almost identical with the complete Aleut suit from Kagamil Island.[141] By comparing the length of our specimen with the slats in this suit, and assuming that the respective wearers were of the same size, we are able to identify our fragment as the first 2 slats of the upper row in front, next to the left armhole. On the Aleut specimen, the slats seem to have had only one hole drilled from edge to edge, not 2. The suit was fastened behind

by means of 2 loops of sinew, buttoned with wooden toggles.[142]

What is probably a third piece of armor was also found in the cave (Pl. 51, 5). This is a wooden slat 9.4 cm. long, 2.3 cm. wide, and 1.1 cm. thick. It is pierced by 2 holes, drilled from side to side, and is decorated by a medial line on the slightly convex outer surface. There are no holes drilled from edge to edge. One end is somewhat whittled down on the convex surface, as if to fit into something. This piece would seem to correspond to one of the 2 end pieces of the upper row of slats in the Aleut suit, which met at the back of the wearer. These are also narrowed at the top although they did not fit into anything. However, our identification must remain tentative, since the end slats on the Aleut suit are about 12 cm. long, while our specimen is only 9.4 cm. long.

Two fragments of worked ivory, one from the upper part of Palugvik 4 (from Section 2C above the pebble layer associated with a hearth) and the other from Layer 3 in Section 2B, fit together to form a rectangular slab, 11.8 cm. long and 3.2 cm. wide (Pl. 51, 4). At one end are a pair of holes drilled near the outer edges. The specimen is worn thin at this end, and the holes are now broken out. This ivory piece may be an armor plate, like those worn by northern Alaskan Eskimo. Hrdlička has also reported of the Aleutians that "on several of the islands occurred artificially thinned slabs of bone, each with several drilled holes. None of these, regrettably, were complete. They may have served as parts of bone armor, or been sewn on a skin garment for the same purpose."[143] Identification of these specimens cannot be made with certainty. If they do indicate the use of bone plate armor, we still know from early reports that the predominant type was of wood.

Cook described Chugach armor as follows: "For defensive armour they have a kind of jacket, or coat of mail, made of thin

---

[141] Dall, 1878, Pl. 6; Hrdlička, 1945, p. 433.

[142] Dall, 1878, p. 18.
[143] Hrdlička, 1945, pp. 457 f.

PLATE 49. Wooden objects. Scale slightly over ⅔ natural size

1, Meat stick (?), Palutat Cave, surface (33-37-682); 2, 2 pieces of withe knotted together, Palutat Cave, surface (33-37-725); 3, wooden nail or tally, Palutat Cave, surface (33-37-693); 4, wooden peg, bottom of Palugvik midden (33-37-474); 5, fire drill, Palutat Cave, surface (33-37-692); 6, wooden hook from pile on top of skull B2, Palutat Cave (33-37-710), see Fig. 35, *1*; 7, undecorated side of wooden bar from pile on top of skull B2, Palutat Cave (33-37-717), see Figure 34, *10*; 8, handle of spoon (?), Palutat Cave, depth 1 to 4 feet (33-37-680); 9, toy arrow, Palutat Cave, surface (33-37-675); 10, meat stick (?), Palutat Cave, surface (33-37-681)

laths, bound together with sinews, which makes it quite flexible, though so close as not to admit an arrow or dart. It only covers the trunk of the body, and may not improperly be compared to a woman's stays."[144]

Sauer has also given us a description of armor seen in Prince William Sound in 1790:

They have armour of wood, which covers the body of the warrior and his neck; but his arms and legs are exposed. This is made of very neat pieces of wood, about half an inch thick, and near an inch broad, tied very artfully together with fine threads of the sinews of animals; and so contrived, that they can roll it up or expand it. This they tie around the body, a flap before reaching down to their thighs; but so made as to rise or fall, and permit their sitting in baidars; a similar flap hangs on the breast, which may be risen as high as their eyes. Straps fasten this armour on their shoulders, and strings tie it round the body on one side.[145]

This armor was evidently not quite of the same pattern as the Aleut suit.

Sauer adds:

The head is well guarded with a wooden helmet; some of these are made to resemble the head of a bear, and cover the face completely. Such wooden caps, or head-pieces, are worn in the chase of the different animals they represent; the native clothes himself in their skins, and approaches within a convenient distance to use his bow or lance.

Cook, too, had mentioned that the Chugach wear caps, "sometimes of wood, resembling a seal's head, well painted."[146] A Kodiak helmet of this type, resembling a seal's head, is illustrated and described by Ivanov.[147] It is quite evident that these wooden animal heads are not helmets worn to protect the warrior in battle but are a form of animal disguise, magical rather than practical, worn on sea mammal hunts. Ivanov, in fact, argues that all the wooden hats of the Aleut, and especially of the Koniag,

are zoomorphic representations on which ears, nose, eyes, and mouth are represented or symbolized, and that both "helmets" and hats are really masks in origin and purpose.

Sauer does not mention shields for a single man, but states: "They have very large screens; I was told (but saw none) of sufficient strength and thickness to withstand a musket-ball, and large enough to shelter twenty or thirty men."[148] Wooden shields were used by the Aleut and Koniag, and the latter, under the challenge of the Russian invasion, devised large movable breastwork screens.[149] It is possible that Sauer is referring in this passage to the Koniag invention, but also possible that it had been adopted or duplicated by the Chugach.

80. WOODEN HOOKS AND BARS

On top of the skull of Skeleton B2 in Palutat Cave (the skeleton of a mature man) was a board on which were piled 12 wooden hooks and 12 wooden bars.

The bars (Fig. 34 and Pl. 49, 7) have a flattened oval or subrectangular cross section. They range in length from 15 to 18 cm. and in width from 1.5 to 2.4 cm. At the upper end, which is slightly narrower than the lower, is a hole or pit, drilled from one side and barely piercing the other. The decorations are confined to the side opposite the pit. (Compare the 2 views of the same specimen illustrated in Pl. 49, 7, and Fig. 34, 10.) Three specimens are broken and lack the end with the pit (Fig. 34, 8, 9, 11); the lower end from another specimen is missing (Fig. 34, 4). The base of the others is slightly concave. On all specimens but one (Fig. 34, 6) on which the lower end is preserved, a triangular area at the base has been slightly cut. On one bar this area is crosshatched (Fig. 34, 5); on another the base is notched (Fig. 34, 9). On these last 2 specimens, and on a third (Fig. 34, 8), this is the only decoration. On the specimen from which the lower

---

144 Cook, 1785, II, 371 f.

145 Sauer, 1802, pp. 198 f. He uses the term "baidar" for both the bidarka (1-, 2-, or 3-hole kayak) and for the bidar proper (large open skin boat, or umiak).

146 Cook, 1785, II, 369. Strange (1928, p. 54) also mentions "The wooden cap, made in the form of a Seals head."

147 Ivanov, 1930, Pl. I, 5, p. 487. Cf. pp. 485-89.

148 Sauer, 1802, p. 199.

149 Coxe, 1803, pp. 190 f.; Hrdlička, 1944, p. 58; 1945, Fig. 35, pp. 131, 135, 433.

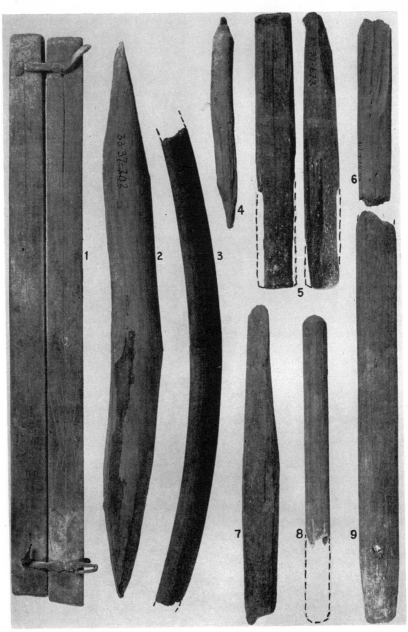

PLATE 50. Wooden objects. Scale slightly over ⅔ natural size

1, Fragment of slat armor with rawhide lashings, Palutat Cave, surface (33-37-672); 2, prow handle for dugout canoe, Palutat Cave, surface (33-37-702); 3, fragment of bidarka rib, Palutat Cave, surface (33-37-709); 4, pin, pointed at both ends (tooth for comb?) Palutat Cave, surface (33-37-684); 5, knife handle with bed for blade, Palutat Cave, depth 6 inches (33-37-673); 6, knife handle (?), Palutat Cave, surface (33-37-674); 7, decorated wooden implement, Palutat Cave, depth 1 to 4 feet (33-37-690); 8, upper end of drill shaft, Palutat Cave, surface (33-37-694); 9, fragment of bidarka rib, Palutat Cave, surface (33-37-704)

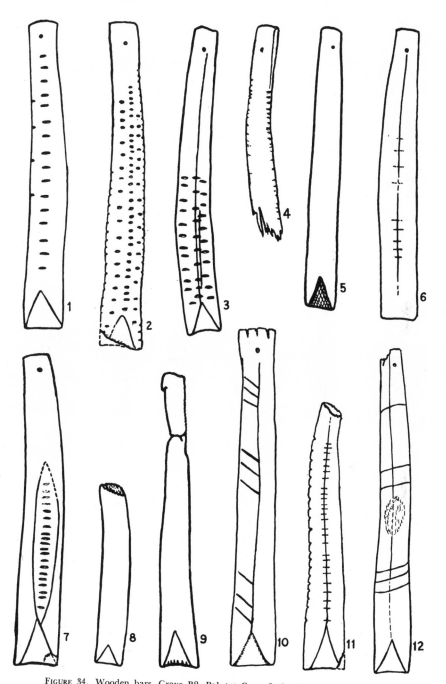

FIGURE 34. Wooden bars, Grave B2, Palutat Cave. Scale about ½ natural size
1, P.1284; 2, 33-37-718; 3, P.1285; 4, 33-37-722; 5, 33-37-721; 6, 33-37-719; 7, P.1283; 8, P.1288; 9, P.1287; 10, 33-37-717, see Plate 49, 7 for undecorated side; 11, 33-37-720; 12, P.1286

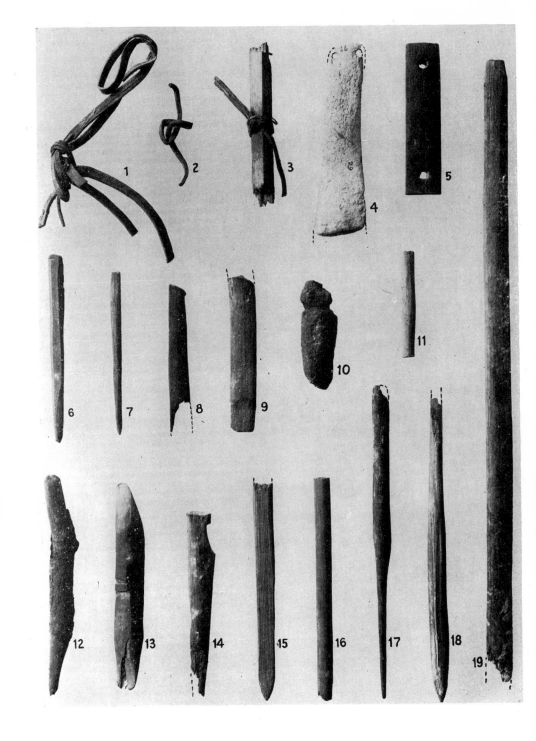

end is broken the decoration consists of the notching of the 4 longitudinal edges (Fig. 34, *4*). On 4 specimens the decoration is characterized by rows of small transverse gouges. The first of these has a single row of gouges and one notched edge (Fig. 34, *1*). The second has 3 longitudinal rows of gouges, those of the middle row more closely spaced than those of the side rows, and the edges on both sides are notched (Fig. 34, *2*). The third bar has a medial line running up from the apex of the triangular area at the base. This line is crossed by small gouges or spurs and is flanked on each side by a row of gouges (Fig. 34, *3*). On the fourth specimen there is an incised pointed oval figure just above the triangular area at the base, and in the middle of this is a longitudinal row of small gouges (Fig. 34, *7*). The 4 remaining specimens have a medial line ascending from the apex of the triangle. On 2 of these, the line is crossed by spurs (Fig. 34, *6, 11*); the second specimen is also notched along one edge. On a third bar the medial line has downward slanting spurs on the left side, arranged in 3 groups of 3 spurs each (Fig. 34, *10*). On the last specimen, the medial line is crossed by oblique lines, slanting up from left to right and arranged in a group of 3 at the bottom, 2 in the middle, and one near the top (Fig. 34, *12*).

The 12 hooks (Pl. 49, *6*, and Fig. 35, except *10*) vary in length from 11.5 to about 17 cm. The width, which is greatest at the notched end of the hook, varies from 1.6 to 2 cm. At the opposite end, the specimen tapers to a point. On one, the notch form-ing the hook is wider at the base of the cut than at the opening (Fig. 35, *6*), but on all the other specimens the lower edge of the notch slopes downward toward the opening. One hook has what may be a decorative incised line up each side (Fig. 35, *7*). On 5 specimens there are small, decorative (?) notches below the larger notch (Fig. 35, *1*, and Pl. 49, *6;* Fig. 35, *2, 4, 6, 8*). One wooden hook is so badly rotted that it is represented only by the lower, pointed end on which is incised a longitudinal line (P.1289). A small flat piece of wood found in the pile may also be the lower end of one of the broken specimens (33-37-713).

In addition to the set of hooks and bars found with Skeleton B2, a stray hook and a stray bar were found on the surface of the cave. The hook measures (11.7) cm. in length; the pointed end is missing (Pl. 51, *14*, and Fig. 35, *10*). The bar was evidently like that illustrated in Figure 34, *2*, but is now represented only by a charred fragment (P.1226).

The hooks are probably part of the trigger mechanism for "Figure 4" traps, but the function of the decorated bars is less clear. The piercing of the decorated side of the bars seems to have been accidental, since the holes were not drilled completely through. Therefore, the bars could not have been attached to anything by cords run through the holes. They may, however, have been placed so that pointed pins or pegs engaged the pits. Such an arrangement would not be inconsistent with the trigger mechanism of a trap or snare, and it seems

PLATE 51. Wooden objects. Scale ½ natural size

1 and 2, Knotted withes, Palutat Cave, surface (P.1257, P.1259); 3, withe knotted around stick, Palutat Cave, surface (P.1233); 4, armor plate (?), ivory, Palugvik 3 or 4 (P.963); 5, armor slat, wood, Palutat Cave, surface (P.1231); 6, wooden tooth for comb, Palutat Cave, surface (P.1221); 7, wooden tooth for comb, near Grave B1, Palutat Cave, (P.1227); 8, grooved and shouldered object, Palutat Cave, surface (P.1234); 9, bidarka rib, Palutat Cave, surface (P.1223); 10, plug or stopper, Palutat Cave, depth 1 to 4 feet (P.1228); 11, wooden nail or tally, Palutat Cave, surface (P.1235); 12, meat stick (?), Palutat Cave, depth 1 to 4 feet (P.1241); 13, toy canoe prow handle (?), near Grave D1, Palutat Cave (P.1245); 14, wooden hook, Palutat Cave, surface (P.1248) (see Fig. 35, *10*); 15, shaft or rod, Palutat Cave, surface (P.1264); 16, wooden nail (?), Palutat Cave, surface (P.1239); 17, meat stick (?), Palutat Cave, surface (P.1238); 18, stake for stretching skins (?), Palutat Cave, surface (P.1237); 19, bidarka rib, Palutat Cave, surface (P.1236)

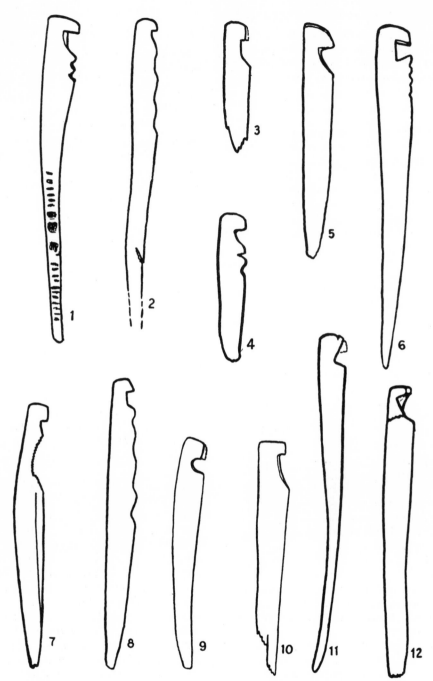

FIGURE 35. Wooden hooks, Grave B2, Palutat Cave. Scale slightly over ½ natural size
1, 33-37-710, see Plate 49, 6; 2, 33-37-712; 3, 33-37-714; 4, P.1281; 5, 33-37-713; 6, P.1278; 7, P.1280;
8, 33-37-715; 9, P.1276; 10, similar hook found on surface in Section D, Palutat Cave (P.1248),
see Plate 51, 14; 11, P.1282; 12, 33-37-711. Fragment of twelfth hook (P.1289) from grave is not
illustrated

likely that the hooks and bars were associated with each other in function. Although they are now badly warped and split, they were evidently carefully made.

81. Wooden Box

A little box, 2.7 cm. long and 2.2 cm. in diameter, was found at the feet of the old woman in Grave III, Palugvik 1 (Pl. 44, *34*). It was evidently carved from a single piece of wood and is now collapsed by the weight of earth so that the original shape is hard to determine. The box appears to have had 2 compartments, separated by a partition across the middle. There is a groove around the middle. It may originally have held an amulet, probably of perishable nature, since the box was empty when found.

82. Basket

On top of the coffin of the mummified body on the small island (Site 26) southwest of Mummy Island was found part of a basket or dish (33-37-736). It is a strip of birch bark, 42.5 cm. long and 12 cm. wide, with 12 holes across each end where the ends had been stitched together to form the side of an oval or circular vessel. Twelve holes, irregularly spaced along the bottom of the bark strip, show where the bottom was pegged or sewn on. The separate bottom, which should have been made of a flat, thin board according to the natives, was not found. Although we cannot be sure of the age of this find, it seems prehistoric but of no great antiquity.

A roll of birch bark with a few holes was found in Palugvik, layer unknown (P.1186). It may have been part of a similar vessel.

A curved willow (?) withe, 0.5 cm. in diameter and 46 cm. long, was found in Palutat Cave (P.1260). It may have been intended for a basket, perhaps as stiffening at the rim.

No archaeological example of a twined basket was found.

83. Sewing

Seventeen fragments of skin with seams were recovered.

Two specimens of heavy depilated skin seem to have been fragments of boat covers. One of these (Pl. 54, 2) was wrapped around the head of Skeleton I on Glacier Island, and was identified by Makari as part of a bidarka cover. The surface which rested against the partly mummified head now has smears of red paint, apparently from the paint on the face of the corpse. The skin, which is probably that of a large species of seal, has seams and patches sewn in waterproof blindstitching. In this type of seam, the 2 pieces of skin overlap; the stitch is a simple running stitch, but the needle passes only halfway through the thickness of the lower skin (not all the way through), so that from the inside of the skin cover the stitching cannot be seen at all. A very heavy depilated skin (sea lion?) was found on the surface of Palutat Cave (P.1293). The seams and patches are also in blindstitching. Along the edge of the piece are holes where the skin was lashed to the frame of a bidar (umiak). Some of these holes are reinforced with patches.

Seven fragments of depilated skin with overcast seams were found wrapped around the mummified body from Site 26, the small island southwest of Mummy Island. Five pieces are of coarse (seal?) skin, stained with purple-red paint, probably from the body (33-37-738a to c, P.1300a, b). One of these has small holes along the edge where the skin was attached for stretching during the curing process. Another fragment is of thinner skins, stitched together, and has a fringe (P.1300c). It may be a part of a garment. The last piece seems to be part of a boot or sleeve (P.1301).

Fragments of skin clothing, too small for identification, were found on the surface of Palutat Cave. These are of sealskin and fur, with overcast seams (P.1290, P.1291, P.1295). A fragment of a fur (sea otter?) garment has a cuff or trimming of depilated skin, about 3 cm. wide, sewn on by over-

PLATE 52. Matting, Palutat Cave. Scale slightly under ½ natural size

1, Mat of shredded bark fibers, part of Plate 53, 2, surface (33-37-745); 2, mat of grass, Grave B2
(33-37-741)

casting (33-37-739 and P.1294). Another piece of sealskin seems to be part of a sleeve for a jacket (33-37-734). The seam is overcast on the fur side, curiously enough. Another sealskin fragment shows the shoulder where the sleeve was attached (33-37-740). The sewing was also an overcast seam on the fur side. In both cases, to judge by the present condition of these fragments, the fur side was worn outside. Although the seams do not have a neat appearance, since the rough edges were outside, they would not have chafed the arm of the wearer.

A fragment of patchwork from Palutat Cave, made by sewing together small diamonds and rectangles of very thin, fine skin, may be part of a bag or a cap (Pl. 54, 1). Our informants described caps of mink or land otter fur, and also of loon breast skin, made of several pieces sewn together. Some had ear flaps which could be tied under the chin; some were decorated with ermine tails. One of the pieces of skin in our specimen is octagonal (?) in shape and was presumably the bottom of the bag or the crown of the cap. The stitching is overcast.

A complete boot was found in Palutat Cave (Pl. 55) and may be the mate to that previously found there by Meany.[150] The sole is of depilated skin, 22.5 cm. long, and is seamed up the center of the heel. The upper is of sealskin, with the hair outside, and is seamed up the front. It is 34.5 cm. long. A triangular piece has been inserted for the instep. The sole is packed with dried grass.

What must have been a similar boot, later cut down for a shoe or slipper, was seen in an abandoned house at Kiniklik. The specimen was of course modern, and the workmanship very poor. There was a pad of hay inside. Unfortunately the details of the pattern were not noted.

In every case the thread used in sewing these specimens was a single strand of sinew, not several strands twisted or braided together.

In addition to the pieces of skin described above, fragments of skin or fur were found in the following graves: Skeleton I on Glacier Island had a fragment of skin near the foot, perhaps representing a boot; there were skin fragments with the bones of the arthritic woman at Site 20 on Mummy Island, and with the bones of the mature man in Grave A, Palutat Cave; and, lastly, fragments of fringed skin were found beyond the feet of the mummified woman in Grave E1, Palutat Cave.

We ought to mention that Meany also found in Palutat Cave "many pieces of sea otter and fur seal garments and ornaments . . . [and] a pair of eagle feathers fastened with sinew thread."[151]

Captain Cook described the common dress of Chugach men, women, and children as a

close frock, or rather robe; reaching generally to the ankles, though sometimes only to the knees. At the upper part is a hole just sufficient to admit the head, with sleeves that reach to the wrist. These frocks are made of the skins of different animals; the most common of which are those of the sea-otter, grey fox, racoon [sic], and pine martin; with many of seal skins; and, in general, they are worn with the hairy side outward. Some also have these frocks made of the skins of fowls, with only the down remaining on them. . . . And we saw one or two woolen garments like those of Nootka. At the seams, where the different skins are sewed together, they are commonly ornamented with tassels or fringes of narrow thongs, cut out of the same skins. A few have a kind of cape, or collar; and some a hood; but the other [i.e., without collar or hood] is the most common form, and seems to be their whole dress in good weather. When it rains, they put over this another frock, ingeniously made from the intestines of whales, or some other large animal, prepared so skillfully, as almost to resemble our gold-beater's leaf. It is made to draw tight round the neck; its sleeves reach as low as the wrist, round which they are tied with a string; and its skirts, when they are in their canoes, are drawn over the rim of the hole in which they sit; so that no water can enter. At the same time, it keeps the men entirely dry upward. . . . It must be kept continually moist or wet; otherwise it is apt to crack or break. . . .

In general, they do not cover their legs, or feet; but a few have a kind of skin stockings [boots], which reach half-way up the thigh; and scarcely any

150 Meany, 1906, p. 467 and illustration.   151 *Ibid.*

PLATE 53. Cord and matting, Palutat Cave. Scale slightly under ½ natural size

1, 2-strand grass cord, surface (33-37-730) ; 2, mat of shredded bark fibers, part of Plate 52, *1*,
surface (33-37-745) ; 3, 3-strand braided cord of bark fibers, surface (33-37-729) ; 4, mat of grass,
surface (33-37-744)

of them are without mittens for the hands, made of the skins of bears paws.[152]

Plate 46 of the *Album* accompanying Cook's narrative shows a Chugach man wearing a gutskin shirt with hood drawn over his head, and a basketry hat on top. Plate 47 shows a woman with a fur cape tied around her neck.

Of the later travelers, Meares merely confirms Cook's observations, especially with respect to the gutskin shirts and the bare legs and feet, and adds nothing new. Sauer mentions the bearskin gloves or mittens, and Sarychef speaks of a "vest of birds' skins."[153] Strange (1786) mentions in his vocabulary the gutskin jacket, the dress of bird skins, the bearskin mittens, and "buskins," which we must interpret as boots. He also writes:

In the Article of Dress, they appear to be well provided, having very comfortable Garments of Fur, and likewise a most excellent Substitute for our thickest and warmest Bath rugs. I used my Endeavours to procure a piece of this Cloth, without however succeeding; altho the Price I offered for it was equal to what would have purchased half a Dozen good otter skins; it was presumable therefore that the material wherewith it is made, is very scar[ce] and in the possession only of their principal Men. I procured a Skin of the Animal of which it is made, which has more the Appearance of a Sheep Skin, than that of any other Animal I know. They are likewise well provided in the Article of Boots; and their Oil Skin Dresses are admirably calculated to keep them dry in rainy Weather.[154]

In this passage Strange evidently refers to twined blankets of mountain goat wool, perhaps Chilkat blankets obtained from the Tlingit, but more likely plain blankets of local manufacture.

Colnett (1788) only noted that the Chugach were warmly clothed in furs and birdskins from head to foot, and in wet weather wore waterproof jackets of intestines. The latter covered all but the face (i.e., had a hood) and could be fastened to the manhole of the bidarka. A few such jackets could still be seen in 1930 and 1933. Merck

writes that he saw one man wearing a parka of ground squirrel skins and another wearing one of young bearskins; over these each wore a rain shirt which reached only to just below the elbows and the knees.

The inhabitants of the shores of Prince William Sound wear skin skirts made of the furs of the ground squirrel, marmot and a marten, which is probably the so-called fish marten (*Martes pennanti* ERXL.); there are also a few bird skin parkas. Often I found these parkas were slit open on the sides under the armpit. The over jacket is of caribou skin.[155]

Our native informants described the gutskin shirt with hood (and we actually saw specimens), a bidarka "half-jacket," hoodless frocks of various furs and bird skins, a combination suit made of a bear's hide, the skin apron worn by both sexes as an undergarment on ordinary occasions and as the sole garment at dances, a skin shirt, skin pants, braided sinew belt, fur headband with feathers, sea otter fur armlets, mittens, boots, fur cap, and twined basketry hat.

As to Chugach skill in sewing, Cook testifies:

They had many little square bags, made from the same gut with their outer frocks, neatly ornamented with very minute red feathers interwoven with it, in which were contained some very fine sinews, and bundles of small cords, most ingeniously plaited. . . . Their sewing, plaiting of sinews, and small work on the little bags, may be put in competition with the most delicate manufactures found in any part of the known world.[156]

84. MATTING

In Palutat Cave were found a number of grass and bark mats. They are made in simple twined technique, the pairs of weft cross strands being widely spaced. These mats may all have been wrappings for the dead, since Skeletons B1 and B2 were wrapped in mats. The scattered position of the fragments may be explained by the pillaging of the cave. In addition to the piece of matting adhering to Skeleton E1 and preserved with it, there are pieces of

152 Cook, 1785, II, 367-69.
153 Meares, 1791, I, xxxiv, lxii-lxiii; Sauer, 1802, p. 187; Sarytschew, Part II, 1907, p. 20.
154 Strange, 1928, pp. 42 f., 54 ff.

155 Jacobi, 1937, p. 133, my translation.
156 Cook, 1785, II, 372, 373 f.

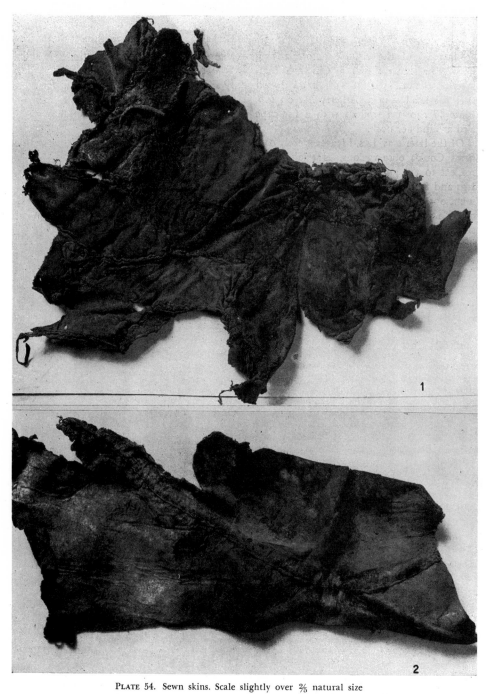

PLATE 54. Sewn skins. Scale slightly over ⅖ natural size

1, Fragment of patchwork bag or cap, Palutat Cave, surface (33-37-733) ; 2, fragment of bidarka cover, wrapped over skull of Skeleton I, Site 43, Glacier Island (33-37-632)

at least 9 additional mats, to judge by variations of the material and the size of the weave. Two mats (Pls. 52, *1*, 53, *2*; 33-37-743) seem to be made entirely of shredded bark fibers; the rest have a warp of grass and a weft of bark (?) (Pls. 52, *2*; 53, *4*; 33-37-742, 746, 747; P.1267, P.1277).

On many fragments the top or bottom edge is preserved; on one both edges are preserved and show that the finish was the same at both ends. The edging is that described by Otis T. Mason: "The warp ends are doubled over on the standing part of the next warp splint—in this case doubled beside the next warp strand—in the direction of the weave, that is to the right, and twined down to it with the weft. This finish is found on the oldest pieces of Yakutat work."[157] On the Palutat mats the first (or last) pair of weft cross strands are so close to the doubled ends of the warp that the effect given is of a braid. Edges of this type are found on 6 mats (Pl. 52, *1, 2* from Grave B2; Pl. 53, *4*; 33-37-743, 747; P.1267). On a seventh mat (33-37-746) the short ends of the doubled-back warp fibers cannot be seen, and it looks as if the warp were one long continuous strand, doubled back upon itself for the entire width of the mat, although we cannot be sure that this was actually the case.

On 2 mats the side edge is also preserved (Pl. 53, *2*; P.1267). Each pair of weft cross strands, as they reached the edge, were twisted to form a cord, brought down the side of the mat to make a loop, and then twined back across the mat. When the weft reached the other edge the same operation was presumably repeated, so that the cross strands form one continuous weft running back and forth across the mat for its entire length.

The direction of the twist of the weft is always upward from left to right. There is no wrong side, no up or down for the mat. The weaving would naturally begin in the upper left-hand corner and proceed from left to right. Before the second row of weft

was begun, the mat would be turned over, or, if the warp strands were suspended from a frame, the weaver would turn to the other side, so that the beginning of each new row was at the weaver's left.

The average distances between the elements of the weave, as measured from the middle of one strand to the middle of the next, varied from 4.5 to 6.5 cm. between weft strands and 1 cm. between warp strands (33-37-746) to 1.75 cm. between wefts (P.1277) and 0.6 cm. between warps (Pl. 52, *1*; 33-37-747). The most common measurements are 4 cm. between wefts and 0.8 cm. between warps (Pl. 52, *2*).

The piece of matting on which both top and bottom edges were preserved is 78 cm. long. The widest fragment of matting, on which, however, there is only one side edge, is (60) cm. wide.

Although most of the Aleut matting was much finer than these specimens from Palutat Cave and was decorated in various ways, mats of the same type, coarsely twined with upward slanting stitches, have been found on the Aleutians.[158] Twining was also done by the Aleut in the opposite direction, i.e., with downward stitches. The Tena Indians of the Yukon Valley made coarse grass mats of the same type as those of the Chugach; examples of such mats were found as shrouds in a prehistoric burial in a pit house.[159] The mats made by the Eskimo from the Kuskokwim River to Kotzebue Sound were also identical with the Chugach specimens, and varied from 4 by 3¾ feet to twice that size.[160]

85. BRAID AND CORDS

From the wrappings of the mummy at Site 26 near Mummy Island a sinew cord was recovered, made of 8 (?) strands braided together (square sennit) (33-37-737).

A 3-strand braid of bark or grass, 1 cm.

---

[157] O. T. Mason, 1904, p. 270.

[158] Dall, 1878, Pl. 7, No. 17468, p. 16, "grass matting, of the coarse common kind" evidently used for the outer wrappings of mummy bundles; Hrdlička, 1945, Figs. 28, 178.

[159] De Laguna, 1947, Pls. XIX and XX.

[160] E. W. Nelson, 1899, Pl. LXXIV, *15*, p. 203; O. T. Mason, 1904, Pl. 136; Oswalt, 1952, Pl. 8B, identified as a kayak mat.

PLATE 55. Sealskin boot, Palutat Cave, surface (P.1292). Scale ½ natural size

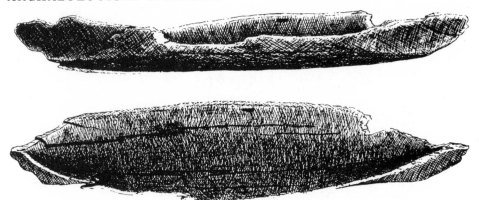

FIGURE 36. Wooden canoe, collected by Edmond S. Meany in Palutat Cave, and now in Washington State Museum. Scale about 1/15 natural size (*Sketch by Victor Castillo*)

wide, was found in Palutat Cave (Pl. 53, *3*); another, 3.5 cm. wide, was found with the mat illustrated in Plate 53, *4*, and may possibly have been the edge of this mat (P.1274).

A cord 21 cm. long, made of 2 strands of grass twisted together, was found with the grass mat wrapped around Skeleton B1 (P.1276). A similar cord was found near by, but not in the grave (Pl. 53, *1*).

Among the types of cord made by the Aleut were square sennit of sinew and 3-strand braids of grass.[161] Strange's Chugach vocabulary contains words for: "A fine twisted fishing line," "A very fine plaited fishing line," "A thick square line made of guts," "A fishing line made of guts," and "The sinews out of which they make their Lin[es]."[162]

86. KNOTS

Ten pieces of knotted withe were found in Palutat Cave. The thinner withes seem to be of split spruce root; the thicker may be of split willow or alder.

Two are simply loops, tied in a loose knot (33-37-726, P.1256). Three are tied in a half hitch; one of these is knotted around a stick (Pl. 51, *2, 3;* P.1258). Two specimens are withes tied together in the incorrectly made square knot known as an

"Old Granny" (33-37-727, 728). Two other knots are variations of the "Old Granny" in which the short ends are both brought together on the same side, instead of being divided, one on each side (Pls. 49, *2;* 51, *1*). Another knot is a bowline, which is commonly used to make a firm loop, not a running noose. The withe is broken so that the size of the loop cannot be determined (P.1296). The tenth specimen is so badly broken that the type of knot cannot be ascertained. It is curious that no example of a true square knot was found.

87. WOODEN CANOES

Meany wrote about Palutat Cave:

The floor of the cave was littered with the remains of wooden canoes. This at first seemed singular, since it is well known that the Aleuts [popular name for the Chugach, used even by themselves] use skin bidarkas. It was learned, however, that some "dugouts" are still used by them. These canoes were by no means hastily made for burial purposes. The numerous adze marks bespeak a long period of careful labor. They are all trim and true in their lines. All were more or less broken by decay and much handling. The best one remaining was secured for the University [of Washington, see Figure 36]. It is carved out of a spruce log, and is twelve and one-half feet long [3.82 m.]. A line from the middle of the bottom to the top of the remaining edge is nineteen inches [about 50 cm.]. All over the relic may be seen the adze marks. On one side is a narrow strip of wood held tightly in place by four thongs of sinew passed through the frame. It was a toilsome, though successful effort to stop a leak.

161 Hrdlička, 1945, Fig. 238b, c.
162 Strange, 1928, pp. 54 ff.

PLATE 56. Dugout canoes, Palutat Cave

1, Canoe (33-37-723) , scale 1/20 natural size; 2, canoe (P.1178) , scale 1/20; 3, bow of canoe Y, left
in cave; 4, canoe X, left in cave

This little evidence, with all the rest of the boat's appearance, indicates that it was at one time in active use. Undoubtedly it was placed by the side of the owner's grave, that he might the more easily paddle into the happy hunting grounds.[163]

We also found the scattered pieces of several wooden dugouts in the cave. From these fragments we pieced together 4 canoes, only 3 of which we were able to remove, because of the limited deck space on our gas boat. The fourth canoe (X) and the prow of a fifth (Y), as well as a number of miscellaneous fragments, had to be left behind. Most of the pieces were in Sections B and C and suggested that the dugouts had formerly been arranged in a row.

These canoes are only 11½ to 12½ feet (3.56 to 3.82 m.) long, 1 foot 8 inches to 1 foot 10 inches (51 to 56 cm.) wide, and 1 foot 2 inches to 2 feet (35 to 61 cm.) deep. Thus they could have carried only one person, and would have been very unsafe except in sheltered waters. It is curious that a people who could make such excellent skin boats (large umiaks, 1- and 2-man kayaks or bidarkas) should have troubled to manufacture these little wooden boats. Unfortunately Meany does not tell us for what purpose dugouts were being used at the time of his visit. It is possible that these small canoes were used by women for short trips, for the kayak and bidarka were men's hunting canoes, and the umiak or bidar would have been too cumbersome for one woman to handle alone. Makari told us a story about 2 little old women who were drowned in the little cove between Palugvik East and West points when they tipped over the wooden canoe in which they were paddling from one settlement to the other. This canoe was supposed to have been very crudely made, however, and was hardly more than a hollow log. The Palutat canoes are not only smaller than the smallest Eyak canoe but lack the graceful lines of the latter and especially the crotch in the prow, so characteristic of Eyak canoes,[164] although

[163] Meany, 1906, p. 466.
[164] Birket-Smith and de Laguna, 1938, pp. 45-52, Pls. 9; 10; 11, 8.

the Chugach specimens are similar in general proportions. Larry Nonini, superintendent of the native school at Chenega in 1933, told us that the natives formerly used dugouts on trips to Port Wells and Culross Island to put up fish. The grandfather of Mike Komkoff, a Chenega native, is supposed to have owned such a boat. Larry Nonini himself has seen, in Jackpot Bay, an abandoned dugout capable of holding 9 persons. This was evidently comparable in size to the large Eyak traveling canoe.

A piece from the gunwale of one of the canoes (Pl. 56, 1) was found in Grave B1, where it had evidently been left by modern grave robbers. This canoe, when pieced together, was found to be 3.68 m. (12 feet 1 inch) long. The inside length is 2.20 m. (7 feet 4 inches). The maximum beam is 51 cm. (1 foot 8 inches), the height at the bow and stern is 35 cm. (1 foot 2 inches), and the inside depth is 30 cm. (12 inches). The bottom is rounded, except at the bow and stern. At the bow the bottom narrows for a distance of 80 cm. to form a false keel, 9 cm. deep, and the prow projects beyond this for a distance of 25 cm. At the stern there is a similar false keel 90 cm. long, and the bottom slopes up gradually to the stern. The gunwales are rounded off amidships, but near each end they show a slight bevel, 1.5 to 2 cm. wide. They lack the graceful flare of Canoe E.

The canoe was evidently shaped with a small stone adz, the marks of which are clearly visible, especially on the inside. The outside has been smoothed off, and the inside is neatly finished except in the narrow angles of the bow and stern. Charring on the inside shows that fire was used in shaping the canoe. On the starboard gunwale, 1.94 m. from the prow, i.e., about 20 cm. aft of the middle, there are 2 small holes, one above the other. The first is about 1 cm. below the gunwale, and the second is 1.6 cm. below the first. These holes are connected by a groove on the outside of the canoe. The opposite gunwale is damaged at this point, but it seems likely that there were corresponding holes, and that these served for the attachment of a thwart or crossbar. This dugout showed no marks in the bow where a prow handle might have been inserted.

The second canoe (Pl. 56, 2) is 3.77 m. (12 feet 4 inches) long and has a beam of 53 cm. It is 43.5 cm. high at the bow, 29 cm. high amidships, and must originally have been about 40 cm. high at the stern, which is now damaged. The sides are 1.5 cm. thick, and the gunwales are beveled on the inside. The stern is rounded and has an overhang of 35 cm. The stern had been broken at one time and repaired, or else extra height had been obtained by adding a separate plank, 4 cm. wide, on the starboard side. Part of this plank, which was fastened on by lashing and pegging, is now broken off. The bow is undercut for a distance of 20 cm., and the false keel at the bow is about 15 cm. long. There was a single thwart amidships, attached by lashings which passed through 3 horizontally placed holes in each gunwale. The outer holes of each group are 5.5 cm. apart, and all 3 holes in each set are connected by a groove on the outside of the canoe.

Canoe E, the third which we recovered and which is now in the Washington State Museum in Seattle, is the smallest found in the cave. We are indebted to Mr. Lionel Holmes for the following description of the specimen:

The canoe has not been assembled and the several fragmentary parts are somewhat warped; consequently the measurements, except for the length, are close approximates. The length is 3.56 meters (11 feet 6 inches). The width taken at midships is 56 cm. (1 foot 10 inches). The average thickness of the hull is 2 cm. The inside depth is 30 cm. (12 inches). The hull is a simple round-bottomed type without a keel. The stern is plain, being formed from the gradual convergence of the bottom and the two sides. The bow has an overhang of 11 cm. above the vertical front of the small [false] keel, 5.5 cm. high. Both the bow and stern show broken surfaces which might indicate that they once extended above the level of the gunwales. The gunwales themselves are the plain rounded edges of the sides at midships, but at about one meter from each end they are modified to conform with the conver-

gence of the sides and are rolled out with a beveled edge on the inside, 3.5 cm. wide. There is no decoration either in adzing or carving.

Canoe X (Pl. 56, 4), which was left in the cave, is 3.66 m. (12 feet) long. One end is defective, and the gunwales are broken. At present the canoe is 56 cm. (1 foot 10 inches) wide, but the true beam was probably greater. The depth inside is 53 cm. (1 foot 9 inches), but it was probably more before the sides warped. The total height is about 61 cm. (2 feet). The bottom is evenly rounded except at the bow and stern, where it narrows to form a false keel. The forward part of the keel is about 61 cm. from the prow, which slopes up abruptly, but there is not the vertical end to the keel which is characteristic of the other canoes. At the stern, the false keel is about 91 cm. long, and the stern itself slopes up gradually.

The bow end of Canoe Y (Pl. 56, 3) is represented by a fragment (2.82 m. long (9 feet 3 inches). The prow is 38 cm. high. The bow is undercut, sloping back about 25 cm., where it meets the vertical end of the false keel, 10 cm. high. The bottom of the canoe is rounded amidships.

The Eyak and Chugach were not the only peoples in southwestern Alaska who made dugouts. That wooden canoes may also have been made by the Koniag is indicated by a passage in the account of Bragin's voyage to Alaska in 1772-76. Referring to Kodiak Island, which he visited in 1776, or more probably to one of the northern islands of the group which are wooded, he says: "In the mountains grow considerable ash and poplar trees from which the natives hollow out even canoes, like those of the Kamchadal, which can carry up to five men."[165] Osgood reports that the Tanaina Athabaskans of Kachemak Bay and Kenai made dugouts in addition to skin boats,[166] which suggests that the wooden canoe, like the kayak and umiak, may have been one of the many cultural items which the Ta-

[165] Pallas, 1781, II, 315, my translation.
[166] Osgood, 1937, p. 70.

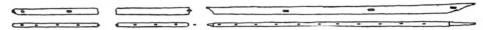

FIGURE 37. Bidarka gunwale, Palutat Cave (P.1255). Scale 1/19 natural size

naina copied from the Kenai Peninsula Eskimo. The boatlike wooden "cradles" in which Aleut mummies were sometimes placed have already been cited as possible evidence that even they had heard about dugouts and about canoe burial, although their treeless land would have prevented them from duplicating the wooden canoe.

88. PROW HANDLES

From the surface of Palutat Cave is a prow handle for a dugout (Pl. 50, 2), similar to one found at the Eyak village, Alaganik, and identified by Galucia Nelson, our principal Eyak informant.[167]

Both handles are made of a naturally curved section of alder (?), the edges of which were sharpened to a wedge. Slots were cut in the angle of the bow of the Eyak canoe, and the sides were forced apart to permit the insertion of the sharp ends of the handle in these slots. The handle and the thwarts were used for lifting the Eyak canoe out of the water. It should, however, be noted that no slots for a prow handle were observed in any of the canoes found in Palutat Cave. The Eyak prow handle is 21 cm. long and 3 cm. wide; the Chugach specimen measures 23 by 2.5 cm.

A much smaller prow handle, possibly for a toy boat (?), was found outside Grave D1 (Pl. 51, 13). It is only 12.5 cm. long and 1.8 cm. wide.

89. BIDARKA FRAME

Fragments of what were probably pieces of a bidarka frame were found scattered on the surface of Palutat Cave.

One of these parts (Fig. 37) is a wooden rod about 3.4 cm. wide and 1.5 cm. thick. It is represented by 3 pieces, (55.5), (42.5), and (155) cm. long, respectively. Since these sections do not fit each other, and are broken at both ends, the total length of the

[167] Birket-Smith and de Laguna, 1938, p. 46, Pl. 11, 7.

specimen must have been over 2.53 m. In these pieces of wood there is a series of holes, drilled from side to side, and in one edge are cut a number of small slots, spaced at intervals of about 11 to 12.5 cm. The first piece has 2 holes and 5 slots; the second, one hole and 4 slots; the third, 3 (or 4?) holes and 11 slots. This rod may be the gunwale of a bidarka or kayak, since it is similar to the gunwale of a modern bidarka photographed at Chenega (Pl. 57, 6). The 20 slots would have received the ends of the ribs; the 6 (or 7?) holes would have been for the lashing of the thwarts. The Chenega bidarka is a 3-hole kayak with 50 (?) ribs and 8 thwarts. The manhole frames rest on a pair of thwarts each, and there are 2 additional thwarts, one near the bow, the other near the stern. However, the fragments from Palutat probably belonged to a 2-hole bidarka, since none of the eighteenth-century explorers, to my knowledge, mentions any but the one-hole and 2-hole types.

Thus Colnett in 1788 sketched and described the Chugach 2-hole bidarka and noted also the one-man type. Evidently the modern 3-man bidarka had not yet been introduced into Prince William Sound, for he remarks that sometimes 2 men sat back to back in one manhole, or the extra passenger was stowed away inside. The prow of the bidarka in his sketch has the same graceful lines as those on bidarkas we saw at Chenega. Lines across the deck in his sketch may represent thongs or thwarts under the skin cover. There is a pair on each side of the 2 manholes, and a fifth between the forward hole and the bow.

The second specimen (33-37-703) is a wooden rod, (2.67) m. long, broken at both ends and triangular in section. Near the ends it is 1.8 cm. wide and 2 cm. thick; in the middle it flattens and widens to a width of 2.3 cm. and a thickness of 1.5 cm. The

PLATE 57. Lance, paddles, bidarka frame. Scale slightly under $\frac{1}{10}$ natural size, except for No. 6
1, Lance shaft, Palutat Cave, surface (P.1254a, b, c) ; 2, fragment of forward section of deck ridgepole for bidarka, Palutat Cave, surface (33-37-678) ; 3, paddle, Palutat Cave, depth 6 inches (33-
37-699) ; 4, painted paddle blade, Palutat Cave, surface (P.1251) ; 5, handle of paddle, Palutat
Cave, surface (33-37-679) ; 6, 3-man bidarka frame, Chenega Village, 1933

rod is pierced by 12 holes, in the plane of
what we have termed the width. In several
of these holes are remnants of root lashing
or wooden pegs. Six holes are near one end
of the specimen, 6 near the other end. The
holes in each group are spaced at intervals of 9.5 to 12.5 cm., and the 2 groups
are separated by a distance of 145 cm.
The spacing of the holes in this specimen roughly corresponds to the distances
between the slots on the first specimen
(P.1255), except that the slots seem to
have been more or less evenly distributed
throughout its length, while there are no
holes in the middle part of the second rod
(33-37-703). The length of both specimens,
allowing for the missing portions of the
first rod, is approximately the same. Both
rods are slightly curved or warped.

The second rod may be compared to the
keel of the Chenega bidarka. The keel is
thicker and narrower at the ends, where it
is attached to the prow and stern pieces,
than it is in the middle. However, we
should note that the keel is pierced by holes
throughout its length for the lashing of
the ribs, while the archaeological specimen
lacks holes in the middle. According to
Makari, the frames of prehistoric bidarkas
and umiaks were lashed with roots, and the
second rod from Palutat Cave has traces of
such lashing (or of wooden pegs?) in its
holes. Both rods from the cave are much
more slender than the parts of the Chenega
bidarka with which we have compared
them. It is not known whether this difference might be explained by the fact that
the Chenega craft is a 3-man bidarka, while
the Palutat specimens may have come from
a 2-man bidarka. The latter would have
had 6 thwarts and about 40 (?) ribs.

A third broken rod or shaft from the

cave may also be part of a bidarka or kayak (Pl. 57, 2). It is subrectangular in section, measuring 2.8 by 2 cm., and is (62) cm. long. At the unbroken end it is 2.5 cm. thick, forming a shoulder, and has a scarf 4.2 cm. long. Through this scarf is cut (not drilled) an oval hole, now broken out, and the scarf is grooved about for a lashing. Evidently another piece of wood was attached at right angles to the scarfed end. The rod is broken through a cut hole at the other end, but there is no shoulder or scarf here.

The specimen resembles the forward section of the deck ridgepole on the Chenega bidarka. This section runs from the edge of the forward manhole to the prow piece, rests at its rear end on the thwart at the front edge of the manhole, and is supported near the middle by the thwart between the manhole and the prow. If the identification is correct, the scarfed end was attached to the manhole frame, and the hole at the broken end held the lashing for the foremost thwart.

Eleven wooden objects found in Palutat Cave may be fragments of bidarka ribs. They are oval in section, measuring 1.7 to 2.8 cm. in width and 0.6 to 0.9 cm. in thickness. All are curved. One (P.1243) seems to have traces of red paint. On 5, one end is preserved. The end of one is simply rounded off (33-37-707); another is slightly flattened and is cut off squarely (33-37-705); a third is narrowed slightly as if to fit into a slot and shows stains left by a lashing which had been wound about it for its full length, (38.5) cm. (Pl. 51, 19). The end of the fourth is beveled or scarfed on one side to fit into a slot (Pl. 51, 9), and the fifth is not only beveled on both sides but has a hole, 3.3 cm. from the end, by which it could have been lashed in place (Pl. 50, 9). Both ends of the other specimens are missing (Pl. 50, 3; 33-37-706, 708; P.1225a to c, P.1229, P.1243). All are from the surface of the cave, except 2 which were found at a depth of 1 to 4 feet (33-37-706, P.1229).

90. PADDLES

Several fragments of paddles and one complete specimen were found in Palutat Cave.

The complete specimen (Pl. 57, 3) came from 6 inches below the surface in Section D. It is 114 cm. long, with a very narrow pointed blade 42 cm. long and only 5.5 cm. wide. The handle is oval in section, 3.1 by 2 cm., the longer diameter being at right angles to the plane of the blade. The handle tapers slightly toward the butt, and there is no knob or crutch at the end. The specimen seems so small and the blade so very slender that it is doubtful whether the paddle was ever intended for actual use. It may have been a toy or perhaps a model for the dead. On the other hand, Meany writes of his discoveries in the cave: "One crude paddle was found, and two fragments that at first looked like substitutes for paddles. Later I learned that they were probably shovels, as the present natives use similar wooden implements to carry heated stones in preparing the sweat baths."[168] These implements were, I believe, used in pairs like tongs; at least Matrona used a pair of wooden tongs for the purpose, although these had simply flattened ends, not paddle-like blades. Our "paddle" from Palutat Cave may, therefore, have been such a tong. Since there is no sign of scorching on the blade, identification must remain uncertain.

A wooden shaft from the surface of the cave may be a paddle handle (Pl. 57, 5). It is (45.5) cm. long and has a subrectangular section 2.6 by 1.8 cm. It tapers toward the butt, which ends in a slightly enlarged knob. The blade is entirely missing.

Three specimens are fragments of paddle blades. One of these, broken from the tip of the blade (33-37-700), is (20.5) cm. long and 7.3 cm. wide. The end of the blade is battered from hard use. As on all the paddles, the blade is thickened in the middle. There seem to be traces of black paint on both surfaces.

[168] Meany, 1906, p. 466.

PLATE 58. Wooden shovel, stake, and house post, bottom of Palugvik midden (see Fig. 4)
1, Shovel blade, found beside house post in Section H (33-37-481), scale slightly under ⅓ natural
size; 2, stake sharpened at both ends, found beside house post (No. 3) in Section 1G (33-37-478),
scale slightly under ⅖ natural size; 3, house post, resting on top of slab illustrated in Plate 59, 1,
in Section 1G (33-37-476), scale slightly under ⅖ natural size

Another fragment, also with black paint on both sides, is a splinter from the edge of a blade (33-37-701).

The third fragment is from the lower part of a pointed blade (Pl. 57, *4*). It is (36.3) cm. long and 8 cm. wide at the broken end. On one side are traces of black paint forming a simple pattern. About 4 cm. above the unpainted tip of the blade is a transverse band of paint, 12.5 cm. wide. One cm. above this is a transverse stripe of paint, 1 cm. wide. In the middle of the unpainted space between the two is a block of paint, 3 cm. long, connecting the band and the stripe. Starting from the stripe there are 3 (or 4) longitudinal lines of paint, 1 cm. wide and spaced 1 cm. apart. These are crossed by a narrow line of black paint, 0.75 cm. above the upper stripe. The other side of the specimen is badly weathered and shows no paint.

We may compare these archaeological specimens with a modern unpainted paddle from Chenega. It is 156 cm. long, with a crutch-shaped handle, carved from one piece of wood. The blade is pointed, measuring 75 by 13 cm., with the greatest width just above the middle. A modern Eskimo specimen from Port Graham on lower Cook Inlet is 151 cm. long, with a separate crossbar nailed at the end of the handle to form a crutch. The blade is 70 by 10 cm., with the greatest width in the middle. The blade is painted black on both sides.

91. WOODEN SHOVEL

A fragment of what may have been a wooden shovel (Pl. 58, *1*) was found at the bottom of the Palugvik midden, driven in beside the house post in Section H. Only the lower end of the blade has been preserved; the upper part and the handle have disintegrated. The specimen has warped and cracked since removal from the moist earth and is no longer as curved as it was when found. It is made of a section of log, carefully adzed inside and out. The adz marks can be clearly seen in the photograph (the small dents or cuts on the surface

were made by accident in the laboratory when the specimen was being boiled in paraffin). The edge of the blade has been beveled off, and the sides are rounded. The specimen is now 41 cm. wide but may have been a little wider originally, for a thin splinter seems to have been broken from the right edge. The fragment is only (24.5) cm. long. When complete, the shovel must have been rather heavy and clumsy. It is quite different in shape from the small paddle-shaped shovels or tongs with pointed blades which the natives used for passing hot rocks into the sweat bath house. It seems to conform, however, to the shovel used for digging (ca·γiutaq), which was described by Makari as made in one piece (?), with a long handle and a broad blade.

92. HOUSE POSTS AND STAKES

Four house posts and 10 stakes were found at the bottom of the Palugvik midden, driven or sunk into the sour soil underlying the shell heap. The lower ends of these wooden specimens were evidently preserved by the constant dampness, but their upper ends have rotted away. The arrangement of the posts and stakes is shown in Figure 4, and House 1, with which they are associated, has been described in Chapter II, section 12.

The house post in Section H (P.1192) was set into a large hole in the mud, and about it were driven 5 small pointed stakes (Pl. 59, *2, 3;* P.1188 to P.1190), probably to strengthen it. A slab of rock was also driven into the hole, and other large stones were piled about the post. Beside the post was found the end of the wooden shovel blade just described (Pl. 58, *1*). The house post is 20 by 27 cm. in diameter and (41) cm. long. It is bluntly chopped off at the lower end. The stakes vary in diameter from 6.2 to 10.1 cm. and in length from (21) to (33) cm. They are roughly pointed.

The second post, in Section 1G, was found resting on top of a flat slab of wood, probably to prevent the post from sinking too deep into the mud. The post is (55) cm.

PLATE 59. House posts and stakes, bottom of Palugvik midden (see Fig. 4).
Scale slightly under ⅓ natural size

1, Slab lying horizontally under house post illustrated in Plate 58, 3, in Section 1G (33-37-479);
2 and 3, 2 of the 5 stakes set beside house post in Section H (P.1191, P.1187); 4, stake beside house
post in Section 2D (33-37-480); 5, house post in Section 3C (33-37-477)

long and about 27 cm. in diameter (Pl. 58, 3). Portions of bark adhere to the surface. The lower end has been rounded off with an adz, the short chopping marks of which are clearly visible. The slab under it (Pl. 59, 1) was split from a log and chopped off across both ends. It measures 22.5 by 15 cm. Beside the post was a stake (P.1194), 5.6 cm. in diameter and (33) cm. long. It had been partially split in two. Lying near the post was a second stake, 35 cm. long and 4.5 cm. in diameter (Pl. 58, 2). The ends have been chopped to form blunt wedges, and the middle of the stake is scored by adz cuts. This may have been only a piece of firewood; it was certainly never used as a wedge.

A stake was found in the northwest corner of Section 2F (33-37-482). It was roughly sharpened and is 6 cm. in diameter. Another stake, (30) cm. long and 5.2 cm. in diameter, was in the northwest corner of 1E (P.1195). It is roughly chopped across the end.

The third house post is from the extreme southwest corner of Section 2D. It is 8.9 to 10.9 cm. in diameter and (30) cm. long (P.1193). It is roughly rounded off at the bottom like the other posts. Close beside it was a stake trimmed to a blunt point (Pl. 59, 4), (27) cm. long and 7 cm. in diameter. Two blunt pegs, 14.5 and 17 cm. long, were found in Section 2C near this house post, and may have been associated either with the house or with Grave III (Pl. 49, 4; 33-37-473).

The house post from the northwest corner of Section 3C is formed of a log (51) cm. long and 12.5 cm. in diameter, which was split in two (Pl. 59, 5).

A wooden peg 11.3 cm. long and 2.4 cm. in diameter, pointed at one end, was also found in Section 3C, about 6 inches above the bottom of the midden (P.1002). Although it comes from Layer 1, it may not have been connected with the house.

Six other wooden pegs, 8.5 to 17 cm. in length, were found at the bottom of the midden (33-37-475, P.1118a to d, P.1003).

It is impossible to say whether or not they were connected with the house.

93. PAINT

Red and black paint were found archaeologically in Prince William Sound. According to Makari, the Chugach used to make paint of the following colors from rocks and earths: red, black, brown, yellow, blue, and gray. The black rock was obtained from Kayak Island. Copper ore was also used for paint (blue-green?). These minerals were crushed in a hollow stone and mixed with water. Stale urine was used to make the colors permanent. Makari did not mention the mixture of animal fat with paint, although the red paint used for pictographs in caves looked as if it had been prepared with fat. The red paint used for wooden bowls was said to have been mixed with blood drawn from the nose. These paints were also used to stain or dye materials used in basketmaking. Other dyes were red and purple from swamp grass, dark reddish brown from boiled hemlock bark, and rose color from blueberry juice.

Samples of red paint were found in the course of our excavations. Lumps of hematite (red iron oxide) powder were found in Palugvik 4 (33-37-65, P.981) and on the burial ledge at Palugvik East Point (33-37-558). A solid lump of hematite was found in Palugvik 2 (33-37-303), and another was possibly associated with Skeleton III at Palugvik East Point (P.1085a). A lump of pyrites with surface alterations to hematite, from Palugvik 4 (33-37-64 and P.980), may have been used for paint or may represent a disintegrated strike-a-light like that found with Skeleton I on Palugvik East Point (section 51). Two unidentified red stones showing marks of scraping come from Palugvik 4 (P.993) and Palugvik 2 or 3 (P.992) and were identified by Makari as materials for paint.

Red paint was found on a whetstone from Palugvik layer unknown, on a "bayonet" or pick fragment from Palugvik 1, on an arrowshaft fragment and bidarka rib fragment from Palutat Cave, and on a relatively modern detachable barbed head in the Chenega Church collection. The blades of 2 paddles from the cave were painted black, and a third had a simple design in black paint.

According to the natives, the Chugach sometimes painted their faces with red or black paint. Warriors covered their faces with black (never red) paint, "so that the enemy could not tell if they were afraid." At potlatches designs were painted on the face with red paint, and at ceremonies simple designs of lines and dots were made with red and black. There is some evidence that each village had its own traditional design. In summer, soot was smeared on the face to prevent sunburn, and the eyelashes were painted red.

The partially mummified head of the man (?) buried on Glacier Island (Skeleton I) was smeared on the cheeks and forehead with red paint, some of which had come off on the bidarka cover in which the head was wrapped. The head was not well enough preserved, however, to indicate whether there was any pattern of face painting. Traces of purple-red paint were noted in the skin wrappings of the mummified body from the small island (Site 26) off Mummy Island, but none was seen on the body itself.

According to Cook:

The men frequently paint their faces of a bright red, and of a black colour, and sometimes of a blue, or leaden colour; but not in any regular figure. . . . Their bodies are not painted, which may be owing to the scarcity of proper materials; for all the colours which they brought to sell in bladders, were in very small quantities. . . The ores with which they painted themselves, were a red, brittle, unctuous ochre, or iron-ore, not much unlike cinnabar in colour; a bright blue pigment, which we did not procure; and black lead. Each of these seems to be very scarce, as they brought very small quantities of the first and last, and seemed to keep them with great care.[169]

Plate 74 in the *Album* shows a woman with what appears to be paint across the forehead and cheeks. A double vertical

[169] Cook, 1785, II, 370, 379.

stripe in the center of the forehead and a dark triangular area covering the chin are probably tattooing, for Cook also reported that the women had tattooed faces.

Meares wrote: "They use a red kind of paint, with which they besmear their necks and faces; but after the death of friends or relations, it is changed into black."[170] (Reference to the use of black paint for mourning is certainly an error.) Portlock merely reports that "they often paint the face and hands," and Sarychef says that a chief who was encountered on Hinchinbrook Island "had his face dyed with a black colour."[171]

Although the Chugach may not have been as expert at painting implements as were the Aleut, yet some idea of the style and extent of painting can be gained from a study of Aleut hats.[172]

94. DECORATIVE ELEMENTS

Only a relatively small number of specimens from Prince William Sound are decorated, and on most of these the ornamentation is very simple. The most important groups of decorated objects are the incised plaques from Palugvik 1 and 2 and Palugvik East Point (section 67), the ivory bears and bone tubes from Grave III, Palugvik East Point (sections 63 and 64), and the set of 12 wooden bars found with 12 wooden hooks on Grave B1 in Palutat Cave (section 80).

The most simple form of decoration can be found in the tendency to exaggerate the shape or part of the shape of the artifact. We have already mentioned the bulge at the front of a few stone lamps which is only an emphasis of the pointed end. Lamps with this bulge or ridge are from Palugvik 3 or 4 (Pl. 23, *4*), Site 7 (33-37-583), Site 23 (Pl. 25, *5*), and Site 26 (Pl. 24, *1*). The enlarged end with octagonal faceting represents the same sort of decorative emphasis of the handle of a pestle. Pestles of this type are from Knight Island (Pratt collection),

[170] Meares, 1791, I, lxi f.
[171] Portlock, 1789, p. 248; Sarytschew, 1807, II, 25.
[172] Ivanov, 1930, pp. 479 ff.

Hawkins Island (Pl. 22, *1*), and the Chenega Church Collection (Pl. 21, *8*).

The edges of a number of objects are emphasized by notching. These include stone plaques from Palugvik 1 to 3 (Pls. 19, *6, 8* to *10;* 42, *50*), 2 of which also have a grooved edge as well as notches. One of the incised slate plaques from Palugvik beach has a notched edge (Fig. 30). Notched edges are characteristic of the wooden bars from Palutat Cave, on which these notches are usually associated with longitudinal rows of transverse gouges or spurs and longitudinal lines with spurs (Fig. 34). The edges of 2 broken bone ornaments from Palugvik 1 are also notched (P.799, P.923).

The rim of the lamp from Palugvik 3 or 4 (Pl. 23, *4*) is emphasized by an encircling groove on the outside, and another from Palugvik 3 has the rim decorated by a ridge between 2 grooves (P.988).

The decorative repetition of a functional element may be seen on the detachable barbed heads with ornamental dorsal barbs (Pls. 32, *1, 2, 4, 5, 10;* 33, *2, 12*), and on some of the wooden hooks from Palutat Cave that have decorative (?) notches below the large functional notch (Fig. 35, *1, 2, 4, 6, 8*).

The decoration on long slender objects is likely to consist of incised longitudinal lines which emphasize the length. Thus, the slender barbed points from Palugvik 1 and 4 (Pls. 36, *23, 24;* 37, *1, 2*) and the side prong for a bird dart from Palutat Cave (Pl. 36, *26*) have a pair of longitudinal grooves that outline the row of barbs. This decoration is closely related to the technique of shaping the barbs. Similar in effect is the single line on one side of a detachable barbed head from Palugvik 1 (Pl. 33, *17*), on another from Palugvik layer unknown (Pl. 33, *3*), and on a fishhook from Palugvik 3 or 4 (Pl. 37, *9*). A single medial line decorated the wooden rods in the fragments of armor from Palutat Cave (Pls. 50, *1;* 51, *5*), 2 of the wooden hooks (Fig. 35, *7;* P.1289), and a wooden

knife handle from the same site (Pl. 50, *5*). The simple decorations on the wooden bars, to which the design on the knife handle is closely related, are also arranged longitudinally. Two or 4 longitudinal lines decorate the bone socket pieces from Palugvik 1 to 4; one pair of these lines emphasizes the notch separating the 2 tangs (Pls. 34, *2;* 35, *2, 3*).

Longitudinal lines border the edges of some of the incised slate plaques (Figs. 26, 28, 32), although the decoration as a whole is made up of transverse lines and bands. One of the few vertically applied elements on these plaques is a band of curve hatching between bordering lines ("ladder" variant) (Figs. 26, 28).

The longitudinal rows of short transverse spurs or gouges on the wooden bars from Palutat Cave have already been noted (Fig. 34, *1* to *3, 7*). Some of the incised slate plaques also have groups of rather short vertical or horizontal lines (Figs. 29, 31, 32), and one has a group of slanting lines (Fig. 27). A group of slanting lines is incised on a wooden peg from Palutat Cave (Pl. 50, *7*), and 2 oblique lines are incised on a socket piece from Site 7 (Pl. 35, *12*).

Other incised elements, applied longitudinally or as parts of a complex pattern, are:

Line with vertical spur on one side—used as part of the designs on the ivory bears and one bone tube from Grave III, Palugvik East Point (Pls. 46, *18, 19;* 47, *2*).

Line with slanting spurs on one side—on a bone pendant from Palugvik 3 or 4 (Pl. 43, *41*, on side not illustrated), and with spurs in groups of 3 on one of the bars from Palutat Cave (Fig. 34, *10*).

Line with alternating spurs on both sides—on an ice pick (?) from Palugvik 4 (Pl. 40, *6*), and as part of the designs on the ivory bears from Palugvik East Point (Pl. 46, *18, 19*).

Line crossed by vertical spurs—on 2 wooden bars from Palutat Cave (Fig. 34, *6, 11*), and as part of the designs on the bone tubes from Palugvik East Point (Pl. 47, *1* to *3*).

Line crossed by slanting spurs—on a wooden bar from the cave (Fig. 34, *12*).

A transverse band of crosshatching was incised on a detachable barbed head from Palugvik 4 (P.579), but with this exception the element is found only on the decorated slate plaques, where it is commonly enclosed between bordering lines (Figs. 27, 28, 30 to 32). Other transverse bands on these plaques were of oblique hatching ("ladder" variant) (Fig. 25), and of zigzag lines and "braiding" (Fig. 32).

Smaller elements in the decoration of these plaques are the "tree" figure (Fig. 32), Y (Fig. 29), V (Fig. 28), and X (Fig. 29).

Small triangular areas were slightly gouged at the base of the wooden bars from Palutat Cave and at the end of the knife handle from the same site (Pl. 50, *5*). On one of the bars this area is filled with crosshatching. A triangular area was gouged out above the line hole of a detachable barbed head from Palugvik 2 or 3 (Pl. 33, *22*), where it is reminiscent of the decoration above the line holes of more northern Eskimo toggle harpoon heads. A small projection below a band of crosshatching on a slate plaque is also filled with crosshatching (Fig. 25). The ears of one of the animals incised on a bone tube from Palugvik East Point are treated in the same way (Pl. 47, *2*).

All of the decorated bone and ivory objects mentioned above were incised with stone tools. There are, however, 2 objects that were evidently incised with metal tools. One of these is a detachable barbed head from Palugvik 1 (Pl. 32, *12*), on which there are a longitudinal line trailing up from the notch of the barb and 2 transverse lines. The other is a bone pin from Palug-

vik 3 or 4 (33-37-51), with 4 longitudinal lines and 2 lines encircling it in a spiral. No examples of compass-drawn dot-and-circle or of the round bored dot were found.

As has already been noted, the patterns of spurred lines on the backs of the ivory bears suggest a man with pointed head (?) (Pl. 46, *18*) and an animal's head (Pl. 46, *19*). Designs of spurred lines on a bone tube from the same grave suggest a man wearing a hat (Pl. 47, *1*), and on another tube seem to represent the heads of 2 animals (Pl. 47, *2*). These figures are highly conventionalized and are the only examples of representative incising, unless we include the slate plaques.

The outline of a pendant from Palugvik 4 suggests a conventionalized eye or a fish (Pl. 42, *48*). A little carving from Palugvik 2 may be a whale (Pl. 42, *30*), and a human face was carved on a slab of walrus ivory from Palugvik 3 (?) (Pl. 42, *40*).

These examples exhaust the list of decorated stone, wood, bone, and ivory specimens from Prince William Sound, except for the few painted objects mentioned in the prevous section and the pictographs described in Chapter IV. There must have been examples of representative wood carving and of painting which have not survived. Nor did we obtain any specimens of decorated baskets, like those described by the natives and represented in a few ethnological collections. Articles of clothing were evidently ornamented with beads, pendants, or buckles, and by the stitching together of different kinds of furs. It would have been very interesting if we had been able to substantiate in any way the report that stone vessels decorated with "flowers" had been found in Port Gravina, since these may have been lamps like the highly ornate ceremonial lamps of Kachemak Bay III.

CHAPTER VI

Conclusion

√ 1. POPULATION

ONE CURIOUS FEATURE about Prince William Sound is that in spite of its apparently abundant food resources the population was evidently very small, to judge by the earliest records. Thus Meares, who wintered in Snug Corner Cove in 1786-87, reports that he saw not more than 500 or 600 natives.[1] Portlock, who visited most of the southern part of the sound, estimates that the natives of Prince William Sound and of the coast to Controller Bay could not muster more than 300 fighting men.[2] Since he did not meet the Eyak, this small tribe is not included, and his estimate presumably applies only to the Chugach. Vancouver in 1794 sent out 2 exploring parties that virtually circumnavigated the mainland shores of the sound, and he expressed surprise that they encountered so few natives and found only one village, a settlement of about 200 (on Mummy Island, Site 20?). "From whence it is evident," he writes,

that the population of this large sound is very inconsiderable when compared with its extent; for if we admit, that all those seen by both the surveying parties, and the four that visited the ship, were all different persons, the total number of people amounted to only two hundred and eighty-one of all descriptions, exclusive of the few we saw amongst the Russians at Port Etches, who most probably belonged to the village that Mr. Johnstone had visited.[3]

Even though the natives at Port Etches were probably a different group from those encountered on Mummy Island, the addition of these does not substantially raise Vancouver's total figure. He did not believe that there had been a recent decrease in population, for he estimated that Captain Cook, during the 8 days that he visited Port Etches and Snug Corner Cove and sailed along the north shore of Montague Island, did not encounter more than 100 persons, although curiosity and a desire to trade would surely have induced all who could to visit the strange ships.[4] Furthermore, Vancouver's exploring parties did not find any deserted habitations. They did see a number of old graves on the western part of the sound, and Vancouver thinks that the lack of fresh graves in that area indicated that the natives had but recently congregated in the eastern part in order to enjoy trade with the Russians at Port Etches.[5]

Although none of these early explorers conducted what could be considered a true census, their impressions of scanty population are in accord with the archaeological evidence. We found only rather small sites, consistently smaller than most of those re-

[1] Meares, 1791, p. xlvii.
[2] Portlock, 1789, p. 250.
[3] Vancouver, 1801, V, 337.
[4] Ibid., p. 338.
[5] Ibid., p. 339.

ported on Kodiak and the Aleutians, and none suggesting a really large village. Some of the sites may even have been the summer and winter settlements for the same community. There were long stretches of shore line where no sites were reported or observed. On the other hand, we did not make a complete census of sites, and, even if we had searched diligently in areas which we were not able to visit at all, we should have no way of estimating how many former villages had been destroyed by the sinking of the land, or of guessing at the former size of such sites as Palugvik which had been partially destroyed.

Early census reports seem to confirm the small sizes of the Chugach population:[6]

1818, Imperial Inspector Kostlivitzof, 360 Chugach (172 males, 188 females).

1819, Tikmenief, in his *Historical Review,* repeats these figures.

1825, Baron Wrangell, 1,563 Chugach (782 males, 781 females).

1837-40, a terrible smallpox epidemic ravaged Alaska and must have reduced greatly the Chugach population.

1839, Veniaminof, 471 Chugach (not including "creoles," i.e., children of native mothers and Russian fathers).

1860, The Holy Synod, in publishing the number of Christians in Russian America, claimed 456 Chugach (226 males, 230 females).

1863, Imperial Inspector Kostlivitzof got the same figures for the entire Chugach population, not including "creoles."

The following figures are quoted from the Tenth and Eleventh U.S. Census reports for 1880 and 1890.[7] The names of the villages have been modified to conform to modern orthography:

1880

Nuchek	60 Chugach, 11 "creoles"
Tatitlek	73 "
Kiniklik	54 "
Chenega	80 "

267 Chugach, 11 "creoles"

1890

Nuchek	120 Chugach, 18 "creoles"
Tatitlek	53 " 36 "
Kiniklik	73 "
Chenega	71 "

317 Chugach, 54 "creoles"

Porter's total estimate for 1890 gives 433 Chugach (217 males, 216 females), but this evidently includes not only half-breeds but also 21 Eyak Indians at what is now Cordova and the population from Ayalik that had recently moved to Port Graham.

The figures for Prince William Sound are strikingly and consistently lower than those for Kodiak Island.[8] Thus, disregarding such exaggerated guesses as those of Shelekof, who claimed 50,000 Koniag in 1784-86, we have the following data:

1790, Register of the Shelekof Company, about 5,000 for the Kodiak Island group.

1792, Delarof, about 6,510 for Kodiak Island and the Katmai area on the opposite mainland which was also inhabited by Koniag.

1796, Baranof, 6,206 for the same 2 areas.

1803, Davydof, about 7,000 for the Kodiak Island group.

1805, Lisiansky, about 4,000. He estimates 10,000 or more in pre-Russian days.

1825, Wrangell, 2,819.

1851, Holmberg, 1,500.

1880, Petroff, 1,943.

1890, Porter, 1,154, but we must subtract from this about 200 for the Eskimo at Port Graham and Seldovia.

Kroeber has used Mooney's careful estimates of aboriginal American populations, although he suggests that the figures are consistently too high for southwestern Alaska.[9] Thus, the Aleut numbered 16,000 with an area of 247,000 square kilometers; the Koniag 8,800 with an area of 287,000 square kilometers; the Chugach only 1,700

[6] Quoted by Petroff, 1884, pp. 33-40.
[7] *Ibid.,* p. 29; Porter, 1893, pp. 4, 158.
[8] Quoted by Hrdlička, 1944, pp. 19-20.
[9] Kroeber, 1939, p. 135.

with a territory of 262,000 square kilometers. The density of population per 100 square kilometers is 64.7 for the Aleut, 30.6 for the Koniag, and 6.48 for the Chugach —a ratio which would appear to be in exactly inverse proportion to the natural resources of the land![10] Since the sea, however, furnishes the main support for these peoples, we may also examine Kroeber's estimate of population density in proportion to length of shore line.[11] For the Aleut he calculates an average of 4.6 persons per mile of coast; for the Pacific Eskimo as a whole, 2.8 persons. He made his own calculation of the Alaskan shore line, at what I suspect was too low a figure, since for all Alaska he estimates 25,000 miles, with 3,500 for the Aleutians and 4,000 for the Pacific Eskimo (with whom he erroneously includes the "Ugalakmiut" or Eyak). Yet, according to Grant and Higgins, Prince William Sound alone has about 2,000 miles of coast line.[12] (Some of this should, perhaps, not be "counted," since it includes the shore of skerries or of ice-filled bays, which are essentially unutilizable.) If we accept Mooney's estimate of 1,700 Chugach, this would mean only .085 persons per mile of shore line, a figure which falls well below the lowest of Kroeber's estimates for any Eskimo group.

I cannot explain the apparent underpopulation of Prince William Sound. The Chugach were perhaps a little more exposed to raids by foreign peoples (i.e., the Tlingit) than were the Koniag or Aleut, yet the latter groups probably indulged in an equal amount of fighting among themselves. Chugach material culture, to be sure, seems somewhat less rich than that of the Aleut or other Pacific Eskimo, yet this impression may be deceptive because the Chugach, more than the others, relied on

wood, which has vanished from the shell heaps leaving few traces, while we have no unrifled caves to compare with the spectacular finds from the Aleutians. The prehistoric remains are, therefore, bound to make a poor showing for the Chugach. Yet Cook writes of them:

Everything they have, however, is as well and ingeniously made, as if they were furnished with the most complete tool-chest; and their sewing, plaiting of sinews, and small work on the little bags, may be put in competition with the most delicate manufactures found in any part of the known world. In short, considering the otherwise uncivilized or rude state in which these people are, their Northern situation, amidst a country perpetually covered with snow [sic], and the wretched materials which they have to work with, it appears, that their invention and dexterity, in all manual works, is at least equal to that of any other nation.[13]

While we ourselves came too late to recover a full account of Chugach social and ceremonial life, our notes would indicate that they shared in the same elaborate social and religious patterns as the Aleut and Koniag.[14] There is no clear evidence here to suggest a markedly poor and very marginal culture, such as would indicate a small population with little wealth. This is not to deny, however, that the Chugach in some respects had a somewhat marginal culture.

2. CULTURAL POSITION

The archaeological material from Prince William Sound enables us to reconstruct a good deal of Chugach material culture as it must have been within the 500 or so years preceding the discovery of Alaska and as it was at the time of the first contact with the white man. The data also suggest some of the cultural changes which took place during that time. These seem to have been relatively minor, or are too scantily documented to be fully apparent.

It would be obvious from a study of the artifacts themselves, even if no further information were available, that the makers of these specimens lived in an area where

---

[10] I wonder whether Chugach territory, as estimated here, may not include a great deal of water, and so be too high; yet this possible source of error could hardly be great enough to conceal an actual density of population comparable to that of Kodiak, much less that of the Aleutians.

[11] Kroeber, 1939, pp. 167, 170.

[12] Grant and Higgins, 1910, p. 9.

[13] Cook, 1785, II, 373 f.

[14] See Lantis' interpretation, 1947.

wood was plentiful, that they were primarily hunters of marine rather than of land animals, and that they wore tailored skin clothing. Probably the most significant fact about their subsistence that might escape us would be the importance of the salmon in their economy. We would also know that they were more or less warlike; we would suspect that they cooked in perishable containers; the presence of offerings in only a relatively few graves would suggest distinctions in social status; masks would give faint hints of ceremonial and religious life. Even if we lacked all records of provenience, the collection as a whole would easily be referable to the Aleut-Pacific Eskimo province. The development of woodworking tools and the possession of copper would further suggest the mainland in the eastern part of that area.

When all available sources of information on the Chugach are considered, we can see that they share in the basic cultural patterns common to southwestern Alaska and that what is most distinctive in their culture is ascribable to their somewhat marginal position in the northeastern part of the area, to the particular resources locally available or denied, and to their more intimate contacts with the Indians whose territories abut their own. Presumably the same general influences have been at work in shaping their culture as have molded those of the other Pacific Eskimo and Aleut groups, and have produced largely similar sequences. I doubt, however, that any of the archaeological specimens as yet recovered from Prince William Sound antedate the period represented by Kachemak Bay III or sub-III and the comparable stages which may be inferred for Kodiak and the Aleutians.

Prince William Sound represents one of the cultural subareas of the Pacific Eskimo-Aleut province. The other cultures are that of lower Cook Inlet and Kenai Peninsula, with which the Chugach was probably most closely related; that of Kodiak, with which it also had much in common; that of the

Alaska Peninsula (though here we are at the borders of the Bristol Bay area); and that of the Aleutians. Aleut culture undoubtedly had important local variations, as yet not defined, so that we ought probably to distinguish at least between eastern and western divisions, if not among smaller units represented by the Fox, Andreanof, Rat, Near, and Shumagin island groups. An important and interesting task would be to discover and formulate the distinguishing characteristics of these several southwestern Alaskan cultures, their many interrelationships, and the common themes on which they are based. The area as a whole was heavily populated by prosperous peoples who had made successful adjustments to rather exacting environments, and whose wealth had enabled them to elaborate the artistic, social, and ceremonial aspects of their culture further than other Eskimo groups, except perhaps their neighbors in Bristol Bay. Their way of life seems to have been distinctive, as compared with that of other Eskimo; it was not simply a northern culture transplanted to the sub-Arctic, but had its own roots and history. The flowering of southwestern Alaskan culture may or may not have been contemporaneous with that of the western Eskimo about Bering Strait and farther north, but for a solution of this problem we need more tree-ring and carbon-14 dates. Southwestern Alaska is one of the strategic areas for an understanding of the culture history of northwestern North America, for here influences were received from and transmitted to the Arctic, the Asiatic North Pacific, the Alaskan interior, and the Northwest Coast, and were locally adapted and transformed to fit indigenous patterns. The Chugach obviously lay in the direct route of some of these cultural exchanges and were touched by the backwash of others.

Since I have already proposed certain hypotheses about the development of culture in this general area, based upon extensive distribution studies of archaeological traits, including a good deal of the

Prince William Sound material, it is not my intention here to undertake a similar analysis of the Chugach data. Any definitive understanding of the complex interrelationships among the various southwestern Alaskan cultures and of the significance of the area as a whole in Alaskan cultural history must await the establishment of local cultural sequences based upon careful stratigraphic excavations on Kodiak and the Aleutians. More extensive material from the Alaska Peninsula, Cook Inlet, and Prince William Sound, especially from the earlier periods, would also be desirable. Until such data are secured, we cannot define clearly the place of the Chugach.

Hrdlička's many seasons at Uyak Bay on the west coast of Kodiak Island were productive of tons of specimens, but his methods of digging were such that we know very little about cultural sequences at this enormous site. It is often very difficult to trace the natural stratigraphy of a shell heap,[15] since the various depositional layers are usually lens-shaped and peter out at the edges, and may be interrupted and disturbed by the digging of graves, house pits, etc. Hrdlička, however, made no serious attempt to understand or utilize the stratigraphy at his site and, in fact, denied that the various layers, so plainly revealed in his own photographs, had any archaeological significance. He writes:

The pre-Koniag exposures showed throughout more or less of stratification, but in no case was any layer continued throughout or even over a large portion of the deposits. The strata were most numerous and best marked in the shell debris, least so to absent in the ashy portions. They varied much in thickness, both among themselves and in different parts of the same stratum, in places showed much warping, a sudden cut-off like cessation, or a general more or less obliterated ancient derangement; and although studied constantly they eluded interpretation.

The stratification could only be a secondary phenomenon, and was shared more or less, experience has shown, by all similar deposits elsewhere on the

island. It evidently had neither chronological nor any other value. It was due, doubtless, to a series of processes acting for a long time on the deposits; yet even thus it was hard to understand. It is a problem, and perhaps a knotty one at that, for the geophysicist rather than for the archaeologist. What confusion it would have brought had it been attempted to peel the deposits layer after layer from the top—such a procedure would in fact have soon proved impossible.[16]

Hrdlička also failed to record the provenience of specimens by the usual method of citing grid and depth coordinates. Instead of dividing up the surface of the midden into squares and excavating these from the top down in measured layers, which would have supplied an adequate artificial stratigraphy with which to correlate the specimens recovered, Hrdlička chose the far easier method of preparing a vertical exposure along the edge of the site and undercutting this cliff. Except for specimens which happened to be exposed in the face of the shell heap and could be carefully removed before the bank collapsed, everything was likely to become mixed up, the younger with the older. This method would also make it virtually impossible to draw plans of the architectural features encountered in the site, and for this reason, perhaps, we are given no reliable details about Kodiak houses.

To be sure, Hrdlička did divide the deposits roughly into 3 levels, and assigned the 2 lower to a "pre-Koniag" and the upper to a "Koniag" occupation. He also noted[17] that the upper level of the site was distinguished from the lower two-thirds by the presence of fire-cracked rocks, presumably used in the sweat bath. Specimens which supposedly came from these 3 levels were marked with pencil: black for the top, red for the middle, and blue for the lowest. Apparently he sometimes changed his mind about the provenience of some specimens, for a number of them, including some especially well-made examples, now have a

---

[15] The number of specimens which I was unable to assign definitely to one of the 4 main layers at Palugvik is a commentary on the difficulties encountered.

[16] Hrdlička, 1944, pp. 208-11; cf. pp. 337 f., and especially Figs. 93-100, which illustrate part of the exposed face of the shell heap, over 300 feet long and from 12 to 15 feet thick at the heart of the site.
[17] *Ibid.*, p. 213.

red mark superimposed over the black. Even if the marking had been carefully and consistently done in the field, we must recognize that there is some danger in applying the criterion of relative depth over so large a site, the different portions of which may not have been occupied simultaneously. Not infrequently, I suspect, the estimates of depth and of cultural chronology were modified to fit the occurrence of "pre-Koniag" or "Koniag" physical types; that is, the skeletons encountered were used as time markers, so that anything found near the grave of a long-headed "pre-Koniag" or near that of a round-headed "Koniag" would be assigned to "pre-Koniag" or "Koniag" cultures, respectively. Certain discrepancies could be explained by the hypothesis that the later "Koniag" had picked up and used some of the finer specimens left by their predecessors.[18] Aside from the obvious dangers inherent in equating culture with physical type, the lack of stratigraphic check prevents us from knowing whether there was actually as abrupt and complete a change in physical type as Hrdlička postulates. His anthropological studies present us with 2 contrasted racial types, but give us no clue to the composition of the population at any period of time, for these types are treated as if they represented chronologically distinct populations.

Because of this faulty methodology, and because Hrdlička too often coined his own names for types of artifacts without explaining what they were like, his summaries of the culture history of the site are not as valuable as they would appear to be. He is probably correct in general about the flowering of culture in the middle period of occupation represented at Uyak Bay and about its subsequent decline in certain respects, but his statements must be used with caution, and the details need confirmation. The cultural sequence on Kodiak Island was evidently similar to that on lower Cook Inlet, for most of the material

can be duplicated in the much smaller collections from Kachemak Bay II or sub-III through the final stage of Eskimo occupation (cf. Port Graham). There are, of course, unique types from Kodiak Island, as well as peculiarities in style and in emphasis and elaboration that cannot yet be adequately assessed. It is fortunate, therefore, that Dr. Robert Heizer, of the University of California, one of Hrdlička's former students who worked for him at Uyak Bay, is at present engaged in a study of the specimens, and it is hoped that his own information obtained on the spot, possibly supplemented by the impressions of others who participated in the digging, may disentangle some of the obvious inconsistencies or correct suspected errors in Hrdlička's interpretations. Until this study is published in full, it would be premature to attempt to make detailed comparisons between Chugach and Kodiak material.

Similar difficulties attach to the use of Hrdlička's collections from the Aleutians. Here again there is no adequate stratigraphic check,[19] and there is no complete description of sites or of artifacts found. Hrdlička recognizes 2 physical types on the islands: the long-headed "pre-Aleut," who were neither "pre-Koniag" nor "Eskimo," and the round-headed "Aleut," who were closely related to the "Koniag" although they possessed a somewhat lower vault. Again, differences in physical type are used as criteria for designating "pre-Aleut" and "Aleut" cultures, although Hrdlička found it virtually impossible to discover any significant differences between these postulated cultural assemblages.[20] The distinction between "pre-Aleut" and "Aleut" could not, in any case, be taken as a chronological guide, except in the eastern islands, where the "Aleut" deposits are said to represent the most recent layer, seldom over 2 feet thick, on top of the larger sites. Farther

---

18 *Ibid.*, p. 324.

19 Hrdlička, 1945. Cf. p. 483 where stratification is described as "secondary and, except as denoting some age, without any chronological or occupational significance."
20 *Ibid.*, pp. 474 ff.

west, Hrdlička reports that the remains are almost exclusively "pre-Aleut." He believes that this physical type survived on the western Aleutians until historic times, but slightly admixed with an infusion of "Aleut" who had begun to spread slowly westward from the mainland in the last centuries before Bering.

The early work of Dall on the Aleutians[21] suffered from a too enthusiastic attempt to establish a cultural sequence with inadequate data. Jochelson's field work was done in 1909-10, and the first draft of his archaeological report was prepared in 1916, only to have the publication in Russia rendered impossible by the revolution. He succeeded in saving the manuscript and illustrations and bringing them to America, and the final version, which included additional material, was not completed until 1924. From my own experiences in preparing the present report, I can appreciate some of the difficulties encountered by Jochelson in completing his manuscript far from the original collections and after such a lapse of time. Although he does not present his material in such a way as to illustrate possible regional and temporal differences, and his field methods are not always clear, he has published sufficiently detailed information on the provenience of specimens to enable a student to make some regional and temporal comparisons, especially if additional carefully excavated collections could be used to amplify and check. Dr. George Quimby of the Chicago Museum of Natural History has been undertaking such a study, and has also published some specimens from a large site on Adak Island.[22] Although the latter material was secured as a result of bulldozer operations during the war, it is divided into an older and a younger group which exhibit significant cultural differences.

In 1948, 1949, 1950, and 1952, Dr. William Laughlin of the University of Oregon and his associates made a series of studies on Aleutian archaeology, ethnology, physi-

cal anthropology, and linguistics. During the first season, Dr. Theodore D. Bank, Jr., of the Botanical Gardens, University of Michigan, collaborated in the field with Dr. Laughlin, but in 1949, 1950, and 1951, Dr. Bank and Dr. A. C. Spaulding of the University of Michigan conducted independent botanical and archaeological studies in the Aleutians.[23]

As yet only a few preliminary papers based on their findings have been published,[24] but when the full results are made available we should be in a much better position to understand the development of culture in the Aleutians. From the material already published, it would appear that the same general trend of development occurred here as on Kodiak Island and Cook Inlet, although the Aleut, especially on the western islands, have developed the most striking local variants of the common cultural patterns.

Laughlin confirms Hrdlička's reported change in physical type from "Paleo-Aleut" to "Neo-Aleut," as he renames them, especially in the eastern sector of the island chain. He and his collaborators argue on the basis of the degree of difference between the Aleut and Eskimo languages that the ancient Aleut separated from the mainland Eskimo some 4,000 years ago. The first known migrants were presumably of "Paleo-Aleut" physical type. About 1,000 years ago a second wave of migration, of "Neo-Aleut" type, began to spread westward from the mainland, and this movement was still in progress at the time of the Russian discovery. At the present time, the physical traits of the earlier type are represented among the central and western Aleuts, while the eastern Aleuts all belong to the newer type.

---

[21] Dall, 1877, 1878, etc.
[22] Quimby, 1945a, b; 1946a, b; 1948.

[23] These expeditions are reported in "Notes and News," *American Antiquity*. XIV (1948), 71; XV (1949), 74; XV (1950), 265; XVI (1950), 182; XVI (1951), 285; XVII (1952), 389; XVIII (1952), 92 f.; XVIII (1953), 291 f.
[24] Laughlin, 1951; Laughlin and Marsh, 1951; Marsh and Swadesh, 1951; Laughlin, 1952; Laughlin, Marsh, and Leach, 1952; Anderson and Bank, 1952; Spaulding, 1953; Bank, 1953, and unpublished MS.

The oldest archaeological remains on the Aleutians *may* be the cores, blades, flakes, and scrapers, found by Laughlin in 1938 at what was presumably a workshop site on top of the island of Analiuliak, near Nikolski. At least Laughlin feels that the material is rather different from that recovered from the near-by Chaluka site at Nikolski on Umnak Island, and may be older, although tools made from blades like those of Analiuliak occur in the lowest Chaluka levels. The greater age is in part suggested by the absence of volcanic ash from the Analiuliak site, although it underlies the Chaluka midden. "If this is essentially a Mesolithic industry preceding that of the Paleo-Aleuts, it would probably be over 5,000 years in age."[25] The situation might then be similar to that farther north in Alaska, where pre-Eskimo industries have been found at Cape Denbigh on the Seward Peninsula and in the northern interior of Alaska.[26]

The site at Chaluka on Umnak Island, a shell mound some 21 feet thick, represents a long period of occupation. A radiocarbon date of 3,018 years ± 280 was obtained from a hearth one meter above the bottom of the mound, and Laughlin estimates that the first deposits must be several hundred years older. The uppermost layers seem to be contemporaneous with the late prehistoric and early historic material from the mummy caves of Kagamil. The culture of the earliest occupants of Chaluka was already essentially like that of the modern Aleuts, and the many minor changes in types and styles of artifacts that occurred intermittently throughout the period of occupation indicate that no sharply marked cultural periods can be distinguished. In late prehistoric times, the appearance of ground slate ulos; flat, shallow, polished lamps; and long socket pieces made in one piece characterize the latest period of occu-

pation and were presumed to have been introduced by the "Neo-Aleuts." However, Laughlin feels that the latter possessed a culture very similar to that of their predecessors, and that whatever innovations they introduced diffused westward more rapidly than the actual spread of the new population.

The published illustrations and the sample collections from Chaluka which Laughlin has shown me indicate that the style of the artifacts, even from the earliest layers, was already "Aleut" in character, different from the styles characteristic of Kodiak and Kachemak Bay. Furthermore, the types seem to be more developed or specialized than those of Kachemak Bay I, except for the predominance of chipped stone at Chaluka (and indeed all over the Aleutians). Moreover, "the earliest missile heads [from Chaluka] are characterized by . . . compass-drawn circle-and-dot design."[27] This design element appears in the Bering Strait area only with the Punuk culture which followed the Old Bering Sea, and at Kachemak Bay appears first only in the Third Period. It was presumably introduced into the Bering Strait area along with iron engraving tools from Siberia. There is no trace of metal-cut decorations in either the Old Bering Sea or in Kachemak Bay I (although straight metal-cut lines suggestive of Early Punuk are found in Kachemak Bay II). The earliest period of Old Bering Sea (Okvik) culture has yielded a radiocarbon date of 2,258 ± 230, and Collins estimates from early Chinese sources, reporting the use of iron in Asia north of Korea in A.D. 262, that the Punuk stage was probably somewhat later in the first millenium A.D. No radiocarbon dates are available from Kodiak or Kachemak Bay, but Giddings' middle layer at Cape Denbigh, which contains types like the Point Hope Ipiutak or Near-Ipiutak, the Dorset, and the Kachemak Bay cultures, has been dated at 1,460 ± 200 and at 2,016 ± 250.[28]

25 Laughlin, 1951, p. 55; see also Laughlin, Marsh, and Leach, 1952; "Notes and News," *American Antiquity*, XVIII (1953), 291 f.

26 Giddings, 1949 and 1951; Solecki, 1950 and 1951a, b; Solecki and Hackman, 1951; Irving, 1951.

27 Laughlin and Marsh, 1951, p. 81.

28 Collins, 1951, pp. 429 f.; Larsen, 1953, p. 602.

The character of the artifacts and the presence of the compass-drawn dot-and-circle in the oldest layers at Chaluka make it difficult to believe that this site is really older than Old Bering Sea and Kachemak Bay I, and one wonders whether the radiocarbon date of about 3,000 years for Chaluka is accurate. In this connection it is interesting to note that Bank (1953, p. 43) reports that the dot-and-circle appears in the "lower part of the middle culture zone" on Amaknak-D on Unalaska Bay. A radiocarbon date for a shellheap on Adak Island has been reported at about 4,600 years, but, since no collection data are given, it is impossible to assess its significance.[29]

These comparisons have been purposely limited to the Pacific Eskimo and Aleut area, although cultural similarities can also be traced farther north along the shores of Bristol Bay.[30] Larsen equates the sites at Chagvan and Nanvak bays with Kachemak Bay II, though they are possibly more like Kachemak Bay sub-III. The Platinum Village site, apparently older, seems to have a culture intermediate in character between that of Kachemak Bay II and the Ipiutak of Point Hope and Seward Peninsula, or the Near-Ipiutak. The Ipiutak has radiocarbon dates of 912 ± 170 and 973 ± 170, and I suspect that the Near-Ipiutak may actually be older, especially in view of the dates for Giddings' middle layers at Cape Denbigh, which is like the Near-Ipiutak. On the whole, however, the Bristol Bay area seems to have closer affinities in both prehistoric and modern times with Norton Sound than with the Aleut-Pacific Eskimo area, that is, with southwestern Alaska proper.

3. Way of Life

Although the following observations will pretend to be neither detailed nor definitive, it may be of some interest to summarize the archaeological material from Prince William Sound to see how far it can suggest Chugach culture as a whole, what

changes it may reveal, and how intimate seems to have been the relationship of the Chugach to other southwestern Alaskan groups.

The Aleut, who had no wood but that cast up by the sea or obtained in trade, produced relatively few woodworking tools, but the Chugach in contrast had a richer assortment than any other southwestern Alaskan people. Especially common was the heavy splitting adz, present even in the lowest levels at Palugvik and increasingly important in the latest period before it was supplanted by the steel ax. I have already suggested that the splitting adz was a relatively late invention on the Northwest Coast, and it is natural that it should appear somewhat earlier in Prince William Sound than on Cook Inlet and Kodiak (late Kachemak Bay III and "Koniag"). It never reached the Aleut. The most elaborate arrangement of grooves and knobs for hafting seems to be characteristic of the western part of the sound, although it is possible that this impression is in part influenced by the large number of specimens obtained from the relatively late sites in this area. In general, the Chugach splitting adz conforms to the general American North Pacific pattern, although most specimens seem to be less well made than those of the Northwest Coast. The splitting adz evidently replaced in part the ordinary planing adz, which was relatively more common in the earlier period in Prince William Sound. Although a few bone wedges and a heavy stone chisel were found, we may infer that most Chugach wedges were made of wood and that such wedges were used to split wood, for our informants specifically mentioned wooden wedges, but we cannot know the relative frequency of wedges as compared to the various types of adzes, nor how wedges may have been affected by the growing popularity of the splitting adz.

Related to the heavy grooved splitting adz are a few individual variants, all apparently from late sites, that have been shaped

---

[29] Anderson and Bank, 1952.
[30] Larsen, 1950 and 1953; Oswalt, 1952.

(or are broken adzes reshaped) as axes or as combination ax-adz or ax-pick. There is also an example of the "intermediate type adz," like a flat planing adz with groove for hafting. In addition, there are a number of grooveless splitting adzes which might be interpreted as survivals from a common undifferentiated prototype of both planing and splitting adzes, or as a hybrid form. The presence of these specimens, as well as the absence of any recognizable adz haft, suggests that the ordinary planing adz blades were attached directly to the wooden handle. Of course wooden hafts might have been used—if so, probably for the smaller blades—and more extensive excavations might reasonably be expected to reveal some examples of the bone haft, since it is known from Kachemak Bay, the Alaska Peninsula, and Kodiak, even though it was nowhere as common as in northern Eskimo cultures.[31] The bone adz hafts of the prehistoric Coast Salish are almost certainly related to the various northern types, and the interconnecting links must involve Prince William Sound, although perhaps at an earlier period than has yet been adequately explored.

It will be remembered that in the last period of Palugvik there appeared a number of very small slate blades which could have been used as delicate adzes or as scrapers. Such blades are found in a number of other cultures, including Kachemak Bay III,[32] but in Prince William Sound they seem to be definitely late.

Other woodworking tools used by the Chugach include small chisels of bear penis bone and small knifelike or adzlike chisels of slate. These forms seem to be local developments in Prince William Sound. Identification of the adzlike chisels was admittedly uncertain, though a relationship was suggested with Tlingit woodworking tools and with the early northern and eastern Eskimo ground burin-like implements.

Knives were obviously used for carving

but are poorly represented in our collections. Aside from the blade for a crooked knife made from a bear canine, none of the other blades of bone, stone, or copper could be identified specifically as knives for cutting wood. The knives of polished greenstone and the rare blades of chipped stone would certainly have been more effective for cutting tough materials than would slate blades. Our informants spoke of crooked knives with copper blades, of stone engraving tools (the latter could also be inferred by designs incised on wood, bone, and ivory), wedges for stripping off bark, and clam shell scrapers for gathering the inner bark of the hemlock, but none of these types could be recognized archaeologically. We do have a wooden knife handle, a porcupine incisor sharpened like an engraving tool, a fragmentary copper knife blade, and a few stone chips which might have been used for carving, but it is evident that our archaeological material fails to give an adequate picture of the contents of the Chugach woodcarver's sealskin tool bag.

For making holes in wood and bone, rarely in slate, we have a number of stone drill points, as well as a hand drill of stone and one of bone. Both the hand and the mechanical drill (operated with bow or cord) were used in all periods, but the mechanical drill was more common. Identification of a bow for a drill and of carved ivory handles for a drill cord was uncertain. Although the natives mentioned a mouthpiece for a drill, this may have been the result of a misunderstanding, for the rest braced against the chest or held in the hand was the only type represented archaeologically, and, in fact, there is no clear evidence that the mouthpiece for the drill was ever used in southwestern Alaska. Bear jaws were utilized as drill rests only in the earlier prehistoric period; bone wedges or similar slabs of bone seem always to have been employed, and such specimens can be duplicated at almost any site in southwestern Alaska.

31 De Laguna, 1934, pp. 58, 173; 1947, pp. 157-59.
32 De Laguna, 1947, p. 186.

The products of Chugach woodworking are represented by the planks used for coffins, by the large posts used for the plank "smokehouse," by dugout canoes, and by many other manufactures. The archaeological collections contain only a few examples of these: armor, masks, paddles, bidarka frames, parts of traps or snares, weapon shafts, etc. Unrepresented are the various wooden utensils used in the preparation and storage of food (except for a fragment of a wooden spoon). These included serving dishes and boxes with the side made of a single bent plank; the latter were used for storing food, water, and urine, or for carrying supplies on boat trips. Some of these utensils were decorated with painted carvings. It seems fairly obvious that in utilization of wood the Chugach approached the patterns of Northwest Coast culture more closely than did any of their Eskimo neighbors.

In manufacturing tools and weapons the Chugach employed hammerstones. These were simply handy ovoid or elongated boulders, now bearing traces of pounding. The elongated forms seem to be relatively late, and may have been used as pestles. There are a few specimens which seem to be pitted hammerstones, anvils, etc. A few grooved maul heads, some of which were made from broken splitting adzes, were probably used to drive wedges and stakes, to break bones for the marrow, and to work copper. Similar specimens are known from Kachemak Bay, the Port Graham area, and Kodiak. Bar, slab, and grooved whetstones and large grinding blocks were common; they showed no especially distinctive forms nor any changes in type during the known period. Thin slabs of sandstone or gritty schist were used for sawing greenstone and slate. Such saws are known from Kachemak Bay, where they appear first in the Third Period, and are scantily represented on the Aleutians. I have suggested that they may have been derived from Asia, and that they ought to be found on Kodiak and the Alaska Penin-

sula.[33] The common Alaskan and Salish type has a single edge, less often 2 parallel cutting edges. Paddle-shaped specimens and rectangular forms with 3 or even 4 edges were especially characteristic of the Chugach. It is to be noted that the paddle-shaped saw was restricted to the earlier prehistoric period when, indeed, saws were more common than in later times. This is perhaps because saws were primarily used in cutting out blanks for planing adz blades, and their importance would naturally decline along with that type of adz.

Only a few specimens of chipped stone were found, aside from some slate ulo blades which may or may not have been finished, a few unfinished weapon blades, and a number of rough scrapers made from slaty materials. The other chipped stone types represented blades for arrow or harpoon, lance, knife, and smaller scrapers. We found only 3 blunt ribs which might have been used for pressure flaking. Presumably slate and schist with slaty fracture were more easily trimmed into shape by battering the edges of the thin slab with a hammerstone than by flaking with a bone tool, and since most slate specimens were finished on a whetstone the roughness of the first shaping was unimportant. The heavy, dense, fine-grained volcanic and metamorphic rocks used for splitting adzes, pestles, lamps, mortars, etc. were blocked out with a hammerstone if a suitably shaped boulder could not be found, and were then pecked into shape with the same implement. Sharp edges or smooth surfaces were obtained with whetstones, grinding blocks, or sand. In winter, we were told, large adz blades were sharpened by fastening them under heavy logs and dragging them over the frozen beach. Bone and slate were, of course, easily shaped and polished by grinding. The general development of all Eskimo cultures, in the Atlantic, Arctic, and Pacific provinces, has been from an exclusive (or predominant) reliance upon chipped flint and chert, often beautifully pressure-flaked,

[33] De Laguna, 1934, p. 175; 1947, pp. 167 f.

to an equally pronounced dependence upon ground and polished slate. With respect to this trend even the oldest Chugach material appears chronologically late, even though it is probably as old as Kachemak Bay III, where chipped stone was still present in significant amounts, though no longer as important as in the First Period. But we are not, I believe, dealing simply with an evolutionary trend which operated with more or less uniform effect over wide areas. Aleut weapon and knife blades seem always to have been made predominantly of chipped stone rather than of polished slate even up to modern times, and, in contrast, Chugach stone work is much closer to that of the northern Northwest Coast, where chipped stone is virtually absent and sawing, pecking, and grinding are the techniques of manufacture. Future archaeological work in Prince William Sound and the Northwest Coast may, however, uncover connections between the prehistoric stone chipping in the Puget Sound area[34] and that of Cook Inlet, Kodiak, and the Aleutians.

Native copper was obtained locally by the Chugach, probably even mined, and was also secured in trade with the Atna. It was worked by hammering, heating, and grinding. While the collections contain only 2 arrowheads, a detachable barbed head, a knife blade, an awl-like nose pin (?), and a finger ring, our informants spoke of copper needles, daggers, and spear points, and the early explorers attest the rather common use of copper for weapon blades. It may, therefore, have been more generally employed than the archaeological material suggests. If it was so valuable that broken specimens were reworked for further use, relatively few finds might be expected in the middens. The archaeological evidence would indicate that copper was not used until the later prehistoric period, which fits the time of its appearance on Cook Inlet after the close of Kachemak Bay III. Copper was apparently not known on Kodiak

and the Aleutians until it was secured from wrecks and later from traders.

Fire is said to have been kindled with a cord drill, but, while we found wooden fire drills and hearths, we know only that the drill was mechanically operated. The strike-a-light of quartz and pyrites was represented archaeologically, but we do not know how commonly it was used. Fires were evidently lit in unprepared hearths at villages and camping places, but at Palugvik a small rectangular fireplace of stone slabs was commonly used. One rather poorly made pit for baking was also found. The hearths at Palugvik resemble those of Uyak Bay on Kodiak more than they do those found on Kachemak Bay, where the baking hearth was common and rectangular slab fireplaces seem to have been unknown. The Chugach, in common with their Eskimo and Indian neighbors, cooked food by stone-boiling in watertight wooden vessels and twined baskets, but no trace of these containers has survived. Some of the wooden artifacts from Palutat Cave may have been spits for roasting meat, tongs for handling hot rocks, and skewers for serving meat. We also found samples of wooden and bone spoons, and probably of bone marrow extractors. We were unable to identify any stone slab as having been used in roasting or frying. There is some evidence that the larger flat grinding stones and slabs from Kachemak Bay were used for cooking, and the Aleut are known to have used stone slabs as frying pans, sometimes with sides of clay, but there is no clear evidence that the slate slabs so common at Uyak Bay were used for such a purpose.[35] The later levels and sites in Prince William Sound, as on Kachemak Bay and Kodiak, contain an abundance of fire-cracked rocks, suggesting the introduction or suddenly increased popularity of the steam sweat bath in late prehistoric times.

Chugach houses were illuminated by oval to roundish stone lamps with a more or less

[34] M. W. Smith, 1950.

[35] De Laguna, 1934, pp. 59 f.; Cook, 1785, III, 107; Jochelson, 1925, Pl. 21, 2, p. 109; Hrdlička, 1944, p. 34.

clearly defined lip for the wick. These reflect most of the various substyles of the North Pacific area, although few are very well finished, and the attempts at decoration are of the simplest. There is only one very unclear report to suggest elaborately decorated lamps. Even on Cook Inlet and Kodiak, where lamps with geometric designs and animal or human effigies are well documented, such specimens constitute only a small percentage of the total number of lamps, so that it would have been perhaps too much to hope for a similar prize in the small collection from Prince William Sound. Although one lamp with human figure has been found on Umnak Island,[36] Aleut lamps are even plainer than those of the Chugach. Elaborately carved lamps seem, therefore, to be characteristic only of the central part of southwestern Alaska and to have been intended for ceremonial rather than for domestic use. Lantis has argued that the Aleut lacked the kashim, or ceremonial house,[37] and this might explain the absence of ceremonial lamps from the Aleutian Islands except for the one example, doubtless secured in trade. Evidence of the kashim among the Chugach is rather uncertain. In addition to ordinary sized lamps, the Chugach, like other southwestern Alaskan peoples, had small lamps which could be carried by hunters on overnight trips.

The Chugach made use of mortars and pestles, presumably for preparing vegetable foods, especially berries, and in historic times for making snuff. No wooden specimens were recovered, although they are known from ethnological examples and descriptions, but stone and whale bone mortars are represented archaeologically. Similar stone and bone vessels, the identification of which is not always clear, are known from Kachemak Bay, Kodiak, and the Aleutians. Some are perhaps mortars, but others have been described as dishes, lamps, lamp stands, etc. They are nowhere very common and are probably not very old.[38] Although the Chugach may have used the elongated hammerstones as pestles, their characteristic pestle was carefully shaped and had an octagonal top. Identification of this is also uncertain, since similar implements were used by the Northwest Coast Indians as hand hammers for driving wedges. In any case, the type has not been reported north or west of Prince William Sound. As far as we can tell, mortars and pestles were used by the Chugach throughout the period represented by our finds, and since they lived closest to the Northwest Coast, where similar specimens were common, it is natural that the Chugach should have possessed the stone mortar earlier than other southwestern Alaskan tribes and that they alone should use the stone pestle (or hammer). There is no evidence, however, that the Chugach used handstones (manos) with large grinding slabs, which are known from Kachemak Bay, Kodiak, and the Aleutians, although in the last two areas these implements seem to have been restricted to grinding paint.[39]

Game was evidently cut up with slate knives. We have a fragment of a large doubled-edged slate flensing knife which could have been used to advantage on a whale, as well as a few broad greenstone knife blades, and a number of smaller slate blades with straight edges ("Halibut Cove type"), the last represented from all periods. Single-edged knives were evidently rare, even though a type with copper blade was described. A few bone knives might have been used for cutting meat or cleaning hides. Women, of course, used the slate ulo. This had a curved or a straight edge, and some of the blades were notched at the back for hafting or for holding a winding which took the place of a handle. The more com-

---

[36] Information supplied by Dr. J. A. Mason, University of Pennsylvania Museum.
[37] Lantis, 1947, pp. 31 f. (Kashims were found in every Koniag village, according to ethnological and archaeological evidence; Hrdlička, 1944, pp. 29, 133).

[38] De Laguna, 1934, pp. 60, 174, Pls. 18, *4;* 21, *4;* Hrdlička, 1944, pp. 334, 345, and unpublished specimens; Jochelson, 1925, pp. 73 ff.; Hrdlička, 1945, pp. 57, 451; Figs. 195, 196.
[39] De Laguna, 1934, p. 60; Hrdlička, 1944, pp. 328, 341; Jochelson, 1925, Pl. 19, *4.*

mon wooden handle was described as having a hole for 3 fingers. There is nothing about the Chugach ulo to distinguish it from specimens from Kachemak Bay, Kodiak, or the Aleutians. Men also, we believe, had a smaller straight-edged knife like an ulo, which is also a common southwestern Alaskan type.

Skins were worked with stone scrapers chipped from thin slabs. Ulo-shaped, rectangular, and irregular specimens were especially characteristic of the earlier prehistoric period, but the more distinctive paddle-shaped form was used throughout. The slate ulos with chipped edge, similar to those of Kodiak and Kachemak Bay, may have been used as scrapers, especially since we were told that a purposely blunted ulo was often employed for this purpose. Curiously enough, there were only 4 boulder chips, 2 of which may have been scrapers, although the type was ubiquitous on Kachemak Bay and Kodiak.[40] Bone scrapers are poorly represented in Prince William Sound, although the scapula scraper (for hemlock bark?), the split leg bone scraper with longitudinal edge (beamer), and small knifelike forms seem to have been known. We were unable to identify the wooden and shell implements said to have been used for dehairing skins. Wooden frames were used for stretching hides, and, although we found no recognizable parts of these, we did secure a number of sharpened stakes in Palutat Cave which may have been used for pegging out skins.

Awls, eyed needles, and needle-like bone implements without eyes (?) were used for sewing. Sinew was used for thread and was also braided into cords and lines. Running stitches, overcasting, and waterproof blind-stitching were represented archaeologically, as was the use of fringes, fur trimming, and beads for decoration. Our collections do not, however, give an adequate picture of Chugach needlework and costume, for we found no samples of the use of feathers, of

embroidery, or of fine skin mosaic patchwork, and few identifiable samples of clothing.

Grass and bark were also used for cords and matting. While we secured several specimens of rather coarse matting that had been used as shrouds, we have nothing comparable to the clothlike matting so well known from the Aleutians, although the Chugach may have made equally fine textiles since our informants described mats made of different colored grasses, decorated with feathers. Woolen blankets, like those of the Northwest Coast, were noted by Cook and Strange. Twined spruce root baskets are also unrepresented in our archaeological collections, although plain and decorated specimens, some of which were watertight, were made by the Chugach for a variety of purposes. The only evidences of basketry we found were a piece of birchbark and a bent willow withe. The first is not part of a folded bark container, like those made by the interior Athabaskans, but was evidently the side of a pail-like vessel with pegged-on wooden (?) bottom, made according to the same pattern as that followed by the northern Eskimo for baleen-sided vessels.

Other tools used by the Chugach were the digging stick and the wooden shovel. The first was not recognized if found, and the second is but uncertainly represented. The shovels usually found in southwestern Alaska have bone blades,[41] but we found no specimen of this material. Large whale bone picks, apparently used unhafted, are shared by the natives of Prince William Sound, Kachemak Bay, Kodiak, and the Aleutians. Although these look like bayonets, I think it is more likely that they were used for digging roots or perhaps for prying up shellfish. The mattock was probably foreign to this area.

Best represented in the equipment of the Chugach hunter is the detachable barbed

---

[40] De´ Laguna, 1934. pp. 60 f.; Hrdlička, 1944. pp. 330, 343, Fig. 84 (?)

[41] Jochelson, 1925, Pl. 26, *36;* de Laguna, 1934, pp. 101, 200 f.; 1947, p. 216; Hrdlička, 1944, Fig. 171 (probably a shovel not a "paddle blade"), pp. 335, 346; 1945, pp. 113, 451.

head with line hole in the tang, used with an arrow for sea otter, with a throwing-board dart for seals and other marine mammals, and with a hand-thrust spear for salmon. These heads are chiefly barbed on one edge, although bilaterally barbed heads, including specimens with ornamental dorsal barbs, were also made during all periods. Heads with a groove for an end blade or with hollowed-out barbs are rare, and the latter seem to be limited to the later prehistoric period. The proportion of heads barbed on both edges is slightly greater here than at Kachemak Bay, and in this respect the Chugach material approaches more closely that from Kodiak, the Aleutian Islands, and Bristol Bay, where bilaterally barbed heads are in the majority and these usually have a shouldered tang to hold the line instead of a hole.

Toggle harpoon heads were also used for sea mammals, but their rarity in Prince William Sound accords with their lack of popularity all over southwestern Alaska in comparison with the tanged barbed form. The only type of toggle head represented in our collections is the form with closed socket and blade (hafted in a bed or slit) at right angles to the line hole. Two of our 3 specimens are from the later prehistoric period; the third fragmentary head is undated. The only 2 recognizable foreshafts for such heads are also late, although one rather doubtful specimen comes from the lower half of the Palugvik midden. We found no open socketed heads, although they may have been made in very early times, since they were especially characteristic of Kachemak Bay I and survived into the Third Period. During Kachemak Bay III and in Hrdlička's material from Kodiak most of the heads with closed socket lacked blades, although the form with blade at right angles to the line hole was fairly well represented on Kodiak.[42] The dating of the Kodiak specimens is un-

fortunately uncertain, but I would hazard that they are not older than Kachemak Bay III, for a number have the same elegant profile as the closed socketed heads of that period from Cook Inlet. Heads with closed socket may be somewhat late in southwestern Alaska. Quimby has found that heads with elegantly shaped spur and bed for the blade are characteristic of the older levels on Amaknak Island, while those with ruder spur and blade slit occur in the younger layers.[43] A similar crude form is also found on Kodiak and may prove to be more recent here. Thus, the type found in Prince William Sound seems to represent the less elegant (but perhaps not less efficient) form characteristic of late prehistoric times in southwestern Alaska.

Bone socket pieces were evidently used to receive the tangs of the smaller barbed heads and the foreshafts of the heads with socket. Evidently no separate socket piece was needed on salmon harpoons. With the exception of a few unfinished and broken specimens from the later prehistoric period, these Chugach socket pieces were short and had bifurcated tangs. We did not find any clear example of the type with central tang or of the form made in 2 parts, both of which are common in other southwestern Alaskan areas.[44] The prehistoric Chugach type with bifurcated butt seems to have been one of the older types found all over the area, and the longer modern version descended from it is equally widespread. It was suggested that the earliest form in Prince William Sound was peculiar in possessing a slit fore end and was replaced in later prehistoric times by one with the more usual oval socket. Modern specimens from southwestern Alaska often

[42] De Laguna, 1934, pp. 80-82, 188 f.; Hrdlička, 1944, Figs. 120 to 122, and unpublished specimens.

[43] Quimby, 1946; cf. Jochelson, 1925, Fig. 8, Pl. 27, 3.
[44] Add Hrdlička, 1945, Fig. 202 to sources already cited in de Laguna, 1943, pp. 194 f.; de Laguna, 1947, p. 201. Laughlin and Marsh (1951, p. 82) and Laughlin (1952, p. 32) find that the 2-piece form is definitely older on the Aleutians than the long slender single-piece type, but give no information about the shorter one-piece form which is probably older than the latter.

have a soft wooden plug or lining to the socket into which the butt of the dart head or harpoon foreshaft can be securely wedged. The slit socket may itself have acted as a spring to grip the inserted butt, and thus suggests an adaptation of the same principle employed on more northern Alaskan harpoon heads to secure the end blade.[45] Only the Chugach seem to have used the slit on socket pieces.

Sealing harpoons were equipped with a bladder float, represented archaeologically by the mouthpiece for inflation and by the plug. No recognizable fragments of wooden shafts for harpoons were found, although there were a number of bone shafts which may have been parts of weapons.

Wooden lances with slate blades were used for killing sea mammals, and we have an example of 2 types. The first of these, undoubtedly used for whales, has a detachable wooden head or loose foreshaft in which the slate blade was set; the other is simply a wooden shaft with a fixed blade. Our example of the second type probably had a chipped stone blade—to judge by the shape of the bed in which it was lashed —although lance blades were more commonly made of slate, and sometimes of copper. It is possible that the Chugach whaler, like his colleagues on Kodiak and the Aleutian Islands, made use of aconite poison,[46] but of this we have no definite information. According to Laughlin's Aleut informants the "poison" employed was not actually effective, but was presumably merely a magical ingredient.[47]

Three main types of slate blades were used for lances, harpoons, and possibly for arrows. The forms most common in the first half of the occupation of Palugvik were the double-edged blade with tang and the slender awl-like point. These lost something of their importance as the barbed slate blade gained in popularity during later times. All 3 types were, however, represented during both the earlier

and the later prehistoric periods. It was suggested that the awl-like forms may never have been used as much in the northern and western parts of the sound as in the southeastern area. They are relatively less important in Kachemak Bay III and sub-III and at Port Möller than on Kodiak Island. The increased popularity of barbed slate blades in Prince William Sound accords with the evidence from Kachemak Bay, where this type probably did not appear until the Second Period and only later became common. Barbed slate blades are not mentioned by Hrdlička from Kodiak Island, although the type is known ethnologically from that region and also from the Koniag area at Katmai on the south side of the Alaska Peninsula. They are virtually absent from the Aleutian Islands, where slate blades of any kind are rare.[48] We found no example of the tangless leaf-shaped blade in Prince William Sound, although the type was common in Kachemak Bay where, in fact, it was the only form represented in the First Period. It was also made on Kodiak, and Hrdlička illustrates a number of specimens with one or more holes for hafting.[49] It will be remembered that slate blades with holes were very rare in both Kachemak Bay and Cook Inlet. A few triangular blades may have been used by the Chugach for harpoon heads.

Except for sea otter hunting, the Chugach employed the bow and arrow chiefly on land. These are represented by wooden fragments of a bow (?) and of arrowshafts, a toy wooden arrow, and a number of arrowheads. The arrowheads include plain unbarbed bladelike heads of bone or copper and a number of barbed bone forms, some approaching in shape the detachable barbed heads with tang and others merging with the type designated as "slender barbed point." There seem to be no temporal distinctions among the various forms,

---

[45] De Laguna, 1947, p. 177.
[46] Lantis, 1938; Heizer, 1943.
[47] Laughlin, 1952, p. 36.

[48] Birket-Smith, 1941, Fig. 16; de Laguna, 1934, p. 183; 1947, p. 175.
[49] De Laguna, 1934, pp. 70-74; Hrdlička, 1944, Fig. 112.

except that copper was late, although our small collections may be insufficient to exhibit a development of types. Two barbed points suggest the presence of the multipronged leister and of the Eskimo bird dart with side prongs.

Fish were caught with spears, some furnished with detachable barbed heads and others with 3 prongs, the outer 2 of which bore incurving barbs. A gaff was also reported by the natives. A number of sharpened bone objects may have served as barbs for the fish spear or for the gaff. The V-shaped fishhook with barbed bone barb and a wooden (less commonly a bone) shank was also used. Some fishhooks seem to have had an unbarbed barb of bird bone. The archaeological data suggest no changes with respect to these devices, and they are all types well known in southwestern Alaska. One bone splinter is pointed at both ends and may have been a gorge. A large needle was probably used for stringing fish and clams. Unrepresented or unrecognized were the bone fishhook made in one piece, compound V-shaped wooden fishhook, dip net, and salmon weir, all described by our informants. No net gauges or netting shuttles were found, and the only known specimens from the area seem to be quite modern. (I think it very doubtful that any of the net gauges ascribed by Hrdlička to "pre-Koniag" culture were older than protohistoric.) [50] The fishline sinker was described as an unworked stone, and so went unrecognized. Curiously enough, we found no notched pebbles, although these were very common in Kachemak Bay from the Second Period to the most recent sites, as well as on the Aleutians, and on Kodiak.[51] Apparently both large and small varieties were found throughout the site at Uyak Bay, although in Kachemak Bay there was a complete shift from the earlier larger form to the later small type. With respect to lack of

[50] Hrdlička, 1944, pp. 316, 318, 347, Fig. 185; cf. de Laguna, 1947, pp. 213 ff.
[51] De Laguna, 1934, pp. 51-54, 167-72; Hrdlička, 1944, pp. 333-44, etc.

notched stones Chugach culture resembles Kachemak Bay I.

A piece of the Siberian spring or torsion trap was found, but was of such recent manufacture as to be an ethnological rather than an archaeological specimen. The wooden hooks and bars from Palutat Cave we have interpreted as parts of traps or snares. We evidently have little material to suggest the various forms of such devices as were described by our informants.

A single dubious example of a bone club was found. The clubs used by hunters were probably made chiefly of wood. Large awl-like implements may have been stilettos for dispatching wounded fish or small game. We found no examples of throwing boards, of quivers, of skin bags for carrying extra weapon points, or of carved seal decoys, although these were all mentioned. According to Cook's observations the kayaker wore a carved wooden hat shaped like a seal's head, which was doubtless supposed to have an advantageous effect on the game pursued. When hunting on land, the Chugach were evidently assisted by a small type of dog, still bred for securing small burrowing fur-bearers.

On the whole, the hunting methods and equipment of the Chugach were like those commonly employed all over southwestern Alaska, although their territory gave them opportunities for hunting a greater variety of land animals than were commonly found elsewhere. Land hunting was most severely restricted on the Aleutians, because of the absence of many types of game found on the mainland and even on Kodiak.

The Chugach warrior was dressed in wooden slat armor of the common southwestern Alaskan type. There is a suggestion that bone plate armor was also known in the area. He was armed with a double-edged dagger. A good bone specimen was secured, similar to weapons known from Cook Inlet, Kodiak, and the Aleutians, but we could not distinguish the slate blades which may have been used for daggers from those used for ordinary knives or lances, and we did not find any copper daggers, although these were described. Another weapon was the double-pointed stone pick, hafted like a splitting adz, and represented by 2 specimens, both presumably late. The Chugach are the only Eskimo group, as far as I know, to have adopted this typically Northwest Coast weapon. Single-edged chipped stone picks may also have been used in war, and one specimen of this type is mentioned from the "Koniag" level at Kodiak.[52] Some of the splitting adzes with very narrow blades might better have served as weapons than as tools, although we do not know, of course, if they were ever so employed. The stone picks may represent the club for striking mentioned by our informants; we found no example of the parrying club. A weapon sometimes used in hunting and especially favored for braining a personal enemy was the grooved stone tied to a cord by which it could be thrown or swung. Most of the specimens we found had a single groove; the only doubly grooved example came from Palugvik 4. In Kachemak Bay the greatest variety of types and the most elaborate forms were characteristic of the Third Period, and an apparently similar series was found at Port Möller and on Kodiak.[53] Our Chugach collections did not contain any plummet-shaped specimens grooved around one end. This was the only type found in Kachemak Bay I, was more characteristic of the deeper layers at Port Möller, and was also represented on Kodiak.[54] Two shaped but ungrooved stone balls from Palugvik 3 were found together and tend to verify the tradition of a 2-stone bola. There is no evidence that the bola was ever used for birds; this was evidently for larger game. Stones were also thrown from a special type of throwing board, but we have no archaeological data concerning this weapon.

52 Hrdlička, 1944, p. 333.
53 Add *ibid.*, Figs. 115 to 117, pp. 333, 344, to the sources cited in de Laguna, 1934, pp. 54 ff., 168 f.
54 Hrdlička, 1944, Fig. 71, p. 344, "stone bottles or flasks."

Almost all travel was by sea, and the Chugach commonly employed the skin bidar or umiak, especially for family removals to and from the summer and winter settlements and for war parties. These are said to have had masts and sails as well as paddles for propulsion and must have been seaworthy craft, since tradition tells of a raid on Kodiak in the dead of winter. The men's hunting boats, which on occasion could carry an extra passenger lying cramped under the skin deck or riding backward in one of the paddlers' manholes, were the one-man kayak and the 2-man bidarka; the 3-man bidarka was an innovation introduced by the Russians for their own convenience as passengers. Double-bladed paddles were used for the one-man kayak, and single-bladed paddles for the bidarka. These skin boats were made according to the common southwestern Alaskan styles. The bidarkas and kayaks in this region have bifurcated prows, but those of the Chugach, to judge by ethnological specimens, had more elaborately curved and graceful prongs.[55] We obtained samples of paddles, of the bidarka frame, and of heavy skin coverings, presumably for boats. The Chugach also used dugouts, some of which seem to have had prow handles and wooden thwarts. The specimens from Palutat Cave could have held only a single occupant, although larger wooden canoes are reported. I have already presented evidence that the dugout may have been more widely distributed or known in southwestern Alaska than we have hitherto suspected. Its greater importance among the Chugach than among other groups in the area reflects easy access to suitable trees and development of woodworking, and also illustrates their marginal position as neighbors of the dugout-using Eyak and Tlingit. Other items associated with transportation, such as snowshoes, skin knapsack and pack strap, sleds (?), and the use of dogs for pulling (?) or

55 Cf. Plate 57, *6*, with illustrations reproduced by Hrdlička (1945, Figs. 31, 32, 33) and by Heizer (1943, Pls. 23 and 23A); Birket-Smith, 1941, Fig. 24.

packing were mentioned by our informants but lack archaeological confirmation.

Personal decoration is represented by labrets, nose pins, ear plugs (?), pendants, beads, buckles, and paint. These show only slight variations from the ornaments worn by other Pacific Eskimo and by the Aleut, except that among the latter beads seem to have been very rare. Beads made of amber are the only type definitely known from the Aleutians before glass beads were obtained. The Chugach, in contrast, seem to have possessed the greatest number and variety of beads. In Prince William Sound, as on Cook Inlet, ornaments of native copper were late and included nose pins and finger rings. Other aboriginal materials used for ornaments were animal teeth, bone, shell, and stone (slate, marble, translucent soapstone?). Scarcity of walrus ivory is perhaps responsible for the frequent utilization of small bits of "ivory" obtained from bear canines. Glass beads seem to have been avidly adopted in the whole area as soon as they were procurable. Ornaments of dentalia and of amber were also described by our informants, and these, too, were prized all over southwestern Alaska. The Chugach evidently lacked red baked shale for beads and oil shale for labrets, materials procurable and used on Cook Inlet. Oil shale seems also to have reached Kodiak Island, where it was used for a few beads and labrets.[56] We were unable to verify a statement of one of our informants that the Chugach used to model beads and animal figures out of clay mixed with oil. The labrets which we found were all of the small lateral type, but it is probably only accident that we failed to secure examples of the larger medial variety, since these are described by early explorers and are also common on Cook Inlet, Kodiak, and the Aleutians. The most elaborately carved pendants

came from the later layers, but again this may be only an accident. Beads and other ornaments were traditionally supposed to be the prerogative of chiefs or wealthy families, and it is interesting that beads, at any rate, seem to have been more common in the earlier than in the later prehistoric period. Can this possibly reflect the growth of a class system?

Wooden splinters found in Palutat Cave may have been remains of composite combs, like those of the Aleut, for dressing the hair. Stone plaques, often triangular and often with notched edges, may have been used as mirrors, like those of Kachemak Bay and Kodiak,[57] although it would be incorrect to identify as mirrors all Chugach specimens included in this group of artifacts.

Stone balls were used for juggling games by the Chugach, as well as by the Aleut and the Eskimo of Kachemak Bay and Kodiak Island.[58] Short, neatly made wooden rods may have served as tallies. Similar tallies of bone are known from Kachemak Bay and Kodiak.[59] We found no other recognizable objects connected with games, although our informants described many types of children's toys, of dice, counters, "men" for games, playing sticks, etc., used in a variety of sports and gambling contests.

The masks published by Dall and the single bone whistle found by us are probably more closely connected with magical and religious ceremonial than with secular amusements. Other musical instruments were the rattle and the drum, of which we found no representatives. The small wooden box in the oldest grave at Palugvik may once have held something precious, perhaps an amulet. Animal and bird bones, claws, teeth, feathers, etc., as well as other oddities, are said to have functioned as amulets, so that a number of objects which

[56] De Laguna, 1934, pp. 105, 109; Hrdlička, 1944, mentions (p. 298) a "lignite" bead and (p. 345) 2 "jet" beads and "jet" labrets, which I believe, after examination of the specimens, to be oil shale like that found on Cook Inlet.

[57] De Laguna, 1934, pp. 78 f.; Heizer, 1946, p. 149.
[58] De Laguna. 1934, p. 104; Hrdlička, 1944, Fig. 166; Jochelson, 1925. Pl. 17, 27, 29.
[59] De Laguna, 1934, p. 104; Hrdlička, unpublished specimens.

we have described as ornaments, such as the pendants of bear or seal teeth, may have had magical significance. A small carving of a fish or whale was more certainly an amulet. The carved ivory bear figures, which were perhaps the handles for a cord drill, the decorated bone tubes, and the perforated marmot tibia, all from Grave III on Palugvik East Point, strongly suggest the paraphernalia of the shaman. The one human effigy is probably a shaman's doll, like those used elsewhere in southwestern Alaska, even though it is very crude in comparison with some of the carvings from other areas. It obviously does not represent the best work of which the Chugach were capable. Of greater interest are the slate plaques with incised designs which probably also had magical significance. They seem to have been restricted to the earlier prehistoric period in Prince William Sound, and are known also from presumably later sites of the Koniag and the Tlingit.

Decorations on artifacts, as far as they were illustrated by archaeological specimens, were relatively simple and in general suggest the persistence in Prince William Sound of very old Eskimo styles.[60] This may have been due in part to conservatism and/or to the marginal position of the Chugach, since they lacked the round bored dot and the compass-drawn dot-and-circle, both introduced from northern Alaska (from the Early Punuk and Punuk) and adopted by other southwestern Alaskan groups.[61] There are only 2 objects, from Palugvik 1 and from Palugvik 3 or 4, which seem to have been decorated with metal tools, although metal-cut lines were already present in Kachemak Bay II and became much more important in the Third Period. The round bored dot and dot-and-circle appear on a few Chugach ethnological specimens, so it is possible that these design elements may have been known earlier (late prehistoric or protohistoric periods?), even though they must have been uncommon. The only decorative motifs which do not suggest early Eskimo styles are the band of "braided triangles" and the band filled with crosshatching, both of which may have been of Indian inspiration.[62] (For examples, see the incised slate plaques.) The latter design also appears on a harpoon head, labeled "pre-Koniag" by Hrdlička and in general appearance suggestive of Kachemak Bay III forms.[63] Another factor which may account for the simplicity of Chugach incising is that their artistic efforts were probably concentrated more on the carving and painting of wood. Makari made some beautiful wooden spoons with animal effigy handles which give some clue to the excellence of this type of art, an impression which one would certainly not gain from the rather poorly conceived and executed masks published by Dall.

The style of Chugach pictographs and their possible significance have already been discussed at some length (Chapter IV). It is sufficient here to remark only that these paintings show the close relationship of Chugach culture to that of their neighbors on Cook Inlet and also the presence among the Chugach of influences from the Northwest Coast which affected the Cook Inlet Eskimo very little. It is curious that much closer resemblances to Northwest Coast art should be found in the Kodiak petroglyphs. This makes us wonder whether the Chugach may not have pecked similar figures in stone which we failed to hear about or to find. If they were on low-lying rocks along the shore, the sea may have covered and obliterated them.

Chugach methods of disposal of the dead have also been treated in considerable detail (Chapter III) and need no review here. Descriptions of the character of the sites in general are given in Chapter II,

---

[60] De Laguna, 1934, pp. 210 f.; 1947, pp. 258-67.
[61] To the sources cited above for these elements, add Hrdlička, 1944, Figs. 50 and 121; Heizer, 1946, p. 149; "Iron-tipped engraving tools and the mechanically drawn dot-and-circle design are old in the site" at Uyak Bay, Kodiak. For the Aleutians, see discussion in Section 3 of this chapter.

[62] De Laguna, 1947, p. 262.
[63] Hrdlička, 1944, Fig. 120, right-hand specimen.

section 1, and what little archaeological information we secured about houses may be found in Chapter II, sections 12 and 15.

To understand more fully the significance of Chugach archaeological remains in the light of the totality of Chugach culture we must turn to the ethnological monograph published by Dr. Birket-Smith. In this work he not only describes all known aspects of Chugach life but by extensive trait comparisons endeavors to show the position of Chugach culture within the framework of Eskimo culture in general. A definitive assessment of the relationships of Chugach culture to other cultural expressions in southwestern Alaska must, however, wait until more complete and accurate data are made available from other areas within that province. The earliest stages of culture in Prince William Sound unfortunately have not been uncovered, and our story there begins about the time when Kachemak Bay III or sub-III had just developed. Whether earlier sites are found will depend on the extent to which subsidence of the land may have spared them from destruction or concealment and on the uncertain luck of the archaeologist. If such remains are never found, we shall be doubly dependent upon carefully documented sequences from other areas in trying to answer the question: "Who really were the Chugach?"

Bibliography

ANDERSON, SVEND T., and THEODORE P. BANK, II
1952 "Pollen and Radiocarbon Studies of Aleutian Soil Profiles," *Science,* CXVI, No. 3004, 84-86.

BANCROFT, HUBERT H.
1886 *The History of Alaska, 1730-1885,* Vol. XXXIII of the author's *Works* (also reprinted in 1890), San Francisco.
1890 *Literary Industries,* Vol. XXXIX of the author's *Works,* San Francisco.

BANK, THEODORE P., II
1953 "Cultural Succession in the Aleutians," *American Antiquity,* XIX, 40-49.
n.d. "Archaeology and Ecology of Aleutian Burial Caves," in press, University of Michigan Press.

BIRKET-SMITH, KAJ
1941 "Early Collections from the Pacific Eskimo," *Ethnographical Studies,* Nationalmuseets Skrifter, Etnografisk Raekke, Copenhagen, I, 16-163.
1951 "Recent Achievements in Eskimo Research," *Journal of the Royal Anthropological Institute,* LXXVII (July-December, 1947), 145-57.
1952 "Present Status of the Eskimo Problem," *Selected Papers of the XXIXth International Congress of Americanists,* University of Chicago Press, III, 8-21.
1953 *The Chugach Eskimo,* Nationalmuseets Skrifter, Etnografisk Raekke, Vol. VI, Copenhagen.

———, and FREDERICA DE LAGUNA
1938 *The Eyak Indians of the Copper River Delta, Alaska,* Det Kgl. Danske Videnskab. Selskab., Copenhagen.

BOAZ, FRANZ
1897 "The Social Organization and Secret Societies of the Kwakiutl Indians," *Annual Report for 1894-1895,* U. S. National Museum, pp. 311-378. Washington, D.C.

BOLLES, LT. T. DIX, U.S.N.
1893 "Chinese Relics in Alaska," *Proceedings,* U.S. National Museum, XV, No. 899 (1892), 221-22, Washington, D. C.

CAPPS, STEPHEN R.
1931 *Glaciation in Alaska,* Professional Paper No. 170 A, U. S. Geological Survey, Washington, D. C.

COLLINS, HENRY B., JR.
1951 "The Origin and Antiquity of the Eskimo," *Annual Report of the Smithsonian Institution, 1950,* Washington, D. C., pp. 8-21.
1953 "Recent Developments in the Dorset Culture Area," *Memoir 9,* Society for American Archaeology, pp. 32-39.

COLNETT, CAPTAIN J.
n.d. "Journal, *Prince of Wales,* 16 October 1786–7 November 1788," Unpublished MS, Admiralty 55/146, Public Record Office, London.

COOK, CAPTAIN JAMES
1785 *A Voyage to the Pacific Ocean,* etc. (2nd ed., 3 vols. and *Album*). London.

COXE, WILLIAM
1803 *Account of the Russian Discoveries between Asia and America* . . . (4th ed.). London.

DALL, WILLIAM H.
1870 *Alaska and its Resources,* Boston.
1877 "On Succession in the Shell-Heaps of the Aleutian Islands," *Tribes of the Extreme Northwest,* Part II (Contributions to North American Ethnology, Vol. 1), Washington, D. C.
1878 "On the Remains of Later Pre-Historic Man Obtained from Caves in the Catherine Archipelago, etc.," *Smithsonian Contributions to Knowledge,* No. 318, Washington, D.C.
1884 "On Masks, Labrets, and Certain Aboriginal Customs, etc.," *Third Annual Report* (1881-82), pp. 67-203, Bureau of American Ethnology, Washington, D. C.

DIXON, CAPTAIN GEORGE
1789 *A Voyage Round the World* . . . *(1785-1788)* (2nd ed.). London.

DRUCKER, P.
1943 "Archaeological Survey on the Northern Northwest Coast," *Anthropological Papers,* No. 20, Bulletin 133, pp. 17-132, Bureau of American Ethnology, Washington, D. C.

EMMONS, G. T.
1908 "Petroglyphs in Southeastern Alaska," *American Anthropologist,* New Series, X, 221-30.

FORSTER, JOHAN REINHOLD, trans. and ed.
1781 *Tagebuch einer Entdekkungs Reise nach der Südsee in den Jahren 1776 bis 1780, unter Anführung der Capitains Cook, Clerke,*

Gore und King, Berlin. (Author unknown, probably an assistant surgeon on H.M.S. *Resolution*.)

GEIST, OTTO WILLIAM, and FROELICH G. RAINEY
1936 *Archaeological Excavations at Kukulik, St. Lawrence Island, Alaska*, Miscellaneous Publications, University of Alaska, Vol. II, Washington, D. C.

GIDDINGS, LOUIS J. L., JR.
1941a "Rock Paintings in Central Alaska," *American Antiquity*, VII, 69-70.
1941b *Dendrochronology in Northern Alaska*, University of Arizona Laboratory of Tree-Ring Research, Bulletin 1, University of Alaska Publications, Vol. IV.
1944 "Dated Eskimo Remains of an Inland Zone," *American Antiquity*, X, 113-34. See also XIII (1948), 267, for further dates.
1949 "Early Flint Horizons on the North Bering Sea Coast," *Journal of the Washington Academy of Science*, XXXIX, No. 3, 85-90.
1951 "The Denbigh Flint Complex," *American Antiquity*, XVI, No. 3, 193-203.

GOLDER, F. A.
1925 *Bering's Voyages*, American Geographical Society Research Series No. 2, 2 vols., New York.

GRANT, U. S., and D. F. HIGGINS
1910 *Reconnaissance of the Geology and Mineral Resources of Prince William Sound, Alaska*, Bulletin 443, U. S. Geological Survey, Washington, D. C.
1913 *Coastal Glaciers of Prince William Sound and Kenai Peninsula, Alaska*, Bulletin 526, U. S. Geological Survey, Washington, D. C.

HEIZER, ROBERT F.
1943 "Aconite Poison Whaling in Asia and America: An Aleutian Transfer to the New World," *Anthropological Papers*, No. 24, Bulletin 133, pp. 415-68. Bureau of American Ethnology, Washington, D. C.
1946 "Analysis of Archaeological Collection from Uyak Bay, Kodiak Island, Alaska," *Year Book of the American Philosophical Society*, pp. 149-50, Philadelphia.
1947 "Petroglyphs from Southwestern Kodiak Island, Alaska," *Proceedings of the American Philosophical Society*, XCI, No. 3, 284-93, Philadelphia.
1952a "Incised Slate Figurines from Kodiak Island, Alaska," *American Antiquity*, XVII No. 3, 266.
1952b "Notes on Koniag Material Culture," *Anthropological Papers of the University of Alaska*, I, No. 1, 11-24.

HOLMBERG, H. J.
1855 *Ethnographische Skizzen über die Völker des russischen Amerika*, Part I, Akten der Finnl. Societ. d. Wissensch., Vol. IV, Helsingfors.

HRDLIČKA, ALEŠ
1944 *The Anthropology of Kodiak Island*, The Wistar Institute of Anatomy and Biology, Philadelphia.
1945 *The Aleutian and Commander Islands and Their Inhabitants*, The Wistar Institute of Anatomy and Biology, Philadelphia.

IRVING, WILLIAM
1951 "Archaeology in the Brooks Range of Alaska," *American Antiquity*, XVIII, No. 1, 52-53.

IVANOV, S. L.
1930 "Aleut Hunting Headgear and Its Ornamentation," *Proceedings of the Twenty-third International Congress of Americanists* (New York, 1928), pp. 477-504, New York.

JACOBI, A., ed.
1937 "Carl Heinrich Mercks Ethnographische Beobachtungen über die Völker des Berings Meers 1789-91," *Baessler-Archiv, Beiträge zur Völkerkunde*, Vol. XX, Parts III-IV, Berlin.

JACOBSEN, CAPITAN J. ADRIAN
1884 *. . . Reise an der Nordwestküste Amerikas*, ed. A. Woldt. Leipzig.

JENNESS, DIAMOND
1928 "Archaeological Investigations in Bering Strait, 1926," *Annual Report for 1926*, Bulletin No. 50, pp. 71-80, National Museum of Canada, Ottawa.

JOCHELSON, WALDEMAR
1925 *Archaeological Investigations in the Aleutian Islands*, Publication No. 367, Carnegie Institution of Washington, D. C.
1933 *History, Ethnology and Anthropology of the Aleut*, Publication No. 432, Carnegie Institution of Washington, D. C.

KEITHAHN, E. L.
1940 "The Petroglyphs of Southeastern Alaska," *American Antiquity*, VI, 123-32.

KROEBER, A. L.
1939 *Cultural and Natural Areas of Native North America*, University of California Publications in American Archaeology and Ethnology, Vol. XXXVIII, Berkeley.

LAGUNA, FREDERICA DE
1934 *The Archaeology of Cook Inlet, Alaska*. University of Pennsylvania Museum, Philadelphia.
1947 *The Prehistory of Northern North America As Seen from the Yukon*, Memoir 3, Society for American Archaeology.
1953 "Some Problems in the Relationship between Tlingit Archaeology and Ethnology," *Memoir 9*, Society for American Archaeology, pp. 52-57.

LANTIS, MARGARET
1938 "The Alaskan Whale Cult and Its Affinities," *American Anthropologist*, XL, 438-64.
1947 *Alaskan Eskimo Ceremonialism*, Monographs of the American Ethnological Society, Vol. XI.

LA PEROUSE, J. F. G. DE
1798 *Voyage de La Pérouse autour du monde . . .*, ed. L. A. Millet-Mureau, 4 vols. and Atlas, Paris (1797).

LARSEN, HELGE
1950 "Archaeological Investigations in Southwestern Alaska," *American Antiquity*, XV, No. 3, 177-86.
1952 "The Ipiutak Culture: Its Origin and Relationships" and "Discussion" by Diamond Jenness, *Selected Papers of the XXIXth International Congress of Americanists*, Vol. III, University of Chicago Press, pp. 22-34.
1953 "Archaeological Investigations in Alaska since 1939," *Polar Record*, VI, no. 45, 593-607.

——, and FROELICH RAINEY
1948 *Ipiutak and the Arctic Whale Hunting Culture, Anthropological Papers*, Vol. XLII, American Museum of Natural History, New York.

LAUGHLIN, WILLIAM S.
1951 "Notes on an Aleutian Core and Blade Industry," *American Antiquity*, XVII, No. 1, 52, 54-55.

1952 "The Aleut-Eskimo Community," *Anthropological Papers of the University of Alaska,* I, No. 1, 25-46.

——, and G. H. MARSH
1951 "A New View of the History of the Aleutians," *Arctic,* IV, No. 2, 75-88.

——, G. H. MARSH, and J. W. LEACH
1952 "Supplementary Note on the Aleutian Core and Blade Industry," *American Antiquity,* XVIII, No. 1, 52-55.

LISIANSKY, UREY
1814 *A Voyage Round the World in the Years 1803, 1804, 1805, and 1806. . . ,* London.

MASON, J. ALDEN
1928 "A Remarkable Stone Lamp from Alaska," *The Museum Journal,* XIX, 170-94, University of Pennsylvania Museum, Philadelphia.

MASON, OTIS T.
1904 "Aboriginal American Basketry: Studies in a Textile Art Without Machinery," *Annual Report for 1901-1902,* pp. 171-784, U. S. National Museum, Washington, D. C.

MEANY, EDMOND S.
1906 "Alaskan Mummies," *Washington Magazine,* I, 459-68, Seattle.

MEARES, JOHN
1791 *Voyages Made in the Years 1788 and 1789 from China to the N. W. Coast of America: with an Introductory Narrative of a Voyage Performed in 1786 from Bengal in the Ship Nootka . . . ,* 2 vols. London.

MERCK, CARL HEINRICH. See JACOBI.

MORICE, A. G.
1894 "Notes Archaeological, Industrial and Sociological on the Western Déné . . .," *Transactions of the Royal Canadian Institute,* IV, (1892-93), 1-222, Toronto.

NELSON, E. W.
1899 "The Eskimos about Bering Strait," *Eighteenth Annual Report* (1896-97), Part I, pp. 1-518, Bureau of American Ethnology, Washington, D. C.

NIBLACK, A. P.
1890 "The Coast Indians of Southern Alaska and Northern British Columbia," *Annual Report for 1887-1888,* pp. 225-386, U. S. National Museum, Washington, D. C.

OETTEKING, BRUNO
1934 "Skeletal Material from Cook Inlet and Prince William Sound," Chapter VIII of de Laguna, 1934, pp. 221-28.

1945 "Skeletal Remains from Prince William Sound, Alaska," *American Journal of Physical Anthropology,* New Series, III, 57-96, 177-205, 277-311.

OSGOOD, CORNELIUS
1937 *The Ethnography of the Tanaina,* Yale University Publications in Anthropology, No. 14, New Haven.

OSWALT, WENDELL
1952 "The Archaeology of Hooper Bay Village, Alaska," *Anthropological Papers of the University of Alaska,* I, No. 1, 47-91.

PALLAS, PETER SIMON, ed.
1781-96 *Neue Nordische Beyträge . . . ,* 7 vols. St. Petersburg and Leipzig.

PETROFF, IVAN
1884 *Alaska: Its Population, Industries and Resources,* Tenth Census, 1880, Vol. VIII, Washington, D. C.

PORTER, ROBERT P.
1893 *Report on the Population and Resources of Alaska,* Eleventh Census, 1890, Vol. XV, Washington, D. C.

PORTLOCK, CAPTAIN NATHANIEL
1789 *A Voyage Round the World; but more particularly the North-West Coast of America, performed in 1785, 1786, 1787, and 1788 . . . ,* London.

QUIMBY, GEORGE I., JR.
1945a "Pottery from the Aleutian Islands," *Fieldiana: Anthropology,* XXXVI, 1-13, Chicago Natural History Museum.

1945b "Periods of Prehistoric Art in the Aleutian Islands," *American Antiquity,* XI, 76-79.

1946a "The Sadiron Lamp of Kamchatka as a Clue to the Chronology of Aleut Culture," *American Antiquity,* XI, 202-3.

1946b "Toggle Harpoon Heads from the Aleutian Islands," *Fieldiana: Anthropology,* XXXVI, 15-23.

1948 "Prehistoric Art of the Aleutian Islands," *Fieldiana: Anthropology,* XXXVI, 77-92.

RICKARD, T. A.
1939 "The Use of Iron and Copper by the Indians of British Columbia," *British Columbia Historical Quarterly,* III, 25-50.

RIOBO, FATHER JOHN
1918 "Alaska in 1779, Narrative of a Voyage There by Father John Riobo, O.S.F.," *Historical Records and Studies,* XII, 76-89, U. S. Catholic Historical Society, New York.

SARYTSCHEW [SARYCHEF], G. V.
1806-7 *Account of a Voyage of Discovery to the North-East of Siberia, the Frozen Ocean, and the North-East Sea* (translated from the Russian), 2 vols. London.

SAUER, MARTIN
1802 *An Account of a Geographical and Astronomical Expedition to the Northern Parts of Russia. . . ,* London.

SMITH, HARLAN I.
1907 "Archaeology of the Gulf of Georgia and Puget Sound," *Jesup North Pacific Expedition,* II, Part VI, 301-441, American Museum of Natural History, New York.

1909 "Archaeological Remains on the Coast of Northern British Columbia and Southern Alaska," *American Anthropologist,* New Series, XI, 595-600.

1927a "A list of Petroglyphs in British Columbia," *American Anthropologist,* New Series, XXIX, 605-10.

1927b "A Pictograph on the Lower Skeena River, British Columbia," *ibid.,* pp. 611-14.

SMITH, MARIAN W.
1950 "Archaeology of the Columbia-Fraser Region," *Memoir 6,* Society for American Archaeology.

SOLECKI, RALPH S.
1950 "A Preliminary Report of an Archaeological Reconnaissance of the Kukpowruk and Kokolik Rivers in Northwest Alaska," *American Antiquity,* XVI, No. 1, 66-69.

1951a "Archaeology and Ecology of the Arctic Slope of Alaska," *Annual Report of the Smithsonian Institution, 1950,* pp. 469-95.

1951b "Notes on Two Archaeological Discoveries in Northern Alaska, 1950," *American Antiquity,* XVII, No. 1, 55-57.

——, and ROBERT J. HACKMAN
1951 "Additional Data on the Denbigh Flint Complex," *Journal of the Washington Academy of Science,* XLI, No. 3, 85-88.

BIBLIOGRAPHY

SPAULDING, ALBERT C.
1953 "The Current Status of Aleutian Archaeology," *Memoir 9,* Society for American Archaeology, pp. 29-31.

STRANGE, JAMES
1928 *Journal and Narrative of the Commercial Expedition from Bombay to the North-West Coast of America . . .,* ed. A. V. Venkatarama Ayyar, Records of Fort St. George, Madras.

TARR, RALPH STOCKMAN, and LAWRENCE MARTIN
1914 *Alaska Glacier Studies,* National Geographic Society, Washington, D. C.

TEIT, JAMES H.
1900 "The Thompson Indians of British Columbia," *Jesup North Pacific Expedition,* I, Part

IV, 163-392, American Museum of Natural History, New York.
1906 "The Lillouet Indians," *ibid.,* II, Part V, 193-300.
1909 "The Shuswap," *ibid.,* II, Part VII, 443-789.

U.S. WEATHER BUREAU
n.d. *Summary of Climatological Data of Alaska, Section 1,* Washington, D.C.

VANCOUVER, CAPTAIN GEORGE
1801 *A Voyage of Discovery to the North Pacific Ocean and Around the World,* new ed., 6 vols. London.

WEYER, EDWARD MOFFAT, JR.
1929 "An Aleutian Burial," *Anthropological Papers,* XXXI, 219-38, American Museum of Natural History, New York.

Index